At Home
in the
Hoosier Hills

Midwestern History and Culture

GENERAL EDITORS

James H. Madison and
Andrew R. L. Cayton

At Home in the Hoosier Hills

Agriculture, Politics, and Religion in Southern Indiana, 1810–1870

Richard F. Nation

Indiana University Press
Bloomington and Indianapolis

This book is a publication of

Indiana University Press
601 North Morton Street
Bloomington, IN 47404-3797 USA

http://iupress.indiana.edu

Telephone orders   800-842-6796
Fax orders   812-855-7931
Orders by e-mail   iuporder@indiana.edu

Library of Congress Cataloging-in-Publication Data

Nation, Richard Franklin.
   At home in the Hoosier hills : agriculture, politics, and religion in southern Indiana, 1810–1870 / Richard F. Nation.
      p. cm. — (Midwestern history and culture)
   Originally presented as the author's thesis (Ph. D.)—University of Michigan, 1995, under title: Home in the Hoosier hills.
   Includes bibliographical references and index.
   ISBN 0-253-34591-X (cloth : alk. paper)
   1. Hoosier (Nickname) 2. Farmers—Indiana—Social conditions—19th century. 3. Agriculture—Social aspects—Indiana—History—19th century. 4. Farmers—Indiana—Attitudes—History—19th century. 5. Community life—Indiana—History—19th century. 6. Local government—Indiana—History—19th century. 7. Ethnology—Indiana. 8. Indiana—Politics and government—19th century. 9. Indiana—Economic conditions—19th century. 10. Indiana—Religious life and customs—19th century. I. Title. II. Series.
   F526.N38 2005
   306'.09772'09034—dc22   2004029321

1 2 3 4 5 10 09 08 07 06 05
Manufactured in the United States of America

In memory of my father,
Richard I. Nation, 1917–1997

Contents

ACKNOWLEDGMENTS

When I ponder the long list of acknowledgments at the beginning of many monographs, I have often thought that the various authors' scholarly lives were not mine. I have fancied myself pursuing a much more solitary life. But like so many others, I have amassed many debts, some to folks who may not remember the small words of encouragement that meant so much to me.

This work began as a dissertation at the University of Michigan, and that dissertation began with the inspiration of a childhood friend, Gib Chew, who, while I was in the midst of studying for my Ph.D. exams, asked for some bibliographical assistance in writing a paper on Indiana in the Civil War. I gave him several citations, and then, sparked by my readings in the rural history of North and South, posited what I thought might be the situation in the state. He read Kenneth Stampp's *Indiana Politics during the Civil War,* among other things, and reported back to me that I seemed to be on the right track. I took the challenge to research the social and cultural roots of the resistance of some Hoosiers to the Civil War, a project that Stampp himself called for in the 1978 edition of his work. Ultimately, I also believe that in knowing Gib, I understand the southern Indiana mind better (even if we both lived in central Indiana).

I was fortunate to work on this dissertation under the guidance of Mills Thornton, a gentleman and a scholar. Few of my cohort at Michigan were so fortunate to have such a humane, yet rigorous hand as the chair of their committee. Mills's most notable support came through frequent Sunday teas at his house, gathering together his small band of dissertation students to discuss one of our chapters. These friends provided much useful feedback, and they included Gerry Leonard, John Quist, Marty Pernick, Cara Shelley, Bil Kerrigan, and Andy Hoag. The rest of my dissertation committee also provided useful feedback and support: Bob Berkhofer, Leslie Tentler, and Patricia Yaeger.

My graduate experience was a bit more turbulent than typical, and I thank Jim Turner, David Hollinger, and June Howard for useful advice and support in getting me through it. That I went to graduate school was thanks to the encouragement of three Wesleyan University professors, Joe Reed, Dick Ohmann, and especially Clarence Walker. I have found great inspiration in the works of various scholars whom I have never met, not only Kenneth Stampp, but most notably Harry Watson, Steven Hahn, Thomas Haskell, James L. Huston, and Paul Johnson.

Acknowledgments

Special thanks must also go the Indiana Historical Society, whose fellowship supported the completion of the dissertation. I spent many hours in the Society's library researching, and in my attempt to sift out what little documentary material remained about nineteenth-century southern Indiana, I sent the staff on many a wild goose chase, for which I apologize and give my gratitude (special thanks to Connie McBirney, Leigh Darbee, and especially Wilma Gibbs). A similar experience befell the staff at the Indiana State Library (I should note Marybelle Burch, Scotty Selch, and Darrol Pierson), the Lilly Library, and the Indiana State Archives (especially Stephen Towne and the late Laurie Meldrum), and I appreciated the friendliness with which all these wonderful people met my peculiar demands. I also benefited from the generosity of the Washington County Historical Society (Dorothy Cottongim was especially helpful), the Salem Public Library (Sue Tengesdel made special provisions for me), and the various county officials in Washington and Franklin Counties (Finis Curry in particular). A special thanks to Dragomir Cosanici, librarian at Ruth Lilly Law Library at IUPUI, for providing a quick and thorough answer to a last-minute question.

After completion of my dissertation, I was fortunate to get a position at Eastern Michigan University—and after six years, I was hired in a tenure-line position. There many good people encouraged me, including Rob Citino, JoEllen Vinyard, Mike Homel, George Cassar, the late Hank Abbott, Matt Mason, now at Brigham Young, Michael McNally, now at Carleton, and Mark Higbee. I thank department heads Margot Duley and Gersham Nelson for their support. Russ Olwell and Dick Goff took great care in looking over my manuscript and offered much advice about how to focus and streamline it. Outside of Eastern Michigan, I got additional encouragement from Drew Cayton, Jim Madison, and Carol Sheriff. Drew Cayton and Jim Madison later would accept this manuscript in their roles of editors of the Midwestern History and Culture series of Indiana University Press, and for that I am appreciative. My thanks also go to many others at the Press who saw this book through the process: Bob Sloan, Jane Quinet, Emmy Ezzell, Jane Lyle, and Elaine Durham Otto.

For nearly twenty years now, LeAnne Martin has been my most important intellectual sounding board. She has always been there for me to talk through my ideas, and she has read drafts of several chapters and articles based on this research. Nevertheless, her devotion as a friend was recently revealed when she used her graphics skills to turn my pedestrian maps into something camera-ready for publication. My brother-in-law, Chris Boone, re-created five other maps and introduced me to the joys of GIS: it's good to have an academic family.

My family has been a constant support to me. My twin sister Marcia, a geographer, took on the role of my cheerleader. Earlier, my sister Peg took me in while I researched in the Indianapolis archives. My father must certainly rank as the single greatest influence on my life; he never went to college, but he valued the life of the mind above all other things. He read every word of this manuscript and probably saved me from more than a few embarrassing errors of writing. The most touching part of my research was plowing through records that my father had once handled when he worked for the WPA's Historical Records Survey in the 1930s.

Debbie, crazy as it might seem, married me at the beginning of the endeavor, and she has stuck by me through thick and thin since then. I would like to say that I never imposed upon her once, but I have several times turned to her when I needed an opinion or a quick proofreading, and for that I am grateful, but not nearly so much as I am grateful just to be with her. Now we have been blessed with two fine boys, Isaac and Elijah, and while they have done little to help with the book, they have brought me unimagined joy.

At Home
in the
Hoosier Hills

Introduction

Looking at the hills of southern Indiana today, many see a backwards place, out of step with the modern world. Sure, tucked into the hills is Indiana University, now a world-class research institution and even in the early nineteenth century often at odds with what the university folk perceived as their unenlightened neighbors. Such perceptions then and now have tended to marginalize the people of southern Indiana, to make them seem an anomaly in the great progression of the United States and ultimately peripheral to that nation's history and even the history of the state of Indiana. I'm often asked, "Why study southern Indiana?" The obvious reply has been "Why not?" For one thing, I do not buy the notion that this nation's history has been one of unending progress with its implicit focus on the victors. For another, I share with many scholars of African Americans, women, gays, and immigrants a distrust of categories that define mainstream and peripheral and thus exclude certain groups from the nation's history. Like many of them, I believe that the history of this nation cannot be understood without understanding the participation of all the various peoples who have inhabited this geographical space. Ultimately, the history of the nation is not merely a sum of the parts but a record of the interactions between the various parts: no community, region, race, or gender exists apart from others.[1]

That the hill country came to be perceived by outsiders (and not a few insiders) as peripheral is largely due to the localism that dominated the region, permitting each of the individual locales to resist the nationalizing and commercializing transformations that had swept much of the North by the Civil War. Certainly some in southern Indiana embraced these notions of progress and joined in projects, both economic and political, that would knit the nation together more tightly. But others in the Hoosier hills were more ambivalent about the changes that were taking place. Like many of their counterparts in the other so-called backwaters, they were not immune to the appeals of progress, but they tended to believe that the world in which they already lived was close to the best of all possible worlds. In particular they questioned some of the costs to their freedom, both economic and political, of tighter integration.[2] Such men could be found throughout America, and the sentiments they expressed lurked in the hearts of even those who embraced progress and integration, but in places like the hill country of southern Indiana, such men tended to dominate the political stage and thus express these sentiments through the political process, by stymieing the forces of progress.[3]

Although many hill country Hoosiers shared their ambivalence about progress and integration with folks throughout the United States, their common ambivalence was rooted in the belief of these various people that their own particular locale was unique. This belief formed the basis for their localism, in which they believed that their particular interests could best be served when governance was local. To them, governments worked best when they were local and thus both responsive to the will of the people and aware of particular circumstances. Such a notion of local governance, however, went far beyond the customary realm of politics and included religion and economics. For these Hoosiers, as for like-minded folks throughout the United States, moral behavior could best be obtained through the close oversight of the local community, a lesson that was reinforced in their churches and in economic activities. In other words, for many in antebellum America, they believed their lives worked best when moral regulation took place within the confines of a small community. Distrusting human nature, they could not depend on internal self-control, but they also believed that those at a distance—especially merchants and politicians—and thereby beyond the oversight of their community would act in ways detrimental to that community and the individuals within it.

The emphasis on human nature here is centrally important, because what often linked these folks together in defense of localism was a belief that humanity could not escape its sinful ways. Protestants who had not left behind Calvinism joined with Catholics in continuing to stress the depravity of man. Without supervision by the church, humans were likely to succumb to sin. Even with the oversight of the church, humans would still sin, but those sins could be kept in check, limited in their extent and their impact. Churches took a central role in maintaining moral discipline, but they were joined by other localized and less formal institutions, especially the family, but also including the "court of common fame."

Such a vision of localized moral regulation had strong implications for these Hoosiers' participation in the marketplace. If distant markets were unregulated, then they were open to manipulation and thus potentially corrupted. Such notions of corruption were broadcast loudly in the agrarian republicanism that was still commonplace in the political rhetoric of the day. Such rhetoric sharpened these Hoosiers' distrust of the marketplace and of the elites whom they believed controlled it, breeding ambivalence about the market economy even in the face of the new opportunities it brought these Hoosiers. Moreover, the rhetoric helped to breed concerns about the rich and powerful that characterized the politics of the mid-nineteenth century.

This localism and its constituent elements of religious belief, economic behavior, and political ideology were not unique to southern Indiana or even to the Upland South whence many of its residents came. I hear echoes of a similar worldview when I read about manorial New York, the industrializing Connecticut Valley, and the Michigan settlements of the New Englander, as well as when I read about the yeoman households of the Deep South.[4] However, by the time of the Civil War, the ascendancy of the Republican free labor vision had created a strong contrast with the slaveholding South, but at the cost of marginalizing voices within the North that were ambivalent about the changes that the Republicans had trumpeted.

Through much of the period under study here, Hoosiers were still engaged in the process of defining themselves, using the cultural values and views that they brought to the frontier, mixing them with those brought by their neighbors, and adapting them all to the new situations they found in the region.[5] That Hoosiers resembled those they had left behind in the East should not surprise any of us. But that they changed in response to their new situations and their new environments should not surprise us, either. And as historians well recognize, time and place change everything: as developments in the wider world take place, they affect people differently. The first sixty years of the nineteenth century were a time of momentous change, and the majority of those in central Indiana reacted to those changes differently than most residents of the hill country, even though many in both regions shared similar backgrounds.

In the process, central Indiana joined significant portions of its neighboring states to create a region that would eventually be called the Middle West and be characterized by the ascendancy of capitalism and a strong nationalist sentiment.[6] This regional development, tied to the rise of the Republican Party, led to the definition of southern Indiana as its own distinct geographical space: call it a subregion, for lack of a better term. The nationalism of the greater Midwest contrasted sharply to the localism of the hill country, but ironically, that very localism meant that among its residents there was relatively little sense of even a subregional identity, sharing a common vision with others in the hill country. The definition of the hill country as unique was primarily the project of outsiders.[7]

By telling the story of southern Indiana, I hope to complicate the history of the North, the Midwest, and ultimately the nation, to tell what Andrew Cayton and Susan Gray call a "counter-narrative."[8] Most of the great community studies on the Middle West have focused on the Yankee reformer cum Republican.[9] My work studies those who resisted these changes, in part to remind us that although their voices have often been silenced, they remain a part of the heritage and the worldview of many of our neighbors even in the twenty-first century. Moreover, I am sufficiently postmodern to believe that by illuminating the peripheral, the marginal, one can better understanding the normative and naturalizing practices of the center, in this case the commercializing, nationalizing Whig/Republicans. In this endeavor, I have an easy task, as I can take what is familiar and dear to many— the hardy pioneer—and use it to expose the contradictions within the grand narrative of the Middle West.

In the process, this book also seeks to answer a much more traditional question that has befuddled many about the politics of the antebellum period: why, if all the rhetoric was about economics, did political allegiances tend to follow ethnic, cultural, and religious lines rather than economic status?[10] At its root, the question makes a false assumption, that an individual's economic status would indicate his economic outlook. After all, a poor man may well have been drawn to the Whig Party, with its promise of opening opportunities. Ultimately, economic worldviews were only tangentially related to economic status, and the exploration of what those worldviews were must focus upon the minds of the historical actors themselves. For the Whig side of the answer, a solid answer connecting evangelical Protestantism with market involvement has been advanced by a number of parties, seeing ultimately the internalization of morality as essential to market production and trade.[11] For Democrats, however, the link between Roman Catholics, Southerners in general, and Calvinists has proven harder to make.[12] I argue that what they shared, a notion that humans were imperfect and doomed to sin, made them viable partners in opposing the perfectionist postmillennialism of the Second Great Awakening evangelicals who populated the Whig Party. Moreover, because they believed that humans were sinners, they looked to local institutions as the best able to keep the sin in check, and thus they distrusted measures that gave tremendous economic power and political authority to individuals beyond the bounds of their local community.

To demonstrate the consistent application of the logic of localism, I will explore religion, economic behavior, and politics in southern Indiana in the antebellum period. For a majority of the region's inhabitants, this localism shaped their response to their own communities and the larger world. As the transportation and market revolutions brought greater integration of southern Indiana into the life of the nation and of the world, localism was both a means of resisting these changes and a worldview that helped Hoosiers negotiate those changes. In both resisting and negotiating change, the citizens of southern Indiana were not alone in the antebellum period, and their localism was not unique.

The Land and Its Peoples

At twenty-one, Enoch Parr wrote that he "was in that difficult perplexity of mind common to poor young men of industrious habits and resolute minds." With few resources to offer, he found he was ignored in his advances to the "worthy part of young ladys." Finally, he "determined not to marry unless [he] could match [himself] to some one that when united we would have some prospect of doing well." Spurning his father's offer of two hundred acres of "sterile" land in Rowan County, North Carolina, Parr decided to leave for Indiana with his sister, Jemima, who had married Solomon Bowers, already a settler in the Indiana Territory. In early 1808, Enoch Parr and the Bowerses put their possessions in the wagon of Jacob Copple and left for the new territory. Upon arriving, Parr quickly began accumulating money with which to purchase land, working for Jesse Hindley at ten dollars a month and later teaching school, all the while tending a small patch of corn for horse feed on land that he had bought for less than four dollars. Late in 1808, a friend came from North Carolina with fifty dollars that was owed Parr and with the news that Parr's father had sold his North Carolina farm and intended to move to the Indiana territory late the next year. Using this fifty dollars and the money he had accumulated, Parr decided to enter land, putting eighty dollars down. Unfortunately, his horse had disappeared, and he was obliged to ask the Bowerses for the use of a horse to travel to the land office; Joseph Bowers, Solomon's son by his first marriage, coveted the same plot of land, and, refusing Enoch the use of a horse, Joseph set off to enter it himself. Others in the neighborhood thought Parr had been treated ungenerously, and once Parr selected another quarter section, he had no trouble finding the loan of a horse. Now a freeholder, Parr nevertheless rented some cleared acres, where he grew a crop of corn for his father. Parr quickly became dissatisfied with his original purchase, and he sold it for twenty dollars in cash and set out looking for the perfect quarter section; he did not find it, but "contented" himself with another he bought. His father arrived soon after and settled on Parr's land, and he was followed by Parr's brothers and sisters, who chose land in the same neighborhood. In the spring of 1810, Parr began to make improvements on his land, building a cabin and clearing five acres for a crop of corn. For two years, though, Parr still slept at his father's house, a mile and a half away, while he worked his own farm, leasing his cabin to the Newton Spence family and eating with the Spences. With his stability established, Parr sought the hand of Nancy Carr, although "being in need of a wife was perhaps too solicitous"; it would be two years before Carr, the daughter of a prominent early settler, would agree to marry him.[1]

Enoch Parr's experiences on the frontier represented much that would characterize life in early Indiana. By 1810, there was already a recognizable community in the hills of southern Indiana, in what would become Washington County. Such a community rested on the group migration of people like the Bowerses, Parrs, and Copples, and it was reinforced by familial ties, some dating back to their earlier lives elsewhere, some established with other families in the new neighborhood, as with Enoch Parr's marriage to Nancy Carr. Such a community judged their members' treatment of others, as with their censure of the Bowerses.

Yet the horse incident suggested another side of this community, as it revealed the way in which hierarchies were established within families. Enoch Parr, as brother of Solomon Bowers's wife, had less claim on Bowers than his son—indeed, Solomon Bowers gave his son the money to purchase the tract that Parr had desired, and it was purchased in Solomon's name. Moreover, despite their neighbors' characterization of their actions, Parr and Solomon Bowers seemed to remain on good terms: Solomon found Parr's lost horse. Within the Parr family, such a familial hierarchy also found expression. Despite having left his father previously and despite being a freeholder in his own right, Enoch Parr returned to and remained within his father's house until the day he was married. Much of his activity, once he learned of his father's imminent arrival, was to prepare for his father. Within a year of his father's settling, his father asked Enoch to return to North Carolina to collect some debts for him. Patriarchal authority played a major role within the families of early Indiana.

Perhaps one reason Parr returned to his father's house was much the same as the one for which he sought the plot of land next to Solomon Bowers: as a single man, he needed the services of a household, namely, a woman. As Parr's anxiety for Nancy Carr's hand revealed, a wife was a necessity to early life in the woods of Indiana. Nevertheless, the patriarchal household of early Hoosiers, although it had a necessary role for the woman, certainly subordinated her. Enoch Parr's snub by the Bowerses revealed the limited voice that Jemima Parr Bowers had.

Yet Solomon Bowers's choice to help his son was dictated in part by his role within the structure. As the father, it was his obligation to assist his children in establishing their own lives. To settle one's children in the same neighborhood was considered very desirable.[2] Certainly the Parr family established an extended family within their neighborhood. Enoch Parr's father helped to ensure that Enoch remained in the neighborhood by giving him about two hundred and fifty dollars in 1811, a sum approximately equal to what Parr still owed on his quarter section. Parr's father would remain in his homestead, surrounded by his children, until his death, and his final years certainly should have been comfortable. Such was the purpose of the family strategies pursued by many early Hoosiers.

Such family strategies depended on the ownership and transferal of familial land. For Parr, as for so many early Hoosiers, the acquisition of land was of prime importance. In his mind, he could not marry until he had land and could guarantee that "when united we would have some prospect of doing well." Upon arriving in Indiana, he set off in search of land. Parr never chose to squat. He even bought the land necessary to support his horse—it could have been hardly more than an acre—instead of just finding a clearing somewhere to plant a small crop of corn. Parr worked for wages, and he leased larger portions of land. All was done with the aim of acquiring title to some portion of property. When he finally settled on a quarter section, he remained for at least the next thirty-five years.

In his persistence, Parr would resemble many of his neighbors. Members of the Carr, Bowers, and Copple families remained in Washington County for decades. Enoch Parr would rise through politics, as a justice of the peace and later an associate circuit judge, and the church, as a prominent lay leader, part of the movement of the Baptist Church into the Campbellite Christian Church. In both positions, Parr would be in a position to assert the community's judgment. Serving in similar roles, persisters often served as the core of the neighborhood, the community. Moreover, as persisters these families were likely to intermarry even more, binding the neighborhood more closely together as a community.

THE HILLS OF SOUTHERN INDIANA

In his desire for land, Enoch Parr resembled many white men of the early American republic: land was the means by which families built farms and gained independence. The European Americans' motivation for developing western lands lay partially in the hopes of ensuring the continued widespread ownership of farms and the accompanying virtue it would engender in the populace.[3] Most who explored the new frontier looked carefully at the land, assessing its potential for agricultural development. The region would be accepted or rejected based on the land's ability to sustain a given society, according to that society's methods of sustaining itself. The land was judged for its worth as farmland.

But to look at southern Indiana today, with its forested hills, it is hard to imagine that early European American settlers saw farmland there. With second-growth forestation, much of the hill country of southern Indiana, which encompasses the southeastern and south-central portions of the state, appears today much as it might have in the early part of the nineteenth century (see map 1.1). What is especially hard to imagine is that these European Americans had once cleared the land of all its trees: first-growth forests are today measured in the tens of acres. Another geographical lesson is plain: southern Indiana, relatively untouched by glaciers, remained hilly, whereas glaciers bulldozed flat central Indiana. The relative wealth of the different regions, a wealth which has been derived in large part from agriculture, depended upon the quality of the soil and the ease with which it could be cultivated. But such simple formulations do not tell the whole story. They presuppose that commercial agriculture was the aim of the earliest European American settlers; moreover, they attribute to those first settlers the ability to see clearly the agricultural potential of a particular parcel of land. For many early Hoosiers the lands of southern Indiana held out not the poverty of contemporary Indiana but the possibilities of building families and communities.[4] There was little consensus about the value of the lands. Some thought it poor. Others saw their future.

Throughout southern Indiana, early European American travelers and settlers gazed upon the landscape and gauged its capacity for agriculture. Most observers, whether positive or negative, were primarily concerned with the hill country's agricultural potential.[5] Some had great hopes, despite the broken landscape, and many, like Enoch Parr, were particular in their desires. Indeed, fears about swamplands tended to be more common than problems with cultivating rolling farm. That the hill country looked like good farm country revealed the observers' roots in other hilly and even mountainous landscapes. It also would suggest that these settlers did not imagine a modern commercial farm, with its acres and acres of grain. Nevertheless, the hills of Indiana, marking the absence of glacial leveling, would have a profound effect on the lives of those who settled there.

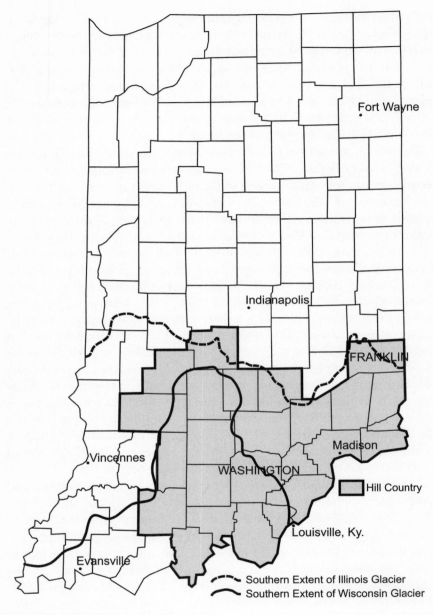

MAP 1.1. THE HILL COUNTRY OF INDIANA
From Robert C. Kingsbury, *An Atlas of Indiana* (Bloomington: Department of
Geography, Indiana University, 1970), 14. (Boone/Nation)

NATIVE PEOPLES AND THE HILL COUNTRY

Native peoples judged the hill country as less desirable than did Europeans. By the time of broad encounters between Europeans and the various native peoples, no indigenous peoples maintained permanent villages in the hill country.[6] Before 1673, the Mosopelea may have inhabited some land west of the Great Miami River in what would be extreme southeastern Indiana, but they were probably driven from this land by the Iroquois.[7] About 1786, a small band of Shawnee dwelt west of the banks of the Whitewater.[8] It may have been to this site that Tecumseh led a band of dissident Shawnee in 1797, living there for about three years.[9] The Delaware, who had settled in what would be central Indiana, had no permanent villages south of the glacial lines, although, at the time of the first Anglo-American incursions, they probably used the resources of southern Indiana more than any other identifiable group. A number of Delaware hunting and winter camps have been noted in the hill country, especially among the headwaters of the Blue River; like many villages of the indigenous peoples of the Great Lakes, these villages were multitribal, with Shawnee and Wyandot.[10]

Why the indigenous peoples failed to establish any permanent villages in southern Indiana has perplexed scholars. One reason for the absence of native groups in the hill country in later years may have been the policies of the Iroquois, who, during the seventeenth century, claimed the Ohio Valley as their private hunting reserve.[11] The Iroquois would later "allow" the Shawnee and the Delaware, whom they claimed they had subdued, to settle on Ohio Valley lands.[12] Certainly Iroquois warfare against more northerly villages had profound consequences, as many Algonquian bands sought refuge on the west side of Lake Michigan. As Iroquois power diminished, these bands, including the Miami and Potawatomi, who had allied with the French, moved eastward, but never settled in the hill country.[13] In this later period, warfare between the various Great Lakes bands and nations further south made the territory in between open to dispute and dangerous to live in. The settlement of Kentucky by European Americans did little to change the situation. For much of the post-contact era, southern Indiana was a buffer zone.

However, for many of the Algonquian Great Lakes tribes, the post-encounter period saw a shift, corresponding with their movement eastward and southward, into greater dependency upon agricultural pursuits.[14] Like the European Americans who would follow them, they raised hogs and corn.[15] Anthony Wayne, while moving on villages along the Maumee, would report "four or five miles of cornfields . . . and there are not less than 1,000 acres of corn around the town."[16] The vastness of these cornfields, to a European from the settled East, suggests a possible reason why the indigenous peoples did not settle in the region: the hill country afforded native peoples little possibility to pursue their forms of subsistence, as there were few places large enough in which to clear and plant the acres of corn that their communal plots demanded. For European Americans, where smaller family plots were the norm, the hill country would not be so restrictive.

Although the hill country was one of the few places in which the imagined "empty land" of the frontier might be conceived as corresponding to reality, such notions of "emptiness" remained profoundly European, tied up in a perception of space that presupposed settled agriculture as the mark of a region used by humans. Without the farms that for many early Hoosiers marked the good society, the natives' claims to the land was suspect. However, the indigenous peoples utilized its forests for the hunting necessary for their survival.

The British had ceded the land to the United States in the 1783 Treaty of Paris, but they had maintained influence among its native peoples until the War of 1812. Westerners resented the British influence—a major cause of the War of 1812—and believed the West had to be open for European American settlement. To a large extent, frontierspeople sought the immediate extermination of the rights of the indigenous peoples, while the government desired a more orderly settlement of the new lands. The federal government had little power to enforce the federal policy. There would be massacres of indigenous peoples, often of the most convenient village; the most convenient village was normally one which believed itself at peace with the United States—otherwise, the village probably would not have been so "convenient." The frontier militia were rarely good for organized warfare—their objectives often differed from those of the authorities who called them out—and the militia often revolted in the middle of a mission. But the cumulative effect of this frontier activity was to drag the federal government along by demanding that it protect its citizenry. The conquest of the indigenous peoples was a "democratic" decision.

The military campaigns that opened southern Indiana to European American conquests occurred primarily to its north. Soon after the American Revolution, the Americans undertook an effort to subordinate the indigenous peoples in what the Americans were now calling the Northwest Territory. After the Battle of Fallen Timbers, where the British failed to come to the rescue of native forces, the Miami chose to negotiate with the U.S. government. The subsequent Treaty of Greenville was the beginning of the end for Indian claims in southern Indiana. Clark's Military Grant at the Falls of the Ohio (Louisville), although claimed in 1783, was confirmed at Greenville. More importantly, the "Gore" of Indiana, a strip of land which encompassed the Whitewater Valley, was ceded to the Americans. With the Miami subdued by the threat of renewed violence, the Americans were gradually able to obtain title to more land in southern Indiana. William Henry Harrison became governor of Indiana Territory in 1803, and he repeatedly set out to acquire land from whatever native group was willing to give it up. Without any permanent settlements in the hill country, various leaders claimed ownership; each sought to gain annuities for their people.[17]

More troublesome to Harrison was the discontent, especially among younger native men, that these treaties bred. The discontent found voice and leadership in the persons of Tecumseh and his brother, Tenskwatawa, the Shawnee Prophet. Tecumseh ranged far to gather tribes into his alliance to oppose European American expansion, arguing that the land belonged to all Indians in common. The Prophet preached a religion of revitalization, arguing that Indians should give up most white ways. Both Tecumseh and Tenskwatawa attempted to transcend tribal affiliations. Because Pan-Indian ideas questioned the leadership of most tribes, the brothers had some difficulty in gathering a strong alliance, but European Americans were scared. In 1811, Harrison invaded Indian territory with one thousand men, camping on a hill within sight of Prophet's Town, near the confluence of the Tippecanoe and Wabash rivers. While they slept, The Prophet—Tecumseh was away at the time—attacked with perhaps five hundred soldiers and was repulsed, but not before inflicting some casualties. In many respects, the battle of Tippecanoe ended as a draw.[18] Harrison actually accomplished his task of ridding Indiana of the Indian threat when he led American forces against a combined British and Indian force at the Battle of Thames during the War of 1812, a battle in which Tecumseh was killed. With Tecumseh's death and the withdrawal of the British, all hopes for native resistance in Indiana were gone. In 1818, two years after Indiana achieved statehood, the Miami, Delaware, and others ceded most of central Indiana, as well as the remaining parts of southern Indiana, in what was known as the New Purchase.

EUROPEAN AMERICAN SETTLEMENT

The English colonists east of the Appalachians had seen the West as new territory, with vast possibilities for farming and commerce; they sought to dispossess the indigenous peoples and take up the land for themselves. These English were joined by a number of other ethnic groups who had settled in the English colonies. With the success of the American Revolution, these "new"

Americans undertook journeys westward. By 1795, European Americans had begun to settle in the hill country of what would be southern Indiana.

For their efforts in the American Revolution, George Rogers Clark's men were awarded land on the northern shore of the Ohio River, at the Falls of Louisville. In 1784, the town of Clarksville was laid out, the first Anglo-American town platted in the hill country of southern Indiana, but even by 1793, it still had only forty residents.[19] Due in part to the pattern of Indian treaties and in part to the relative access to waterways, southern Indiana was settled from the Ohio, Wabash, and Whitewater valleys inward.

That waterways played an important role in the settlement of southern Indiana is of little surprise; transportation routes and access played an important role in determining exactly who would settle the region. The two most obvious routes that most early settlers took were the Ohio River and the trail through the Cumberland Gap. Hence the vast majority of early southern Indiana residents were from the Mid-Atlantic and Upper South states. There was no northerly route, and therefore there were few New Englanders and New Yorkers among the early settlers. Iroquois dominance in much of New York and Algonquian dominance in the Great Lakes had limited the decades-long westward thrust that had placed over 60,000 people in Kentucky by 1798; settlement in Kentucky had been aided by the relative absence of indigenous peoples on both sides of the Ohio River.

Both migration paths eventually led back to eastern Pennsylvania or, more generally, the Mid-Atlantic area. Those who came down the Ohio River seem to have come directly from east of the Appalachian ridge, although some may have lived in western Pennsylvania before migrating to the hill country of southern Indiana.[20] The other major migratory stream had started in Pennsylvania and headed down the Shenandoah Valley into the Upland South of Virginia and North Carolina. The large number of Southerners who settled in Indiana were overwhelmingly from the Upland South, not from the large plantation areas of the lowland.[21]

While these two migratory streams met in the hill country of southern Indiana, each predominated in certain parts. In the south-central portion of the state, there was a heavy concentration of settlers from the Upland South, but this migration pattern extended much further north than what was typically considered southern Indiana (see map 1.2).[22] Both southeastern and southwestern Indiana had relatively fewer Upland Southerners in them; southeastern Indiana, while part of the hill country, was settled primarily by residents of the Mid-Atlantic states. Despite these larger patterns, ethnic enclaves were apparent in both my sample counties: for instance, over two-thirds of Franklin County's Maryland natives resided in three of its thirteen townships. Likewise, Quakers made up a sizeable portion of

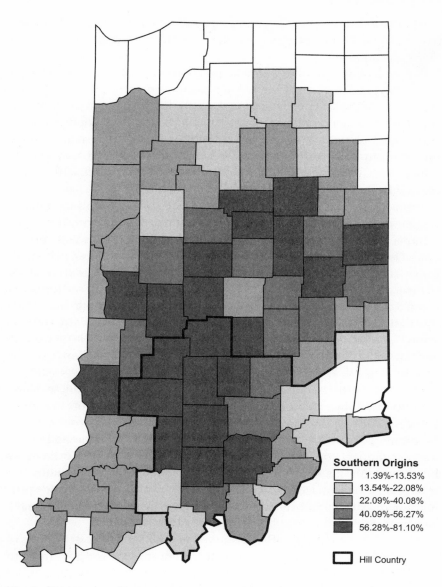

Southern Origins
- 1.39%-13.53%
- 13.54%-22.08%
- 22.09%-40.08%
- 40.09%-56.27%
- 56.28%-81.10%

☐ Hill Country

MAP 1.2 RESIDENTS OF VIRGINIA, NORTH CAROLINA, AND TENNESSEE, AS PERCENTAGE
OF HOOSIERS BORN OUTSIDE THE OHIO VALLEY STATES
Derived from Gregory S. Rose, "Hoosier Origins: The Nativity of Indiana's United
States–Born Population in 1850," *Indiana Magazine of History* 81 (September 1985): 201–
32; Rose, "The Distribution of Indiana's Ethnic and Racial Minorities in 1850," *Indiana
Magazine of History* 87 (September 1991): 224–60; and United States Census Office, *The
Seventh Census of the United States, 1850* (1853; reprint, New York: Arno Press, 1976).
(Boone/Nation, using Jenks Natural Breaks)

Washington County's North Carolina population. By far the most important enclave in Franklin County was the settlement of German Catholics in the 1830s and 1840s.

These German Catholics were a major component of southern Indiana's ethnic mix, and they were centered in two locations: one, in the southeastern corner of the state, included Franklin, Ripley, Jennings, and Dearborn counties; the other, in the southwestern portion of the hill country, was in Perry and Dubois counties, as well as Spencer County. German Catholic migration to both these areas began in the mid-1830s, and they quickly achieved prominence, with priests and early German Catholic settlers purchasing land to make available to later immigrants.[23]

Even before the German Catholics arrived, there were Germans in Franklin and Washington counties; many Germans came through Pennsylvania and followed the two migratory streams west. Remnants of this older German culture remained in the Church of the Brethren. Although some Irish came to southern Indiana to work on railroads and canals in the 1840s and were probably from the Potato Famine exodus, they rarely formed themselves into identifiable communities. The Scotch-Irish Presbyterians did form a number of small communities.[24] And other ethnic groups also formed communities: German Protestants in Jackson County and elsewhere; Belgians in Perry County; French Catholics in Floyd County; and the Swiss of, aptly enough, Switzerland County.[25]

Nor was southern Indiana's diversity limited to foreign immigrants. Lying next to the slave state of Kentucky, the hill country was home to a number of free African Americans.[26] These African Americans often found homes in communities with large Quaker populations, such as Orange and Washington counties, as well as in the bustling Ohio River towns. In 1820, many hill country African Americans lived with European American families, and several were categorized as slaves, despite the Northwest Ordinance's prohibition of slavery; probably a number of those listed as free were actually held as slaves.[27]

Almost all these early settlers came to farm. In 1820, over 97 percent of the workers tallied in Washington County were engaged in agriculture; in Franklin County, the percentage was 88 percent. With the development of these counties, the percentage of farm workers slowly dropped. By 1840, only 87 percent of Washington County laborers engaged in agriculture, and it would drop again in 1850 to 73 percent. Franklin County's drop was sharper: by 1840, 72 percent of the workers were farming, and by 1850, only 67 percent.[28] While the opportunities for nonagricultural employment increased as the society grew, these new jobs were not taken by the earlier settlers. Ninety-seven percent of working 1820 residents who remained in

Franklin County in 1850 were farmers; 93 percent of similarly persisting residents in Washington County pursued agricultural employment.[29]

To look at much of the land of modern southern Indiana is to see rolling hills, again covered with a dense forest. With the knowledge of the wealth and abundance of the Great Plains and even the flatlands just north of the glacial line, it becomes hard to understand how any imagined the hill country of southern Indiana to be an agricultural mecca. Yet in the early nineteenth century, few trusted flat country. And a glance at these people's origins suggests that many were accustomed to an even more broken country: the Upland South and the mountains of Germany. Because they imagined southern Indiana as a place where the land could sustain them and their families, as a place where they could achieve independence, as a place for farms, they demanded the removal of those—the indigenous peoples— who did not use the land as the European Americans thought fit, as independent yeomen farmers. In their version of agrarian republicanism, men who lived as the indigenous peoples did could hardly be called civilized. Land was for farms.

BUYING THE LAND

Communities in the hill country of southern Indiana were built around the households that farmed the land. To build the good society was, in the eyes of many early Hoosiers, to create a world in which households were able to acquire the means of production, land, without interference from government, individuals, or indigenous peoples, and to use that land to ensure the prosperity and independence of the family and its descendents.

The European Americans who settled southern Indiana were willing to kill for its land. Yet despite Enoch Parr's relentless search for the perfect farm, it would be wrong to suggest that simple greed was the motivator. Land was necessary to building the family, the basic unit of the community, as it was the means of access to the resources of production and thus the means of ensuring the reproduction of the family. And land had political meanings as well as economic. Property, to most early Hoosiers, was the foundation of independence and thereby of equality; only a man who owned his own property could be beyond the manipulations of others and thereby control his own destiny. Arguing for laws to protect debtors in the wake of the 1819 depression, "Hector" asserted, "You take my life, when you do take the means whereby I live."[30] As late as 1850, a Hoosier could argue, against the claims of usurers, that "an inalienable right to the earth is a right not to be divested of."[31] In addition, this independence conferred upon a property owner virtue at the ballot box, thereby ensuring that a band of well-to-do men

17

could not manipulate those in their employ and control and lead the government to tyranny. Equality between men was guaranteed by property as well, because in any system in which one was beholden to another for employment, equality was in danger; many Hoosiers, like Parr, took on wage labor, but as a means to acquire land. Ownership of land by the individual was the desired norm, as it guaranteed subsistence and equality.[32] Hoosiers, therefore, sought property.

Despite this emphasis on independence, communities were formed, sometimes against great odds. The rectilinear division of the land was not conducive to the establishment of close neighborhoods, as the grid dictated that only four families could erect houses within shouting distance. Despite these obstacles, tracts were not purchased in random order.[33] Early land purchases were often defined by the valleys of small streams. In sample townships of Washington County, a number of distinct communities formed, with early land purchasers avoiding floodplains and sharp ridges. Nevertheless, social units also emerged, as early purchases formed neighborhoods in these valleys. For instance, in Springfield Township of Franklin County, although it saw a great deal of speculative buying in the 1810s, by 1820 resident landowners, with only two exceptions, lived adjacent to other resident landowners.[34] As Enoch Parr's story suggested, communities were quickly established in southern Indiana, often on the basis of mutual migration from earlier homes and often through extended families. Certainly in 1809, Parr and his neighbors also feared attacks by the indigenous peoples still inhabiting the northern portion of the Indiana Territory, and communities were often formed around blockhouses. Nevertheless, with Harrison's vanquishing of Tecumseh, such imperatives diminished, yet the settlement patterns continued.

Certainly the first place many new Hoosiers looked to purchase land was the United States Land Office. Southern Indiana was served by land offices in Jeffersonville, Vincennes, and Cincinnati, the last of which was moved to Brookville and then to Indianapolis.[35] Given the great distance to land offices, many settlers had to travel several days to enter land; for want of a horse, Enoch Parr was prevented from entering his choice of lands. Sometimes they sent neighbors and relatives or traveled together. For instance, on the same day in 1832, George Chastain and Absalom Stark entered land in Vernon Township, Washington County, splitting a quarter section between them.[36]

The distribution of the public lands in southern Indiana occurred under three basic eras. Prior to 1820, land was purchased in quarter section tracts, normally of 160 acres. The land could be purchased on credit from the government for two dollars an acre, with 25 percent down, and the rest to be paid regularly within four years. Despite these liberal terms, Congress passed laws almost every year for the relief of debtors. With the Panic of 1819, the delinquencies became so great that Congress scrapped the entire credit system, ushering in the second era of land purchases in southern Indiana. Congress made up for the denial of credit by offering the lands at $1.25 per acre and lowering the minimum purchase to 80 acres. In 1832, the Congress reduced the minimum purchase to 40 acres. On the heels of this reduction came the boom years of 1834 to 1836, in which much land in southern Indiana was purchased. Even with the reduction in acreage, Hoosiers demanded further cutbacks in the price. In 1833, the Salem *Western Annotator* had argued for the reduction in the price of the public lands, claiming that although such a reduction might lower the price of lands previously bought, perhaps even below their original purchase price, only speculators would be hurt: For the true farmer, "the same number of acres will yield the same number of bushels of wheat, corn, or potatoes"; the question for virtuous men was not the value of the land but the potential to produce. Hopes for further reductions in prices were not fulfilled until 1854, by which time all but the poorest swamp land in southern Indiana had been entered.[37]

Before 1820, a settler would need eighty dollars to enter a tract of land of 160 acres, and he had to be prepared to come up with a like sum in the second, third, and fourth years. For actual settlers, the costs were potentially prohibitive. Most settlers would have to take into account that their new farm would not begin paying immediately. A few chose to halve these costs by purchasing land together; some were obviously kin, like John and Christopher Stroube, but many others had as partners more distant relatives— in-laws, cousins—and as friends, like William Clark and Stephen Gregg.[38] They faced the task of clearing a dense forest from their land. In the interim, the family still needed to be fed and clothed, needs not yet readily met by the farm's production. The woods, with its game and furs, met some of these demands, but others had to be fulfilled in the marketplace, thus requiring cash or barterable goods. The Ingleses, who settled near Princeton, Indiana, estimated their first year expenses to be $1,240.

Entry of half section, or 320 acres	$160
House and stable, $80; smoke-house, pigsty, and henhouse, $40	120
Two horses, good, $160; two ploughs and harness, $40	200
Four axes, four hoes, $16; wagon, $100; harrows, $12	128
Spades, shovels, $6; two cows, $36; four sows in pig, $20	62
Corn crib and barn	60
Clearing 20 acres of land first year, foot and under, and fenced well	130
Ploughing, planting, hoeing, and turning	130
Twelve months' maintenance of family	250
	$1,240[39]

The Ingleses, part of the relatively affluent English settlement, were unusual among early settlers of southern Indiana: they paid to have their tasks done. Ingles did insist that in the second year they would not hire labor; the labor was necessary to make a viable farm in as short a time as possible. But even people who constructed their own buildings, cleared and broke their own land, and brought with them their own stock would still have many expenses in the first years, and they might not have a fully functioning farm after just one year.[40]

As a consequence, especially before 1820, some families were not able to buy land, even with the government's credit terms. Often families worked for others before being able to purchase their own land, as Enoch Parr did. John and Mary Watson, immigrants from England, landed at St. John, New Brunswick, and pulled a sleigh loaded with their children and possessions on a frozen river and then overland to the St. Lawrence, where John built a light wagon, which he then pulled some 400 miles to Kingston. From there, a kind gentleman paid their passage across Lake Ontario; they stayed in New York for a time and then left for Indiana, rafting down the Allegheny and Ohio, to settle in Dearborn County. They quickly found a position whereby they leased land on half shares. As their circumstances improved, they wrote back to England to report that "we are not much concerned with Michaelmas and Lady-Day here, for as many farms as we chose, we could have for paying 1/3 of the produce," and that prospects appeared good that they would soon purchase land.[41] Some who sought land were assisted by speculators and mortgage writers; at Brookville, within a year of the establishment of the land office, there were eight "banks" in town.[42]

The expenses faced by early settlers certainly created an impediment to settlement. Of the four townships that I examined extensively, the two in Franklin County saw the most activity before 1820. After 1820, while the price on the barrelhead increased $20 to $100, the title was clear, and settlers no longer had to balance their families' needs with additional payments to the government. Unfortunately, though, with the Panic of 1819, few would have any money; some took advantage of the reduced acreage in 1821, but sales then dipped. It would not be until the middle of the 1830s, with a combination of even smaller acreages and greater prosperity, before large numbers of purchases would resume. By the time the bubble burst again in 1837, much of the land was gone in three of the sample townships, but in Gibson Township, Washington County, sales took several years to subside, only to resume slowly again in the 1840s and 1850s, until all land was purchased.[43]

Who purchased the land? In southern Indiana, argues historian Paul Wallace Gates, settlers "made the land system more democratic in its operation than its framers intended."[44] At first glance, it hardly looked democratic. In Franklin County, only a quarter of all land purchasers from the previous eleven years were residents by 1820. By contrast, though, Hamilton Township, Hamilton County, Iowa, had only 9 of its 149 purchasers still farming in the county in a similar eleven years after it was opened for sale.[45] But smaller tracts after 1820 improved residency. By 1840, over a third of the Highland Township purchasers, primarily from the 1830s, still lived in Franklin County. Although Franklin County showed higher levels of residence among original purchasers than other areas surveyed in the historical literature, Washington County was off the charts.[46] In 1820, 54 percent of those who had purchased land in Washington County remained. By 1830, the number had dropped to 46 percent, and by 1840, only 36 percent of those who had purchased public land in the previous thirty-one years made their homes in Washington County.[47] In sum, the relationship between land purchases and actual residence was stronger in southern Indiana than elsewhere.

Nevertheless, about half of Washington County public land purchasers and up to three-quarters of Franklin County purchasers were not, or at least did not remain, county residents. Who were these people? Speculators would be the obvious answer. Speculation may well have played an important role in the development of southern Indiana. Such speculation had the potential to threaten the independence of its residents, by concentrating the resources of the community in the hands of the few.

The hand of the speculator is revealed by a glance at the largest purchasers in each township. At the far extreme Gibson Township, Washington County, had over 22 percent of its land acquired by just 5 percent of the purchasers. A more detailed look at the individuals who constituted the largest purchasers reveals that many actually resided in the county in which they made their purchases. In Gibson Township, thirteen of the fifteen largest purchasers—320 acres or more—were present in the county the census year immediately following their first purchase.[48] In general, though, the relatively small acreages of purchases contrasted sharply with other areas in Indiana and the Midwest.[49] None of these people was about to control the destiny of southern Indiana.

Large-scale speculating did exist.[50] Nevertheless, in 1833, no one, resident or nonresident, owned land in more than two townships of Franklin County.[51] Widespread domination by certain individuals was not the norm. Even so, the speculator was never a popular figure in southern Indiana, although a distinction often was made between resident and nonresident speculators. One of the biggest differences between resident and nonresident speculators was that resident speculators often leased their land, while nonresidents left the land unimproved and unavailable, except to those whose livestock ranged. By 1844, unimproved tracts held by nonresidents of the township accounted for 13 percent of the acreage in Gibson Township and 12 percent of the acreage in Highland; by contrast, most of the nonresidents' land in Vernon and Springfield Townships had some improvements due in large part to their earlier settlement.

Speculative activity was not always a hindrance to settlement. Speculators sought profit, of course, but they were often willing to grant credit, before 1820 on more liberal terms than the government and after 1820 as the sole source of credit. John Henry, exploring for lands upon which to speculate, wrote to his wife:

> About 8 miles above the [Hindostan] Falls and five or six from the [White] River in a straight direction, I found some land, which I think will be valuable. It is sufficiently level for any species of cultivation, and the soil is of a very excellent quality. . . . It is within three miles of a mill, about to be erected on a stream sufficiently large + surrounded by a country which must populate as soon as the rage for the Wabash subsides.— I confidently hope to see the whole country settled by good industrious farmers in a few years.[52]

While Henry recognized that having the neighborhood fill with "good industrious farmers" would profit him, he had a sense of pride and accomplishment in playing a role in creating a society where there had been none before. Few Hoosier speculators played great roles in developing southern Indiana by building roads and railroads, banks and factories.[53] Nevertheless, the speculator as source of capital cannot be dismissed, as evidenced by the large number of people who purchased land, not from the government but from individuals.

Those speculators who left their lands fallow were open to scorn and a little depredation. As long as speculators did not prevent Hoosiers from gaining access to land, their potential to disrupt the community was minimized. Speculative activity in southern Indiana appears to have been relatively minimal; Hoosiers had little to fear from outsiders' buying up their lands. When speculation did take place, it was often by members of the local community who did not deny access to the land. But as the improvements suggest, much of the land, even that owned by outsiders, was being placed in the hands of actual settlers.

Many nonresident speculators may have had the services of a local agent. In 1820, the Brookville law firm of Caswell and Drew offered a number of properties for purchase, lease, or rent.[54] Perhaps some speculators owed the Land Office money when cash was in short supply. Interestingly enough, several of the properties had specific terms: one was to be sold "very low for *cash* or *whiskey,*" while another was available for ten years. Among the

propositions offered was "to lease several quarter sections of good land ...
on improving leases." Many early settlers who did not have the means to
buy land took on such improving leases. Benjamin and Mary Mace, who
settled near Lexington and were unable to find land to suit them, took such
a lease:

> [Benjamin] has leased 25 acres of land for 5 years there is a log house and
> barn on it & smoke house 2 acres of pasture cleared of and 15 acres of the rest
> the timber is all dead and no under brush we are to have all we can raise of
> from it for five years for clearing it.[55]

John Hicks's father also first settled on such a lease, holding the land for
nine years for the mere task of clearing and fencing it; Hicks's father would
later enter land in the same neighborhood.[56] Such leases met the needs of
all concerned: the owner got a cleared field, and the tenant got all he could
raise. More traditional leases, like the ones into which Enoch Parr and the
Watsons entered, also gave individuals access to land.

The lands cleared by people like the Hickses and the Macys would be
prime lands sought by newcomers to the region who wished to establish
farms quickly. When the labor of clearing was considered, federal land was
hardly a bargain. Many sought land with improvements. In 1823, Elisha
Hughes

> bought a small farm of 125 acres and crop of corn and hogs; moved in July,
> got a deed and paid in full. Four hundred dollars was the price of this small
> farm, with twenty acres cleared—two cabins, which are comfortable in time
> of storm, a tolerable barn and other buildings and six good springs of water.[57]

Twelve years later, George Kennedy's brother would buy thirty acres for
$190, "with tolerable improvement."[58] It was not only the speculator that
sold this land. Not far from where John Henry located his plots, "land ...
may be bought Second Handed by paying In Addition to the Congress price
the work of the Improvements."[59] Others reported that they had purchased
improved land of a backwoodsman, who was only too glad to move further west.[60] Not all land sold privately had improvements on it. Jacob Weaver
bought some land, "no improvement made there on" for "six dolars an
aker, to be paid in ten years time."[61] Such contract purchases may well have
been common. For stable speculators, both resident and nonresident, the
ease and reduced risk of land contracts may well have made them a favored
instrument for conveying land.[62]

These contracts and leases help explain the large number of southern
Indiana residents who had not purchased land. Family assistance may have

been an even more important element. In the 1820 Franklin County sample, only about 40 percent of male-headed households owned land.[63] However, over 60 percent of those without land had families in Franklin County, with most in the same township; many could well have been farming family tracts, even after they had set up their own households. This strategy certainly would explain why Elisha Hughes's farm had two cabins.

Tax records tell a similar story. In the four sample townships in both counties, more than 40 percent of the males over twenty-one residing in the township were without property in each of the available tax years (see chart 1.1).[64] However, in most of the tax years, almost half the landless residents had families in the township who owned land.[65] Information given in the 1850 census confirmed that large numbers of these were sons who, like Enoch Parr, remained at home before being married. Certainly many of these were young men who had yet to receive their legacy.

Some, of course, may have been squatting. However, since squatting took place outside institutions, few records survive of squatters. The period before 1820 probably saw the most squatting on the public domain. The disparity between the year of first settlement and the year of the first land entry gives a hint that some arrived before the land was auctioned off. At the time of the auctions, though, too few had actually settled in southern Indiana to lend credence to historian Paul Wallace Gates's notion that the "section was early overrun by squatters who settled promiscuously over the land before it was offered for sale, made improvements, and organized claim associations to provide quasi-legal land and title registration system in the absence of government action."[66] The 1807 Indiana Territorial Census found few eventual Washington and Franklin County land purchasers already resident. None of the early land purchasers in Franklin County was there by 1807, except John Conner, who had a trading post on the Whitewater. In Washington County, there were at most only four 1807 residents among the 244 people who bought land between 1809 and 1819.[67]

There were squatters in southern Indiana, but squatting often took place after the land had been offered for sale and there were no buyers. By 1820, in Washington County, only eight individuals could be identified who probably were squatting on land they would eventually purchase; in 1830, a similar number squatted.[68] In Franklin County, only one person jumps off the pages of the 1820 census as a squatter. The low level of access to land recorded by the 1821 tax roll for Highland Township in Franklin County, however, suggests that others must have been squatting. Only 59 percent of residents taxed had access to land, when the township would achieve 83 percent access by 1835. It would seem improbable that with all the public land, settlers would be renting at a rate far in excess of any later seen.[69] If later rates of

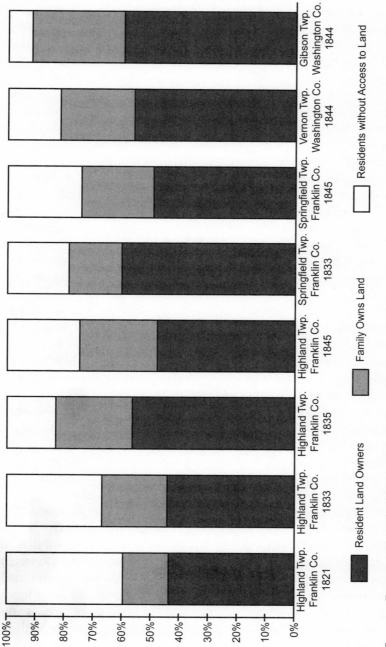

CHART 1.1 EXTENT OF ACCESS TO LAND, 1821–1845

Derived from Franklin County, Highland Township 1821 Tax Roll, Auditor's Office (attic), Franklin County Courthouse, Brookville, Ind.; Franklin County, 1833 Tax Roll, microfilm, Genealogy Division, Indiana State Library, Indianapolis; Franklin County, 1845 Tax Duplicate, Auditor's Office, Franklin County Courthouse, Brookville, Ind.; and Washington County, 1844 Tax Duplicate, Auditor's Office, Washington County Courthouse, Salem, Ind.

access to farmland are held constant, the most generous estimate would be that before 1830, squatters could have made up no more than 20 percent of the population.

For instance, in 1830, a Hamilton Shaw resided somewhere in Franklin County; by 1833, he was assessed a poll tax in Highland Township. The 1835 tax assessor placed Shaw in section 24 of Highland Township (T8n R2e); in 1836, he purchased 120 acres in the southeast quarter of section 23, abutting section 24.[70] The line between the two sections followed a small valley, with the best soil in Shaw's purchase and the most likely spot for his home. If the tax assessor failed to distinguish the lines correctly, not altogether impossible, Shaw very well may have been squatting by 1835, if not sooner.[71] While certainly the land was by modern agricultural standards quite poor, it supported various oaks well and, given the proximity to the proposed Whitewater Canal, would have been a prime timber source; the land was no worse than much that was entered in the heyday of the mid-1830s.[72] Given that, Shaw was fortunate enough to be able to enter as large a tract as 120 acres at as late a date as 1836, unless he had already taken possession of it, with the agreement of his neighbors. His neighbors very well may have agreed: fourteen landless people in the Highland tax duplicate for 1833 were to enter land in the township in the next three years, and Shaw was one of six in the 1835 tax roll who would buy a piece of the public domain in the next year. Nevertheless, it is perhaps telling that of all the archived and published primary materials by southern Indiana residents, although they mention farming on family land, leasing, and contracting to buy land, nary a one speaks to squatting on the public lands.

Squatters believed that the land belonged to those who used it. And they probably were not the only ones in southern Indiana to hold such beliefs. It had been the justification that Hoosiers used for stealing the land from the indigenous peoples. Such beliefs were projected not just on the government's land but on private land as well. For many in southern Indiana it did not matter much whether the land was entered or not. Even by 1850, Springfield Township, which was the most developed of my four sample townships, over half of its acreage, all privately owned, was still unimproved.[73] Township resident Joseph Hewitt would write to his father in Ireland that "a man can go out with a gun and a dog and there is no gamekeepers to watch him."[74] Even private property, if it was not being used, was appropriated for others' use, occasionally to the owner's consternation. William Jones demanded of George and Levi Jennings that "the board tent which you built on my land near Rice's Campground . . . must be removed with in thirty days of the date of this notice or I shall proceed to remove the said tent at your cost and damage."[75] As long as much of the land was unimproved and unfenced, livestock could run wild by custom, if not by common law. Many Hoosiers ignored the formal distinctions of property.

Despite these beliefs, squatting was far too risky. Always leery of the manipulations of others, southern Indiana settlers could not risk their family's production and reproduction by not owning their own land. They took advantage of the high wages of the settlement period to pay off their obligations. By actions like Hamilton Shaw's, their ideological allegiance to the complete system of land and capital was limited; rarely questioning the individual proprietorship of land, they often questioned the marketplace in capital which dictated that only those with money could use land, feeling justified in using unutilized land. But because only landownership guaranteed independence, they were landowners. By 1820, most residents had legal possession of the land upon which they lived, whether it be through ownership, family plots, leases, or land contracts—extralegal means were too risky.

EGALITARIANISM IN THE HOOSIER MIND

Too many southern Indiana settlers did not own land for it to be considered an egalitarian distribution. But in contrast to many parts of the country, land belonged to a greater proportion of the population. A perfectly egalitarian distribution of land was hardly important to early Hoosiers. Some might take more than others, often with the community's blessing; few Hoosiers scorned such accumulators, as long as the speculator's activities did not interfere with the Hoosiers' access to resources. What was important was that most Hoosiers retained some form of access to at least some land, for the land guaranteed their independence and thus their political and social equality. Perfect economic equality was not necessary.

Lamenting her servant woes, Susannah Pering had identified landownership at the root of her problems; she wrote back to England:

> Many of them require to sit down at the table, and be treated in all respects as one of the family. . . . The reason that they are so independent here seems to be that they are not obliged to live out; most of their parents own a larger or smaller portion of land, on which they can maintain their family.[76]

A Napoleon, Indiana, landlady echoed Pering, reporting to Virginian James Davidson that "these servant girls are very proud and cannot brook the idea of being called servants." Davidson added, "May God protect me from these Free States."[77] The egalitarianism showed up, in large part, because it offended the sensibilities of the more aristocratic visitors. Captain William

Newnham Blane, detouring off the main roads, was astonished by the backwoodsman: "It is true they always treated me as their equal; but at the same time, there was a sort of real civility in their behavior"—as if Blane had never considered that civility and equality could coexist.[78]

Without the perspective of aristocrats, few Hoosiers themselves commented on their egalitarianism. Bazil Edmonston suggested that if his children "could turn their property into money they may lay it out here to a good advantage in a free country of equality that flows with milk and honey."[79] Despite having come from places where inequality was more the rule, for most Hoosiers, the belief in their equality to their neighbors, as well as to their visitors, was so imbedded in their understanding of the world that it rarely was voiced, except when it was called into question. Captain Blane tapped into the "imponderability" of their equality, when he described stopping for the night at a cabin in southern Indiana and having "to rub down and feed my own horse":

> Those who have not tried this after riding all day, do not know how disagreeable it is. At the same time, I am certain that no kind of incivility was intended. All the people living in the same neighbourhood being nearly equal in point of wealth and education (with little enough of either), are not accustomed to show one another any attention, and therefore extend the same want of ceremony to the strangers who might chance to come to their houses.[80]

As Blane suggested, these Hoosiers acted in accordance with their notions of equality, not out of spite for their betters; as Blane's description conveyed, the householder treated the situation as completely natural.

Talk of egalitarianism was, of course, prominent in political rhetoric. Within the political realm, many of these hill country Hoosiers sought to protect what they believed to be their equality. Enoch Parr's actions illustrated how deeply engrained equality was in the southern Indiana mind. By the 1840s, Parr had risen to prominence in Washington County, as both Democratic politician and church leader. With the coming of the Mexican War, he sent three of his sons off to fight. Two did not survive. Morgan died of sickness, and David was killed while aiding a wounded man. The citizens of the county requested of Enoch Parr that David be buried under a public monument as a "son of Washington County." Enoch consented but, perhaps thinking of Morgan, stipulated that the monument be erected in memory of all those from Washington County who died in the service of their country.[81] A cynical reading might have Parr seeking to honor both his sons and recognizing the political capital to be made in honoring the other four county men who had died. Yet Parr chose not to make distinctions between heroes and those who merely served, clearly seeing that despite the cause of death, both his sons had made the valiant choice. Moreover, even if it were only a good political move—and Parr's deep religiosity suggests to me that it was not—it would suggest that Parr understood how deeply Hoosiers responded to assurances of equality. Parr was elected later that summer to fill out a term of a judge who had died.

Hoosier social equality did not rest upon an equal distribution of wealth. Instead, equality was granted by access to land, the means by which most hill country Hoosiers could sustain themselves. Therefore, the most important criterion would be what percentage of the population had access to land. Referring back to access to land (see chart 1.1), in the years from 1821 to 1845, at least three-quarters of southern Indiana residents had access to land, whether through ownership or through family. Among those who owned land, acreage was fairly evenly distributed, in large part thanks to the minimum purchases required by the federal government. By the mid-1830s, there were significant differences between townships in the proportion of the taxpayers who actually owned land; much of this difference, as we have seen in Highland Township, reflected the resurgence of settlement which had just begun in 1833. The townships with the highest proportion of actual landowners in their midst were the ones which had been earliest and most thoroughly settled. By 1844, distinctions in rates of landownership disappear; about 57 percent of taxpaying males owned land in most of Franklin County.[82] Only Ray Township, the center of Franklin County's German Catholic community, had a significantly higher landownership rate. In any given neighborhood, most landowning farmers had a rough equivalency in wealth with their landowning neighbors; when aggregated across the entire county, with its varying soils, terrains, and market opportunities, wealth proved to be more unequally distributed. Fewer distinctions appeared in Washington County.[83] Like Franklin County, about 60 percent of Washington County taxpayers owned land, with several townships surpassing 70 percent. The 30–40 percent without land still often had family resources upon which to depend. Few places in nineteenth-century America equaled southern Indiana's access to land.

Nowhere was dependence on family resources more apparent than in the changes over the life cycle. Ownership of land was very much a function of age; whereas only about half the male heads of household in their twenties were fortunate enough to own land, around 80 percent would own land by the time they reached middle age.[84] Among all landless men over twenty, more than half were only in their twenties. These life cycle patterns of landownership could suggest an agricultural ladder at work, but many of these heads of household had families in the same township.[85] As their fathers passed middle age, they slowly distributed their holdings, passing them along to their children; some began to live with these children.

In a breakdown of wealth by place of birth, Germans in Franklin County stand out, both for the lowest average landholding and for the greatest percentage of landowners. The acquisition of land, no matter how small the acreage or third-rate the soil or terrain, was profoundly important to the German immigrants.[86] Little distinction in wealth appeared between migrants from the various parts of the United States.

The vast majority of Hoosiers had access to property. If land were controlled by the few, access to land would be limited. Such was not the case in southern Indiana. The only identifiable census group with a unique pattern of wealth in these counties of southern Indiana was the Germans, many of whom were Catholic. As I will argue in forthcoming chapters, these Germans were bound into a vision of independence, community, and morality—a vision which demanded they control their own piece of soil. In this desire they were joined by many other inhabitants of southern Indiana, defined not by their place of origin, their age, or their township but by their attitude toward the market, their political ideology, and their religious and moral beliefs. These Hoosiers, like their new German neighbors, sought land as necessary to their future independence and the independence of their children. Many may have accumulated large land holdings in the process—indeed, it was necessary if a man had a large family—but for many, too, their fears had the potential, as we shall see, to limit their accumulation of wealth. For that reason, these Hoosiers, like their German neighbors, may well have had smaller holdings. Their interest was not wealth—although they never turned down a dollar—but in providing for the future of their families.

A PERSISTENT PEOPLE

Implicit in the family strategy was a commitment to the particular area in which these families settled and carved out their future and the future of their progeny.[87] Through buying land and creating families, Hoosiers made long-term commitments to life in the hills. Indeed, if they found a society in which they could be as assured of the continued pursuit of their desires, they would remain. And they did. Both Franklin and Washington counties showed persistence rates at or above the norm for nineteenth-century America.[88] From 1820 to 1830, at least 44 percent of the 1820 heads of household remained in Washington County.[89] Franklin County showed a slightly lower percentage: only about 36 percent remained.[90] In the 1830s, fewer people persisted, as both counties dropped 5–8 percent, only to rebound in the 1840s and 1850s.

Land and family were two key factors in determining persistence among Hoosiers in the hill country. In the 1820s, those with families persisted at a rate about 5 percent greater than those who did not have families. These trends continued through the 1830s and 1840s, with families playing such an important role that by the 1840 census, in Franklin County, family members persisted at over twice the rate of nonfamily types, 48 percent to 22 percent; almost as large a contrast was found in Washington County. Land also played a major role in promoting persistence. Owners in the 1820 sample persisted at a greater rate, peaking at nearly 9 percent greater in Washington County. By the 1850s, land had increased in importance in determining whether residents would stay or go, with landownership boosting persistence by about 15 percent. The size of the holdings made some difference, although in Washington County, values above $500 showed fairly consistent persistence. Place of origin was of little significance, save one: the German population of Franklin County persisted at a rate over 15 percent higher than the general population of the county.[91] These Germans helped ensure that Highland Township had the highest persistence rate in Franklin County. The German factor begins to explain why, unlike in Washington County, in Franklin County there was great variation between townships in terms of persistence.

All the townships in the northwestern part of Franklin County showed low persistence. The primary reason for the low rate of persistence may well have been the demise of the Whitewater Canal, which had originally drawn many with grandiose dreams of commercial success. People who persisted in southern Indiana were those who had found some semblance of success, however they defined success. For some in Franklin County, that success came in the form of accumulated wealth. Adjusting for age, it appears that persisters had a much greater percentage of wealth than did the general population. Not surprisingly, Franklin County showed a far greater willingness to participate in a commercial economy, and its citizens had had the advantage of the Whitewater Canal. In Washington County, persisters did not hold much greater wealth than did the general population. Nevertheless, in both counties, access to land was of primary importance. Persisters equaled or exceeded the general population in landownership. Because access to land ensured independence and made possible the re-creation of the family, it is of little surprise that those who held land stayed.

Southern Indiana was not immune to the mobility that characterized much of nineteenth-century America. In two short years, from 1833 to 1835, 37 of 115 residents had left Highland Township, about 32 percent, or almost half of the total turnover recorded for Franklin County in the 1830s.[92] If multiplied by five, this number would suggest that in the ten-year periods of the census, the population would have turned over more than one and a half times. Since at least 30 percent of the population remained, that did not happen; instead, a segment of the population probably turned over several times with great rapidity. There was a transient population, characterized by the nonownership of property and the absence of family. Those with property remained; those without property only remained if they had family.[93] For those without either, there was a good chance they would be moving on.[94]

These themes were repeated in more muted form in the other parts of southern Indiana sampled. Despite the stress on community and persistence, there was geographical mobility, some of it quite rapid in southern Indiana, and transients were characterized by having less access to land and fewer ties to family.

PATRIARCHAL FAMILIES

Families were a means by which communities were formed and land was transferred. Each landed household stood in rough equality with the next, but within the household, one person, usually the patriarch but sometimes a matriarch, ordered the lives of all the members of the family. The authority of the family leaders was nearly absolute, yet for many early Hoosiers, there was no distinction between the advance of the family and the advance of its patriarch.[95] Households were the basis of the nascent economy. Each member of the household had a role to play, and households in which either the father or mother was unable to fulfill the assigned role stood at great risk. Nevertheless, risks were minimized by the community, which often was constructed on the skeleton of kinship networks.

Certainly the persistence of family members suggests that the family served as a means of gaining access to property. Many of the landless who had family were in their twenties, still living in their parents' home. It was a rare man, from an unusually distressed family, who would find his way into another's household.[96] Even fewer single men established their own homes—as early as 1820, over 95 percent of the households in southern Indiana had multiple persons—or even households in conjunction with a group of men.[97] Households typically included an adult male and an adult female. Until young men acquired wives, they belonged to other households, much as Enoch Parr did. Once married, most couples established their own households. However, many of these had not received their legacy from either of their parents, and so they were often landless, living near one of their sets of parents and drawing their subsistence from these parents' farm. Many remained, not only because the parents' farm provided their livelihood but also because their parents had promised land to them if they remained.

If sons, like daughters, were expected to remain within their parents' household until marriage, and while within the household to provide labor toward the family's survival, the duty of many parents was to accumulate enough land or money so as eventually to establish their children as independent householders. Although Enoch Parr had gone off on his own, his father would provide essential funds for Parr to purchase his own land. When Joseph Wynn turned twenty-one, his father promised him he would give him a farm if Joseph would remain at home and work until his father could accumulate the funds to purchase the land.[98] Although marriage often brought about the creation of a new household, it did not always diminish a son's obligation to his parents. At the most rational of levels, a farm with more than one adult laborer would have more likelihood of success than two separate farms. More importantly, parents depended on some of their children to support them in their old age.[99] To retain control over their children, they retained control of the family land. However, the motives were not nearly so sinister. Many of these parents remained capable of farming in their own right, and they were certainly unwilling to give up their land until they believed themselves unable to fend for themselves; in a society which promoted independence, few parents wished to be dependent on their children until it was necessary.

Of course, they placed their children in such a role of dependence. The family in early southern Indiana was not an egalitarian institution. Highly hierarchical, its roles were firmly established, and adult children were expected to defer to their elders. Even at a distance, parental authority was exerted. Bazil Edmonston admonished his children who remained in North Carolina: "Now I can only say this, that I always sat an example before you all in the several particulars to wit: industry, truth, honesty, justice and civility."[100] Replying to a paternal exhortation from afar, Asa Rosenbarger thanked his parents: "Entreating us to give heed to our own and our children's ways—to live circumspectly ourselves, and thereby set an example of true piety before our children (which we believe is stronger than precept)."[101] As these examples of paternal authority suggest, the patriarchal family was not merely an economic unit. Even within the same household, that all family members were necessary for the family's survival did not make them equal. Sons were expected to bow to the wishes of their fathers. Wives and daughters were to subordinate their desires to the patriarch. Yet their labor was essential if the family was to prosper. For all the pride and independence which the male head of the family claimed as a landowner, that independence rested in many ways on the labor of his wife and children, rendering him, in the ultimate irony, dependent. Nevertheless, too great a stress on this dependency would obscure the power that underlay these relationships. It was, after all, the man's household.

Contemporaries did recognize the important, if subordinate, role that wives played in the household economy. Jonathan Hardy realized that the source of his sister's family's difficulties revolved around her illness; without his wife's assistance, Benjamin Mace had to hire a woman to help.[102] With good "wives it is not difficult to raise large crops, propagate fine stock, increase in wealth, live in peace and prosperity, and finally, in a good old age, to die happy."[103] The goals remained the man's. Looking back through Victorian eyes, Noah Major condemned the hardships through which wives were put. The wife's work was "never done in the beginning of a new settlement, where, to the ordinary cooking and washing of dishes, pots, pans, and washing and ironing clothes, were added picking geese, shearing sheep, making soap and punkin' butter, washing and picking wool . . . carding and spinning, reeling and coloring, warping and weaving webs for beds and tables and cloth for wearing apparel. . . . She was, indeed, the mainstay of the family, notwithstanding the more pretentious boastings of the "lords of creation."[104]

Major's biases aside—for one, he saw fishing and hunting as leisure activities for men—there can be little doubt that most southern Indiana women labored intensively. Their contribution to the family economy was real and important. The relationship was best captured in John Watson's description of his wife's work: "Mary has just made a bushel of soap, which cost me nothing but her attention and a little labour."[105] For Watson, his needs were shorthand for the needs of the family, and his wife's labor ("attention") was a cost to him. That women's work was essential for the survival of the family did not make the household egalitarian.

On occasion, women were called upon to take over the husband's role, because he was away, sick, or dead. A southern Indiana legend, probably apocryphal, captured the ability of women to take care of themselves and their families. The husband of Betty Frazier was crippled, and it fell on Betty's shoulders to acquire the cash necessary to buy the land upon which they were squatting. Like many southern Indiana farmers, she chose to raise hogs. Also like many settlers, the Fraziers had debts, and when the sheriff came to foreclose on their property—their horse—she led him to the barn, but when he entered the stall, she locked the gate behind him. After a night in the stall, he was agreeable to a compromise, and she released him, shouting after him, "I guess the Brookville officers will let me alone now until I have sold my pigs and bought my land." Left alone, Frazier fattened her swine, and then drove them to market, stopping only to bear a child, and arriving in time to sell her hogs and buy the land at auction, her newborn screaming in her arms.[106] The final touch of the pregnancy emphasized Betty Frazier's ability to take on both gender roles of the family, as nurturer and as guarantor of the family's independence.

Certainly the husband did not even have to be dead for the woman to play an important role in what might have been considered the husband's area of expertise. J. S. Wynn paid a social call on Mattie Stout, but "I understand you were out riding with Leanine Stout and breaking a colt to the saddle."[107] That the gender roles could be blurred, however, did not mean that in most matters, the husband, when present, did not speak as head of the family.

The death or disability of either parent put the family enterprise at risk. Even while legend celebrated the ability of women to raise a family alone, one reason that men rarely struck out on their own was that within the prescribed gender roles, a household could not succeed without two adults to provide their gender-inscribed types of labor. The loss of this labor proved devastating to many early Indiana households. Most men sought quickly to replace wives who had died. In 1837, John Hicks's "wife died leaving me with four small children. In 1838, I married Elizabeth M. Nichols."[108] When Enoch Parr's wife died in 1833, Parr "knew I could not reasonably think of raising of my family without the assistance of another woman," even though his eldest daughter was seventeen.[109]

Like so many women, Nancy Parr had died from complications of childbirth. Bearing children was always a danger in an unsettled country, and, given the higher rate of childbirth in the backcountry, the risk was even greater. In early Indiana, those who lived in the most rural of areas and pursued farming tended to be more fertile than their "urban" and nonagricultural counterparts. Historian John Modell argues, however, that fertility was not a product of the availability of land; population density had little effect upon the fertility rates of Hoosier women in 1820. Instead, the fertility rate was related to age at family formation, economic pursuits, and the degree to which there were towns in a given county.[110]

Perhaps few ever fulfilled both gender roles with the audacity of Betty Frazier, but many women found themselves in the unenviable position of heading the family. When men died, women often moved into more settled areas, where they worked as seamstresses or kept boarders.[111] Others tried to maintain their farms, however. Those with older sons had greater potential to succeed. Fanny Booth became a landlord, renting half her cleared land to a John Wheeler.[112] Father Joseph Thie recounted the trials of his mother, widowed by the cholera death of her husband; she was up to the rough life of southern Indiana farming, complete with ranging livestock: "She was then still young and strong, and fearless as a genuine frontier woman, never there was a thought of her returning home without her cattle."[113] Others found themselves able to make do, much as some men made do without wives. Fatherless families would often place children on neighboring farms as laborers or domestic servants. These children would be less likely to gain access to land and thus to establish their own independent household.

Such problems were, of course, mitigated when families were part of an extended kin network in the neighborhood. Such kin networks were established when second generations intermarried. Often, like that of the Parrs, they resulted from mass migration from an earlier area.[114] These kin networks often were the basis for the local community, and the authority of certain patriarchs and matriarchs was certainly extended through the neighborhood. Early southern Indiana egalitarianism was bred within a highly structured authoritarian world; it was profoundly a relationship between male landholders and not within families.

Within the organic world of the family, roles were hierarchical, but the independence these worlds created was not merely the dominion of the patriarch alone. As Susannah Pering suggested, her servant problems were the result of the independence of the young women who served her, young women who gained independence through their fathers' landholdings. The independence of the household and the family was an independence from all external to the household and family; given that the communities of southern Indiana were often based on kin networks, the independence to be gained was in fact an independence of all outside the neighborhood. Despite each household's, each family's, each community's having a firmly established hierarchy, that hierarchy existed in order to establish the independence and equality of the members vis-à-vis the larger world. Sons and daughters were expected to defer to their parents; parents, in turn, were expected to establish their children as freeholders in their own right. Although southern Indiana families were profoundly authoritarian, they demanded their equality; indeed, their strategy was to ensure access to land, by which they claimed equality.

The egalitarianism was most forcibly asserted, not within the community but between communities, in these Hoosiers' relationships with the outside world. Family strategies worked to provide access to land, the resource which ensured independence, not from one another but from the outside world. The control of land was, therefore, an important goal of

Hoosiers. Squatting, although sometimes a useful temporary strategy, could not ensure the long-term success of the settler and his children. Speculators, although not absent from southern Indiana, did little to impede Hoosiers' access to the land. Families came to the hills of southern Indiana and put down roots, entwining their lives with those of their neighbors and buying land. Through their access to land, they asserted their social equality and created legacies for their families.

Religion and the Localist Ethic

❦ ❦ ❦ ❦ ❦ ❦

The neighborhood's church stood as an institutionalized reflection of the southern Indiana community. Drawing its membership from the community, it reinforced the authority of the families that made up the neighborhood, and it often acted as the primary institution to regulate the behavior of the neighborhood. Whether Methodist or Roman Catholic, Brethren or Baptist, the church served as moral arbiter of its members. Nevertheless, each of these churches looked at the world with different eyes, seeing the role of the church and its individual members in the temporal affairs of humans in ways that shaped and reflected not only religious belief but also economic behavior and political ideology. While some people were predisposed by their religious beliefs to certain economic practices and political alignments, others joined a particular church because its beliefs corresponded to their previously held political and economic notions.

The focus of my story is on two seemingly divergent groups: the Primitive Baptists and the German Catholics.[1] Both groups were centered around the local congregation, with great distrust of anything that took place outside the scope of their community's authority. Although both therefore opposed the great reform efforts of mid-nineteenth-century evangelicals, they were not necessarily opposed to the reform of the individual, just to the means by which such reform was undertaken. Both groups tended to represent the smaller farmers of southern Indiana, as opposed to the more evangelical churches like the Methodists, Christians, Presbyterians, and mainstream Baptists, which by 1850 drew their membership from the wealthier inhabitants of southern Indiana towns and neighborhoods.

To detail the role of religion, I will first examine the breadth of religion in the region, using both narratives and the surviving census and membership records. Next, I will look at the depth of religious feeling. Having established a certain depth and breadth, I will then examine religious communities that re-created themselves in the Hoosier hills, pausing here for an extended discussion of the German Catholics. From there, I move toward the more voluntary religious communities of many of the Protestant sects, detailing how discipline and geography helped these communities to cohere. While many of the Protestant sects shared a democratic spirit, they were moving in different directions.[2] In particular, distinctions between many of the Second Great Awakening Protestant churches and the Primitive Baptists had come into sharp relief by 1850, and although within many of the churches southern Indiana believers tended to be more conservative than their brethren elsewhere in the North, the continued appeal of the Primitive Baptist creed for the farmers of the hill country demands my close examination of the sect. I end by showing how, despite far different logic, both German Catholics and Primitive Baptists came to share much in common and how these commonalities would find expression in the economic and political life of the region.

THE BREADTH OF RELIGION

While the churches of southern Indiana played an important role in creating the communities out of neighborhoods, their influence only reached as far as the devout. For some early visitors and settlers in southern Indiana, the idea that religion played an important role in most Hoosiers' lives was laughable indeed.[3] They saw southern Indiana, like much of the early West, as filled with heathen who needed the redemptive powers of the Word. Hence frantic letters back East, especially by transplanted New Englanders like Lucinda Kittredge of Salem, complained of the absence of a religion: "If Christians at home could only see the spiritual wants of the West, they would come here in colonies [?] and bring with them the privileges of the gospel."[4] Others thought they saw more dangerous tendencies than the absence of religion. American Home Missionary Society envoy B. C. Cressy advised his superiors that "it is generally acknowledged by those capable of judging, that [Salem] contains more infidels and influential opposers of religion than any other place in the State of the same population."[5]

Communities in southern Indiana were not without a certain irreligious element. In Salem, Thomas Allen broke with the Presbyterian Church, expressing "to them his disbelief in the Divine Inspiration of the Holy Scriptures."[6] Elsewhere, Joseph Hewitt wrote back to his father in Ireland that:

> I dond attend any places of Religious Worship not because their is no places near but like the most people in this Country I have got tired of Religious

dogmas and Popular Theology, and would like to see its downfall & see erected on its ashes something more better for the cause of Humanity.[7]

Underlying much of southern Indiana's relationship to religion was a distrust of the ministry and of organized denominations. In particular, Hoosiers distrusted the missionaries sent by New Englanders, not just because the farmers were Southern in origin, but precisely because these missionaries often acted as if hill country farmers were incapable of creating their own churches.

Yet despite their disdain for southern Indiana folk, many of these missionaries still conceded that there was a religious spirit abroad in the region. Despite complaining of the "thick darkness which covers the people," John Parsons had identified the problem as "too great a profusion of ministers & church members."[8] From his new home, Elisha Hughes reported "Methodists, Baptist, Presbyterians, United Brethren, New-lights, and a large settlement of Quakers or Friends nicknamed."[9]

In outright numbers, by 1850, the Methodists had one hundred more churches in the hill country than the Baptists, seating nearly twice as many people.[10] The Baptists remained the second most important denomination, having twice the churches and half again as many seats as the Presbyterians, who barely edged out the Christian Church, composed of the New Lights of Barton Stone and the followers of Alexander Campbell. The Roman Catholics and the Friends had significant strongholds, as did the Lutherans.

Fifteen of the twenty-five hill country counties had seating for at least 75 percent of their populations. Smaller, less densely populated counties did not appear to have reached the population density at which they could support the erection of church buildings.[11] Congregations without permanent buildings well may have been the norm for less densely settled areas, and many residents were certain to gather any time a preacher appeared in their neighborhood. In 1839, P. I. Beswick reported that his endeavors on the Nashville circuit—Nashville being the county seat of Brown County— served some 350 souls, comprising "some of the most simple-hearted kind and affectionate people of Indiana."[12] Eleven years later there was only one Methodist church in Brown County recorded in the census, with just 200 seats.[13] Typically, membership seems to have been at least 45 percent of the seats, regardless of a given church's policy upon children's membership.

There is little reason to suppose the other half of the seats remained empty. Key to understanding the influence of religion upon the people of southern Indiana is to understand that women made up a large number of those in attendance, up to 75 percent.[14] Most churches began with approximately an even number of men and women; coming together as husbands and wives, two by two, the churches were formed by families, families who occupied the given neighborhoods and were intertwined. As time passed and churches grew, however, they tended to attract women in greater numbers than men. One reason was that women tended to join at an earlier age.[15]

For many of these women, their husbands were involved in the community formed by the church, even if they did not belong. When work needed to be done around Big Cedar Grove Baptist Church, twenty men stepped forward, yet only nine were members. Of the other eleven, however, at least seven had family members in the congregation, including four whose wives belonged.[16] Although they may not have been members, these men had an obligation to the church and the community formed by the church. While wives and mothers may have been the only ones to join formally, the entire family belonged to the community.[17]

Although they may not have belonged in as great numbers, men were quite likely to be at church on Sunday. In churches that required a conversion experience, like Big Cedar Grove, those who related their experiences were rarely subjected to rigorous scrutiny, yet the fact that men whose wives belonged may have attended regularly for most of their lives without relating an experience suggested the respect all had for the faith. One could believe without being able to belong, and others believed enough to be frightened by the consequences of a false declaration of a conversion experience. Churches in southern Indiana were widespread enough that they involved a substantial portion of the region's stable population, even including nonmembers, within the moral communities they created.

THE DEPTH OF RELIGIOUS BELIEF

The church, as some wags noted, was as much a social gathering spot as it was a religious affair, especially in the early days.

> What surprised Ralph was to see that Flat Creek went to meeting. . . . In fact, few were thinking of the religious service. They went to church as a common resort to hear the news, and find out what was the current sensation.[18]

At revivals and camp meetings, whiskey wagons may have appeared, and bands of ruffians sometimes sought to disrupt the gatherings. Certainly many a courtship was carried out in the midst of a revival. Yet despite the social aspects of the religious services, most sat respectfully through the service. Some certainly were moved by the sermon. Converts, including those "thrown into the jerks," may have originally attended church for its social functions, but they became believers.

The social role of the church would suggest that many hill country people joined the church established in their own neighborhood. It does not necessarily follow, however, that these Hoosiers were shallow in their beliefs. They were often willing to fight for the soul of their church. If those outside the congregations showed deep respect for the churches, they probably learned their lessons from the deep faith of church members. Certainly a range of piety and faith existed within any congregation, but many hill country Hoosiers spoke eloquently of their religious belief. Even some Eastern missionaries testified that many Hoosiers were deeply religious. To suggest the depth of their faith, it may be informative to look at the religious experience of three Hoosiers.

Like many who settled in southern Indiana, Benee Hester was descended from Scottish Presbyterians, but due in part to the absence of a Presbyterian church in her childhood neighborhood, she attended the local Methodist church, which her widowed mother thought only better than no church: "She did not think it was according to scripture to say, 'she knew her sins were forgiven,' and could not join with a people that held such a doctrine." Despite her doubts, Hester's mother was gradually drawn into the Great Revival, and she "read Wesley on Christian perfection" and "became convinced that there were higher attainments in the Christian sphere than she had ever enjoyed." Four years later, Hester's youngest sister and stepsister joined the church, but Benee Hester "stood aloof, believing [she] was a sinner and not fit to die, yet not fully sensible of my danger, nor yet persuaded that it was now time to give myself up and forsake my vain companions and worldly amusements." Later that year, attending a love feast, Hester listened as a preacher "related a solemn scene through which he passed during his distress." The words that moved him moved Hester as well: "Sinner! every sin you commit pierces the Saviour's wound afresh." "I saw in a moment, as I never saw before, that Christ had loved me, had suffered and died for me; that I had been, against better light and knowledge, grieving his spirit, and sinning against him." At this point, Hester realized that her damnation was just, and she fell unconscious. She "went home a true penitent—joined the church the first opportunity; but did not find relief" immediately.

> The manner in which the Good Lord revealed his mercy to me was as strange and powerful as my conviction was. . . . On Saturday evening, I was called to assist in taking my sister in the tent, who was powerfully exercised. When we laid her down, she looked up in my face and commenced praying for me. I had felt much opposed to having the jerks, with which she was exercised. But when I looked upon her heavenly countenance, saw her uplifted hands, heard her fond and pathetic prayer for her poor sister, I felt abashed; the pride in

my heart was completely subdued; I bowed my head and hunkered down beside her, laying my hands across my knees and my head upon her hands;—as I did this I said, "O, Lord, if thou wilt grant me the blessing which she seems to enjoy, I will willingly have the jerks or anything else thou may please to put upon [me]." I cannot recollect another thought passing through my mind till I heard my own voice saying "Glory, glory," and felt my hands slapping together. I then asked myself, "Why what is this?" I instantly felt the reply in my inmost soul, as sensibly as if some one had spoke to me, "This is what you have sought for."

From that moment on, Hester believed her entire nature had changed: "I felt as if I had been snatched from an awful gulf; and so grateful did I feel for it that my soul was all ecstasy." In her conversion, Hester laid aside all "fashions and foolery," all things which "did not accord with true piety." Her deep, abiding faith would be strengthened in her marriage to a Methodist circuit rider. Her story, like so many others, revealed the intellectual torment that preceded the simple "emotionalism" decried by so many observers.[19]

Enoch Parr labored with many of the same issues in coming to his Christ. Having resolved to reform himself, he nevertheless feared that he would backslide, and so resolved

> to make no open profession [of religion] but trust to the Lord alone for life and do all the good I could and if I could do no good do as little harm as posable or in other words to persue the best light I could obtain as nearly as I could and say but little to any body on the subject of religion and if I failed to perform what I thought was my duty to be my own admonisher and test my conduct by the *book of God.*"

Parr continued to meditate on his situation, reading the Bible closely, as did many hill country farmers, to seek his Lord in the Word. He distanced himself from both Baptists and Methodists, as both "held out that to get religion you must become, a doubter before you could be a believer"; Parr instead sought merely to follow God's law. Attendance at a Baptist association did little to provide Parr with the instruction he sought, though he "viewed the members as the people of God but felt dispare because I did not believe that I was fit to be a member." Soon after the meeting, still searching for meaning, Parr thought of these words, long familiar but newly encouraging: "If the son shall make you free ye shall be free indeed." Thus began for Parr a long series of revelations, ending with

> "Because I live ye shall live also" I knew the words ware the words of the Saviour and they appeared addressed to me I received them as such with great joy and was very happy in the hope they created in me—I praised God.[20]

With this revelation, Parr's confidence was increased, and he related his experience, to be accepted into fellowship within the Baptist Church.

Parr remained content with his church for the next fifteen years, until about 1825, when the Baptists were struck with a number of divisions, centered around the Manichean "Two-Seed" doctrine of Daniel Parker, to which Parr attributed heathen origins. Parr argued to the contrary: "For it is of the Grace of God that any of us are hear, great or small, noble or ignoble." It would not be until 1843 that Parr would be induced to leave the Baptist church, "tho not with out a pang," and join the Campbellites, as his old church asserted itself as wholeheartedly "Two-Seed," despite Parr's bold protest.[21] Such splits occurred throughout the association and inspired the formation of a new Baptist association.

If Enoch Parr reflected the intellectual soul-searching of Benee Hester, then Siegfried Koehler, a German Catholic immigrant to Franklin County, mirrored her deep devotion. Originally from Alsace, Koehler came to America in about 1836, bringing with him, so the story went, a statue that his family had rescued from a church threatened with destruction during the French Revolution. During his journey over, the ship appeared in danger, and Koehler led the litany of the Blessed Virgin, adding to the ritual his own promises to build a shrine for his statue of the Virgin. Koehler fulfilled that promise, but his poverty could provide only a log hut. He wanted to do better, and so, obviously, did his neighbors, for around 1871, Koehler made a pilgrimage through his neighborhood to collect money for a brick shrine. At Easter, Koehler walked all the way to Cincinnati for the holy oils.[22] In this act of devotion, Koehler was as deep in belief as his Protestant neighbors. He was not simply Catholic because he was German; he did not simply act in reaction to the nativism of those around him. His religious beliefs were deeper than that; he thanked the Lord who, through the intercession of the Holy Mother, had saved his life.

The depth of religious feeling and thought among many who settled southern Indiana can be grasped in the lives of Siegfried Koehler, Enoch Parr, and Benee Hester. They loved God, and they feared Him. One thing that emerges from these portraits of their relationship with God was the immense humility they all exhibited before the Almighty. Whether Catholic or Protestant, all believed themselves to have acted in ways unworthy of God. Both Parr and Hester thought themselves unworthy of being a member of the church, even though they believed. And for thirty-five years Koehler believed he had yet to fulfill his promise to the Blessed Virgin. This humility would be an identifying feature of religion among many southern Indiana residents.

WHY BELIEVE?

However, it would be unreasonable to suggest that Benee Hester, Enoch Parr, and Siegfried Koehler all traveled similar roads to arrive at similar ideas about humility. Although humility had long been part of the Christian tradition, Parr, Hester, and Koehler may well have embraced it for different reasons. Part of the reason for such different paths came from the historical time and place. In ordinary times, church traditions, whether Protestant or Catholic, were part of the acculturation of youths raised within these churches. For the Catholics, little had changed in this regard. Yet the years preceding the European American settlement of southern Indiana had been filled with change within the religious worlds of many Protestant Upland Southerners. Most had felt abandoned by the Presbyterian Church of their forebears, an abandonment which was driven home by the condescension of Presbyterian missionaries to southern Indiana.

Even before the American Revolution, the Baptist Church had made great inroads in the Shenandoah Valley of Virginia, wresting souls not only from the Presbyterians but from the various German Protestant groups. After the Revolution and by the time of the Great Revival, the democracy of the new faiths—Methodist, Baptist, Cumberland Presbyterian, and the various sects which eventually would be united as the Disciples of Christ—would provide these newly empowered, newly free, newly enfranchised "Americans" with a "democratic" church.[23] Having been freed from the Presbyterian Church, southern Indiana Protestants had the unique opportunity to join churches that reflected their own beliefs about the world.

Certainly there was a limit on the churches to which one could belong: especially in the early years, there was not much chance that more than one church might exist in a given neighborhood. Not surprisingly, among the churches to thrive were those that gave great autonomy to local congregations, the Baptists and two of the sects that would become the Disciples, the Campbellites, and the Stoneites. The laity thus participated in the creation of their own belief system. The individual congregation, composed from the local neighborhood, thus could form a church in its own image, with its own beliefs.

Sometimes individuals played important leadership roles. Through their evangelizing, the Wright family, for instance, made Jackson Township, Washington County, solidly a Christian (Disciples) Church township in 1860; all four township churches were Christian, accounting for a third of Washington County's total.[24] Certainly some were more gifted in spreading the word and in organizing and sustaining congregations. But even these ministers were constrained by the beliefs and needs of hill country Hoosiers. As they spoke a message that intersected with the beliefs of these farmers, they gathered congregations. On the other hand, the beliefs of the various churches did not merely reflect their congregations; in part, the members were also shaped by the theology they encountered in their new churches. For instance, as countless critics of revivalism have noted, the initial excitement of the moment may have been responsible for the conversion. Yet, despite the large incidence of backsliding, those who remained within the church certainly found sustenance and substance in the church's doctrines and creeds. The emotional appeal of the revival, in the true believer's mind, was not separate from the rational. A doctrine that was capable of creating such an atmosphere was certainly powerful.

Much of this dynamic within the Protestant sects will be explored in greater depth below. At this point, what is important to note is that there were two distinct sources of the religious communities of the hill country. The first, based in the church of one's parents, prompted a process whereby the church community was "re-created" in its new Hoosier home; most notable among the "re-creators" were the German Catholics. As we shall see, such a community included far more invention than might be supposed, yet nothing on the scale of the "created" communities of the neighborhood Protestant congregation. In sum, there was no one reason why southern Indiana farmers believed. Some were indoctrinated from birth, while some chose a religion that reflected their views and others followed leaders who seemed to know the way. Whatever the reason, they believed with fervor and depth.

RE-CREATED RELIGIOUS COMMUNITIES

That some were born into the faith of their parents and raised in the community of believers did not necessarily mean that they did not have a deep and abiding faith. There were many re-created communities of the faithful. The German Catholics were the most successful. Certainly others tried.

In their movement from North Carolina, the Friends attempted to create communities centered around their faith, most notably in Morgan, Orange, and Washington counties. Their communities would often be made up of extended families from North Carolina. The nurturing of the community was readily apparent. After the death of her husband, Priscilla Cadwallader moved to the new country of Indiana and settled on a farm, bought for her by her father; although a widow on the frontier, she lived amidst other Friends, and she soon became a minister. Elsewhere, Quaker itinerant William Forster reported the disappointment of some White River

Friends that no other Friends had followed and said that they therefore thought of moving. Despite the best intentions of the Quakers, their communities could not be contained. To keep the community boundaries tight, Quakers disowned those who married out of meeting, and this practice, rather than strengthening the community, may well have served to limit its reach. Coercion was not sufficient to maintain the community of the faithful.[25]

Another unique set of communities involved the various Scotch-Irish Presbyterians—Covenanters, Seceders, and Reformeds—who founded their own tight-knit churches in several hill country counties.[26] The most intriguing of the "closed-corporate communities" was the short-lived utopian community in Monroe County, based on the nearby Harmonie and New Harmony experiments, but centered around a Disciples of Christ church.[27] The Protestant transplanted communities of the faithful, but they made up one form of the moral communities of southern Indiana.

By far the most successful of communities centered around religion were those of the German Catholics. One of the most compelling reasons for their greater success at maintaining their separate communities was their perceived difference from their neighbors. Unlike the Friends or even the Scotch-Irish Presbyterians, language reinforced German Catholic separatism from their English neighbors. Ethnicity existed not only in the minds of the ethnics but in the minds of those who defined them as ethnic. Nativism was no stranger to the hill country, and the Catholicism of the German immigrants put them at double risk. At Leopold in Perry County, Nativists attempted to burn the local Catholic church in 1858.[28] Earlier, in Lawrenceburg, a group attacked a German coffeehouse and murdered a German farmer.[29] But nativism had less appeal in the farming neighborhoods of the region. The nativist spirit tended to dwell within those who sought capitalist expansion, and such men were more likely to be found in the growing commercial villages.

Certainly other southern Indiana non-Germans welcomed their German neighbors. Bazil Edmonston, local Jacksonian politician, was excited by their arrival in Dubois County: "They nearly to a man are democrats."[30] Yet Edmonston's enthusiasm was not completely opportunistic. The local priest, "a very friendly gentleman," boarded with Edmonston, and Edmonston's granddaughter, Missouria, "goes to school with him to learn the German language."[31] Edmonston's admiration for Father Kundeck revealed that, although a deeply religious Protestant, Edmonston did not fear the Catholics. Edmonston's trust was shared by other non-Germans in the community. In 1840, Father Kundeck reported, his English-speaking neighbors attempted to draft him for the legislature. Father Kundeck declined, insisting that "he was a missionary, not a senator."[32] And in 1842, Father

Kundeck noted that, although the parish had grown considerably in the three years he had been there, another reason that the children's procession for the bishop's visit was so large was "the presence of a number of non-Catholic youngsters who gladly took part in the unusual celebration," youngsters who three years earlier had "whispered 'Priest! Priest!' in suspicious tones whenever I had to pass them."[33]

The insularity of the German Catholic community was brought about as much by their own acts of self-definition and community-building as by the ideas of their English-speaking neighbors. At the center of these acts was often the parish priest.[34] Not all priests played these seminal roles. Many lacked the resources, the initiative, or the commitment. The establishment of these German Catholic communities was part of the greater struggle within the American Catholic Church over the creation of "national" churches, serving the needs of Catholics of particular ethnic backgrounds. Three priests stood out: Father Kundeck, of Dubois and Perry counties; Father Ferneding, of Franklin and Dearborn counties; and Father Rudolph, of Oldenburg, of Franklin.[35]

Croatian-born, Father Kundeck played an important role in establishing German Catholic churches, not only in southern Indiana, but in cities like New Orleans. Kundeck first learned of the missionary fields of the United States through the bulletins of the Austro-Hungarian Leopoldine Foundation.[36] The Foundation played an important role in the financial health of the early Catholic Church in southern Indiana, and Kundeck honored that assistance by naming one village he platted Leopold. Although many of the early German Catholic settlers in Dubois, Perry, and Spencer counties were drawn from American cities where they had first settled, Kundeck also used the Leopoldine Foundation and the pages of its bulletin to encourage German-speaking Catholics to come to these new communities in southern Indiana.[37] Upon arrival in the United States in 1838, Father Kundeck reported to the bishop of Vincennes, who assigned him to the newly formed parish at Jasper, where some German families had begun settling several years earlier. These early settlers envisioned a German community— they had purchased land to settle about one hundred families—and Father Kundeck shared their vision. Not content just to tend to this flock, Kundeck pursued additional settlers with vigor, using the funds at his disposal to purchase land for resale to the immigrating German Catholics. Nor was Kundeck content just to develop his own community of Jasper; he established Ferdinand about twelve miles southeast of Jasper, and later several other settlements; in all these instances, Kundeck played a major role in acquiring land and drawing settlers.

Although Father Ferneding, whose circuit was primarily in the southeastern part of the state, may never have directly bought and sold land, he worked closely with German Catholic land speculators to establish communities centered upon the church.[38] According to one source, Father Ferneding, "from his early experience as a young immigrant working on the Louisville Canal in 1825, had learned the need of grouping Catholics in order to prevent loss of the Faith through isolation."[39] A native of the province of Oldenburg, Ferneding was initially assigned by the Diocese of Bardstown (which covered much of southern Indiana until 1833) to provide for all the Germans in southern Indiana and the Louisville area.[40] Within months of the advertising of the new community of Oldenburg, Father Ferneding was there to provide the sacraments.[41]

Although not the first resident pastor at Oldenburg, Father Franz Joseph Rudolph, an Alsatian, most obviously took up Ferneding's legacy in developing the German Catholic community in the Oldenburg neighborhood. Like Father Kundeck, Father Rudolph actively bought and sold land. In addition, he served as missionary to the several outlying congregations in Franklin County, as well as schoolteacher, builder, laborer, and lawyer; in short, he was, as one historian put it, the patriarch of this community.[42]

Although their experiences proved similar, Kundeck, Ferneding, and Rudolph were not the norm for priests; many priests sent to serve with Father Kundeck found themselves incapable of the task. These priests stood out for aggressive leadership; they stood out for their vision of a German Catholic community; and they stood out because they created an ideal of that community. In the minds of many who settled in those communities, the church was an important center to the community, and the priest was a man to whom to defer. As organized leader, the priest could call upon the labors of the community. When the Dubois County courthouse burned down and the county's contractor gave up with only the foundation complete on a new courthouse, Father Kundeck mustered the aid of parishioner craftsmen, who completed the building.[43]

Yet just as certainly the relationship between the community and the priest was not without tensions. When Father Rudolf's contractor failed to complete the Enochsburg church, some parishioners felt that it was Father Rudolf's fault, and it allegedly took the bishop's intervention to silence some of Rudolf's critics.[44] Tensions between the hierarchy and the laity suggest the immense importance that the laity placed in the church itself, that they were willing to go head to head with such powerful men to fight for the soul of their church. The church and its standards were their possession, stood at the center of their community, gave their lives much of its meaning. As a group, the German Catholic community found its expression in the German Catholic congregation, and as a group, they demanded a certain amount of control over the church. As individuals, German Catholics were expected to defer to the church and to the priest, for the church was the expression of the community, and the priest was its leader.

In neither Dubois County nor Franklin County was the German Catholic constituency as homogeneous as "German Catholic" might indicate. German Catholics who settled in southern Indiana, even within tightly delimited neighborhoods, had roots in various parts of Germany.[45] Yet such varied peoples, considered "Germans" by their English American neighbors, and more importantly, by their priests and the French hierarchy, became reconstructed as such.

The German Catholic communities of southern Indiana hill country were, like all "communities," constructed; they did not occur naturally. The bonds provided by their "difference"—Catholicism and German language— from the communities surrounding them served to reinforce, however, a desire among German Catholics to live in such small, locally oriented communities.[46] In many places, German Catholics exhibited a far greater desire to create small, closed communities than their non–German Catholic neighbors. The Old World form of the "German hometown" inspired many German Catholic immigrants to attempt to re-create the independence, self-government, and consensual community that lay at the base of the ideal. Historian Jay Dolan suggests that for many Germans in the new world, "the church was certainly one such surrogate hometown."[47] In this respect, even the German insistence upon lay government of the church was part of the creation of the hometown. The desire for community and the demand for consensus within the community certainly played a role in the creation of community, with the church at the center, in many German Catholic neighborhoods.

That the German Catholic communities were constructed made them no less meaningful to their inhabitants. Not only did the community exist within their minds; it also existed within a specific space. Their community was tied to the neighborhood in which they earned their bread and lived their lives. In many, but not all, cases, communities that corresponded to neighborhoods demanded a different and more intense investment from their members. For many of the German Catholics of southern Indiana, indeed for many of the region's inhabitants, the arena in which they pursued most of the activities of their lives encompassed a very limited geographical space. They were localist in nature.

The community was constructed around the parish church, often by the priests who performed Mass and heard confessions. Although residents might differ with the priest upon occasion, the church was a primary source of meaning in their lives, and the priest's judgment was one to be sought. They had come to southern Indiana because they knew there would be a church there in the hills, one which could provide spiritual sustenance and moral guidance, but note, it would be a church that was so enmeshed in their lives that it might well have been the priest who sold them their land or got them a job.[48] Such a priest could well command their respect. The German Catholic peoples of the hill country, then, were extremely localist in orientation, and the communities that they constructed in their new neighborhoods would center around their local parish church. As Father Kundeck's early experience in Jasper revealed, German Catholic communities could and did find ways to coexist with their neighbors. One of the most important of these ways would come with shared allegiance to the Democratic Party.

CHURCH DISCIPLINE

Certainly hill country German Catholics were not alone in their localism, nor were they unique in placing their neighborhood church at the center of the local community. For many in the hill country, the neighborhood church served, as we have already seen, as the gathering spot for the neighborhood. The church often acted in a neighborly guise. The Lost River Regular Baptist Church promised in its very Covenant to contribute "cheerfully for the relief of the poor."[49] Sinking Spring Baptist Church created "a subscription to assist Brother Robertson in paying for his land" ($20).[50] Catholic or Protestant, the church, by its very nature, united the neighborhood, not merely on the grounds of voluntary association or social needs but as a moral institution. With churches at the centers of their communities, the community thus took on a moral flavor. Within the Catholic Church, judgment took place in the confessional as well as in the far more effective, if less institutionalized, court of local opinion. Such an informal court also existed in the Protestant communities, but there, in many of the denominations, the membership of the church gathered formally to judge the transgressions of the faithful. Indeed, in this church discipline, community was created and defined.[51]

Hill country Hoosiers proved their devotion by bowing to the wishes of their congregations. Discipline was an important role of the church. Members were expected to settle their disagreements within the confines of the church; those who sought redress elsewhere, in the secular courts, were guilty of transgressing the covenant of the church. The church was the ultimate source of moral judgment. At periodic meetings of Protestant churches, members bearing grievances would come forward and state their cases. The defendant would then offer his side. In many cases, the primary purpose of the discipline was to get the sinner to recognize his sins and ask for forgiveness, in a manner not unlike the Catholic confessional, albeit in front of the community gathered as a whole. For instance, in November 1823, Lucy Highnote was accused of fornication, and in December she was excluded; by February of the next year, however, Highnote had satisfied the church and she was restored to membership.[52] Sometimes the complainant was the sinner himself, baring himself to the congregation and asking for mercy, much as Reuben Shields, who "came forward and protest to be agrieve with himself for oferen to fite and he gave satisfaction to the Church for the same."[53] In many ways, members were expected to internalize their community's values; at the very least, they were expected to bow to its judgment. For many, contrition was enough. For those who refused to accept the church's judgment, exclusion from the church was the most common punishment. Since such exclusion was an exclusion from the fellowship of one's closest neighbors, it carried great weight. Having been judged unworthy of their fellowship in church, they were also unworthy of the variety of aid proffered by neighbors, including employment. There was an appeal process, but it was invoked mainly when the church as a whole was split; the appeal process often involved a fight for the soul of the congregation.

After making a promise to take care of the poor in their covenant, members of the Lost River Regular Baptist "Old Union" Church declared, "We also engage to work circumspectfully in the world; *to be just in our dealings,* faithful in our engagement and exemplary in our deportments, to avoid all talking, *backbiting,* railing and excisive anger."[54] As the covenant suggested, peace within the church was often the primary goal. The mention of "backbiting" pointed to the very real and probably common experience of divisiveness within the churches.

> Sister Hannah Combs states to the Church that she feels distrest with Sister Sarah Wilson for saying that she had heard that Sister Cathrine Gray had not told Sister Combs that she had not voted in a decision of the church when Sister Combs had said she had not voted and that she had abused Sister Wiatt and had begun like she had in Clark County a raking up things and if she told any boddy so that they would not believe her and Sister Wilson had said that she never was so abused in her life.[55]

The actions of churches did suggest that many bent to fit the differences among the membership. In 1837, Lost River Baptist Church judged that the "washing of feet . . . is a duty, but we will not make it obligatory up for those that do not see it their duty."[56] Likewise, the issue of missions was not always allowed to split churches: "The church amend a certain item of last meating saying we ase a church object to modorn mishons but do not make it a bar to fellowship but leave each member at liberty to exercise there own views on the several subjects."[57] As we shall see below, both the washing of feet and the missionary question were important elements among hill country Baptists, yet they were not automatically division points within the church. As a community, the church was committed to maintaining harmony and order within the geographical neighborhood in which it served as the social and moral center. Peace within the church was an overwhelming aim, and division of the church, while certainly not unknown, reflected special circumstances.

Much as within the Catholic Church, challenges to moral authority within many Protestant churches rested on whether the transgressions were individual or group in nature. The neighborhood found a certain bond within the local congregation, and that bond sealed a variety of relationships within the neighborhood; if that bond were rent by division, many of the other relationships within the community were endangered and so preservation of harmony within the church was important. Individuals were expected to defer to the judgments of the church. Likewise, the church could afford to be magnanimous in granting latitude to those citizens of the neighborhood who differed in their beliefs in some ways. Only divisions that involved large minorities of the neighborhood pitted against bare majorities were likely to evolve into open conflict, as each group fought to establish its vision as the vision of the church and thus of the community. For instance, both the footwashing and missionary statements involved an attempt to include those who felt excluded by an earlier pronouncement on the question.

In its claim to be the supreme judge of the moral character of its members, the church handled a variety of cases. Many were the sorts of matters that churches still claim as part of their moral oversight: fornication, drinking, and swearing. Gossip played an important part in the church discipline network: "A report being in Circulation of our Brother Adam Ribble frequenting the Groceries and on one occasion offering to fight." Ribble admitted the charge, claiming self-defense, but refusing to stop frequenting drinking establishments. He said that if he were such a disgrace to the church, they could erase him from the books, which they eventually did.[58] Although drinking and fighting were serious offenses to many mid-nineteenth-century churchgoers, sometimes the charges could be of an even graver nature: "Brother J. M. Hodges stated that Bro. Elias Richards was guilty of base conduct and on motion that the church have cause for grevance against him in consequence of his having an illegitimate child by his stepdaughter and acknowledged the same to be the fact and on consideration of the case the church say by [the church's] act that he be excluded."[59] Justice could be swift; some crimes carried little room for forgiveness. However, in the majority of sins, forgiveness was available to the contrite.

Hill country churches, through their claim to be the ultimate authority on the moral behavior of their members, understood moral behavior as encompassing almost all the actions of their members, not merely adultery, profanity, assault, and drinking. For instance, Catharine Johnson was excluded for mistreating her stepchild.[60] Within the Scotch-Irish Presbyterian Church, one man was brought to trial for failing to report his entire taxable property.[61] As the Lost River Regular "Old Union" Baptist Church Covenant stated, members were expected to be "just in dealings." Such sentiments were echoed in the Methodist Discipline; a member would give evidence of his desire for salvation in many ways, including:

> By doing no harm, avoiding evil of every kind, especially that which is most generally practiced, such as:
>
> . . .
>
> Fighting, quarrelling, brawling, brother going to law with brother; returning evil for evil; or railing for railing; the using many words in buying or selling.[62]

These were not merely empty words; Methodist Bishop McKendree admonished a congregation for engaging in economic exploitation of their new neighbors:

> Yes, it frequently happens, that some take advantage of the poor emigrant too, that has removed to your fine country to become your neighbour and fellow-citizen; you sell him your corn or other produce at double price, . . . and receive it too from the poor man who has to grapple with misfortunes to support his family.[63]

The neighborhood church took upon itself the role of regulating a member's economic activity, and its members had internalized this role: "Bro. Moore lays in a report against himself in regard to a mistake in changing money with Bro. Phelps in Salem. . . . A second report Bro. Moore lays in against himself with regard to borrowing flour of James Jones and paying flour and corn."[64] Other charges of fraud were more serious, and the devout member humbly attempted to regain the trust of his church and thus of his community.

> Mr. McPheeters having sometime since been requested to keep back from communion in consequence of a rumour against him, in which common fame had accused him of unchristian conduct in his dealings.

McPheeters had been accused of "receiving more money for halling goods than was due him," a charge he agreed was true, although "without any design to defraud."[65] While McPheeters's appearance of fraud may well have been an incident within the capitalist framework of exchange, that a local institution, using its own set of localized rules, would presume to judge his actions, especially since they did not even involve a second member, placed it outside the realm of capitalism, which demanded a universal and common set of rules. Even if there were a remedy in law, good church members were not allowed to take that course against their brethren. When Ansel R. Pease sued Brother Samuel Goudie, he was excluded from Big Cedar Grove Church; he had to appear before the congregation to ask for forgiveness, whereupon he appears to have been restored.[66]

Through their claim to ultimate authority, the neighborhood church could actually find guilty a man cleared in the court of law. James Alvis was a constable in Washington County and a member in good standing of the New Providence Baptist Church. In the course of his duties as constable, he attempted to arrest one Leonard Carnes and, in the resulting melee, killed him. Although Alvis was cleared of wrongdoing by the secular courts of Washington County, the church declared that Alvis "was no longer of them for killing Leonard Carnes." Obviously, this declaration caused some consternation within the congregation because, a year later, the church sent for a committee, to be composed of messengers from neighboring churches, to decide whether the majority was correct in excluding Alvis. The committee was unanimous in support of the majority: "We exhort the minority in committee to submitt to said decision believing it will be one amongst all things that shall work for good."[67] That there was a strong minority willing to divide the church on Alvis's exclusion indicates that not all were willing to abide by the church's claim of superior authority to act in this matter. The unanimity of the visiting messengers, made up of the elite of the other churches, made clear that among the most faithful there was little leeway given to the secular world in moral matters.

Certainly there were some who thought they could do without the church and the community it embodied. Nancy Chasteen refused to see the harm in dancing and fiddling.[68] Adam Ribble told the church to erase his name from the records if he was a disgrace to them, although he was sorry for what he had done. No one was more forthright than Uriah Anderson:

> Anderson had understood that the Church was agoing to turn him out and that he had come to speak for himself . . . said he did not deny selling . . . and would do it again he said that he would prefer having his name raced off the list of the Church Book of members.[69]

Defiance of the moral community created through the church did, of course, occur, increasingly as the countryside developed. Adam Ribble and Uriah Anderson belonged to communities outside the church, to communities whose norms included the buying, selling, and drinking of intoxicants. For Uriah Anderson, in particular, his relationship to the neighborhood was not predicated on pleasing all his neighbors. He had discovered, as so many would, that an economic livelihood could be obtained outside the cooperation of all his neighbors. But the transition to this phase was hardly completed in the antebellum period.

Much as was the case with the patriarchal family, the church as community complicated the egalitarian individualism that many Hoosiers thought was their birthright. The community was hardly golden. It demanded a level of conformity from its members that many would increasingly find impossible and intolerable. Whether Protestant or Catholic, the moral community placed tight reins on its membership. Church discipline was the institutional form through which the church constricted its members; certainly it takes little imagination to recognize that the moral community policed its membership in other, less structured ways. As James Alvis discovered, its discipline could be more demanding than that of secular justice. In return, however, the church, the moral community, offered the rewards, both spiritual and material, of fellowship. In its rituals, it bonded the neighborhood.

NEIGHBORHOODS AND VOLUNTARY COMMUNITY

Moral community, at some level, depended upon voluntary adherence. Yet it also depended on some sense of geographical proximity. In the earliest days, neighborhoods were often defined by their church. Allen Wiley reported that areas along the banks of Big and Little Cedar Grove Creek in Franklin County were known as Baptist neighborhoods.[70] Big Cedar Grove Church, established in 1816, was an offshoot of Little Cedar Grove Church, and it helped define its part of Springfield Township, Franklin County, as solidly Baptist. Mapping the membership in 1833, one can see how the core of members was from two very small areas (see map 2.1). The Big Cedar Grove Church was built on an early Springfield Township neighborhood; the secondary neighborhood also was apparent as early as 1820.[71] Much the same neighborhood quality can be found in the membership of the Livonia Presbyterian Church. The primary community was made up of those living around Livonia, with an intriguing secondary community north and west of the town (see map 2.2). The land in this latter area, which included the majority of the farmers in the church, was purchased fairly early—

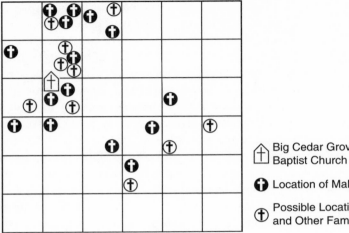

MAP 2.1 MEMBERSHIP OF BIG CEDAR GROVE BAPTIST CHURCH, 1833
Derived from "Members of Big Cedar Grove Baptist Church, Franklin County, Indiana,"
transcript, Weidenbach Collection, Indiana Division, Indiana State Library,
Indianapolis; and Franklin County, 1833 Tax Roll, microfilm, Genealogy Division,
Indiana State Library.

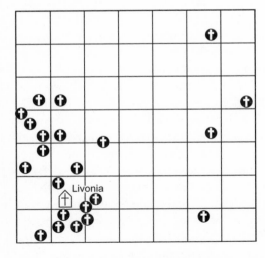

MAP 2.2 MEMBERSHIP OF LIVONIA PRESBYTERIAN CHURCH, 1844
Derived from Livonia Presbyterian Church, membership list, 1831, transcript,
Presbyterian Church Records, Washington County Historical Society, Salem, Ind.; and
Washington County, 1844 Tax Duplicate, Auditor's Office, Washington County
Courthouse, Salem, Ind.

earlier than the land around Livonia—and it was characterized by some of the flattest terrain in the entire county. To have two distinct neighborhoods in each of these churches underlined the importance of neighborhood in the creation of the moral community. The church did not just draw only upon the immediate neighborhood to create the moral community; rather, it may have built upon distinct neighborhoods, even those at some distance. A single church may have stood at the moral center of two unrelated neighborhoods. In other words, the moral community encompassed by the church did not emanate in any purely geographical sense from the church itself.[72] It did not draw its membership from a diffuse area but from distinct, tightly bound neighborhoods. In areas where the church had members, it was likely to have multiple members.

The geography of the church was an important element in the creation of the moral community, especially in the earliest days of European American settlement. As the country grew, more and more churches came upon the scene and, coupled with better roads, residents gained choices in churches.[73] It would be a mistake, as I have argued above, to suggest that the membership did not at every stage believe deeply in the doctrine of their neighborhood church. Yet as choices were made available to hill country Hoosiers, doctrine took on greater importance. The moral community became defined, in an ever-increasing way, by adherence to particular doctrines. A caution remains in order, however. The most important differences among the churches that emerged by midcentury may be between those that still attempted to create the earlier world of the moral community and those that attempted to adjust to the fundamentally secular changes wrought by the denser populations and better roads.

In all of the Protestant faiths, the community of believers was essential. Discipline was at the core of the churches, as each church provided the moral guidance for its neighborhood. But as the hill country became more settled, the correspondence between neighborhood and church community became less geographical. Sects began to compete with one another. As neighborhoods began to support more than one church, different churches began to represent not primarily the neighborhood but different ways of understanding how one's neighborhood related to the larger world. These changes in southern Indiana paralleled larger theological changes within some of its sects. Some churches, notably the Primitive Baptists, did not necessarily change. But because the role of the church in the neighborhood and in the society was the topic of the new Christian order, all denominations were irretrievably drawn into the debate.

For the most part, Protestantism in southern Indiana represented what Nathan Hatch has called the "Democratization of American Religion."

Religion was to be the experience of the commoner, and the emphasis was on emotionalism, not the intellect. Certainly the foes in all these battles were the Anglicans, Presbyterians, and Congregationalists, who saw religion as a matter of intellect. Nevertheless, the primary guilt of the "Presbygationists" may not have been their religious belief so much as it was their adherents' positions within the society as its economic and political elites. In the postrevolutionary period, the appeal of the new, "democratic" churches—Baptists, Methodists, Campbellites, and Stoneites—came in part from their rejection of the established order. Their rise accompanied the rise of a new "democratic" polity, and it found some of its greatest resonance among people at the margins of the new commercial world, among them those living on the so-called frontier.[74] Settling in areas where they were deemed incapable of governing themselves, as evidenced in politics by the Northwest Ordinance, these people reacted as strongly against the clerical prescriptions of their unfitness to practice religion without guidance.[75] Much as these frontierspeople cried that they were capable of governing themselves politically, they believed that they were capable of religious devotion without the assistance of learned elites. Indeed, the struggles were one and the same. Both revolved around the notion of self-government and whether the lowly born were capable of governing society and themselves. In both cases, Westerners claimed that they were not savages, that they were capable of acting morally, that they were, by birth, equal to any other man. The democratic appeals of Methodist, Disciple, and Baptist leaders resonated for many southern Indiana farmers, who clung to their republican and democratic notions of their equality with every other man, an equality ensured by their ownership of land.

The democratic religions made the laity more central to the religious practice of the church and denied special abilities to the clergy. Many joined Enoch Parr in seeing a connection between the democratic sects and democratic politics:

> All laws usages and customs that opperate unequal or oppress all is directly or indirectly the works of the devil and must be distroyed by the brightness of this coming. The gospel teaches to rule as you would be ruled. Democracy is one of the blesing we obtain or receive by the coming of christ or by the brightness of his coming.[76]

In the democratic sects, the ability to express conviction in deep theological terms was unnecessary; what was necessary was the ability to bare emotion. In rejecting much of the theological baggage, some popular sects insisted on the ability of ordinary men to preach. To many of the sects, the theological and creedal battles that engaged what seemed to them the majority of the attention of the learned clergy were the stuff of much nonsense.[77]

Revivals were common places for this emotionalism to be expressed. The large crowds gathered at these events may have acted to release inhibitions—a "domino" effect—as well as served as a kind of mass surrogate for God, to whom the penitent repented his or sins. In other words, for the sinner, his or her known world gathered in judgment. This submission to the community as surrogate for God was not altogether different from the contrition the church expected from its members. However, the broader mass of the revival, drawing from beyond one's own immediate neighborhood, surely made the sinner in the crowd feel as if the eyes of the world—read God—were upon him or her.[78]

The religious ecstasy that characterized the revival was only an extreme example of the new sects' emphasis on religion of the emotions.[79] The Holy Spirit emanated not from the preacher but from the community. As historian Donald Mathews notes, "Substance for early Methodists . . . was the spoken word, the event and act of preaching and responding, the fusing together of individuals who poured their interior life out into a sharing community through testimony, song, shout, and laughter."[80] In its communal form, Methodism, as well as many of the other new, popular sects, emphasized the great equality of all the members of the community. Caught in the uncontrollable grip of the Holy Spirit, penitents suffering the jerks were reduced to equals; one's social status had no meaning before God. Therein lay the radicalism of the revival and, by extension, of all of the new popular sects.

Although the popular sects endorsed and encouraged these extreme outbursts of passion, they sought to transform their followers into self-disciplined, pious persons. These qualities were precisely the qualities that the emerging capitalist society demanded of capitalists and workers alike: sobriety, self-discipline, and industriousness. The embrace by many capitalists of the new evangelical order, while it served their personal spiritual and status needs, also reflected a recognition that its values served their needs for a trustworthy and industrious workforce and civil polity.[81] The new evangelical order, through its various missionary and tract societies, reaped the beneficence of the wealthy capitalists, who shared its vision of extending evangelical values. For the emerging capitalists, the increasing distance of commercial relations emphasized the need for common moral values over the distances: each party to a commercial contract needed to share a common understanding of the obligations rendered by the contract.[82] Other reform activities pursued by these emerging capitalists reflected the concerns of the more thoughtful of the advocates of expanding commercial activities; they realized that, although commercialism could bring rewards and untold wealth to many of its participants, it required certain minimal abilities—hence reforms in education—and that those unfortunate by birth or accident might be excluded from the benefits—hence institutes for the deaf, blind, and insane.

These examples of beneficence should not obscure a larger trend within the evangelical tradition, one that speaks volumes about the divisions that animated the southern Indiana landscape. Even within reform movements, there was increasing emphasis on ideas of perfectionism, the notion that in the rebirth humans could escape sin. With its increasing emphasis on sobriety and self-discipline, the evangelical culture moved toward an understanding of "good works" as an absence of sin, rather than as responsibility for others. Edward Eggleston, novelist and later historian, began his adult life as a Methodist minister in the Hoosier hills. In his novel *The Hoosier Schoolmaster,* Eggleston portrayed religion and belief as necessary for a properly working society, but he condemned the churches of the era immediately preceding the Civil War as inadequate, thus necessitating the creation of the "Church of the Best Licks," whereby his backwoodsman, Bud Means, could vow to put in his "best licks for Christ." All the heroes of Eggleston's story were those who act to help others. The contrast was laid out between his hero's very own Aunt Matilda, an upstanding member of the Methodist congregation in the county seat, and Miss Nancy Sawyer, "a providence, one of those old maids who are a benediction to the whole town," whom Aunt Matilda thinks "lets people impose upon her and keep her away from the means of grace." Aunt Matilda was shocked that Nancy Sawyer had missed prayer meeting to tend to a sick baby.[83] Although Aunt Matilda, of course, participated in all the required benevolent committees, sewing garments to be sent to some far-off mission, she could not countenance the idea of housing a pauper woman. In Eggleston's eyes, Aunt Matilda represented Methodism's turn to respectability, a respectability defined in large part by the virtues of sobriety, industriousness, and self-discipline—in other words, the absence of sin—but missing a generosity of spirit toward others, especially her own neighbors.[84]

This shift in Methodism toward respectability mirrored similar trends among some Disciples and Baptists and, when coupled with the movement of the Presbyterians toward the popular evangelicals, helped to build an American evangelical movement.[85] It was a Christianity safe for both the masses and the elites, and by midcentury it seemed to have gained a following in southern Indiana, much as it had in the rest of the nation, even though reform movements never had quite the force they had in other parts of the North.[86]

That following was built, in large part, on the continued power of the Methodist Church, coupled with the presence of Presbyterians in smaller numbers yet concentrated among the most powerful citizens. Like the Presbyterians, many Methodists remained within the church of their fathers (and mothers), despite shifts in theological emphases. Methodism was able to consolidate its power because of its hierarchical structure, which also allowed the Presbyterians to exercise influence beyond their numbers.[87] This hierarchy was part of the organization which had made them so effective, especially when compared with their greatest potential rival, the Baptists. Their organization made it possible for every neighborhood to be visited by a Methodist itinerant; their emphasis on evangelical conversion made all people potential targets for proselytizing. Indeed, the "democracy" of Methodism had little to do with hierarchy and far more to do with the availability of grace. If, in the early days of Methodist success, the authoritarian hierarchy was of little consequence, in the latter days, such a hierarchy meshed closely with some people's ideas of the proper control of society.[88] Much as they began to recognize that far-flung endeavors, whether the government or a business enterprise operating over great distances, needed large-scale organizations with rigid authority to succeed, so they recognized that the organization of the Methodist Church was its blessing.[89]

The Methodist Church, with its rigid hierarchy, also taught some hill country Hoosiers that such authority was not antithetical to democracy, that indeed it was only through such structures that Hoosiers could be led to their own experience of grace. Such practices paralleled the new Whig, evangelical insight which argued that people would be free if they were released from many of the shackles that bound them: ignorance, alcoholism, vice. By exercising self-restraint, people could truly be freed.[90] From the Methodists, some hill country Hoosiers learned the necessity of such organizations and began to appreciate the possibilities of acting beyond the local community.

Hidden within Methodist practice was another element which worked to extend the moral horizons of some hill country Hoosiers. Ministers were rarely assigned to the same circuit or station for longer than a year. In this way, one minister was seen as little different from another. Despite the immense pressure on Methodist preachers to evoke the emotions of their audiences, ministers were treated as interchangeable. The Methodist discipline was to be exact, not dependent upon the judgments of any one man. It was precise; it was, as we have seen, written down, drawn up by the leading minds of the faith. There was no meeting of the minds of the neighborhood, coming together to condemn "backstabbing." When disciplinary actions occurred, they often took place not in the neighborhood but in the

Yearly Conference, with the leading pastoral figures of the region in judgment; unlike the practice in Baptist or Disciple faiths, the sanctity of the minister was only for his superiors to decide. Morality was universal. For this reason, Methodist—and, I would argue, much of the evangelical—morality was often more a set of prohibitions than an admonition to act decently and humanely. In this way, Methodist discipline paralleled the rules of the emerging capitalist economy.

By 1850, a hierarchy of sorts had come to be accepted among the major denominations in the hill country. The mainstream Presbyterians clung to their status among the elites of some communities, but their dependency on an educated ministry concentrated their strengths in areas with particularly devoted and able preachers. With their reach for respectability, Methodists claimed the elites of many towns and neighborhoods, especially those where Presbyterians had not been able to make a stand. The Disciples were perhaps the most enigmatic. With their offer of free grace and absence of creed, they could appeal to some commercializing elites, yet their congregational nature certainly conformed to the worldview of more localist denizens. In some neighborhoods, they seemed to appeal to the most successful; in others, they were the means to grace for those on the lowest rungs. The Baptists were perhaps the most diverse, because the Baptist faith encompassed so many divergent opinions. Free-Will and missionary Baptist churches followed a path similar to that of the Methodists, although anecdotal evidence suggests that they never quite reached the prominence in their neighborhoods as their Methodist colleagues did. It was, however, the highly Calvinist strains of what would later be known as the Primitive Baptists that would prove attractive to a number of ordinary southern Indiana farmers and their families. With its highly congregational nature and its distrust of distant activities like missionary work, these Primitive Baptists particularly appealed to the less commercialized hill country farmers.

THE PRIMITIVE BAPTISTS

To understand the worldviews of some southern Indiana farmers, it is necessary to understand the Primitive Baptists. Yet the congregational nature that made them so appealing to localist Hoosiers also makes them very difficult to describe. Each congregation could be different; moreover, at times congregations could choose to ignore differences among them—"footwashing shall not be a bar to fellowship"—while at other times, the congregations could explode over theological controversies. Primitive Baptists were not unique to the hill country of southern Indiana; they had broad appeal throughout the Upland South, as well as the western portions of some of the Mid-Atlantic states, and they could be found throughout Indiana. The key split for Primitive Baptists focused on whether missionary work was permitted, but this division was not absolute. Moreover, even churches and associations considered to be "missionary" shared with their antimissionary brethren a willingness to accommodate a variety of beliefs including those later labeled Primitive; although, for instance, southeastern Indiana had no "antimissionary" associations, there were many in that part of the hill country who adhered to that more conservative position while remaining members of nominally "missionary" churches and associations. The confusion might be summed up by detailing the situation in the Blue River Baptist Church: while it believed in general atonement, as contrasted to the limited atonement embraced by most Primitive Baptists, it opposed the modern missionary system, but did "not make it a bar of fellowship but leave each member at liberty to exercise there own views on the several subjects."[91]

Some of the confusion surrounding these conservative Baptists centered on the nomenclature. The term "primitive" did not come into widespread use until late in the nineteenth century.[92] Unlike many of the names, it was not an outsider's deprecation of their beliefs, but referred to the Baptists' claims of origin in the "Primitive" Apostolic Church. Many still went by "Regular" Baptist, although in areas where "modern" ideas had taken hold of the "Regular" Baptist Church, they used the name "Old Regular." Other names they used to denote themselves included "Old School," "Old-Fashioned," "Predestination," and "Particular," although within many of these different appellations were different theological positions. "Antimissionary" was perhaps the most common contemporary name for these conservative Baptists. Although it identified a spirit that infused many of them, some were open to particular kinds of "missionary" activity: after all, John Taylor of Kentucky, theological hero to hill country Baptists, did begin ten churches in Kentucky.

Moreover, the antimissionary spirit was not limited to Baptists.[93] Many Methodists were wary of the new organizations, and some of the impetus to their struggles with their hierarchy lay in this antimissionary spirit; likewise, the issues surrounding the New School/Old School split within the Presbyterian Church can be viewed as a manifestation of a similar reluctance to engage in large-scale missionary and reform activity. This antimissionary spirit, although not confined to the conservative Baptists, provides a solid key to understanding the moral worldviews of many southern Indiana farmers and their families, Baptist and non-Baptist alike.

Despite my difficulty in defining these Baptists, their enemies had little problem ridiculing them: "Hardshell," "Square-toed," or "Hard-rined." Edward Eggleston snorted:

> The "Hardshell Baptists," or, as they are otherwise called, the "Whisky Baptists," and the "Forty-gallon Baptists," exist in all the old Western and Southwestern States. They call themselves "Anti-means Baptists" from their Antinomian tenets. Their confession of faith is a caricature of Calvinism, and is expressed by their preachers about as follows: "Ef you're elected you'll be saved; ef you a'n't, you'll be damned. God'll take keer of his elect. It's a sin to run Sunday-schools, or tempr'rince s'cieties, or to send missionaries. You let God's business alone."

Eggleston added: "Of course the Hardshells are prodigiously illiterate, and often vicious. Some of their preachers are notorious drunkards."[94] American Home Missionary Society envoy John Parsons frothed when reporting on his Baptist neighbors: "One devoted intelligent Baptist Missionary could do more to save the west than a dozen Presbyterians other things being equal." Presbyterian Parsons invoked the image of the shared purpose of Presbyterians and enlightened Eastern Baptists: "We have stood side by side with you, & helped to roll the great machine that is to move the moral world, & felt perfectly united in our efforts to spread the Bible & the sabbath school to every neighborhood." Parsons feared that without some type of reform, the millennium could not occur; the sectarianism of the "Hardshell" Baptists ran contrary to his notion of the shared purpose of all Protestants, which was to make the United States a Christian nation, in preparation for the millennium. Parsons ends his digression on the Baptists by confirming Eggleston's comments on the Baptist minister: "He will preach on the sabbath & be reeling from the Grocery on Monday; & sometimes be half intoxicated while preaching."[95] To many churched elites, the conservative Baptists represented the nadir of religion in the hill country. Certainly all the Eastern elite characterizations of southern Indiana religion—and "frontier" religion in general—found double force in the characterizations of the conservative Baptists.

One reason for these negative portraits of Primitive Baptists was the perception of the membership. In the minds of Easterners, Primitive Baptists represented the epitome of the "frontier" type: unable to govern themselves. Although not all Primitive Baptists were dirt farmers, that was how they were characterized, and they, probably more than any other sect, drew upon the mass of ordinary people. In other words, the characterization of the Primitive Baptists as being drawn from the masses had some validity; the anathema which Easterners pronounced upon the Primitive sects was derived from those Easterners' disdain for the Western masses.

The American Home Missionary Society's missionary activity itself was an insinuation that the religion practiced by southern Indiana dirt farmers was not religion at all—indeed, that without proper training, Hoosiers were unable to practice religion—and it probably struck deeply in the hearts of these farmers and their families, many of whom had had honest spiritual experiences of the sort described by Benee Hester and Enoch Parr. In the minds of these Hoosiers, the validity of their experiences was being questioned. Moreover, their ability to govern themselves, in the widest sense of the word, was also being questioned. They felt capable of seeking religion themselves, without the aid of intervenors. And they felt capable of governing themselves, of regulating their behavior and the behavior of their family members and their church community. The insistence with which such missionaries were thrust upon Westerners fed a certain paranoia about intentions, which led them to oppose, not only missionaries among themselves but missionaries among the heathen of the world.

Much of the paranoia surrounded the perception of the Presbyterians and Congregationalists, with their New England ties, as being part of a Federalist plot to establish a state church.[96] The Southern and Middle Atlantic roots of many southern Indiana residents abetted the fear of a New England plot. Despite the disappearance of the "Federalist" party as an entity, antimissionary Baptists, like many in their socioeconomic class, detected Federalist machinations in various "Presbygationist" programs and Whig policies. Cooperation between various churches, beginning with the Presbyterian and Congregationalist Plan of Union, appeared particularly unusual to Baptists, who were more inclined to split than to join. That this union produced the American Home Missionary Society missionaries who so antagonized the Hoosiers underlined the undesirability of such activity. When plans for Sunday schools—seemingly ecumenical—were proposed, Primitive Baptists could not understand how such efforts could be advanced without adhering to some church's version of Truth, and the universality of the Sunday schools indicated that they might well be an insidious plot to capture the minds of Baptist children. In their opposition to the Evangelical Protestant mission to "Christianize" America, they were joined by their Catholic neighbors, who, as we shall see, shared similar economic circumstances and political beliefs. Baptists primarily opposed state religion because it interceded in their personal relationship with the Lord.

The class position of these southern Indiana farmers begins to explain what animated the sect. For the farmers who found themselves thus put at the bottom of the social order, the Calvinism of the Primitive Baptist Church offered compensation for the Easterners' dismissal of them. Much as in the Methodist Church, shared grace served as the great leveler. The Baptists' Calvinism added an extra dimension to this compensatory system: that worldly attainments were no reflection at all of inner grace. In fact, since grace was undeserved, no amount of human endeavor could attain it; predestination foreordained the elect and, by extension, practically every aspect of the human experience.[97] As opposed to the leveling in Methodism, where God's grace was available to all, the leveling within the Primitive Baptist sects reflected a view of all human beings as depraved, thereby making any earthly burden just and any relief from one's fate unearned. To toil the livelong day was a human affliction, and all were to share the same fate. Those who achieved grace were to see themselves not as somehow singled out but as merely lucky, and they were to remain properly humble before God. Likewise, those who escaped the toil of the human endeavor were viewed with suspicion, especially when they began to claim the agency of God.

Despite their own fears of being subjugated by others, their Calvinism endorsed their own subjugation of other races. Part of the animus against missionaries was the activity of some evangelicals among the indigenous peoples still living in the northern portion of the state.[98] The success of the missionaries in "Christianizing" the northern Indiana natives and turning them into farmers somewhat in the image of their conquerors delayed the appropriation of their lands. For hill country Hoosiers, these Indians stood in the way of further development of the state and impeded their claims to the land. Many a hill country farmer must have looked north and seen land for his progeny, yet was prevented from claiming it by the success and support of the missionaries for the natives. For many Hoosiers, only those of European descent seemed destined to receive God's grace, since among the heathen races not even heretical forms of Christianity existed: God had not even seen fit to provide his Word, the Bible, to such people. Such beliefs reinforced the racism of many early Hoosier Baptists, and their emphasis on human depravity made the lowly position of indigenous peoples and Africans seem to be the just position for all humans, save for the grace of God. Since missionary activity was for naught—Indians would become Christians only through God's predestined will—it was futile to pursue and a waste of money to fund such activity.

Missionary activity among native Americans merely underscored for early Hoosier Primitive Baptists the futility of all human creations. This skepticism about all human institutions outside those described in the Bible was central to the Primitive Baptist critique of the Evangelical Protestant crusade to Christianize America: none was part of God's plan. To those who pointed to the biblical "missionary" work of the Apostles, the Primitive Baptist answer was plain: "God calls and sends his Ministers to preach his gospel, without money and without price."[99] The skepticism about human institutions was rooted in their belief in the depravity of humanity; no human creation, funded by human money, could fulfill God's plan, because the human was tainted by the flaws in human intellect and emotion.

This skepticism certainly promoted the divisiveness that characterized the various sects of Primitive Baptists. Since they believed that it was only by the will of the Lord that humans received grace, they could not be content with the means that brought the greatest number of sinners to the Lord; rather, Primitive Baptists reflected at length about the proper structure and beliefs of the church. Like all written words, the Bible was open to interpretation, and it was the conflicts over these interpretations which caused splits, as each side accused the other of introducing human ideas into its interpretation.

The character of each individual church depended to a certain extent on the local interpreter; however, when an individual felt the calling to preach, he found his license in the company of believers. To Elim Baptist Church, "Brother Isaac Worral states that he has an impression of mind to exercise a public gift."[100] Such communal authority limited the ability of the interpreter to stray far from the beliefs of the community, and sometimes that company could choose to revoke the license: "The Church takes into consideration the gift of Jacob Tash and the Church says they think it is not profitable for him to take texts but exercise his gift in exhortation and prayer."[101]

Such local control reinforced the congregationalism, but since such preachers often traveled on the Sundays on which no church was held in their own neighborhood, their ideas traveled, too. Such visiting could prompt the divisions that so animated the Primitive Baptists, as new neighborhoods were exposed to perceived heresies and chose to sever ties with heretical congregations. For this reason, many of the divisions within the Primitive Baptists were not within churches but between churches. These divisions, prompted by the importance of adhering to the means and beliefs of the apostolic church, gave the Primitive Baptist sects a direction opposite that of the evangelical Protestant denominations: instead of moving toward a "Christian America," wherein differences between faiths were subsumed, within the Primitive Baptist sects the emphasis was on distinguishing correct belief.

In this arduous task of distinguishing correct belief, three definable camps emerged within the conservative Baptist congregations of southern Indiana: Means, Anti-means, and Parkerite.[102] All opposed the mission system. The Means camp believed that "God used preached word as means or medium of conversion" but that missionary boards were human institutions. The Anti-means crowd rejected such a notion, believing that the "preaching of the gospel had no power to convert [a] dead sinner."[103] A majority of Primitive Baptists in the hill country shared this latter belief, which gave to the church gathering an emphasis less on conversion than on "community." The final group was influenced by the writings of Daniel Parker, who posited that humanity was born of two seeds, one of God and one of Satan. While congregations and associations might differ on other issues, it was the split between the means and anti-means camps and the split between the Parkerites and the "Regular" (normally anti-means) Baptists which truly divided congregations and associations.

Yet despite these divisions, there were imperatives within congregations to remain together. If, as in the case of anti-means Baptists, grace only occurred through divine will, then the purpose of preaching was merely to obey the edict that God's people—both saved and damned—should hear God's word, and the primary purpose of gathering centered far more on sharing among God's elect. As the Blue River Association preached in 1825:

> A particular, visible, gospel church, is a congregation of men and women, called of Jesus Christ, from darkness and ignorance, to the knowledge and practice of the truth, in which the pure word of God is preached and the ordinances of the Gospel duly administered, after the example of Christ and the Apostles. The members of which, by mutual agreement, must be in union, all which requires a coalition of a number of persons feeding in one pasture, under one Shepherd.[104]

In other words, community was central to many conservative Baptist sects.

The Baptist emphasis on the local community, institutionalized in their congregationalism, begat their antimissionary stance. Congregationalism gave all control to the local church. These churches chose to maintain loose relationships with other churches in their region which they believed held similar beliefs, in associations, and associations often corresponded with neighboring ones that shared similar doctrine. Interference in the affairs of other churches within the association animated the divisions. In the midst of Parkerite divisions, Bethlehem Church questioned Unity Church's call for a council to deny Bethlehem the preacher of Bethlehem's choosing (who had originally been licensed by Unity, but then had been discovered to preach the Parkerite heresy).[105] At the center of the controversy was the tricky question of the preacher, Martin Ellis, who was practicing at other churches although Unity had revoked the license that it had previously issued. Bethlehem could have issued their own license to Ellis, but because Unity was Ellis's neighborhood church, Unity claimed the sole prerogative to issue and revoke any license that could be given to him. This Baptist tradition of requiring one's neighborhood church to issue the preaching license was part and parcel of the localist ethic, and therefore the conflict was between two churches, both claiming their own local authority.

Ironically, the associations, one of whose primary functions was to help resolve doctrinal disputes within the local church, often served to fan the flames of dissent. These unintended consequences worked to justify, in the Primitive Baptist mind, their aversion to an even more authoritative church structure. This aversion paralleled their political fears, as they resisted the increasing power of federal and state authority. Such political roots were voiced in the White Water Regular Baptist Association's resolution of 1852, addressing "the Modern Missionary, and kindred institutions of the day."

> *Resolved,* That we, in all sincerity and brotherly love recommend to the Churches with whom we stand in connection; and advise our brethren generally to maintain the ground on which they were originally constituted, and to stand aloof from the modern inventions of men called benevollent, and from all *entangling alliances,* which have not the word of God for their support; or a thus saith the Lord for their creation.[106]

Echoing George Washington's Farewell Address, the leaders of the association suggested that the "sovereignty" of the church would be threatened by participating in the modern institutions of man, with their "entangling alliances."

For these reasons, all associations with other churches were seen as temporal and readily broken, while the major emphasis remained a commitment to the sanctity of the local church and the maintenance of peace within the local church. The error of the "missionary" movement, as the leaders of the White Water Association saw it, was not primarily the preaching of heresy, but the disruption of the peace of the church, the interruption of brotherly love. Primitive Baptists viewed divisions within their associations with sadness:

> Until 1844; an epoch in the history of this Association long to be remembered in sorrow by many that yet live; when the terms Means and Anti-Means began to be excited, and some seeming to forget their high and Heavenly calling, and to engage in speculation on, and misrepresentation of, the views of others until those who had long went to the house of God in company, and had taken sweet councel together, could no longer meet in harmony and good feeling, to consult on any matter pertaining to the kingdom of God; nor could churches go on in the even tenor of their way, nor in their (heretofore acknowledged) independence.[107]

Yet despite their sorrow at the rending of the association, the offense was against sovereignty of the local church, which was to remain inviolate and in harmony. All Primitive Baptist churches asked, "Is there peace in the church?" and business could not proceed until peace was achieved.

Maintenance of communal harmony was the highest goal for these conservative Baptists. In its Circular Letter of 1825, the Blue River Association asserted: "The law of love should never be forgotten—love one another with a pure heart fervently," adding that "nothing is more pernicious to a church state, than want of love."[108] Enoch Parr opposed the name "Regular Baptist" because some of the church disliked it, and one of his major complaints about "Two-seedism" was that it was "better calculated to scatter flock than to gather it."[109] This emphasis on communal harmony permeated the minds of all who gathered, even those who questioned the ruling theology of the body. In the midst of the Parkerite controversy in the Sinking Spring Church, Gustavus and Catherine Trabue withdrew from the church in the interest of harmony:

> Brothers and Sisters in as much as there are reports in circulation against myself and wife, over which the cause of Christ is sorely bleeding, and feeling interested for the welfare of the Church, and not being suficiently able perhaps, to give the church entire satisfaction relative to said reports, we therefore rather than the cause shall longer bleed, request the church to suffer us to withdraw from its fellowship.[110]

Not all went so willingly, and the interest in communal harmony forced these conservative Baptists to exclude members. Highest on many lists for exclusion were those "who gender strife."[111] During an 1834 dispute, Brother McGee was excluded from Lost River for "refusing to attend with us saying hard things of us which we believe that we are clear of & for trying at our August meeting [to] split the church by making a motion for the majority to sit together to do church business alone."[112] McGee's offense, it appears, was to ignore the minority, thus slighting the Baptist imperative for communal harmony. Exclusion was a particularly harsh way to maintain "community." Possibly for this reason, conservative Baptists felt compelled to defend it: "Lepers were to be put out of the camp, that they might not infect others."[113]

Of course, exclusion was not reserved solely for those who engendered strife in the church. In addition to those who by their nonattendance excluded themselves and "all erroneous and heretical persons, who hold doctrine contrary to the word of God," the Blue River Association classified as lepers worthy of exclusion:

> All such are busy bodies, going from house to house, tatling and making mischief, 2d Thss. 3d, 6th and 14th. All who commit crimes and continue in them unrepented of, as fornication, covetousness, idolters, railers, backbiters, drunkards and exponers [sic], 1st Cor. 5 and 11. Eph. 5 and 5.[114]

Backbiters and tattlers undermined the community; in his second epistle to the Thessalonians, Paul mandated that:

> And if any man obey not our word by this epistle, note that man, and have no company with him, that he may be ashamed.

> Yet count *him* not as an enemy, but admonish *him* as a brother. (2
> Thessalonians 3:14–15, AV)

Certainly transgressors were not to be removed readily from the community, for they remained brothers. Yet the Primitive Baptist emphasis on *unrepented* crimes indicated a key aspect of this conservative Baptist understanding of morality and community. The Lost River Association suggested that its churches "deal mildly with offenders; and labour hard to restore such in the spirit of meekness."[115] When Gustavus and Catherine Trabue withdrew from the church, the church formally "excluded" them, withdrawing "from them the watch care and fellowship of the church."[116] Part of the community was such "watch care"; part of the structure that formed the community were the labors with transgressors. Such a community was very constrictive. All members were expected to watch over all others. And if a member transgressed, the other members were, as Paul ordained, to make him or her ashamed.

Since humans were destined to sin, yet the community was to keep watch over and care for its brothers and sisters, the moral horizons of the Primitive Baptist were quite limited. Behavior was to be regulated, and it could only be regulated within the local community. It was only within the tightly circumscribed local community that the inevitable human failings would be visibly manifest and their consequences mitigated. Moral regulation over a distance, with its formal rules that the distances demanded, could not respond to the unique sins of the individual. Formal moral regulation could only condemn those who transgressed its rules; it featured no efforts by concerned acquaintances to reach out and embrace each other as sinners, undeserving of grace. Actions outside of the moral community, inevitably dangerous as they were because of human depravity, took place outside of the watch care of the community and therefore were without the necessary regulation. They were in a moral and cultural morass where Christians trod at their own peril, because they had no means to bring the watchful eyes of the community to bear.

Part of what determined the community of the Primitive Baptist congregation was the involvement of all members in the regulation of morality. Yet because their communal needs created an opposite impetus to "deal mildly" with transgressors, Primitive Baptists were often portrayed as amoral and sinful. In many ways, they would have agreed with such a portrait, believing, as they did, that all humans were sinful; the emphasis within the Church was not on weeding out sinners—all had received the Grace of God without merit—but on ensuring that the sinner recognize his or her sins—in other words, that he or she was repentant—and thus was properly humble. As part of their Calvinist tradition Primitive Baptists did not believe that doing good was necessarily evidence of God's grace.

Despite their insistence on human depravity, conservative Baptists frowned on excessive drunkenness and debauchery. Many of the disciplinary efforts within the Baptist Church were directed toward the same sorts of sins against which the more evangelical sects arrayed themselves: Swearing, dancing, and fighting. Nevertheless, the Baptist attitude toward the sinner was subtly different. In many ways, it confirmed the Christian edict to "hate the sin, but love the sinner." Sin was not always a cause for exclusion from the church, but merely confirmation of the depravity of humanity. As long as the sinner recognized his sin and repented, then he might be forgiven. Some sins, of course, remained beyond redemption—child molestation, for instance. Yet Primitive Baptists viewed sin as part of the human condition: innate depravity.

Baptists regulated morality because they believed themselves keepers of their brothers in Christ. While sin could not be eliminated, the elect were expected to be obedient. "The love of God is the main-spring of all their obedience to his commands."[117] Their obedience came in part from the action of the Spirit: "James says that even faith if it hath not works, is dead being alone, and by works was faith made perfect, the wisdom of the Lord is not merely to say I believe, have faith &c."[118] Primitive Baptists expected the elect to pursue good works. In many respects, to act morally was inherent in grace. But for Primitive Baptists, the converse was not necessarily true: acting morally did not reveal grace.

For Primitive Baptists, morality and religion were separate issues. Baptists chose to regulate morality for the good of their familial and communal life. Joel Hume argued:

> The man that is in the habit of getting intoxicated, and cursing and swearing or that is in the habit of any immorality, no matter what, possesses the power to lay the habit aside; does not only possess the power but if he has respect he ought to have for himself, will do it; not because he is expected by doing so to work his passage to heaven. No, verily, but that he might render himself and family more respectable and happy and set them an example that would be worthy the imitation of all who knew him. But let me ask you, is that religion? Is that the first step toward Christianity? I maintain that every man ought to be a moral man, but that every truly moral man is not truly a pious man.[119]

Despite their belief in innate depravity, Primitive Baptists granted humans some power over their behavior, however weak they appeared next to God. Their emphasis on innate depravity actually reflected a realist's vision of the world, where humans stumbled but still were supposed to continue on.

But they were to act morally for the good of family and society, their community, "all who knew" them. Such moral actions were not necessarily Christian. "A man may be a moralist and not a christian; but to be a christian and not a moralist is contrary to the teachings of the Redeemer."[120] This distinction between moralist and Christian lay at the heart of the Primitive Baptist critique of the Arminian heresy: "Their faith of external evidence, in obeying God, no supernatural change, but a mere belief in the son of God; but the children of God hath the spirit itself bearing witness with their spirits."[121] Anyone could obey the laws of God, but only the children of God felt the action of the Holy Spirit within. Salvation, within the Calvinist credo of these conservative Baptists, was beyond the choice of mortals. God had predestined the unmerited election of a number of humans. In the eyes of Primitive Baptists, those who made the Arminian error "offer Christ and salvation as a reward for the works of depraved mortals."[122] The essence of innate depravity was that humans could never act well enough to merit salvation; this inability did not preclude them from trying to do good.

DEPRAVITY AND HUMILITY

Innate human depravity stood at the core of the Primitive Baptist worldview, informing their skepticism about human creations, their distrust of the claims of education, their adherence to a doctrine of limited atonement, their attitudes toward treatment of different races, and their understanding of the limitations of human reform. This belief in the baseness of humanity has not always been the most illuminated part of Calvinism—many focus more on limited atonement—in part because it was not unique to Calvinism. Yet in the mid-nineteenth century, as many of the evangelical sects were moving toward postmillennialist perfectionism, the Primitive Baptist insistence on innate human depravity stood in greater relief and gave it common ground with Catholicism. At the theological level, of course, most of the Protestant denominations never really abandoned the doctrine. Yet the emphasis of their preaching undoubtedly changed, stressing the perfectibility of man, and it was this stress which Primitive Baptists condemned.

The doctrine of innate human depravity produced in its adherents a profound sense of humility. Next to the divinity of Father, Son, and Holy Ghost, the baseness of humanity was evident. And the great beneficence of the Creator to elect a poor sinner to join Him was more evidence of His magnanimity. God was on a different plane from mortals. And to understand the mind of God completely was impossible. Explaining why the damned were not believers, Joel Hume attempted to answer the question: "Why did they not believe?"

> Here is the reason why some people do not believe—because they can not. As to why they can not, that is not my business. I have never attempted to arraign Jehovah, neither do I intend to apologize for the conduct of my Lord, for he is too wise to err.[123]

God had revealed in the Bible what he had chosen for humans to understand. Beyond that lay mysteries.[124] Such mysteries often were at the root of the conflicts that engulfed their congregations from time to time.

> Whereas there is contention among us some charging others with believing and preaching a created Christ, while others charge them with believing and preaching an Eternal flesh and bone or material substance Christ *all which are questions and charges to no profit* and only tend to the subverting of the hearers and if such a course has been indulged in by use and we have thus preached we have thus far departed from the simplicity of the gospel and from the plain declaration of the Bible and therefore have wandered out in *the ocean of mysterys* and on our return therefrom have brought with us opinions yet knowing from whence they originated we should not attempt to enforce others to receive them they having equal rights with us in matters of opinion.[125]

In their humility, Primitive Baptists were taught to respect the mysteries of God's ways.

The emphasis on humility was an attribute that Primitive Baptists shared with their Roman Catholic neighbors, along with related beliefs about the innate depravity of the human heart and the mysterious ways of the Lord.[126] In both churches, humility was and is ritualized in the ceremonial washing of the feet, following Christ's example at the Last Supper, when he washed the feet of his disciples. In recommending the "ritual," the Lost River Baptist Church, after much consideration, said, "We believe washing of feet is an example of humility given to us by our Saviour & a manifestation of our love to each other."[127] While the image of the poor farmers of southern Indiana, Protestant and Catholic alike, participating in this rite of humility may seem too pat, it forms a useful contrast to illuminate their common difference from those in the postmillennialist perfectionist camp, who believed, truly believed, through evangelizing and reform in the legislatures that they could form a Christian America that would host a thousand years of peace.

For Catholics and Primitive Baptists, such a program was nothing short of blasphemous. As they characterized it, to believe that one needed to be perfect to be saved and that one who was saved was perfect contradicted their own experiences and their own understanding of human possibility. The idea that humans could perfect themselves for the millennium surely seemed preposterous and arrogant. Humanity was not divinity. For these reasons, Catholics and Primitive Baptists opposed the evangelicals' efforts, especially in the legislatures, and in doing so, they found themselves together on the Democratic ticket, while the Whigs, and later the Know-Nothings and Republicans, served as the means to evangelical ends.

Yet their affinity for the Democratic Party did not end there. As small producers they were, as we shall see, ambivalent about the expanding marketplace that was part of the Whig vision of the world. Primitive Baptists in their independent congregations and German Catholics in their ethnic parishes were both part of tightly bound local communities, by which the morality of their members was governed. Within the community, economic activity could be regulated; outside the community, moral regulation, in the minds of the Primitive Baptists and German Catholics, was diminished. Therefore, trade at a distance entailed the danger of dealing with amoral men and, as we shall see, had to be approached with great caution. The great hope of the evangelical camp, that all capitalists would internalize a moral code, seemed far-fetched to Catholics and Baptists who believed that humans could not escape sin.

"Surplus Produce" and Market Exchange

When Mr. McPheeters was excluded from communion while charges about his "unchristian conduct" in his economic dealings were investigated, he encountered the ambiguous relationship between Christianity and capitalism. Yet McPheeters's difficulties derived from an ancillary problem, that of the moral judgment of the local community. In his southern Indiana community, members took it upon themselves to define what was "just," and they did not acquiesce in the values of the broader world. This demand for local regulation emphasized the localized morality of many of the communities of southern Indiana. Moreover, McPheeters's case pointed to a larger, noninstitutionalized community in judgment of its members' economic behavior: McPheeters was charged "in consequence of a *rumour* against him, in which *common fame* has accused him."[1] Although local churches could bring much force—promises of heaven, fears of hell—to bear upon those who transgressed their moral codes, the multiplicity of churches and hence restricted memberships certainly limited their ability to regulate their neighborhoods. Rather, they served as institutionalized manifestations of beliefs that permeated their neighborhoods. As McPheeters's case demonstrated, "common fame" judged his "Christian conduct in his dealings."

Such local moral regulation was central to the way in which many southern Indiana farmers pursued their life's work, through a strategy encompassed in the term "surplus produce." As we shall see, at the most basic level, Hoosier farmers sought both to survive and to ensure their children's survival, and these twin goals explained both their dependence upon the local community and their involvement in more distant markets. Central to these pursuits was hog-and-corn farming, certainly not the best adapted form of farming for the Hoosier hills, but one which fulfilled the goals of its inhabitants.[2]

One cannot really understand antebellum southern Indiana—and probably much of the United States—if one does not understand hogs. Hogs were at the center of an orderly economic strategy pursued by many southern Indiana farmers, through which they sought to preserve their survival and the reproduction of the same opportunities for their children. Pork was the primary source of meat for antebellum Americans. For one thing, pork was relatively easy to preserve by pickling or smoking. Moreover, the hog was the most efficient means of turning grain into meat. Hoosiers depended upon hog-and-corn farming, and residents recognized its importance.

Hog-and-corn farming provided a steady source of food and, when nature cooperated, could also provide the income necessary to set up one's children in a similar operation. In other words, a Hoosier farmer could reap the benefits of the market without incurring much risk to his family's immediate survival. Minimizing risk was important, because the distant marketplaces that served as occasional sources of income for Hoosier farmers were beyond the oversight of the local moral community, and since morality was localized, distant markets were by definition immoral, as they inherently depended upon different moral standards. Moreover, these distant markets were often perceived as manipulated by immoral men to increase their own ill-gotten gain. Nevertheless, food was not the only essential for survival, and for these other necessities Hoosier farmers turned first to their neighbors, depending upon local moral regulation to ensure that their independence and survival would not be threatened.

There was hardly what one might term consensus among all the inhabitants of southern Indiana about the risks and benefits of the distant markets, and some sought to maximize their profits. Profit maximizers were not in the majority, and theirs is not my story. Over the years, as members of the communities of the southern Indiana hills, the activities of such capitalists helped to draw their neighbors into the expanding capitalist economy, and while I will allude to this development in my story, my emphasis is not upon the "roots of rural capitalism" or the "agrarian origins of American capitalism," but upon the effort to show a certain limited logic to the worldview of many—not all—southern Indiana farmers, a worldview which circulated around their localism.[3]

The relationship between localism and economic activity is my central concern. The destruction of community and the rise of capitalism have been often connected, yet these two events have been variously dated from the 1640s to the 1890s and beyond.[4] The decline of a geographically located form of community and the rise of capitalism have been a continuing process over the nearly four hundred years of European presence in North America. With the ascendancy of capitalism, relationships defined by formal and limited knowledge replaced relationships conditioned upon knowledge of the whole person. The traditional community, where persons bore the burden of being judged in the court of common fame, could prove very limiting. It was no golden age. Conflict abounded, and accommodation, rather than justice, often prevailed. In many ways, the ascendancy of capitalism made it theoretically possible for individuals to escape some of the constrictions of the geographical community, as they no longer needed to depend upon their neighbors for their survival.[5] In most regards, it was a movement from one form of community, defined spatially around the neighborhood, to new forms of community, defined by economic relationships, by training and expertise, by voluntary cooperation.[6] The shift, therefore, was for some a liberation, but as it was a move from one form of interdependence to another, it at best only gave the illusion of individualistic independence. The invisible hand of the marketplace could have seemed far more just than the arbitrary actions of the local moral community, but as a member of that community, a person also had a voice into the community's decisions.

Nevertheless, my division of the peoples of the Hoosier hills into those who embraced distant markets and those who feared them is an artificial one. Hoosier farmers were not so neat in their beliefs—although the two-party system tended to force them into more distinct positions—but rather existed along a continuum, from those who embraced the market without hesitation to those who attempted to exist completely outside these markets. My choice has been to focus upon those ambivalent about the market. Yet even within this group, there were conflicts between competing ideologies in their own minds. Their fears of dependency, which drove them to fear the distant markets, could also cause them to fear dependency upon their neighbors, thus leading to the peculiar circumstance that their neighborhoods were both the home to much communal activity as well as a compulsive behavior to record in their ledgers much of their mutual aid. Much of the impulse came from a purely ideological commitment to independence: they did not want to be beholden to anyone.

THE UTILITY OF WORK

What was most astounding about early life on the frontier was not the self-sufficient subsistence farming but the almost immediate involvement in commerce.[7] Of course, many participated in the market to accumulate money to purchase land. The federal land system treated land as a commodity. But as I have already suggested, land was purchased for reasons that had little to do with commodities: raising a family, guaranteeing equality, ensuring independence. That settlers participated in the market economy did not mean that they acquiesced to the control of the market. Nevertheless, from the beginning of European settlement of the region, Hoosiers sent a large variety of commodities out of the hills, from meat to lumber products, from cloth to alcohol.

The earliest commodities were products of the forest. The selling of furs and skins, of course, continued practices of the conquered indigenous peoples, but the fact that Hoosiers were involved in international commerce was underlined by ginseng exports.[8] Yet even forest products were not merely harvested, but prepared for market, passing through a complex marketing relationship:

> A [deer] haunch will bring only 20 cents . . . or the value of 25 cents, if the hunter will take powder, lead, or goods. The shopkeepers who buy the haunches, the only parts of the deer that are thought worth selling, cure and dry them much in the same manner as the Scotch do their mutton hams, and then send them for sale to Louisville or New Orleans.[9]

With the differential cash and goods price, the embeddedness of the backwoods hunter in commercial markets was evident, and certainly the rise of agriculture did little to change that situation.

Transportation difficulties were an impediment to commerce before the coming of improved roads, canals, and railroads, but farmers in the Hoosier hills found ways to get their surplus goods to market. Flatboats, requiring little investment, were the preferred means. Both flatboats and wagons had a limited capacity, and many farmers found it profitable to reduce their fruit and corn to brandy and whiskey. However, the most notable example of overcoming transportation problems was the driving of livestock, thus creating a four-legged means of getting goods to market. As early as 1816, men like Enoch Honeywell traveled through Indiana, buying hogs for driving back to eastern markets.[10] Very quickly, Cincinnati became a major destination, earning the appellation "Porkopolis," although other towns throughout the hill country opened meatpacking plants, the most prominent of which was Madison.[11] In the fall of 1834, some 30,000 hogs passed through Brookville, although many of these were undoubtedly from central Indiana.[12] Living on the road to Madison in the early 1840s, Harrison Burns related that "droves on some days . . . would be almost continuous, there being scarcely a half hour but that a drove would be passing along the road."[13] Hogs were the mainstay of the hill country economy.

Nevertheless, the region produced diverse products. In 1825, John Scott reported that in the state, then comprised primarily of the hill country, "horses, cattle, swine, whiskey, flour, sugar &c. compose the principal domestic articles of exchange for foreign commodities. —These articles are taken, in great abundance, every year to the southern and eastern markets."[14] Salem in particular furnished a wide variety of products for export:

1,250 barrels, flour
285 barrels, whiskey
614 barrels, pork
18,500 barrels, bacon and lard
208,000 pipe staves
15,000 yards, tow cloth
1,000 pounds, bees-wax
3,000 pounds, feathers
50 barrels, linseed oil

Additionally, "large quantities of butter, eggs, chickens, &c. &c. [were] exported." All of the exports were products of farms, including domestic manufactures. Save for the linseed oil, manufactured from flax, absent from the locale's exports were any products of the town's already considerable manufacturing base: "2 cabinet makers, one cotton spinning factory, 3 wool carding machines, one fulling mill, one oil mill, one tin and copper manufactory, 3 blacksmiths, 3 saddlers, 2 wheelwrights, 2 brass clock makers, 2 watch makers and silversmiths, 3 tan-yards, 2 shoemakers, 2 tailors, 2 chair makers, . . . 3 brick makers and brick layers, . . . one tobacco manufactory, and 4 hatter shops."[15] These manufacturers and artisans produced not for export but for the local community, and they received in return for their goods the agricultural produce and domestic manufactures detailed above, which they exported to outside markets.

The local market was a good place for residents to sell their goods. The constant influx of new settlers made a ready market for food products. Many of the counties did not reach the height of their nineteenth-century population until after the Civil War, although most had minimal growth after the 1850s.[16] "Thus it is probable there will be a market for all the spare produce for a series of years, arising from the accession of strangers as well as the rapid internal growth of population."[17] One resident told William Faux, "We can always sell all the produce we raise from the land to travellers like you, and others, new comers."[18] Noting that they lived better than most in the community, Patrick Henry Jameson remembered:

My father would kill about thirty hogs every year, more than we could use. We had a big smoke-house . . . and we hung up that meat and smoked it, and as Hoosiers came through they would come there to buy, so it was another source of revenue; and then some improvident fellow would always want to buy a middling or a ham, and we got part of our ready money in that way.[19]

Faux also encountered another fellow, Ferrell, who believed that he would always have "a market at his door . . . because of the number of idle people who do not, or cannot raise produce."[20]

The perception held by Ferrell of many Hoosiers as lazy and improvident certainly was an image that permeated much of the outside elite's account of southern Indiana; Faux called Ferrell himself "improvident." Perhaps the accounts of large-scale commerce were merely fictions of aggregation, the result of a small population of families like the Jamesons. Yet the irony of Faux's labeling of Ferrell underscored that there were a variety of conceptions about the value and purpose at work abroad in the hill country. Some of the differences were probably based in the commentators' social and economic backgrounds. For instance, many observers were part of the English gentry, and their sensibilities were offended by the democratic notions of hill country Hoosiers, if not Americans in general. Yet the characterization of Hoosiers as lazy falls flat once one recognizes that few went hungry, despite George Leavitt's insistence otherwise:

> The others who reside in this neighborhood are poor *Devils* not worth a picayune apiece and too lazy to earn enough to subsist on decently in this land of plenty—there are men of enterprise and perseverance here who nearly all become rich and there are also lazy worthless scum in abundance.[21]

These characterizations reflected the conflicts between different perceptions of the utility of work, and these condemnations revealed an upper middle class frustrated by what it saw as lost opportunities for profit. If there were indeed lost opportunities, it would suggest that a majority of Hoosier farmers were not living up to capitalist ideals.

In the minds of many observers of southern Indiana, Hoosiers did not want to better themselves.[22] Richard Lee Mason reported that he "slept in a house without glass in the windows and no fastenings to the doors. The inhabitants imprudent and lazy beyond example."[23] Mason was not alone in characterizing Hoosiers as lazy, nor was he the only one to measure laziness by the yardstick of glass windows. In Baynard Rush Hall's fictionalized account of early Indiana settlement, one of Hall's neighbors, upon purchasing window glass, laughs:

> "Ain't it a sort a funny theme ere settlers what's been in the Purchus longer nor us ain't got no sashes?—I allow, it looks a sort a idle in 'em."[24]

Charles Sealsfield, annoyed when Troy residents tried to sell him a half-barrel of apples for ten dollars, when in Louisville a whole barrel went for three dollars, "advised them to keep their apples, and to plant trees, which would enable them to raise some for themselves; and to put panes of glass in their windows, instead of old newspapers."[25] This insistence upon glass windows reflected a calculus of consumption, in which "needs" were created as part of the civilizing and modernizing enterprise; without consumption, there could be no economic growth.[26] Certainly, without the impetus of consumer "needs," many Hoosier farmers saw less utility in working hard.

Hoosiers of the day probably did not work as hard as others. Southern Indiana farmers were alleged to have shinnied up trees in the springtime to judge how many acorns, butternuts, and beechnuts would be available for the hogs to eat in the fall, and then they planted their corn accordingly.[27] Hoosier farmers often raised more than they could use, for reasons we shall discuss below, and sometimes crops were left to rot in the field.[28] Certainly the time they saved by such decisions may have been put to more profitable use—the record does not speak—but the sense of many was that hill country Hoosiers were not afraid of leisure. As William Borden recalled, "In those easy days, the farmer had no ambition for a great farm and great crops of cereal, such development in life had not been attained." Nevertheless, other pursuits demanded early Hoosiers' time. Borden added that in that day, hunting had been more a profession than an amusement.[29] Such a notion was beyond the grasp of Charles Sealsfield: "Two [other bears] which were skinned, indicated an abundance of these animals, and more application to the sport than seems compatible with the proper cultivation of these regions."[30] William Faux "stopped at another quarter-section farmer's, who has never cleared nor inclosed any of his land, because sick or idle; being, however, well enough to hunt daily, a sport which, as he can live by it, he likes better than farming."[31] For Faux and other observers, time spent hunting was time spent at leisure, despite his recognition that they "could live by it." In many ways, Faux's comments recalled an earlier generation of Englishmen in America, who could not conceive that Native American males worked, since they hunted, a leisure activity reserved for the gentry in England. The purpose of labor, to many early Hoosiers, was to provide for their families. If that could be done with little effort, so much the better.[32]

For Hoosiers, laboring for another individual could be a threat to an individual's control over his own life. Morris Birkbeck, who, on the whole, was impressed with the industriousness of southern Indiana residents, noted on passing through Lexington:

> We see in every village and town, as we pass along, groups of able-bodied men who seem to be as perfectly at leisure as the loungers of ancient Europe. This love of idleness, where labour is so profitable, is a strange affection. . . . If you enquire of hale young fellows why they remain in this listless state, "we live in freedom," says they, "we need not work like the English."[33]

One settler reported to William Faux "that hiring when you can, in a free state in the west, may sometimes pay, but as nearly all feel themselves masters instead of labourers, it is impossible to be regularly supplied with hands."[34] English emigrant Susannah Pering complained that the availability of land made servants independent. Pering added much vitriol:

> The first [servant] we had took umbrage at my asking her to go down in the town for three dozen eggs; said she had never been sent on an errand before, and left me at the expiration of a week. Many of them require to sit down at the table, and be treated in all respects as one of the family. . . . I had four young women successively, neither of whom staid longer than a week and at intervals was out of one several days together.[35]

The Perings circulated in the same Bloomington crowd as Baynard Rush Hall, and he recorded similar complaints: "Did a girl fancy, too, herself undervalued?—was she not asked to the first table with company?—not included in invitations sent us from "big bug" families?—not called Miss Jane or Eliza?—she was off in a moment!"[36] Lewis Peleg reported that "girls here think it a disgrace to go out to work."[37] Certainly servant difficulties were not unknown elsewhere, but in the hill country, the option not to work, when coupled with the high wages current, angered the elites.[38]

The "laziness" of Hoosiers seemed incomprehensible to many like Morris Birkbeck, because "labour is so profitable." Birkbeck did not exaggerate; letters back East promised high wages in the hill country. Lorenzo Chapin wrote that Leavenworth was "a good place for a man that wants to work out for wages is high."[39] George Kennedy reported that "in general wages here are very good a hand gets from 10 to 12 Dollars per month," and he closed the letter by adding:

> Job work is tolerable plenty makeing Rails 50 Cents per hundred white oak timber Chopping wood 50 cents.[40]

Evident from many of these exchanges was that the hill country promised greater opportunity than the settled East.

> I would inform Joseph Brubeck that this is an excellent country for a blacksmith, and that I have selected a good place for him, to which I want him to remove. If he does, it will certainly be a great exchange, for he can undoubtedly make more than a livelihood here, which is more than he can do where he now is.[41]

Although all forms of laborers seemed to benefit in the early days of European settlement, none was perhaps in more demand than skilled craftsmen like blacksmiths and tailors. As late as 1840, Jehiel Goltry noted that "a very good blacksmith could have plenty of business here and a shoemaker need not be idle."[42] Charles Arms used the growing consumerism to entice his brother:

> taylering is good busyness the young men have to go 15 or 20 miles to get a coat cut and made ther are still dressing beter some broad cloth is worn and the making costs ver high you have now good learning and a good trade come a head[43]

The high wages made farm laboring, as well as skilled and semiskilled trades, good avenues for accumulating the funds necessary to purchase one's own farm.

Despite the high wages reported by visitors and residents alike, poverty seemed widespread to many who looked upon the Hoosier landscape. While visitors might acknowledge early Hoosiers' abilities to provide for themselves and their families, this success did not prevent the elites from imagining the Hoosier as poor. In a particularly haunting passage, Richard Lee Mason described one southern Indiana household:

> In the midst of one of those long and thick pieces of woods, we passed one of the most miserable huts ever seen—a house built out of slabs without nail; the piece merely laid against a long pen such as pigs are commonly kept in; a dirt floor, no chimney. Indeed, the covering would be a bad one in the heat of summer, and, unfortunately, the weather at this time [Nov. 4] is very severe for the season of the year. This small cabin contained a young and interesting female and her two shivering and almost starving children, all of whom were bareheaded and with their feet bare. There was a small bed, one blanket and a few potatoes. One cow and one pig (who appeared to share in their misfortunes) completed the family, except for the husband, who was absent in search of bread.

Although the circumstances seemed dire, Mason was surprised to find the woman apparently "happy."[44] Countless travelers published similar statements, erroneously depicting southern Indiana as poor. Certainly poverty existed, but few visitors successfully separated that poverty from the general image of southern Indiana. Quaker leader William Forster reported that somewhere in Lawrence County, he stopped at

> the house of a man who readily gave us shelter for the night; and it was well we had not occasion to ask for more, as the family were bare of meat of any description and were then living on hominy, with plenty of fat pork. This was almost the only family we met with that was not abounding in the necessaries and ordinary comforts of life.[45]

Forster recognized that poverty was not ubiquitous in southern Indiana, but his impoverished were hardly starving, as he failed to see that salt pork and hominy were at the center of Hoosier subsistence strategies.

Forster's equation of poverty with the absence of "ordinary comforts" suggests that he, at least, had accepted a more modern conception of the purpose of work, one that saw labor not as driven solely by the need to survive but as a means to accumulate wealth and consumer goods.[46] The older conception—necessity compels labor—and many of its ancillary ideas colored the perceptions of some visitors and residents of southern Indiana, especially those from England. However, despite some contradictions within the minds of these outsiders, much of their disdain for Hoosiers resulted from the elite's adherence to free labor and free market ideologies. Although Charles Sealsfield suggested a "just price" for a barrel of apples, Susannah Pering's husband would find ways to avoid usury laws. And William Faux was a monomaniac on the question of markets for produce. Certainly self-interest played a role. When Faux was told that capitalists would find better opportunities in a slave state than they would in southern Indiana, capitalism was defined as a system whereby the person investing the money could get others to work for him.[47] In southern Indiana, where high wages still could not engage laborers, such a form of capitalism had come to a standstill. Yet for Faux, Birkbeck, and others, whereas the refusal of Hoosiers to labor for wages may have limited opportunities, what was more troubling was the refusal of many Hoosiers to pursue profit in any form. While their critique of "idleness" mimicked earlier thoughts of leisure's being reserved for the "leisured" classes, the problem was not that Hoosiers failed to adhere to the role of the "common" classes. Nor did their idleness prove a drain on the resources of the community, nor, to go to a more modern interpretation, was it perceived as a failure to labor for the common good. The problem, simply put, was that these Hoosiers somehow resisted the opportunities of the marketplace; they did not work when labor was so profitable.

Whatever the motive of these observers and whatever their internal consistency, their comments underline the fact that many early Hoosiers did not adhere to contemporary notions of proper economic behavior. As countless labor historians have observed about work in the nineteenth century, elite condemnations of work patterns and idleness revealed differing cultural norms. Early Hoosiers were obviously not lazy—the large amount of produce shipped to foreign parts certainly would suggest otherwise—but they held a different conception of the utility and purpose of work. It certainly was not feudal, since it glorified private landownership by the masses. But, if the disdain of the observers can be read, it was not capitalism as they knew it.

THE MARKET AND ITS RISKS

Most Hoosiers understood their economic system in terms of "surplus produce," a concept that incorporated their moral relationship to both local markets and more distant ones, and that allowed them to pursue both their short-term goal of sustaining their family and their long-term goal of accumulating for their progeny the land necessary to repeat the process in the next generation.[48] "Surplus produce" emphasized that the primary purpose of production was to directly sustain the family, and any surpluses above sustenance were traded locally, nationally, and even internationally. Moreover, this concept had multiple layers. Individual farmers were considered to have "surplus produce," but so were communities, counties, and even states. Farm production, thus seen, was primarily for the farm family itself; surplus from it was traded within the local community for goods not produced on the family's farm and then traded at the county level, whence surpluses were shipped greater distances, most often for "luxury" goods and money. Competency, after all, was not subsistence but a level of basic comfort, and its pursuit meant the purchase of some nonnecessities.[49] The primary objective was to take care of the family as well as possible—"safety-first" farming—and then to depend upon the local community to meet most of the family's other immediate needs.[50] Distant markets, beyond the control of the local moral community, were useful primarily for long-term goals and for luxuries, and for this reason, "surpluses," but not the central part of the farm's production, were sent there.

"Surplus produce" and its synonyms were practically ubiquitous in discussions about southern Indiana farming. Birkbeck and Faux repeatedly spoke of "surplus" or "spare" produce. Recalling his Grandfather Vawter's farm upon which he had lived in his youth, Harrison Burns reported:

> While the farm of my grandfather was not very productive, and there was not a large area in cultivation, yet there seemed to be enough produced to support his family, but I do not think there was any surplus for sale, unless it was cattle or horses.[51]

The situation of the Vawters reflected exactly the purpose of farming, as embodied in the term "surplus produce." Yet not only individuals were understood to have "surplus produce." The interior of Perry County in 1853, according to Richard Fisher, "furnishes little or no surplus."[52] Of course, surpluses were also something to be cheered. In an 1843 address, Governor Samuel Bigger reported that "there is an evident upward tendency in prices, and a briskness of demand for our surplus productions, from which we may augur the return of a prosperous business."[53] Defending Whig tariff policy, the Salem *Indiana Phoenix* argued in 1833 that "we have secured by the same tariff a permanent market for the surplus produce of the country."[54] Bazil B. Edmonston bragged that his son Enoch had 360 acres of the richest land: "He can make a surplus boat load annually of corn, pork, and other articles of produce."[55]

Certainly the enthusiasm of Edmonston and the uses to which political discourse put the notion of "surplus produce" could call into question whether the term itself, although it seemed to involve a distancing of farmers from the marketplace, was not merely an empty phrase from an earlier age. When Morris Birkbeck asked William Faux what he thought of Birkbeck's reply to William Cobbett's critique of Birkbeck's emigration project, Faux replied: "I pointed out what I conceived to be a grand omission, that of not noticing 'no market for surplus produce.'"[56] Given Faux's details on internal markets and Birkbeck's emphasis on how well labor paid, such an exchange would seem strange, unless "surplus produce" was understood in a commercial manner. In a similar light, the various schemes to engage internal improvements often hinged on creating markets for "surplus produce." As early as 1822, hill country farmers met "to consult on the most eligible mode of sending their surplus produce to market, and of receiving returns for the same."[57] Sentiments became more pointedly capitalistic in a similar notice thirty-six years later in neighboring Orange County: "We want an outlet for our surplus products—an outlet that will enable us to compete with our more fortunate neighbors."[58]

Markets were never far from the minds of hill country Hoosiers. George Kennedy praised the convenience of markets near Fairfield in Franklin County:

> Cincinatti is distant 50 miles Hamilton 25 miles Brookville 5 which is a County seat. Indianapolis the seat of government of the state is 70 miles there are numerous small villages all through the County.[59]

The multiplicity of markets suggested no loyalty to any one place but rather a willingness to pursue the best price. Hoosiers also recognized how markets affected farming decisions. Arguing for a road to be built to Bloomington, Clinton of neighboring Brown County noted:

> In the first place it would make Bloomington a kind of headmaster for several counties. No longer then would the farmer be discouraged in raising large crops of wheat (to which our soil is so nobly adapted) for want of a convenient market.[60]

Finally, not a few southern Indiana farmers had grand schemes for accumulating much profit. John Durham wrote a relative that "I wont to make five hundred dollars at [hog raising] this fall hogs are worth $3.50 here now."[61] The blessings of the market were apparent to many southern Indiana farmers.

Among those blessings were consumer goods. We have already seen the role that glass windows played in defining the civilized and industrious from the lazy and barbaric. In a similar vein, Simon Ferrall reported that in one otherwise plain southern Indiana home:

> the good dame had a side-saddle . . . which would not have disgraced the lady of an Irish squireen. This appears to be an article of great moment in the estimation of West-country ladies, and when nothing else about the house is even tolerable, the side-saddle is of the most fashionable pattern.[62]

Morris Birkbeck lauded Indiana residents for their consumerist habits: "Those who are now fixing themselves in Indiana, bring with them habits of comfort, and the means of procuring the conveniences of life."[63] Susannah Pering was astonished at the availability of goods: "There is no article of domestic use which I have not been able to obtain here, but mops and scouring brick."[64] Account books detailed the luxuries purchased in stores. Limited transportation did not completely prevent the flow of produce out of southern Indiana, nor did it prevent the flow of consumer luxuries into the region.[65]

It was the rare family who chose from principle not to participate in the market. Yet they did not go blindly into the market, believing that it would automatically reward their hard work. They trusted neither markets nor nature. Their strategy, encompassed in the term "surplus produce," sought to limit the potential risks of farming. The strategy existed not in opposition to capitalism but rather in symbiosis with it. For farmers, one could seek large profits, while still viewing one's yield as "surplus," if two conditions were met: one, that a large portion of the family's day-to-day needs were met by the family's production (and the rest were met by the local community); and two, that one did not make a large investment (beyond the purchase of land) in search of profits. Both were part of the larger risk-aversion strategy embodied in "surplus produce."

Farming was an uncertain enterprise. Neither nature nor the market was certain. Farmers attempted to hedge against uncertainty by overproducing, especially in the crops and livestock that they needed to subsist. For this reason, the large surpluses that seemed to indicate early American farmers were full-fledged capitalists proved little at all. When Harrison Burns's grandfather "raised in one year more than enough for family use, it was usually kept over for some subsequent year when there might be a shortage."[66] The word to the wise was: "Farmers raise all you can, and save all you raise, as if you expected a regular drouth next year."[67]

Nature was not always friendly. Army worm depredation destroyed Jacob Weaver's meadow: "They started in the meddows about the first week in May and in a few days they would cut down the howl meddow so naked you could have seen a snake crawl on the ground at 10 or 15 yards distance with all eas."[68] By far the greatest problem, though, was the weather:

> Prospects are rather discouraging we have not had a good rain since last spring I think corn will make about half a crop wheat was pretty fair oats was not worth cutting vegitables is an intire failure Provodience has smiled on us a little we have a prospect of a verry good mast in the woods.[69]

Without the mast in the woods—the acorns, beechnuts, and other nuts that hogs fed upon—Hoosiers might have been doomed.

By far nature's most severe blow, one which lingered in the minds of many southern Indiana farmers, was the drought that came in the summer of 1832. Its cruelty was exacerbated by the cholera epidemic of the following fall and winter that struck the more densely populated villages. These twin events, coupled with Black Hawk's War and the close encounter of the Comet Encke, had divine import to some in southern Indiana. The end was near: "We were told by religious old folks that God had appointed a time when the earth should be destroyed by fire as it had been by water, and that undoubtedly the time was rapidly approaching when this catastrophe would take place."[70] The burnup occurred not from the comet but from the great drought. According to Bazil Edmonston, 1832 was the second straight year of poor crops, undoubtedly undermining the strategies of Harrison Burns's grandfather and others of keeping produce over a year. Fortunately, "we also had a good Mast."[71] For Isaac Reed, the scarcity of 1832 had been unimaginable:

> It was a spring of more difficulties to procure seed corn, which would grow, than I have ever known in my whole life. People went for it 50 miles, some 100 miles & some 150 miles & planted three or four miles [times] as much as usual in a hill. I this year learned what I had before supposed would never be, that in these western states there would be a famine of corn.[72]

In 1832, the corn crop failed. Yet the overall strategy of "safety-first" farming worked:

> There was an extremely short crop of corn that year, and no means of importation from other places; in consequence of which during the ensuing winter a great deal of stock died from starvation; but still there was enough

left for the family's meat, and enough stock cattle and hogs to go over into the next year, and the horses were taken care of some way. There was no want of corn or meat, or whatever we wanted to eat.[73]

Not only did nature make farming uncertain. The market was fickle, too, and those who placed too great a faith in it soon discovered the pitfalls. Some pitfalls were quite simple; writing to his employee who was flatboating potatoes down the Mississippi, James Reader admonished him: "The man that you sold the 200 barrels of potatoes to gave you a $5.00 counterfeit bill."[74] Creditors were always a problem. In Orange County, Enoch Millis had "Bean for about two years trading in stock, + every thing else that he could trade in, + makeing money verry fast (as he boasted)." Unfortunately, "he got in debt over one thousand dollars," and he chose to abscond for California, leaving his family behind to have their farm sold out from underneath them by his pushing creditors. Millis's kinsman condemned not only his flight but also his entire emphasis on trade, with its risks of credit and immersion in the market: "I disaprove of the course Millis has bean pursuing for the last two years."[75] In Jackson County, John Parker put his hopes in the marketplace and regretted the hole he had dug:

> I have give up my home and I never exspect to bee at home again I never expect to bee satisfide any more I fear my little children will come to sufer exsept one simple thing will make me something that is wine graps that is all my hope as I have bought a place that has a spot that is nice for that business five or ten acreas that is hy and roling to the east all reddy cleard. . . . if this will not make us something I fear wey will suffer wey live harder now then wey ever lived someways but thire may bee something for us again but, my time will be hard now.

Parker recognized his mistake: "if I had ove kep my place tell this year I would ove bin *independent* and could ove restted the ballence of my days."[76] Yet he continued to perceive the opportunities of the world; looking to Kansas, he fretted over the potential for speculation. For many other southern Indiana residents, independence was the better choice; the marketplace bred uncertainty and danger to their independence.

Perhaps nowhere was the fickleness of the market more apparent than in the experiences of Benjamin and Molly Mace and their family. The Maces moved to Indiana with Molly's brother Jonathan Hardy and his family, and they began with great expectations. Writing to their kinsman Ely, Molly relayed Benjamin's advice: "You must come up and go with him to the Indiania if ever you mean to have a farm."[77] Yet quickly upon arrival she became disenchanted.

> Benjamin has not bought any land yet he has been one journey onto one branch
> of White rivver but he did not like it and there is know land to be bought
> here that is good for anything So he has leased 25 acres of land for 5 years.

Nevertheless, the land they leased was "excelent for wheat and corn and evry thing else." Still, they did not "know as we shall stay here half of the time [of the lease] if he can find land to suit him."[78] The Hardy branch was faring little better, forced into cash-crop farming in 1818.

> Jonathan has lost his place he bought and has least some land for five years
> he has let him out a hopyard this year and I hope he will be able to pay all he
> owes in a year or two if hops keeps up there price.[79]

Hardy "had bought one farm since I mov'd to this country but got cheated out of it after clearing 10 acres of land and lost 117 Dollars into the Bargain."[80] By 1819, hard times fell on Benjamin Mace, as they had on so many in the West, and he was forced to travel into the interior of Kentucky to get work.[81] But ague struck Benjamin, and he returned, and the Maces looked to Jonathan Hardy's solution for their troubles, hops: "Hops will always fetch the money here if nothing else dont and there is nobody here that knows how to raise them but Benjamin and my brother." Cash had become a necessity: Benjamin Mace had probably squandered the sum with which he had arrived, in his fruitless search for a farm that could produce more than merely a competency. The Maces were not completely destitute—"we have raise good crops of corn and wheat the two years past"—but their aims were higher, looking for the day when they could have a good pasture, raise more cows, and make cheese.[82] They had two cows but only one old sow. Like many settlers, they sought to reproduce the world they left behind, but perhaps their neighbors from the South had desires and practices more in keeping with the southern Indiana landscape. Mace's desire for profit doomed him to failure.

Jonathan Hardy did better. He informed Benjamin Mace's parents that things were far worse for the Maces than they probably admitted—"they have too much pride and ambition to let you know their real circumstances." Molly Mace's sickness had forced them to hire a woman at a dollar a week, and the debts they had incurred from that had placed their family in grave straits. Hardy had already settled two judgments against them of twenty or thirty dollars. The purpose of Hardy's letter to his sister's father-in-law was to settle a debt. The money Hardy had was valueless in the East—one of the serious flaws of the marketplace that Indiana farmers had to avoid—but Hardy proposed that he would give the sum he owed Benjamin Mace's father to Benjamin himself—as part of the father's bequest to his son—for the cash had value in southern Indiana and Benjamin Mace desperately needed it.[83]

Some of Mace's misfortune can be laid on the depression that began in 1819. Molly Mace reported that "our wheat is good and we shall have corn enough to eat and fat our pork I hope and if we had ever so much to sell we could not sell it."[84] The periodic economic downturns often signaled to Hoosiers the dangers of market embeddedness, and the 1819 downturn was particularly destructive.[85] The contractions from the period sent shock waves through the communities, as one person's calling in loans begat another group who called in their accounts. Debts forced farmers onto the market, selling the goods they needed to survive: "The farmers . . . indebted to the store-keepers, are now forced to sell all their corn at one dollar a barrel, and buy it again for their spring and summer use at five dollars, a fine profit for the monied merchant."[86] Jacob Weaver believed that transportation problems were part of the difficulty, but he detailed the difficulties brought on by the panic:

> Our cuntry is very extensive and perduses in abundunce gits to be thick set-tled and abundunce raised and has but one sea port no foren-trade at presant so the markets are glutted and people can scarse sell anything at all but what they sell amungst another then cumes on the wors of all no mony to be had if any good for nothing so you must sell on credit or not at all When a farmer goes to a store to buy any thing he wont take anythin the farmer can rase his cry is mony cash in hand no credit can be geven.[87]

The problem spawned by the panic was not the "trade amongst themselves" but trade tied into more distant markets. For this reason, the panic of 1819 spawned much condemnation of the Second Bank of the United States, as well as of combinations of aristocratic wealth, and led to much political activity, as we shall explore in the next chapter. Perhaps the greatest effect on Hoosiers' economic understandings was the fate of both Jacob Weaver and Jonathan Hardy: the seeming arbitrariness of money, whose value differed from day to day and location to location. In the minds of many Hoosiers, this instability was manipulated by the moneychangers and merchants for their own profit, and therefore made trade at a distance—normally conducted with money and not barter—open to manipulation. Long-distance trade could not be trusted for a family's day-to-day survival.

In sum, farming in the first half of the nineteenth century in southern Indiana was risky business. Neither nature nor the market could be trusted. Those who were too optimistic about the outcomes of the market put themselves at risk, much as did Benjamin Mace or John Parker. It would be wise to note that this situation was not unique to southern Indiana. Because farmers could neither control the value of their produce at market nor predict the ravages of nature, they made rational choices to reduce the impact of the things they could not control. To put it another way, why would farmers make risky decisions about what to plant in the spring with no knowledge of what weather would be like in the intervening months and no knowledge of what the market was going to be like in the fall?

Yet to speak of fickle nature is perhaps going too far. Hoosier farmers certainly did not expect every year to be like 1832. If nature did not correspond perfectly to the needs of the marketplace with bountiful harvests every year, it did provide a wealth of resources over the long run. And Hoosiers built their economic strategy around this long-term beneficence as much as they built it around the possibility of short-term scarcity. In the short term, for the basic day-to-day necessities, one's household and one's community provided; the vagaries of nature demanded a tight interdependence. But in plentiful years, the beneficence of nature made it possible for Hoosier farmers to release that surplus to more distant markets and gain the wealth necessary to set up their progeny in a similar situation. This long-term familial goal did not necessitate good crops every year, but depended upon regular surpluses.

Despite the drought, farmers continued to expand production for the market. In 1834, just two years after the drought, the first societies were formed in the state to promote agriculture. Franklin County had one of the first, yet in the newspaper announcement of its formation there was little indication that the drought had ever occurred:

> It *has been* heretofore not so great an object among the individuals of the Western Country to excel, as it has been to realize a subsistence, and the soil being salubrious, and easily cultivated—a living is easily attained, it being all that was desirable. Hence the majority rested satisfied with their slender attainments, and set down contented beneath the shade of the forest, having "cleared" a few acres of land, and raised there on a sufficient quantum of "*hog and hominy.*"[88]

Instead, the newspaper's emphasis was on the "inevitable" progress of the age and an admonition to the residents of the region to leave behind their "safety-first" ways to embrace the opportunities of the marketplace. The editor claimed that those who pursued these, as he thought, outmoded forms "have dived deeper into the wilderness" and have been "succeeded by men of enterprize and industry." Despite such predictions, "hog and hominy" farming continued to be the norm in the region for many years, because of the merits of the "safety-first" strategy embodied in "surplus produce." Certainly many Hoosier farmers found the market in later years "safer," but periodic economic downturns reinforced the sagacity of their strategy. In the wake of the 1857 downturn, Ripley County's Jesse Hamilton would write that "times are hard," and "in main, the people are all thinking about planting corn," for they were unwilling "to trye to raise something to sell."[89]

The "safety" of the system of "surplus produce" included its multiple layers. Surviving the drought of 1832, town-dweller Bazil Edmonston wrote, "Corn is scarce in this county but [there] is a good supply for the citizens with care."[90] Surplus produce was a strategy for maintaining the household, but it also contained within itself a strategy for maintaining the community. Not only did individual farms have surplus produce, but so did neighborhoods and counties. In Jennings County, for instance, "agriculture furnishes little for export," although there was no indication that food had to be imported.[91] Discussing how raising large surpluses did not pit one neighbor against another, but benefited the entire community, the *Franklin Democrat* noted that the benefits accrued after the local demand had been met:

> For it is a well known fact, that the greater the quantity of grain raised, and the greater the surplus of any other staple, after filling home demands. The greater will be the flow of capital to that place, to secure that surplus, and to make it an item of profit.[92]

Nothing precluded profit, but the home demands had to be met first. These multiple layers of "surplus produce" not only reflected a policy of risk aversion but suggested the moral vision that made trade in the local community "safer" than trade at a distance.

In their farming practices, southern Indiana farmers pursued a policy, "safety-first" farming, attempting to meet most of their families' needs with their own production while using the local market to fill in the necessities of life, but trading their surplus produce on more distant markets for nonessentials and for the means to establish their children on their own land. These distant markets could not be depended upon to support the short-term needs of Hoosier farmers. Not only were these markets more volatile, fluctuating with the whimsies of the world economy, but exchange within them was unregulated in the eyes of the Hoosiers, because they understood moral regulation as solely within the purview of their local communities. With such moral regulation, Hoosiers could place their immediate survival in their neighbors' hands, although their desire for independence always made them fearful of too much dependency.

To illuminate this economy, first we shall examine the extent to which individual households were able to support their own subsistence, and then we shall examine the workings of the local community, to suggest the ways in which it could be depended upon to provide the day-to-day necessities of life in southern Indiana. Finally, we will examine the relationship of most Hoosier farmers to more distant markets.

FEEDING THE HILL COUNTRY

The things that are truly the necessities of life are rather limited. We need food and water, and in temperate climates we need clothing and shelter. In a society in which these necessities are commodified, cash or barter becomes a necessity, but that should not obscure the fact that the purchase of some seed, a bull and several cows, a ewe and ram, and a sow (leave it up to some nearly wild boar to impregnate her), and, especially, forty acres of the southern Indiana landscape could create an almost self-sustaining means to procure most of these necessities. Of course, a horse or two would have been nice and more efficient than using the cows as oxen, and there was always the question of tools. These desirables could add up to a considerable sum, and probably most farmers accumulated these items over time.[93] Shelter was readily available, as wood was plentiful, and a crude cabin could be replaced rather quickly by a house of finished lumber. The forest also could provide the railing to build fences, and of course the trees needed to be cut anyway to clear fields for grains and pastures. In the interim, game was plentiful. The sheep could produce wool, and many planted flax and even cotton, especially in the earliest days. And water was never far beneath the surface, when it did not rush by in a stream. Such a vision seems close to idyllic, a romanticized past, but perhaps the disgust in the voices of the patricians who urged southern Indiana farmers forward might suggest that the availability of most of life's necessities impeded "progress." Water and shelter were so readily available as not to warrant further investigation, although the procurement of shelter often required communal activity. Food and clothing, on the other hand, were the necessities which demanded some form of "production" and thus merit closer examination.

"Hog and hominy" was the image of southern Indiana subsistence, and the importance of corn and pork in the diet cannot be overstated, because it played the crucial role in the economic strategy pursued by many Hoosier farmers. Nevertheless, the hill country dinner table often included far more than just ham and cornbread. Hoosiers grew a variety of crops for their consumption, and there was far more diversity in their livestock than many have recognized. Such diversity, however, did not impede the larger aims of southern Indiana farmers; indeed, too much specialization in "hog and hominy" would have been dangerous.

This diversity was apparent in early reports about the productivity of the land:

> The soil of this land is peculiarly adapted to the culture of small grain, and for grazing. The last harvest produced several crops of wheat, in the neighborhood of this place that weighed from sixty-five to sixty-eight pounds a bushel; and the best crops of grass I have ever seen, are produced without aid of manure. Corn, oats, rye, flax, hemp, sweet and Irish potatoes, &c. &c. are produced in abundance.[94]

And this diversity reflected the variety of crop choice of individual farmers within the hill country. Elisha Hughes reported on his new farm: "It is good for wheat, rye, corn oats, sweet and Irish potatoes, cabbage, tobacco, flax, hemp and any quantity of water and musk melons, turnip plenty—still growing in the fields."[95] Probate records confirm this diversity in crops. Although in 1830, everyone raised corn, at least half the farmers also raised either oats or wheat.[96] By 1850, in Washington County oats still were raised by 88 percent of farmers, while wheat was raised only by 75 percent, but in Franklin County, wheat was second only to corn in the number of farmers raising it (over 60 percent), while oats were raised by fewer than half of all farmers.[97] Other crops seemed to be less important, although by 1850 Irish potatoes were still raised by half the farmers, and the census failed to record garden and orchard products for household consumption.

Many singled out cabbage for their gardens and no wonder. Save for potatoes, Irish and sweet, no other vegetable was more mentioned in probate inventories. Sweet potatoes have often been associated with the Southerners who predominated in the hill country, and although New Yorker Samuel Whedon reported that his Carolina neighbors used sweet potatoes in place of bread, they did not remain common in the region.[98] Like potatoes, and like turnips and onions, two other vegetables that made the inventories, cabbage had a long shelf life—one reason it was around to be probated—but unlike the rest of them, it was a green vegetable. Harrison Burns described the manner in which they were kept:

> Almost everything required for the use and support of the family of my grandfather was raised or produced on his farm; all vegetables and fruits were so obtained. Some vegetables and fruits were stored in the cellar, but the principal portion was "holed" up as it was called. Piles of potatoes, cabbage, turnips, and apples would be made in the garden, over which would be thrown straw or hay and then dirt would be thrown over the pile until it was covered some eight or ten inches which would be sufficient to keep the contents from freezing.[99]

Cold storage was not the only means of preserving fruits and vegetables, however. Probate records did indicate preserving tubs, used for fermenting and pickling, and again, cabbage shone, this time in the form of sauerkraut. Cabbage was not the only vegetable that was preserved. Cucumbers had their devotees; George Fitzhugh related that "Mrs. F. has put up 300 Cucumber pickles—equal to *500* of the favorite size—all from our own vine."[100]

The pumpkin played an important role within the household economy. Their ease of cultivation and their use for human as well as livestock consumption fit well into the larger economic strategy:

> [Settlers] scatter seeds of pumpkins in corn fields & no further care until they are to be picked[;] along with corn fodder, are sufficient stock feed for winter.[101]

For humans, pumpkins were dried, as were many fruits. Peas and beans were also raised.

> We had the ordinary white bean we called Yankee beans too, but we did not have them in the garden. They were grown in the fields with other crops and sold to people in town. We had all we could possibly use and to spare, sometimes as many as twenty or twenty-five bushels. We found them a source of revenue.[102]

Living near a community with a number of New England residents, Jameson's family found white beans a source of revenue, but they also incorporated the white bean into their own diet, selling the surplus to Madison townspeople.[103] Other beans and peas were probably more common among the Southern majority in the hill country, although by 1850, pea and bean cultivation remained only in concentrated pockets, and few grew anywhere near the twenty bushels of the Jamesons.

The Jamesons were, of course, always looking for a buck, and in that way they probably were not much different from many of their neighbors. When their orchards produced in abundance, they would dry the fruit and offer it for sale at a dollar a bushel, a welcome treat in the spring.[104] Winter apples brought twenty-five cents a bushel, as a young Harrison Burns delighted in discovering.[105] Yet perhaps the best evidence available that early settlers of southern Indiana were not improvident were the orchards they quickly planted. By 1816, Enoch Honeywell noted that along the Whitewater River there were "plenty of apple and peach orchards . . . both hanging with fruit."[106] By 1844, Charles Arms could entice his kinsman: "I will now inform you that thare is good chances here of farms with apple and peach orchards good buildings for sale and very cheap 4 or 5 hundred dollars."[107] That farms with orchards could be bought so cheaply, albeit in Perry County, suggests the ease with which Hoosiers could create orchards on their farms. Despite the successes of Harrison Burns and the Jamesons, most fruit was kept for the family's own consumption, with apples muddled with sugar providing a tasty winter treat. By 1850, despite the literary evidence of orchards, there was little trade in fruit.[108] While fruit may not have made the market, brandy may well have reached it. As early as 1810, John Bradbury related that "farmers often make cider into brandy."[109] Like drying apples, distilling them reduced the size of the goods, thus making them more transportable. Moreover, it provided a less perishable product, one that could be held for a favorable market.

Meat was the centerpiece of the southern Indiana diet. Cows were prized possessions because they provided milk and thus butter as well as serving as meat at the end of their milk-producing years. Cows were individually assessed in probate records, and their value at auction reflected common knowledge about their productivity. By 1850, a hill country farmer was slightly more likely to have a milk cow than to have swine.[110] Since it was impossible to control for the sex of the cattle, steers were raised for meat alongside the cows.[111] Sheep, necessary to provide the wool for clothing, found their way to the table. "At the end of the year [the spring] the meat would run pretty low, and then we would sometimes kill a lamb."[112] Barnyard fowl were also prevalent, providing eggs on a regular basis, and they included chickens, turkeys, ducks, and, the most common, geese.[113] Most of this meat was eaten fresh, but beef was occasionally corned or pickled, although neither seemed very prevalent.

> It was very seldom that the people in the country had any fresh beef. Once in a great while some one in the neighborhood would kill a small beef which would be divided among the neighbors for immediate use as there was no way of preserving it fresh in warm weather. The pork that had been put up and chickens furnished the bulk of the summer meat.[114]

"Hog and hominy" was the keystone of the strategy of "surplus produce." Production of fruits, vegetables, other grains, other livestock, and fowl were all accomplished as a supplement to the family's emphasis on hogs and corn; only the milk from the dairy cows could be considered as central to the family's survival, and that could be replaced by other parts of the diet, as many Southern migrants well understood.[115] With an emphasis on pork and corn, Hoosiers produced for the market goods which, in times of low yield or low market prices, could also be eaten. Visitors imagined the majority of southern Indiana residents as poor, but most of the region's wealth was to be found not around the barnyard but scrounging the forest in the form of ranging swine. Far from the view of visitors passing through the region, the inhabitants of southern Indiana invested in their families' continued prosperity and independence.

Stock laws permitting the ranging of livestock were at the center of conflicts throughout the nineteenth century. Before the 1850s, the custom permitting the ranging of livestock came into conflict with the common law, which forbade it. In 1852, new laws were established allowing the county commissioners to permit the ranging of livestock.[116] Such a law allowed for much of the hill country to continue the ranging livestock, while permitting the states' other regions to forbid it.[117] Not until the late nineteenth century would the practice be completely eliminated, to the cheers of the men of prosperity:

> It took Indiana fifty years to learn that it is the duty of every man to fence against his own stock. There are those who yet think that they ought to be permitted by law to forage the unfenced lands and public highways.[118]

By the early twentieth century, Major's anger had hardly calmed. Nor had H. H. Pleasant's condescension: "Many thought that it would ruin them if they had to build fences and keep up their stock."[119]

But many small farmers had little choice. In an era when fields themselves were small, pastures had to be large, and fencing sufficient to enclose such pastures was expensive. While roaming hogs were not the only livestock on the range, their rooting abilities posed a real threat to crops, more so than sheep or cattle. Nose rings could be required. Smart and tough, hogs were able to range at will, being able to fight off most predators and to find their way home, virtues not shared by other domestic animals.[120] In the forest, swine fattened on the mast, only with winter returning home, to be fed maybe a few bushels of corn to prepare them for slaughter.

English settler Cornelius Pering was amazed by the ease of hog farming:

> One of the farmer's most profitable employments is raising pigs and this is done with least possible trouble and inconvenience as they live almost entirely in the woods three fourths of their time. Towards winter they come to the house to be fed, when they can find no more acorns in the woods, and a few ears of Indian corn are thrown over the fence to them. Many farmers kill more than a hundred annually.[121]

Harrison Burns related how every part of the hog was used:

> My grandfather usually fattened some twelve or fifteen hogs, which were slaughtered in the fall or early winter and the different portions preserved or cured. The hams and shoulders were smoked with hickory wood in a smoke house, the sides were made into pickled pork or salted down, sausage was

made of the lean portions and put away in different manners, while the fat was made into lard.[122]

The fat not made into lard was turned into salt pork, the seasoning of choice, and the intestines served as casings for the sausage. The ease of preserving pork, especially when coupled with the ease of raising it, made it a splendid choice for southern Indiana farmers.

And, of course, pork and hogs could bring plenty of money on the open market. Probably few raised as many as the one hundred reported by Pering—as a moneylender, he may well have had "friends" in desperate need of cash—but in 1844, Charles Arms wrote home that "i killed and sold 26 head last fall."[123] Patrick Henry Jameson reported a similar number killed, with meat available for sale to newcomers. The twelve to fifteen hogs of Burns's Grandfather Vawter, slaughtered to provide for his large extended family, was less than the 1850 median value of livestock slaughtered reported by my sample of southern Indiana farmers, around fifty dollars. Such a sum was the equivalent of thirty to forty hogs, despite the fact that in Franklin County, hog farmers only owned at census time seventeen hogs apiece, although in Washington County, the mean was twenty-eight.[124] Although the value of livestock slaughtered included other animals, most notably beeves at about six dollars a head, certainly the difference between Vawter's slaughter and the average numbers would suggest that, as planned, surplus was being sold. Many of these hogs were driven to meat packing plants in Madison and Cincinnati. Others were slaughtered in the hill country itself. Writing from Brownstown, Aaron Stryker noted:

> Pork has went off quite dull C. S. Wayman has packed about 400,000 pounds hear and bought the most of it on time Consequently that has cut off that amount of money that would have been in circulation at this time that wont come in till May or June he Bought all his meat at $4.00 net and it ranged from four to four 20 cents 30 and fourty at the river.[125]

Men like Wayman played an important role for farmers in marketing their surplus produce, even as the marketplace began to shape farmers' strategies. Wayman had the farmers over the barrel; few probably had the corn necessary to tide the hogs over until spring, and since Wayman offered as much as may have been available at the river, the potential for any compensation for the effort to drive the hogs there, plus the weight lost on the drive, certainly made Wayman's offer, despite its being on time, very appealing. Yet it is important to recognize that the farmers could give the note because the profit from the sale of surplus hogs was not integral to their day-to-day survival. If it had been, they would have probably taken the hogs to someone with cash, even if it meant the loss in driving them to the river.

Beyond its use as hog feed, corn found its way onto many hill country dinner tables. When she linked the independence of servant girls to their family's ownership of land, Susannah Pering added: "They subsist a good deal on Indian corn of which the Americans are very fond; it costs very little and can be cooked a variety of ways."[126] While wheat bread was often served on special occasions, cornbread was the basic breadstuff in most southern Indiana households.

> Then we had corn dodgers and corn pone. All the year round we had corn bread every day once, and sometimes several times. Sometimes we had corn fritters in the morning.[127]

Corn also was the base for the ubiquitous hominy, a form of preserving corn with lye.[128] Corn was not only important as feed for livestock; it served alongside pork as the primary food of southern Indiana farmers.

When droughts came, the corn crops were reserved for human consumption, and hogs fattened themselves solely on the mast of the forests. Such a strategy would explain production figures for individual farms in southern Indiana. When foodstuffs are expressed in corn bushel equivalents, most farms, after feeding livestock and household members, produced anywhere from a 100 bushel deficit to a 100 bushel surplus.[129] In the most productive sampled township, Springfield Township in Franklin County, only 20 percent of its farmers were producing over a 1,000-bushel surplus, compared with 5 percent of Highland Township farmers and 2 percent of Washington County farmers. One thousand bushels, however, would have garnered only three hundred dollars, and with the majority of farmers producing less than one hundred bushels, valued at just thirty dollars, the surpluses, although they sound large, certainly would have required several years of accumulation before even a single child could be established on a farm.[130] At the township level, no township in Washington County showed the surpluses found in the more prosperous Franklin County townships. High production occurred in parts of southeastern Indiana and in Morgan, Jackson, Lawrence, and Bartholomew counties, with prime White River bottomlands (see map 3.1). In general, heavy production was dependent far more on location than on the ethnic makeup of the settlers, especially comparing Upland Southerners with Mid-Atlantic and New England settlement areas. However, German settlers tended to be far less successful in producing large surpluses than their Anglo-American counterparts, perhaps due to the Germans' relatively recent settlement.

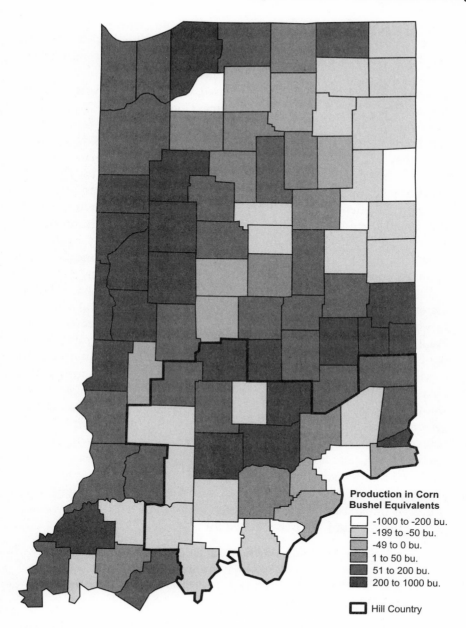

**Production in Corn
Bushel Equivalents**

- ☐ -1000 to -200 bu.
- ☐ -199 to -50 bu.
- ☐ -49 to 0 bu.
- ☐ 1 to 50 bu.
- ☐ 51 to 200 bu.
- ☐ 200 to 1000 bu.

☐ Hill Country

MAP 3.1. INDIANA FARM PRODUCTION, PER FARM, 1850
Derived from United States Census Office, *The Seventh Census of the United States, 1850*
(1853; reprint, New York: Arno Press, 1976) and *Statistical View of the United States . . .
Being a Compendium of the Seventh Census* by J. D. B. De Bow (Washington: A. O. P.
Nicholson, Public Printer, 1854). (Boone/Nation)

A number of farms, both German American and Anglo-American, appeared to have insufficient production to meet household needs. Much of that deficit centered around insufficient meat and dairy production, but there was no evidence of a trade of butter and meat into the hill country. The year 1849, upon which the 1850 census was based, was a poor crop year in southern Indiana.[131] From Jennings County, James Goodnow wrote: "We have had an uncommonly dry season here."[132] For well over half of the farmers with deficit production, their yields would have been sufficient to feed their families if they had withheld corn from hogs. However, for German Catholics with deficient production, this strategy only worked for a third. That German Catholics, farming smaller farms than their Anglo-American neighbors, could produce deficits and yet still persist at a greater rate than these neighbors would suggest that much economic activity that escapes the historians' gaze was occurring within southern Indiana communities. Yet for many, the mast in the forest was sufficient. And there was always some game to survive upon, although large game had begun to disappear by the 1850s.[133]

Few cash crops were grown. The probate records revealed that in Washington County, circa 1830, of thirty-six estates probated, two had hemp and two had tobacco; in the same period, the only cash crop detected among Franklin County's seventeen estates was a single crop of hops, despite Timothy Flint's earlier report that the area had "acquired a reputation for the excellence of its tobacco."[134] By 1850, tobacco, the most frequently grown cash crop in Washington County, was raised by fewer than 5 percent of the county's farmers; in Franklin County, hops led the cash crops—not surprisingly in a county settled by Germans—but they were raised by only 3 percent of the farmers. Cash crops, while they promised great returns, were also risky; hogs and hominy revealed a strategy by which Hoosier farmers sacrificed easy returns for certain survival.

In the 1850s, some agricultural reform writers were again lamenting southern Indiana farmers' heavy dependence upon hogs and corn, suggesting that the land was better suited for pasturage.

> The minds of our farmers appear to be entirely engrossed with hog raising—
> they seem to think there is no money in anything but hogs—yet, as a general
> thing the corn they feed to their hogs is worth more money than the hogs
> will sell for when they are ready for market.[135]

Indeed, a simple calculation of prices current would uphold the reformers' arguments. But such arguments were premised on a completely market-driven economy and assumed that the market would be able to provide. These ideas often carried with them the anxious cry that hog-and-corn farming was depleting the soil.[136] However, to go to stock farming necessitated building fences and seeding pastures. Such an investment in labor and durable fencing was beyond the means of many hill country farmers and ill-suited to their risk aversion strategies. Through the Civil War, Hoosier farmers would place their families' survival on hog-and-corn farming.

One aspect of hog-and-corn farming was important in coloring outsiders' perceptions of Hoosiers. Unlike many crops, such as sugar, cotton, and wheat, corn did not require intense labor discipline. There was no short period of time in which the crop had to be brought in. For this reason, there was little imperative to gather in the crop in the disciplined manner that many by midcentury had begun to equate with a free labor spirit. And for that reason, there was little need to hire additional labor. Farmers could potentially raise as much corn as they had fields cleared. Moreover, unlike other crops, there was also little need for machinery.

However, in 1850, the potential for investment in machinery was slight, since the technological revolution had just begun; a farm wagon valued at maybe fifty dollars could encompass much of the investment, and probably many census takers did not even include a wagon among farm machinery. A comparison of the machinery investments of hill country farmers with their Hoosier neighbors suggests that in 1850, major distinctions in investment in farm tools and machinery had not yet occurred (see map 3.2). There was some variation in the hill country, with counties along the Ohio and those on the Whitewater showing elevated investment, as did Jennings County, located on the Madison and Indianapolis Railroad. Outside the hill country, few patterns emerged; only in west-central Indiana were there beginning to be large investments in farm machinery, perhaps because these areas placed greater emphasis on wheat production for the market. Corn production demanded neither intense labor discipline nor machinery investment.

Hoosier farmers pursued a strategy that limited the risks of both marketplace and nature, while preparing to reap the benefits of their "surplus produce." "Hog and hominy" stood at the center of this strategy, yet the production of the soil was such that a variety of crops were grown, most of which could find their way either to the family table or to the market. Hoosier farmers sought to avoid a pattern identified by William Faux during the 1819 Panic, of selling to the merchant and then having to buy back the same goods at an inflated price.[137] Production of foodstuffs was geared toward ensuring familial survival. If there were surpluses, that was good: the long-term reproduction of the family demanded the accumulation of assets to endow the next generation.

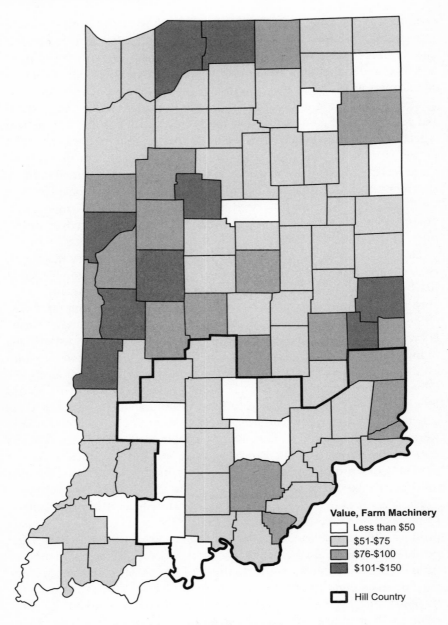

MAP 3.2. INDIANA FARM MACHINERY AND IMPLEMENTS, PER FARM, 1850
Derived from United States Census Office, *The Seventh Census of the United States, 1850*
(1853; reprint, New York: Arno Press, 1976) and *Statistical View of the United States . . .*
Being a Compendium of the Seventh Census by J. D. B. De Bow (Washington: A. O. P.
Nicholson, Public Printer, 1854). (Boone/Nation)

TEXTILES, WOMEN, AND THE COMING
OF THE MARKET ECONOMY

Clothing was the other human necessity with which Hoosier farmers were faced, although it was not a need in the intense, day-to-day sense of food. For this reason, it probably should be no surprise that it was in the area of clothing where Hoosier households first turned to the marketplace to secure their needs. Nevertheless, cloth manufacture had an important place in the household economies of early southern Indiana, and the permanent shift to manufactured cloth was an important aspect in the internal dynamics of the Hoosier household.[138]

Part of the image of the Hoosier hill peoples as poor came from the description of their clothing, or lack thereof: "the uppermost [settlement] three years old, but very little advanced, has a family of children and their mother almost naked."[139] At Mt. Pleasant, in Martin County, one of the first families lived unusually: "They slept in troughs, and if a neighbor dropped in, the children would run to hide their nakedness to the troughs and pull the skins over them."[140]

Quickly, though, animal skins were dressed and buckskin became the fashion for all. Nevertheless, the era of buckskin was a short one, probably shorter than most remembered. John Hicks reminisced:

> Our clothin was buck-skin pants, flax shirts, linsy round-about and mocca-sins. The women would spin flax and care and spin cotton to make clothing.[141]

Very quickly cotton, flax, and wool were raised and formed into cloth. Despite the climate, Timothy Flint related that "some sheltered valleys have had considerable crop of cotton in favorable years."[142] Nevertheless, cotton did not figure in the 1830 era probate records, and by 1850, no cotton was produced in the hill country. Pursuing a risk-aversive strategy, Hoosier families could not afford to depend on "favorable years."

Flax and wool were by far the more important farm products for clothing Hoosiers, and in the earliest years much of the weaving was done at home. The only exception to the general need for skilled craftsmen, Jacob Weaver advised his weaver brother Llem, was there was little need for his skill: "for most of them do thair own weving."[143] Not everyone had looms—only two of eighteen estates probated in Franklin County around 1830—but many had wheels of some sort—eleven of the eighteen—and looms were often shared by several families. About half of the probated farmers had flax crops, and almost two-thirds had sheep or wool on hand at their death around 1830.[144] If the flax crop failed, the women and children headed to creek bottoms to gather nettle stalks that would be treated as flax, an indication of flax's status as a necessity.[145] In the earliest days, each family produced a significant portion of its own cloth.

On Harrison Burns's grandparents' farm, the flax was raised, hackled, spun, and woven at home, but the wool was picked and carded, then sent off to a mill to be made into rolls, and returned to be spun and woven.[146] The promise of the technological age, with its capacity to reduce arduous tasks, helped to draw families into the specialized world of capitalism, although the fact that they chose to retain much of the production process in their household reflected the appeal of the family economy. The potential for textile manufacturing to embed Hoosiers into the marketplace was also evident in the case of the Watsons, poor English emigrants who rented land; they had a loom, from which they produced "between 40 and 50 yards of linen . . . from last years crop."[147] Certainly the Watsons sought to buy land, and linen production offered a viable means to do so.

The flip side of this movement toward specialization was that many Hoosier households bowed out of textile production altogether. Warning cries shot out from advocates of the "surplus produce" model:

> [Many] contend that we should make bacon, flour, &c., because it is easily made, and purchase our clothing because it can be bought at a lower rate than a farmer can make it for.—Such doctrine will do for a man who thinks lightly of subjects; but one who investigates in a thorough manner the economy of the times, will denounce it as sophistry, and inconsistent with farming policy.

"Grazier" argued that sheep should not replace a good-sized herd of well-fed hogs, but could supplement such an enterprise, as wool brought cash in the marketplace. He ended:

> The times are hard Mr. Experience, and suppose you had no money on hand, and produce so plenty all to bear no price—but you had the means of raising sheep, and manufacturing the clothing of your own family—to purchase you have not the means—to manufacture you have.—I now ask, would it not be policy for you to manufacture or not?[148]

For "Grazier," the hard times brought on by the Panic of 1819 demanded that Hoosier farmers pursue familial self-sufficiency in clothing. Such a strategy made sense in food, although in clothing, the failure to pursue a policy of "surplus produce" only produced a series of lamentations, this one a humorous play on the tariff debate:

> Much has been said about Protection of home manufactures, and as I am in the habit of speaking my own opinion, on whatever comes up, I will also ven-

ture to give my idea of Protection. It is this.—Let every family adopt old fashioned, Protections, such as our grand fathers practiced, to wit: Let it be a first object, in every family, to have plenty of wool &c. also good wheels and Looms.

Yet the author then revealed that even he could not imagine a time of pure household manufacture: "Let the Hatter, the Shoemaker, the Spinners of Cotton, the carders of wool and the fullers of Cloth, be almost our only manufacturers of cloth."[149] Two transitions were actually taking place in these years. The first was that flax production was seriously diminished, probably with the rise of cotton goods, while the second was that the production of woolen goods became more involved in local and more distant markets.

Although as early as 1822, "Grazier" believed Hoosier farmers were neglecting household manufacture of textiles, the numbers would suggest that many had followed or would follow his suggestion to raise sheep. Where the decline occurred was in the production of flax. In 1840, flax was still being produced in some quantity in parts of southern Indiana, but by 1850, there had been a general falling off.[150] Both Washington and Franklin counties had far fewer growers than the 50 percent recorded in 1830s probate records. In Washington County, about one in six still raised flax while barely 1 percent of Franklin County farmers still produced any.[151] Governor Joseph Wright suggested that the reason for the decline of flax production lay in "the cheapness of cotton and cotton goods, and our rich soil, upon which we raise hogs, corn, and cattle in such abundance."[152]

By contrast, wool production actually grew from 1840 to 1850, although there were mixed changes in the percentage of sheep herders.[153] From around 65 percent of all farmers who raised sheep in 1830, Washington County saw an increase to almost 80 percent, while in Franklin County, the percentage dropped to less than 50 percent.[154] Southern Indiana farmers continued the trend of apportioning some of the work to people or businesses outside the household. When she first came to southern Indiana, Mrs. Karl Tafel, whose family were German 48'ers, had to be taught by a neighbor to shear their four sheep, dye the wool, and spin. "Later I had enough wool to have our clothes woven, and I paid for the weaving with a third of the yarn."[155] Such a system was not unusual, but with the coming of greater technology, by the early days of the Civil War, the Miller family, living in Jackson County, would send their 175 pounds of wool at least twelve miles to a mill in Vernon, county seat of Jennings County, to have it "spun wove and colored all ready for the scissors," made into flannel, linsey, jeans, stocking yarns, and blankets.[156] In many ways, this splitting of the production of the family clothing between farm and factory was emblematic of the general relationship between southern Indiana farm families and the larger marketplace.

In the production of cloth, the importance of wives and daughters to the entire household economy was illuminated, and shifts in that production, while they perhaps revealed an element in how gender relationships within the household were negotiated, also underlined the importance of women's roles in the man's achievement of independence. Leaving aside the irony of the dependence of the male on his wife in an era where dependence implied subordination and vice versa, it is important to note that women's production—not the selling of surplus corn and pork—formed the basis of most trade essential to the household's day-to-day survival.[157]

While men's labor appeared in account books, it was in the form of working for each other to pay off debts. Most of the bartering took place with goods that women produced: eggs, butter, and feathers. As Mrs. Karl Tafel related: "It was also up to me to exchange butter, eggs, chickens, and so forth for coffee, sugar, shoes, in short, for everything which we needed and did not have ourselves."[158] Harrison Burns concurred: "I think that the receipts from butter and eggs sold paid for most, if not all, of the tea and coffee that was used."[159] Both Tafel and Burns saw butter and eggs as an integral part of the household economy, as a means to meet the day-to-day wants—note how Tafel turns these into "needs"—of the family.

"Needs" like coffee and tea drew southern Indiana farmers into the world of luxuries, as well as embedded them within the larger frame of international trade. Nowhere are these changes more evident than in the actions of Mrs. Gibson of Mt. Pleasant, Martin County: "One morning, she took her child and some linen thread and went a mile, wove six yards of goods, took it a half a mile to a little store, and got six yards of calico and came home by night."[160] Calico, made from cotton, was superior in the minds of many Hoosiers, and the homespun was exchanged for the superior cotton. While homespun linen was a valuable market item early in the antebellum era, production shifted away from it in the later period. The difficult elements of wool production began to be shared with skilled tradespeople and small mills, but linen production nearly disappeared, replaced by consumption of cotton, cotton grown in more distant places, thus embedding hill country families in national trade. To purchase more cotton goods, Hoosier women seem to have shifted the emphasis of their production onto butter and eggs.

This shift represented a larger transformation in the mentality of southern Indiana farm families, a movement toward greater dependency upon the marketplace. While clothing was not a necessity of immediate, day-to-day subsistence, and that eased the transition, the decision to shift production points to how the marketplace offered many—possibly including wives and children—a better life with less patriarchal control. Women and men may even have had conflicting interests within the household, certainly undermining the equation that the interests of the household and the interests of the patriarch were the same.[161]

Yet patriarchs may well have made the choice themselves. The development of the ideology of "separate spheres" created a female gender role which was not negative in connotation but complementary to a masculine definition of self. Such a gender role was profoundly middle-class—indeed, contributed to the definition of the middle class.[162] This new conception of gender roles ranged beyond its birthplace in the middle-class world and affected many husbands' understanding of their wives, as well as women's own understandings of themselves. By the late nineteenth century, Hoosier men recollected that women had been nearly worked to death, and it is the ascent of the ideology that permitted such a perception to which I am attempting to point.[163] Certainly few Hoosier farmers embraced the ideology completely—they could not have afforded to do so—but the ideal of true womanhood may have influenced a move away from more strenuous forms of production. In other words, it was not just the allure of consumer goods but also the reordering of gender roles which may have contributed to both women's and men's desiring a shift away from some of the strenuous tasks of home textile manufacture. Such a change, of course, was possible only because of the availability of cheap consumer goods.

Nevertheless, far closer to the general strategy of "surplus produce" may have been another source of the shift. If Mrs. Gibson at one time could exchange six yards of home-manufactured linen for six yards of calico, that situation did not remain true. Homespun linen gradually lost value, as few chose to use it for anything but toweling, and the ability of southern Indiana farmwives to sell their surplus linen in the market lessened. Without a market for the surplus, the production of linen lost some of its strategic importance.[164] Goods, even if they were useful for subsistence, were not desirable unless they could also be turned into cash. The movement away from textile production emphasized how the strategy of "surplus produce" was market related and how many southern Indiana households were embedded in the market, although not dependent upon it. By choosing to use eggs and butter to purchase cotton clothing, the farmer and his wife may still have been choosing the least risky strategy. Even if the market was bad, butter and eggs could be used to feed their family and free up other produce for sale.

While both husbands and wives may have produced within the strategy of "surplus produce," each of their productive efforts were directed at different goals of the family. The husband, with his production of grain and livestock, used the surplus from that production to meet the long-term goal of the household, to replicate the ownership of land for his off-spring. Although they dined on hog and hominy, much of the day-to-day survival of the family rested on the efforts of the wife—who prepared the meals, after all—and her surplus produce often went to meet those day-to-day needs which were not met by the household's own production. These two goals had different markets: the wife sold her goods locally, and the husband, although he met some local demand, sold most of his surplus to more distant places. Over time, the perceived importance of such distant markets would help to obscure the wife's substantial contribution to the family's survival.[165] Nevertheless, in antebellum southern Indiana, husbands and wives, and their children, too, were engaged in a pursuit of the family's basic welfare.

THE LOCAL ECONOMY

Of course, few if any farms ever were fully self-sufficient, producing all their necessities within the household. As we have seen, women sold their surplus produce at local markets in order to purchase necessities and comforts that they did not or could not produce themselves. They were joined in this marketplace by men, who, although primarily farmers, traded other skills with their neighbors. This local economy served an important aspect in the "surplus produce" strategy, as it was the sector within which southern Indiana households secured the necessities of life that they could not produce on their own farms. They could not depend upon more distant markets, because those markets were not within the oversight of the local moral community, the only apparatus, for many hill country folk, that could ensure that those with whom they traded would act morally. In return for supplying the necessities, all the community asked was that farmers ensure that the demands of the local community be fulfilled before goods were shipped to more distant markets.

As we have already seen, the assumption embedded within the notion of "surplus produce" was that surpluses from the local community would be shipped elsewhere but that it was a "surplus" from the production of the entire community, not just individual farmers. However, in the early spring of 1835, the editor of *Rising Sun Times* took local farmers to task for not keeping back enough provisions for the community.[166] That this moral demand was crumbling was confirmed by a similar complaint in the Vevay *Village Times and Switzerland County News:* "It is hard to get farm goods. . . . Most farmers trade them on account with merchants, rather than selling them for cash on market days." The indignation underlined the moral precept at issue, although many farmers would not have included themselves in the same "community" as these residents of Ohio Valley market towns. Moreover, farmers in the vicinity of these two towns had imbibed the spirit of the market more than many in southern Indiana, and some of them may well have transcended the earlier moral demand. For many farmers in southern Indiana, however, the moral demand remained, so entangled in their understanding of the world that they could speak of the great profits to be received "after filling home demands."[167]

This demand was just one element of the locally regulated economy, an economy not in opposition to capitalist ideals, but one whose highest goal was to ensure the competency of all members of the community. That, in reaching for that goal, certain capitalist ideals were ignored should not be understood as "anticapitalist," nor should the ease with which other capitalist ideals insinuated themselves into the community's notion of competency be taken as evidence that they were capitalists. Rather, the localism of many residents and their need for the products and services of their neighbors necessitated a local economy regulated by a vision of justice and morality that ensured the survival of most residents.

Cooperation was one key way in which the community concerned itself with the survival of all its members. Men and women who were unwilling to help their neighbors often found themselves scorned in the community. There was a sense that each needed the other, as Reverend George Hester recalled:

> Their dependence on each other served to endear them to one another in their several associations. These remarks will apply with peculiar force to the professing community of our Church—in those early times—from the parson to the humblest of the flock.[168]

The fluidity with which Hester moved from interdependence for survival to the community of the church underscored the importance of that institution in creating the communities of southern Indiana, communities which were as concerned with the material world as with the eternal one. Neighbors looked after each other; when John and Mary Watson arrived in Dearborn County after their long journey, they were destitute strangers: "But no sooner was our situation known, than we had plenty of provisions brought to us."[169] As already noted, looms and probably other implements of textile manufacture were shared through the community, and sometimes neighbors, often kin, would together purchase some farm implements.[170] This spirit of cooperation even pervaded the practice of running swine at large:

> Pompey had a "hog ranch" somewhere between Cox's Mill and Lamb's Creek. He did not exactly own, but exercised a sort of supervision over it, looking after his neighbors' as well as his own swine herd.[171]

Pompey, one might surmise, exchanged the opportunity to run his hogs on his neighbors' land for looking after their hogs on the loose. Mutuality was an important element in creating the communal life in southern Indiana, as neighbors cooperated to achieve their desires.

In discussing mutuality, one cannot discount completely the romanticized visions of log-rollings, barn-raisings, and corn-huskings. For wealthy English émigré Cornelius Pering, the free assistance was something to write home about: "People are accustomed to assist each other gratuitously (on invitation) at corn-husking, log-rolling, and house-raising."[172] Log rollings could be an effective way to clear land: "Ten or fifteen hands will log ten acres in a day."[173] Although log rollings and barn and house raisings were probably more common in the earlier days of settlements, mutual assistance also included wood choppings, quiltings, wool pickings, and apple cuttings.[174] Much of the mutual assistance that continued to be rendered happened within the female roles—quilting, wool pickings, and other textile manufacturing—but in one of the most integral elements within male production, hog killing, neighbors of both genders gathered to help: three or four men for the outdoor work and their wives to make the sausage. Without this assistance, the pork that was central to hill country survival would never have made it into the smokehouses and pickle barrels; perishable, meat had to be preserved quickly.[175] For many southern Indiana residents, mutual obligation was a necessity, and one that created networks of reciprocity outside the world of cash.

This world of mutual obligation was so strong that cash could not absolve indebtedness, as many a traveler discovered: "A man, therefore, who receives a traveller in his house, and gives him a bed and food, considers with justice, that he confers a favour on his guests, even though he charges some trifle for his hospitality."[176] For many Hoosiers, favors were as important as the cash that was exchanged, for in their relationships with their neighbors, mutual dependency was central. Certainly this necessity was not part of the exchange between traveler and host, but the sense that there were favors which cash could not absolve would suggest that in southern Indiana, Hoosiers understood that survival could not depend upon the availability of cash. Even when there was a cash price arrived at, that did not mean that one's indebtedness was relieved.

In another sense as well, money did not always represent the resolution of bargaining, the result of supply and demand. Prices, in the minds of many Hoosiers, should represent "an equality in the value of each man's time." The writer added, "The profits of the labor of one man must bear a reasonable proportion with that of his fellow citizens, else trade will be disordered and 'times will be hard.'" The failure of mechanics and merchants to recognize that as the value of farm produce went down, so should their prices, had led, according to this writer, to the hard times after the Panic of 1819. The availability of money, this Hoosier asserted, should have no bearing on exchange, as it was only a useful means of representing resources, for shoes lasted as long whether they cost two dollars or four.

> It can make no difference with the farmer whether he sells his wheat at one dollar per bushel and buys his salt at four dollars or sells wheat at twenty-five cents and buys salt at one dollar per bushel: the result is the same, as twenty-five cents in the latter case is worth as much as the dollar in the former case.[177]

While the notice of the usefulness of money for trading at a distance spoke to the importance of such trade, if the primary purpose of accumulating money was to purchase land, then, as a later correspondent pointed out in a different context, the reduction of the price of federal land, although it depressed settled land prices, did not change the value. "Even if it did reduce the price of improved land, it would do so in no greater proportion to their reduction in public lands." Even if a farmer sold the land at a lower price than he paid for it, he still could command the same buying power. If he chose not to sell his farm, "the same number of acres will yield the same number of bushels of wheat, corn, or potatoes."[178] This emphasis on what modern economists would call either "use-value" or "labor-value," as opposed to the "exchange-value" of the world of supply and demand, conditioned much of the trade which took place among southern Indiana farmers.

Distinction in the value of work did exist. Skilled tradesmen commanded even higher wages than ordinary laborers. Such distinctions were even made to depend upon the skill of the job performed. The 1823 account of John Redish with Burr Banks reflected this distinction, as Redish's ordinary "work" was valued less than his making of a cupboard.[179] Yet the importance of exchange of work should not be underestimated, nor should the hidden skilled trades of many southern Indiana farmers. Although the persistence of skilled and semiskilled tradesmen was low, fully one-quarter of 1850 tradesmen who persisted from 1850 to 1860 identified themselves in 1860 as farmers.[180] The trades were one means up the agricultural ladder, but the skills that these farmers had acquired certainly could continue to be put to use within the local marketplace. Nevertheless, this movement into agriculture affirmed the ultimate appeal of farming as a way of life. As in the case of Redish, hill country Hoosiers used both their skills and their brawn to pay off their debts.

They also paid off their debts in kind. Even within the world of female work, debts were incurred. We already have seen that Mrs. Karl Tafel paid her weaver with one-third of the yarn. Molly Mace paid "my girls in cloth."[181] Much of the bartering at stores occurred with goods produced by women: linen, butter, and eggs. But the economy was structured such that even manufactured goods, like cotton calico, could be bartered back to the store in payment of debts.[182] Store accounts were generally settled up every six months to a year, although some were carried longer. If there remained a debt, a note bearing interest was issued. Until that point no interest had been assessed on the account, although there were definitely different cash and credit prices.

The issuance of the note may well have propelled the obligation into the second marketplace of the Hoosier hills, the marketplace where much of the grain and livestock was traded. Rather than being carried on accounts, much of the grain and livestock was traded within a different world of obligation, a world defined by notes bearing interest. Some was traded within the local world of the account book—Burr Banks did sell John Redish grain—and probably the merchants who prepared the "surplus produce" for shipment elsewhere could be enticed to sell some locally, although the complaints from Vevay and Rising Sun suggested otherwise.[183] When individual farm households had deficiencies, they were usually quite small, so only a small portion of others' surpluses went to feed their neighbors. At the township level, most townships came close to being self-supporting. Butler Township, Franklin County, and Brown Township, Washington County, probably had made up their deficiencies by withholding corn from hogs, but Washington Township, Washington County, home of Salem, the county's major marketplace, drew some of the surpluses from the more productive parts of the county.[184] For the most part, though, grain and livestock that were surplus at the farm level were also surplus at the county level and were rarely drawn into the market defined by the account book. Two worlds of defining debt; two ways of exchanging goods; two familial goals: these are the differences between the world of the account book and the world of the note. Both were present in the hill country.

Nevertheless, the exchange with notes may well have been made with the same person as were trades on account, and both parties could well have remained within the oversight of the local community. For this reason, even exchange on notes had the possibility of judgment in the court of local opinion and could be regulated in extralegal ways, as John Bollin's advertisement made clear:

> All persons are forbid from taking an assignment of, or trading in any way
> for a note, given by me to Christopher Peelman, dated September 26, 1834,

calling for one hundred bushels of corn, to be delivered next fall at 25 cents per bushel. It was given for a consideration which has entirely failed, being illegal and void. Therefore I will not pay the same unless compelled by law.[185]

In Bollin's mind, the law existed outside the moral community, here defined to a certain extent by the readership of the local newspaper. The actual courts, in many respects, were the domain of outsiders, who sought recourse in the judicial system when long-distance transactions failed. For some local trades, churches forbade their members to sue each other. It was not until late in the antebellum period that the majority of plaintiffs in Circuit Court debt cases in both Washington and Franklin counties were residents.[186] Some of the difference undoubtedly had to do with the sum involved, as local justices of the peace handled most small claims matters.[187] Smaller debts, those that undoubtedly were kept in account books, were decided by these justices, most of whom, it must be added, did not have formal legal training and thus relied as much on personal and communal standards as on the body of law.[188] By 1860, it did appear that larger debts were being contracted between county residents, and they were more willing to go to court to recover them.

For much of the period, however, most local exchange took place in the world of the account book, a world in which barter and labor exchange fulfilled the basic needs of hill country households. The circularity of that exchange emphasized the interdependence of the community. As Baynard Hall, whose family operated a store and tanning yard/cobblery, described it:

Hence, occasionally when a wood-chopper must have shoes and yet had no produce, but offered to pay in "chopping," we, not needing that article, and being indebted to several neighbours who did, used to send the man and his axe as the circulating medium in demand among our own creditors, to *chop out* the bills against us.[189]

Such circles can be found in many account books from the period.[190] The account book of a storekeeper could also be used in some ways as a local clearinghouse, as various transactions from outside the store were recorded there.[191] Similarly, John Ketcham wrote to Absalsom Morgan: "Please let the bearer (Wm. H. Tredway) have the Brandy coming to me from Thomas Cliff—the amount due me is $3.20."[192]

The mutual bonds reflected the mutual interdependence of the community. That interdependence had its negative side. John Hicks complained about his inability to say no when others asked him to be surety:

About 1842 I with others bailed our Sheriff of Owen county at that time, and he failing in his duty caused me to have to pay eight hundred dollars. I had no money at the time and my property was sold, George Parks bid on my land and gave me a chance to redeem it; it took all I could make for eight years to redeem my land after supporting my family.[193]

Despite Hicks's condemnation elsewhere of "mere money power," he saw this situation as one of his own making, and saw George Parks as a good neighbor who gave him the opportunity to regain his substantial holding of 240 acres. Parks probably did not lose money on the deal, but one purpose of his endeavor was to preserve the competency of his neighbor. Whether it be a sum of eight hundred dollars or three dollars, the community gathered to ensure the economic well-being of its members.

Barter, account books, and notes all point to the larger problem of the unavailability of cash. The absence of cash was a problem during economic downturns, especially following the Panic of 1819, when much of the specie in the West was drained off. Many merchants would not give cash for any but the most liquid of commodities. Pork often could get cash, but for the Maces, the choice had been hops. Most merchants in the hill country had no more access to cash than the farmers with whom they traded. The relationship remained fair; if a piece of linen was "worth ten cents in silver," a merchant would "give twelve in trade."[194] Likewise, there were separate cash and barter prices. Reverend George Hester commented on the general absence of cash:

> Money was hard to be obtained, so much so, that it became proverbial that 5 dollars paid all debts which occurred among the first settlers. When one individual would get into straitened circumstances, he would borrow this amount, and so of the next, etc.[195]

The image of a single five-dollar note circulating around a neighborhood captured the essence of the scarcity of cash, and the idea that five dollars could relieve all debts spoke to the arbitrariness of the values on commodities and services.[196]

However, as Hester's comment suggested, there were circumstances facing residents that required cash. In many instances, small loans might be obtained from persons with whom a farmer already had an account; on account, these "loans" would not draw interest until the account was settled up into a note, although they may have been discounted.[197] For larger loans, there were residents of the hill country always willing to oblige, sometimes without regard for local custom or law:

> The way the law is avoided, where it exists, is in this manner. Suppose a person wants to borrow 500 dollars for a year, the state allows but 6%, but you have no money to lend at that interest. He will then draw a Bill in this form,—
> "Twelve months after date, one or either of us (if a security) promise to pay

Mr. ———— five hundred dollars in silver or gold with lawful interest of 6% &c." You charge the party besides, say, 10% and deduct $50, and if you please the 6% also—$30., pay him $450 or $20, and take his note for $500, send the bill to the Bank, and when due the money is paid. In this way many realize immense sums annually; but it requires some time to know the parties you have to deal with.[198]

Cornelius Pering was a modern businessman, using formal means to accumulate immense sums. But despite the rigor of his efforts, he realized that the borrower had to be a known quantity—a member of one's community, in a sense—someone who saw a contract, even an illegal one, as higher than law or custom and would not challenge the debt when it came due.

Many southern Indiana farmers would not have been so malleable. Enunciating a producerist ethic, a J. E. of Everton questioned the practice of lending in an 1850 exchange on usury: "The sacrifice is too great, to keep up a system that robs the mouth of labor."[199] This Everton citizen opposed lending as a drain on the wealth of the producers and thus a drain on commerce itself, as well as a threat to the independence of the producer, who must be controlled by the lender. Unfeeling creditors were despised creatures. When Enoch Millis left behind his wife and huge debts, his kin were angry with him, but they also reserved some venom for his creditors: "Lord Campbell + the Royall Bratt (H. Henley) are the most pushing creditors of all."[200] The rendering of the creditors as aristocracy paralleled J. E.'s insistence that creditors posed a threat to the independent man.

Despite widespread ideological opposition to lending, some Hoosiers did borrow. As we have seen, Benjamin Mace and his brother-in-law Jonathan Hardy borrowed money, and they were not alone. Relatively few Hoosiers took on mortgages, at least through 1830.[201] Yet the borrowing, as in the case with Cornelius Pering, reflected somewhat the localist, face-to-face nature of commerce in southern Indiana. Mr. Hughes of Elizabethtown wrote to Ezekiel Tyner: "I must settle up with you this fall by getting what money I can from my claims there + borrow the rest at the same interest I pay you."[202] While Hughes's emphasis was on using his creditors' money to settle his own debts, the role of locale was key. Hughes had obviously moved from Tyner's neighborhood—probably somewhere in Franklin County— and just as he owed money in that neighborhood, he also had "claims there." He did not expect to recover enough to pay off his account with Tyner, and he undoubtedly would have to borrow money from others—not write a new note to Tyner. Who these new lenders were to be, Hughes did not say, yet it would seem reasonable to suspect that they were his new neighbors in Bartholomew County. Hughes was compelled to settle his accounts in his old community, perhaps creating new debts in his new one. To many hill country Hoosiers, debt was only safe within the confines of the local community.

The sense of debt as a moral obligation—after all, it appears that Hughes initiated the contact—rather than just a legal one underscored the importance of the local moral community. Others felt the impulse of Hughes. Aaron S. Bullard wrote that he would like to join his son, Joseph Bullard, but obligations kept him in Vernon.

> I still have a great desire of coming into that country but it appears I hav not got the faculty that some are in possession of a starting and coming at any time. neither have I any desire to be in possession of any such a faculty I am determined to pay my debts before I starte.[203]

The abundant production he reported in the letter would suggest that his debts were substantial and that he must have been somewhat enmeshed in the market system. Nevertheless, Bullard still felt a moral obligation to remain in his community until he could pay them off. Such obligations were evident when the community church demanded that its members adhere to a local morality:

> Church prefer charge against Brother John Wright for refusing to offset a debt by work when the opportunity was offered him, also leaving other debts unsettled outstanding against him.[204]

By not working when he had the opportunity, John Wright ignored the community's tradition of exchange and spurned the economic bonds that held the community together. For that reason, he was brought before the institutional embodiment of the community, the church, to be charged with economic sins. In a court of law, there would have been no remedy for Wright's failure to take the opportunity; within the community itself, there was a powerful one.

Most "regulation" took place within the "court of common fame," which had sometimes become institutionalized in the church courts. Trying to distinguish between the common situation of mutual assistance and dishonesty, church courts sometimes found themselves in a quandary. In the Livonia area, rumors had circulated that Susan Redus had purloined fish, flour, and coffee from Dr. W. F. Patton. Redus admitted that she had taken the items but not dishonestly.

> On the grounds of mutual familiar intimacy between her own family and family of said Dr. Patton, she had at different times when she found none of the family at home, taken said articles, with the design of returning as much in place, or of paying for them, which in said cases she stated she had already

done. Session having heard these statements felt that nothing further could now be done in the matter: and could only hope that God in his providence would throw light upon their path of duty in this embarassing matter.[205]

Although the unwillingness to judge may indicate the retreat of churches from regulating the lives of their members, the root of the impasse remained the fine line between the sanctity of personal property and the traditions of mutual assistance.

While in a purely legal sense Redus was wrong, hill country Hoosiers did not tend to judge their neighbors so formally, nor did they show respect for the law when they believed that it was impeding their God-given right to independence and survival. Betty Frazier, who allegedly confined the sheriff who threatened her opportunity to sell her pigs and buy her land, represented this tradition. Likewise, boatmen on the Lost River in Orange and Martin Counties tore down a mill dam constructed by a Mr. Pine, thus precipitating an acrimonious conflict. Unbeknownst to the farmers of the region, Pine circulated a petition among certain parties and was able to convince the state legislature to pass a law removing the designation of public highway from the Lost River, though "the fact that it is navigable has already been proven by the number of boats that have descended it for many years past."[206] Although a dubious compromise was reached— it was redesignated a public highway, but nothing under seven feet was considered an impediment—Hoosiers who had depended upon the river to get their goods to market were willing to undertake extralegal means to secure passage of their rafts. Most often, however, Hoosier "justice" found more passive expression, much to the chagrin of some:

> A practice prevails to some extent, in this county, which ought to be discountenanced and discontinued; that is, at sales of decedent's personal property, if the widow bids for an article, no other person will bid against her, so that the article is struck off to her, at whatever price her cupidity may induce her to bid, and even clerks who act under oath, and criers, will exert themselves to influence bidders, to affect the same object.[207]

Despite the editor's fears that the creditors and infants were ill served by such traditions, few Hoosiers probably thought that infants would be well served by an impoverished mother; as for creditors, surely many of them were in attendance and participating, although major creditors—often those at a distance—may well have been victims of the Hoosiers' desire for the widow to be well situated.

Such local regulation, as we have seen, was part of a moral world that sought to ensure the independence of each family. Most of the cues for their behavior came from the capitalist world of exchange, but Hoosier families never adhered closely to rules when the rules threatened their independence or the independence of their neighbors. By pursuing a strategy of "surplus produce," hill country farmers achieved a certain level of independence, and by depending upon their neighbors to meet their other needs, within the tightly controlled local economy, they did not need to be too dependent upon more distant markets. Many Hoosier farmers recognized that dependency upon such marketplaces came at great cost, and they feared these distant marketplaces.

TRADING ON DISTANT MARKETS

Yet as much as they feared distant marketplaces, it was only in such commerce that Hoosier farmers could achieve the second of their two goals in "reproducing" their families: to accumulate the cash necessary to set up their children on their own farms. That such a goal was rarely fully achieved did not mean that Hoosier parents did not feel the impulse. The goal was there, and hill country farmers looked to more distant markets as the places where they could sell off their "surplus produce" for the cash necessary to buy land for their progeny. That these markets were necessary for the long-term survival of the family did not mean, however, that Hoosiers acquiesced in the values of the markets.

The major problem with more distant marketplaces was that they were beyond the control of the local moral community. Hoosiers' ambivalence was bred within the moral communities to which they belonged, notably "Primitive" Baptist and German Catholic. Many were ensconced in tightly bound local communities, in which the economic activities could be regulated. Outside such communities, however, not only were these markets more volatile, fluctuating with the whimsies of the world economy, but exchange in them was unregulated in the eyes of the Hoosiers, because they understood moral regulation as solely within the purview of local communities. For these traditional believers, the evangelical-capitalist emphasis on internalizing a moral code seemed a road to anarchy; only through the tight control of a local moral community could the worst impulses of humans be subdued.

These distant markets were to be feared; that was one reason Hoosier farmers chose not to depend upon them for the day-to-day survival of their families. When "Grazier" advocated sheep as a proper safety-first strategy, he condemned visions of hog-and-corn farming as enormously profitable, "whereas wool always bears a reasonable price—is a cash article—is not dependent on the New Orleans market and the speculation of traders."[208]

The issues were complicated. Wool was praiseworthy because it could bring cash, necessary for long-term familial reproduction, and because it insulated farmers from the vagaries of distant markets and the synonymous speculation of traders. Certainly the appearance of this letter in the aftermath of the Panic of 1819 would explain the emphasis on distancing oneself from the market and speculation. The Panic was a seminal event in defining Hoosiers' attitudes toward the marketplace, and the subsequent periodic economic downturns would reveal to them repeatedly how much they were involved in the marketplace—"the depression that the price of produce has received in foreign market, has reduced its price at home"— and therefore how susceptible they were to its manipulations.[209] The Panic had hit southern Indiana especially hard because many Hoosiers were buying their land on credit from the federal government, and the absence of cash had the potential to force them to default on their payments. By the 1837 downturn, public land was purchased cash on the barrelhead, and therefore economic depressions had less immediate effect on the family's livelihood. However, by that time, much of the public land in southern Indiana had been patented, and while some looked further west for their progeny, those who chose to buy locally were potentially still in danger of defaulting on private mortgages and land contracts. Still, John Sloan thought he saw a silver lining: "I am rather disposed to think the present hard times will have a good tendency in the end & tend to equalize the distribution of property."[210]

To achieve their long-term goals, hill country farmers needed distant markets and the collapse of these markets was cause for concern. While Jacob Weaver recognized that local exchange continued unabated, that there was "no foren-trade at present" was of enormous importance.[211] Such an interest about more distant markets was almost universal. Their importance was underscored by a letter in the *Rising Sun Times* which bragged that the streams leading into the Ohio "bear off productions of our country to the best market in the world."[212] George Leavitt added that in Crawford County people traveled to New Orleans so often that "they talk of that city which is 1,400 miles distant as if it were but a few miles distant."[213]

Part of the reason that Hoosier farmers could to some extent relax about their relationship with these distant and morally suspect markets was that the opportunity costs of such activity were minimized. Farming was a seasonal activity. Once the hog killing had been completed in November or early December, only livestock tending and maybe a little fence mending would occupy a farmer's time until April. During that time, a farmer could pursue many profitable activities, both in manufacturing and in marketing.

Farming was not the only pursuit of hill country farmers. When discussing the mill dam on the Lost River, Representative Benjamin Edmonston of Dubois County, son of Bazil B. Edmonston, joked that the flatboats were loaded with hoop-poles and whetstones.[214] Some Hoosier farmers had backgrounds in skilled trades. Others used the winter months to manufacture a variety of items that could be marketed in more distant markets. Again, the gender division reappeared. Whereas women's manufactures were often sold locally within the barter economy, the men's production was shipped greater distances for sale for cash. The forest was the source of much of the men's possibilities. Just by clearing it and burning the brush, Horace Stow's family saved the ashes and made them into black salts, potash, and pearlash: "They brought good price & sold for cash."[215] Others turned the timber to other purposes: "In order to earn money, Papa made railroad crossties in winter, which he would haul to the station during the summer."[216] By far the most lucrative pursuits were the making of staves and hoop-poles, the first stage in the manufacture of barrels.

> Levi is nearly reddy to go out with a boat load of staves he will go the firs good rise he has about 25 thousand staves ready.[217]

Even as late as 1860, such trade continued.[218] These forest products, often cut and manufactured during the winter months, were an essential part of the household income of some southern Indiana families, as they used the lull in farm activity to pursue other forms of surplus.

For many who moved surplus farm produce and home manufactures down the rivers, the late winter was the common time to travel, as the thaws provided an extra measure of water to get through shallow parts of the inland rivers. In late winter, few chores kept one down on the farm, so the opportunity cost was minimal. Some complained that "no produce they could make would pay to haul to the Ohio River, seventy miles."[219] Others saw their own labor as costing them little. The loss of weight to hogs and other livestock cut into profits, but even after the railroad had come to Franklin County, some German settlers still drove their livestock to Cincinnati.[220]

For longer distances, flatboating was the preferred means. Some young men, like Owen County's John Hicks, found employment taking loads down the Ohio and Mississippi: "I commenced flat-boating in 1826, and followed it for many years, making as many as five trips to the mouth of the [Ohio] river during one season, and occasionally to New Orleans."[221] Young men like Hicks were hired by farmers to help with the loads and by merchants like Samuel Gibson Brown of Dubois County, who took the goods he had purchased from farmers and sold them down the river.[222] Flatboating for merchant or farmer was a risk. Both could suffer the sinking of their boats, but for the merchant, prices might not have paid for a trip, whereas for a farmer pursuing a safety-first strategy, all profits were in the clear.

Because opportunity costs were low and because they did not depend upon distant markets for day-to-day survival, the money that hill country farmers received in trading on these markets was almost pure profit in their minds. In the long term, such profits were necessary to replicate opportunities for their children. Yet these Hoosiers recognized that not every year would bring such profit, and they had arranged their economic lives to account for these variations. A strategy built around "surplus produce" had the potential to meet both their short-term needs and long-term goals.

BUILDING STRONGER LOCAL MARKETS

The involvement of merchants like Samuel Gibson Brown in the marketing of the agricultural produce of the hill country pointed, however, to changes in marketing strategies. Surely many farmers encountered the same deluge of flatboats on the river every spring, with the excess supply driving prices down, maybe to a point at which they may have begun to question the efficacy of their journey, despite the minimal opportunity costs. Advocating the building of the Louisville and Salem Railroad, the Louisville *Journal* noted that "all the citizens of the interior of Indiana want is a certain and cheap mode of conveyance for the surplus products of their soil," but the problem was that Lawrence County alone sent nearly 100 flatboats, and "all these things produce glut in New Orleans in spring, when most of this travel takes place." According to the newspaper, a railroad would open up the market to the entire year.[223] Such a leveling off would introduce a degree of certainty in the marketplace, something that was lacking in all farmers' economic strategies.

Yet the activities of merchants like Samuel Gibson Brown also introduced a new element of certainty to the economic strategies of hill country farmers. By marketing their "surplus produce" to local merchants, farmers now had the potential to deal with members of their own moral communities. Such a possibility was part of the appeal of the new internal improvement projects. Despite the failings of the Wabash and Erie Canal, the Worthington *Valley Times* credited it with having "given a home market for all the surplus produce of the country."[224] And urging wool production, the Salem *Washington Democrat* pointed to "home markets" again, created undoubtedly by the new railroad: "Now that we have a home market for all the wool that can be grown, we may reasonably hope that, ere long Young America, under the symbol of the lamb, will be seen sporting and skipping on every grassy slope in the land."[225] Home markets, of course, reduced transportation and other opportunity costs and thus appealed to capitalists, but considering the minimal costs to many farmers, the added security of dealing with members of the farmers' own moral community must have been an element in their allure. No longer would a farmer have to deal with amoral strangers but rather face-to-face with men whom he knew.

The security promoted by the local moral community obscured the ways in which these changes allowed the values of capitalism to insinuate themselves in the neighborhoods of southern Indiana. The community's aim was to protect the competency—"the possession of sufficient property to absorb the labors of a given family while providing it with . . . a degree of comfortable independence"—of its members; when that competency was threatened by actions based on capitalist values, the community could mitigate the damage, with offers of mutual assistance.[226] But as some members of the community—particularly merchants—had to meet capitalist obligations to maintain their competency, they introduced the full logic of capitalism into the local community. To protect these members, the community respected their need to charge interest, collect debts in a timely manner, and deal only in cash. Certainly all Hoosiers recognized that distant markets were beyond their control—that was what was wrong with them—and they could sympathize with their neighbors who were bound by those markets' prices. Capitalism and the local moral community were not in immediate opposition to one another; it would be only as capitalism threatened people's competency that conflicts would emerge, and fortunately for Hoosier farmers, their strategy embedded in "surplus produce" served to protect their competency for a long while.

A transition was taking place in southern Indiana in the years before the Civil War, but it would not be until after the war that the conflicts would begin to erupt. Nor did this transition begin during the period under investigation. Interest, for instance, had always been present in the hill country. The extent to which these economic changes were occurring has thus been obscured. It is worth noting that the changes detailed above were revealed by newspapers, newspapers which had seen the possibilities of capitalist marketplaces, as evidenced by the embrace of "Young America" by the Salem *Washington Democrat.*[227] And the individualistic, property-holding aspects of the agrarian, localist ethic provided a solid foundation for these capitalist endeavors. Certainly many southern Indiana residents who sought the rewards of capitalism did not see its potential conflict with the values they held, which circulated around the local moral community.

The failure to see the conflict should not be surprising, since the strategy of "surplus produce" itself pulled Hoosier farmers in two directions. On their own farms, these hill country residents sought to achieve the utter independence of their households, while within their community, they were embedded in circles of mutual dependency. What held these two oppositions together was a common ambivalence about distant markets.

In their farming practices, southern Indiana farmers pursued a policy of "safety-first" farming, attempting to meet most of their families' needs with their own production while using the local market to fill in the necessities of life, but trading their surplus produce in more distant markets for non-essentials and for the means to establish their children on their own land. These distant markets could not be depended upon to support the short-term needs of Hoosier farmers. These markets were unregulated, beyond the moral oversight of Hoosiers' local communities.

The Democratic Party would respond to these fears of distant markets, identifying the problem as the actions of a rapacious moneyed aristocracy. While the Democrats would confirm Hoosiers' worst fears about these marketplaces, they also proposed solutions to the problem, which would allow hill country residents to achieve their long-term goal of providing for their progeny. And the Democrats, by opposing Whig reform efforts, endorsed the vision of local moral communities held by many of these Hoosiers.

The Politics of Localism

Concerns over the economy, religion, and morality found their widest and most divisive expression in politics. The expansion of market opportunities and the creation of a uniform moral code coexisted at the center of political conflict in the antebellum period in southern Indiana and in the whole of the United States. In the Democratic Party, southern Indiana farmers found a means to express vociferously their vision of the world, a vision built in part around their localism. The Democratic Party was a vehicle to preserve and regain the world of "surplus produce" farming and of freedom of choice in religion, as well as the equality of all white men. In picking up these themes, in creating new issues, and in redefining some concerns, the Democrats also played a role in molding the mentality of early Hoosier farmers. And the two-party system, because it had the effect of dichotomizing issues, sharpened beliefs. Political ideology joined religious beliefs and economic pursuits as part of a holistic worldview of southern Indiana farmers, one which centered around a localist understanding of human morality.

For Hoosier farmers, raised within the confines of local moral communities where the only secure transactions were carried on with neighbors, fears of more distant markets were confirmed by the Jacksonians' identification of the enemies of the people in the Bank of the United States, in various internal improvement projects, and in various corporations granted special privileges. Jacksonians alerted Hoosiers that the "moneyed aristocracy" manipulated markets to increase its wealth, at the expense of ordinary people like the farmers. Although Hoosiers' economic strategy of "surplus produce" shielded them from some of these market vagaries, their long-term goal of providing for their progeny required that they market some goods, and therefore they demanded that control of markets be wrested from this aristocracy. The Democratic Party had taught that this control was unnatural, the result of an activist government that granted special privileges to certain individuals, and it promised that if these privileges were removed, Hoosier farmers could find safe markets to sell their produce and provide for their offspring.

The elimination of governmental privilege was part of the larger Democratic program of promoting equality among all white men.[1] Because all governmental decisions had the potential to favor one individual over another and one locale over another, they were to be looked upon with distrust. Only those governmental actions were condoned which tended to smile broadly upon the entire populace, whose social benefits outweighed the minor advantages they would give to certain individuals.[2] Thus legislation designed to fill the needs of the vast majority of the people fulfilled the demands of this "localist" ideology, even though it might bankrupt the government. The egalitarian impulse of the Democratic Party corresponded well to the egalitarianism of the local communities in which Hoosier farmers lived, and the success with which Democrats painted Whigs as "aristocrats" certainly touched upon Hoosier experiences of being treated as second-class citizens by Eastern politicians and missionaries.

Despite the condemnation of these missionaries, Hoosiers considered their communities to be as moral as humanly possible, yet they understood that this tenuous morality was only achieved through tight local regulation. When Whig and, later, Know-Nothing and Republican legislators attempted to impose a new moral order, the Democratic opposition paralleled many a Hoosier's belief that humans could not perfect themselves, but that only through the strict control of the local moral community could their worst impulses be subdued.[3] For many Hoosiers, Catholic and Protestant alike, humans were very far from divinity, and the postmillennialist dreams of Whig evangelicals were predicated, in many Hoosiers' minds, on the impossible hope of human perfectibility.

Not surprisingly, the two denominations most identified in southern Indiana with the Democratic Party, the Catholics and the Primitive Baptists, both embraced the Democratic Party because it refused to endorse one particular vision of the sacred, as befit their egalitarian and localist roots.[4] The German Catholics also found the Democrats more welcoming than nativist Whigs. Yet despite this particular appeal, many German Catholics shared with their Protestant and Democratic neighbors a similar approach to farming, a similar commitment to their progeny, and similar moral communities. Unlike the experience of their Protestant neighbors, their political ideology played little role in shaping these Germans' choice of churches, but in many ways their stories were comparable, as German Catholics responded to the Democratic Party's defense of localism.

129

The Democratic Party also argued vehemently for decisions to be made on the most local of levels, where decision makers would be the most representative of the constituency at hand. For this reason, Hoosier farmers struck out at actions by the federal government which they believed should be addressed by the Indiana General Assembly. Their localism explained their great concern over national issues. While their belief in limited government was important, much of the concern was more about the overexercise of the federal government's authority than it was a general ideological opposition to government action at any level. Many times, the issue rested in the federal government's doing what Hoosiers believed the Constitution reserved for the states: "states' rights." Moreover, they sought more local jurisdiction for projects within their own communities. In this way, the Democratic Party not only pursued policies that reflected Hoosiers' concerns in religion and economic activity, but Hoosiers also directly affirmed the importance of localism in legislative activities.

Localism, in other words, was the glue that held together significant parts of the antebellum Democratic coalition. For years historians have debated the relative importance of economic versus ethnocultural issues in delineating the political lines of the Second Party System. For some historians, the continued focus of political debates on economics means that surely these were the ideas that moved men to vote.[5] For other historians, sophisticated statistical analysis reveals much stronger relationships between religious and ethnic identifications and politics than between wealth and political identification.[6] The difficulty for statistical analysis was that actual wealth itself was a poor indicator of attitudes about economic policy. Those that placed great faith in the market might well be young and poor—wealth, after all, was a function of age in this period—and they would have seen in the Whig Party policies great hope for their future.

Whig economic ideology and its relationship to ethnicity and religion have long been recognized by historians, but they have had more difficulty in finding a similar pattern among Democrats, whom have often been labeled a coalition of people opposed to various aspects of Whiggery.[7] The Democratic Party certainly had less cohesion than the Whigs—for one thing, within its ranks were a small number of men who saw the Democratic Party as a means to end special privileges that were enriching their Whig competitors, and from these men a disproportionate number of Democratic leaders were drawn. Nevertheless, I would argue that the main body of Democratic voters shared similar convictions about localism, seeing that the best government was that which was most local and thus most responsive to the will of the people and the peculiar needs of a given locale.

Nevertheless, localism was not the only thing on which the Democratic Party based its appeal to Hoosier farmers. Wrapping themselves in the rhetoric of agrarian republicanism, Democrats shied away from its more "elitist" elements and used the language to reinforce the equality, indeed the virtue, of the simple farmer, whose hard work and honesty would enrich the nation in the marketplace and preserve the nation at the ballot box. Modifying the language to include the increasingly large mechanical and artisan classes, such a producerist rhetoric also fit nicely into the party's indictment of the moneyed aristocracy, whose pursuits added nothing to the true wealth of the nation. While not necessarily "backward-looking," Democrats tended to lean far more on the accomplishments of the past, attempting to preserve the gains, whereas Whigs, though rarely thumbing their noses at their forefathers, tended to see endless possibilities in the future.

However, we should not be misled into believing that politics was merely a battleground for these ideas or a place where they became manifest. At an ideological level the party taught its adherents to fear distant markets and to seek out religions that corresponded to their God-given equality. The Democratic Party's rhetoric helped to shape the religious beliefs and economic activities that we have already detailed. It is, of course, a complicated story, one that resonates in a different timbre for different hill country Hoosiers. A German Catholic, as I have already suggested, would not have chosen his religion based on Democratic ideology, but the politics of the day may well have made him more fearful of doing business with an evangelical Whig merchant, especially one who had expressed Nativist sentiments during the previous election season. On the other hand, his neighbor from the Upland South may have had little problem dealing with that merchant, maybe a not-so-distant cousin, but would have become a "Primitive Baptist" because that faith's insistence on the equality of all men before God and on the sanctity of the local congregation corresponded to what his political ideology had already taught him.

One aspect of the voting record may well give voice to the inarticulate fears and frustrations of many hill country farmers. Throughout the region, there was a tendency for those townships most removed from the centers of commerce and power—county seats and position on major trade routes— to vote Democratic. Such a tendency was, of course, muted by other forces, especially ethno-religious affiliation. The local-cosmopolitan cleavage has been noted before.[8] The cosmopolitan Whigs were already establishing new forms of communities based on their commercial ties, and their success in such economic endeavors led them to fear less these new ties that bound. Whigs tended to live in closer proximity to small rural villages—hardly urban meccas to the modern eye, but places where multiple churches thrived and kinship networks were far looser. In this regard, they learned forms of trust outside these institutions. Yet the new communities they created shared a characteristic with all communities: they were defined as much by whom they excluded as by whom they included. Despite the myth of the market-place as open to all, the new forms of the market world could seem alien to outsiders, and the differences multiplied, taking on cultural and economic meanings. In many ways, the Democratic Party spoke to this feeling of ex-clusion, arguing that a small band was depriving the people of their rights.

My story is not a natural progression from religion to economics to poli-tics, but an interwoven one, in which politics was as much an influence on these other factors as it was influenced by them. However, it is in politics where some of these ideas may be seen most clearly to have coalesced, in part because the division into two parties sharpened differences about morality and economic activity that stretched across a continuum. The very success of Andrew Jackson in limiting the threat from the aristocrats helped to move the conflict to the state and local scene, where the state granted monopoly privileges not to aristocrats but to friends and neighbors of hill country producers. In this way, the discussion of political ideology will also follow the changing scene, from concerns about the federal government's embrace of banks and internal improvements to the embrace of these same projects by figures from both parties at the state level, only for the Demo-crats to back away again, followed not long after by the Whigs and then Republicans.

THE LOCALIST ROOTS OF THE DEMOCRATIC PARTY

Throughout the antebellum period, republicanism had not yet died, but remained, along with liberalism and other strands of Enlightenment thought, as part of a common political vocabulary that served various needs in the early republic.[9] For Hoosier farmers as late as the 1850s, agrarian republican ideas reaffirmed their special role in the nation's politics, and paeans abounded.

> In this last place we will say that farming may be regarded as a source or fountain, which from its very nature, largely contributes to the independence of the man who devotes his energies to its pursuit. We do not simply or only mean, that kind of independence which is the result of a competency of wealth to meet all our diversified wants: we allude to an independence of a higher character—one that will place us beyond the influence of the views, the opin-ions, or the stratagems of other men.[10]

Nevertheless, Hoosiers also praised the independence of farming for its role in securing to a man the means by which to live and raise his children to live as well:

> The genius of our system is to build up a democracy ... to identify the masses with the soil, and make them, in fact as in theory, a part of the government, to furnish homes for the people, or, at least to place it in the power of every man to secure a spot of ground which shall be to him a home . . . where, under his own vine and fig tree, free and unmolested, he can enjoy life, worship God according to the dictates of his own conscience, and by the honest labor of his hands support his family and train up his children in the paths of industry and virtue.[11]

And Hoosiers were proud of the relationship to the past embedded in their use of republicanism. Speaking against monopolies and incorporation, Enoch Parr intoned that "I think I am and always have been a sound republican and my father before me, of the true Jefferson school."[12] Despite the inconsistencies and the melding of republicanism with liberalism, republicanism was embraced in part because, in its agrarian mode, it created a special place for tillers of the soil. When Parr spoke of the "moneyed aristocracy," he used the language of republicanism because it contained a far better critique of market activities and the wealthy than the liberalism which he invoked on other occasions.

Nevertheless, one of the most important gifts of republicanism to the early history of politics in southern Indiana was its condemnation of parties. In the early Republic, a great antipathy for political parties existed, emerging out of a republican suspicion that such groups were the home of intrigue and vice that threatened to corrupt and destroy the government, as individuals used the parties to pursue private ambitions rather than the common good. Parties, to early Hoosiers, were to be shunned because they were the means by which the aristocracy gained control. In the early nation, aristocracy—identified by republicans as the greatest threat to the government—was a label filled with much loathing, as it hearkened back to an earlier era of English rule and corruption.

For most Hoosiers, what had activated politics during the territorial period had been the constant quest to achieve the equality with other Americans that they believed was rightfully theirs. Their limited voice in territorial government served as a constant reminder that certain aristocratic parties in the East regarded Hoosiers as incapable of self-government.[13] Hoosiers' experience with appointed territorial governors found expression in the new Indiana constitution with its weak governor. Statehood was favored by over four-fifths of the delegates to the constitutional convention. The move into statehood was the final and, in many ways, symbolic step toward democracy and away from the elite limitations of the Northwest Ordinance.[14] Moreover, the ease with which Indiana achieved statehood, absent intrigue and secret cabals, affirmed Hoosiers' republican belief that parties were not necessary.

Without parties, politics in the first years of statehood were based in the personal, often in which an individual's character was paraded and smeared, but in its purer and more local forms, it depended upon common knowledge. In 1833, Enoch Parr ran against S[amuel?] Peck, a man who "had been useful to the distressed" during the cholera epidemic just prior to the election, and Parr himself observed, "If I had got beeten I was beeten by a man."[15] Within the face-to-face communities of southern Indiana, knowledge would prove important for many years to come; well into the 1840s, some townships still tended to swing massively to a favorite son. Obviously, such personal knowledge was not available at higher levels, although Patrick Henry Jameson noted that his father, an otherwise apolitical man who did not allow political papers in his household, "was a 'Clay man' because he had known Clay in Kentucky."[16] Indeed, the language used to describe national candidates often attempted to replicate this personal dimension: Adams was a friend to Indiana, Jackson was a fellow Westerner. The familiar was an important aspect of "personal politics," because it assured voters of the virtue of the candidate.

Surprisingly enough, then, conventions for nominating candidates began at the local level. For instance, in Harrison County, in 1820, delegates from the various militia companies gathered to recommend a ticket to the electorate at large. They recognized how open to criticism their actions were:

> They do not wish to dictate to the people but it has been a course pursued by States older than the one of which we have become citizens; . . . in our opinion, the people ought, if they attend to the interests and feelings of the farmers and mechanics of this district, to support the candidates which they have designated in the above resolutions.
>
> . . . We explicitly state that we wish to support the farmer and mechanic—they are the mainstay of our country—they are the firm supporters of our republican constitution; and we, as a committee, wish to prevent an evil which has long prevailed, *viz:* of electing persons who do not really feel an interest in the general welfare.[17]

While two of their three nominees for the Indiana House of Representatives won, the impetus for the convention was unclear: speaking in the voice of neither the farmer nor the mechanic, the convention nevertheless claimed to bring a voice to the people. The following year, Harrison County again came together for a convention, an act which the Corydon *Indiana Gazette* praised as "a very salutary purpose in getting forward modest men of talents whose interests may be identified with the great agricultural and farming interests of the country; and have a tendency of putting down that uncouth and baneful method of a candidate starting up, and to gain a popularity riding all around the country to electioneer for himself, treating at every town or grog shop he comes to as long as he has money or credit."[18] The specific motivation behind the call for conventions was again unclear, but certainly these conventions signaled an adherence to the idea that politics should emanate from local concerns.

In 1820, some of the legislators from Franklin County called for a convention of the people specifically to provide instructions for the legislators, a course of action condoned by Indiana's 1816 Constitution: "that the people have a right to assemble together, in a peaceable manner, to consult for the common good, *to instruct their representatives,* and to apply to the legislature for a redress of grievances."[19] The meetings had been called by three of the four members of the General Assembly from the county, perhaps to give their legislative actions the imprimatur of republican legitimacy.[20] Even in 1857, a Franklin County Democrat would call for a party convention in terms of a meeting of a majority of the people.[21] As late as the eve of the Civil War, the Democratic Party occupied a place on the fence between an organization and a series of local meetings of the people, and this awkward position reflected deep-seated anxieties about parties.[22]

The most frequently offered justification for conventions was the cry of the rule of the many against the rule of the few and distant. The characterization of early Hoosier settlers by Eastern elites was of a people incapable of governing themselves, whether in politics, as reflected in the early stages of the Northwest Ordinance, or in morality, as reflected in the impulse to send missionaries among them. For men who believed themselves fully capable of self-governance, such a characterization smacked of an "aristocracy." Many Hoosiers would have agreed with Enoch Parr's remark that "there always has been and always will be an aristocrascy in the land disguiseing themselves with various prentons [*sic*] and under various names but always striving to assume for the government powers not granted."[23] Without a birthright aristocracy in America, many Hoosiers believed, this aristocracy was determined by power, of which wealth was the principal source, but these wealthy aristocrats needed the government because, without the government's potential for preferential treatment of some citizens over others, differences in wealth would have little impact on the society as a whole. The reverse was also true to the minds of many Hoosiers. The government's preferential treatment was the major source of inequality in wealth; as they well knew, any man could provide for his family if he was willing to work.[24] With this fear of an aristocracy's taking over the government, conventions began to be seen, not as the agents of such a takeover, but as the people's best defense against such an action.

For Hoosiers, conventions were an effective means of combating aristocracy, and as such they formed the literal and ideological underpinnings of the Democratic Party in Indiana. In 1824, the acceptance of gathering in convention to nominate the "people's" candidate for office found its way into the Hoosier hills during the presidential campaign. In Greene County, men gathered near Point Commerce to poll themselves as to who should be the next president, and they put forth the name of Andrew Jackson. Moreover, they resolved "that the people of this republic on this occasion ought to meet not only in cities and towns, but on their farms and in the forests, and express their opinions, and have them published, throughout the United States," adding that their meeting was held in the "wilds of Indiana."[25] Perhaps rhetorical, the conflation of urban and rural hearkened back to the republican virtues of the yeoman farmer, while also suggesting the dominance of urban elites in directing politics and thus provoking feelings of exclusion among Hoosier farmers.

Soon afterwards, a number of Hoosiers gathered in Salem, Indiana, to put forth a final electoral slate for Andrew Jackson. The primary impetus here was far less ideological: as outsiders in the Hoosier political process, Jackson's supporters belonged to no ancillary organization like the State Bar or the Indiana General Assembly, and so they had created three separate Jackson electoral tickets, a situation the convention sought to change. And the feelings of exclusion from politics may well have motivated the Jackson delegates; few Jackson followers were among the leading politicians of the day.[26] Jackson had the support of only one newspaper in the state, albeit the most influential one, Elihu Stout's *Western Sun* in Vincennes.[27]

Jackson appealed to those who began to feel left out of the democratic process, both as Westerners within a political world dominated by Easterners and within Indiana, as persons hostile to deferring to the small group of men who ran the state government. Furthermore, Hoosiers also had reason to believe that their economic lives were being controlled from afar. By 1824 Westerners had just begun to emerge from the impact of the Panic of 1819. The Panic had taught Hoosiers how deeply embedded they were in the economy of the nation, as its ripple effect throughout the economy threatened many farmers' independence. Heretofore, one of the blessings of the political economy of the new nation had been its seeming imperviousness to the downturns that plagued the aristocratic nations of Europe.

Large-scale panics were often attributed to the machinations of aristocrats and large companies which had gained special privileges—e.g., the South Sea Bubble—but in a political economy built on a large number of free-holders, in whom sovereignty rested, such economic downturns were to be limited if not eliminated.[28] Because economic distress was expected to be constricted by both the political system and the economic strategy of "surplus produce," when it did occur, such distress signaled to many Hoosiers, as it did many other Americans, that the rotten corruption of aristocracy had crept back into the politics and the economics of the state and nation.

Convinced that forces of economic aristocracy were arrayed against them, they turned to Andrew Jackson, a man whose character was unassailable, for the reason that he defended his honor. In Jackson, his supporters found a man whose life replicated that of the Founding Fathers, in his glorious defense of New Orleans and thus the defense of the nation at large. In an era in which the Hartford Convention came to represent to many Westerners the symbolic attachment of many Easterners to the aristocratic pretensions of the English, a man like Jackson who had literally repelled a British invasion could be expected to repel figuratively the more insidious ideas of Anglophiles, such as aristocracy, whether moneyed, natural, or birthright.

Jackson was the winner in the 1824 election in Indiana, capturing a plurality that approached 50 percent.[29] Thirteen of the sixteen Indiana counties in which Jackson obtained a majority were in the hill country, and he won a plurality in seventeen of the hill country's twenty-three counties (see map 4.1).[30] His strength, reflected in the Salem convention, was concentrated in the central part of southern Indiana. Adams and Clay voters were concentrated in the interior of southeastern Indiana, above the broken country where streams cut their way down to the Ohio River, in townships where the "land is more level, more susceptible of cultivation, and will yield a greater amount of produce with less labor."[31] In many ways, the Whiggish tendencies of the region were probably the result of both the Mid-Atlantic origin of its residents and the region's commercial potential, but other smaller areas of Whig support emerged in hill country sections with Upland South majorities.[32]

Outside these specific Whig strongholds, the nebulous feeling of being left out of the political processes received substance with the "corrupt bargain." Hoosiers joined with many other Americans in detecting antidemocratic dealings when Henry Clay threw his weight behind John Quincy Adams. And when Adams offered Clay the position as secretary of state, it appeared to many that the offer came in exchange for Clay's support. For Enoch Parr, an avid Jackson supporter, such dealings paled next to Clay's greater crime of ignoring the will of the people:

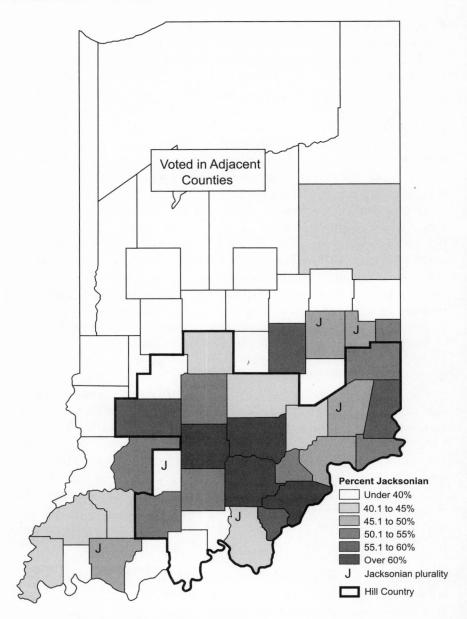

MAP 4.1 JACKSON'S STRENGTH IN INDIANA, 1824
Derived from *Indiana Election Returns, 1816–1851*, comp. Dorothy Riker and Gayle
Thornbrough (Indianapolis: Indiana Historical Bureau, 1960). (Martin/Nation)

It was discouvered that if Clay had been out of the way Jackson would have been elected by the people. Clay was a representative from Kentucky and the Legislature of that state instructed their Representatives to vote in Congress for Jackson as Adams got no vote in the state of Ky.[33]

By failing to obey the instructions of the Kentucky legislature, Clay had proven to be an enemy of the people, and his acceptance of the cabinet post, then considered a stepping-stone to the presidency, merely confirmed the antidemocratic corruption in Washington. Hoosier voters had been attracted to Jackson precisely because of his virtue, and to see their wishes denied by an act of corruption merely confirmed to many of them that they had been correct in their embrace of the Hero of New Orleans. By 1828, Jackson had solidified his support in the hill country, and much of the rest of Indiana joined with hill country farmers in supporting him (see map 4.2).

Jackson's positions were never clearly articulated. While Adams's supporters extrapolated from Jackson's opposition to the American System to suggest that he might be generally opposed to tariffs and internal improvements, they could not actually pin him down, and his replies to inquiries from Indiana's Governor Ray, who quietly supported Adams's administration, remained obscure.[34] Those who felt strongly about tariffs, internal improvements, and banks knew they had a secure friend in John Quincy Adams. But men who supported those measures, it would appear, could also support Jackson. Despite Enoch Parr's assertion that "the exertion made against Jackson from the start had been on account of his known hostality to a national bank," the bank was not an issue in the 1828 campaign. Jackson maintained the highest decorum of a man *standing* for office, by avoiding campaigning on issues. However, the actions of the banks in the wake of the Panic of 1819 helped to create the feelings of exclusion in which Andrew Jackson arose, and his eventual opposition to the Bank of the United States would tap into hill country Hoosiers' bad experiences with the bank and with banking in general.[35]

BANKS AND THE APPEAL OF ANDREW JACKSON

The Bank of the United States did not have a branch in the state of Indiana; its 1816 constitution, reflecting agrarian-republican fears of banks, forbade any bank not chartered by the state.[36] Many Hoosiers of the time believed that banks were a means by which others gained control over them, and they attempted to avoid just such dependence. In 1816, protesting the Presidential Proclamation against squatting, someone calling himself "Farmers & Patriots Rights" argued that such proclamations were issued

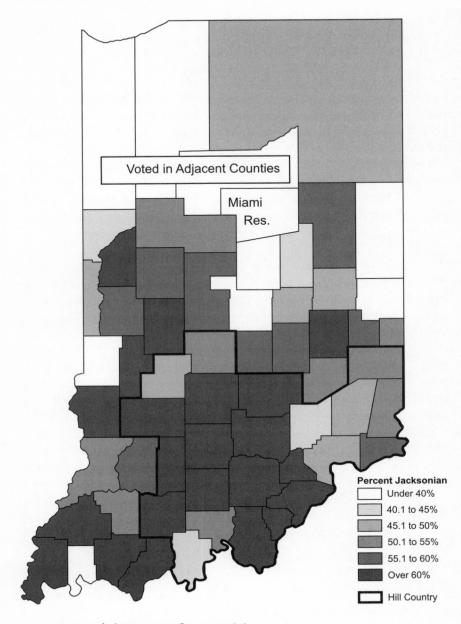

Voted in Adjacent Counties

Miami
Res.

Percent Jacksonian

☐ Under 40%

☐ 40.1 to 45%

☐ 45.1 to 50%

☐ 50.1 to 55%

☐ 55.1 to 60%

☐ Over 60%

☐ Hill Country

MAP 4.2 JACKSON'S STRENGTH IN INDIANA, 1828
Derived from *Indiana Election Returns, 1816–1851*, comp. Dorothy Riker and Gayle
Thornbrough (Indianapolis: Indiana Historical Bureau, 1960). (Martin/Nation)

by men who were "enemies to republican government, who deny to the people the exercise of rights which [the constitution and the laws founded thereon] secure to them." Going on, "Farmers & Patriots Rights" identified a second phase of this threat: "That our industrious and brave citizens may . . . from necessity and inability to move, be forced to come to the Bank of Vincennes to pay for *its credits,* use the notes issued upon that credit, to pay for a few acres, although they may be compelled to give their title as collateral security!"[37] This aversion to mortgaging and the belief that actions by the government served to force unwilling farmers to mortgage themselves helped to animate Hoosier fears of banks. Banks, to their mind, were ways for people to make money without working. As a wag in 1854 put it, "[Both bankers and brokers] want laws that will support hordes of non-producers at the expense of the producer." He ended by exhorting: "Watch well the course of the money mongers—the educated idle of all classes—it will not hurt even the college made preachers to look a little after them."[38] In this advice to the churches he was not alone: "When the Legislature shall have made these sections a part of the code of Indiana, the Churches will divest their bodies of such avaricious excrescences[;] of all shavers that infest the land, those praying shavers cut the deepest, longest, and most foul gashes."[39] Such calls for clerical oversight recalled the tradition of church discipline, absent within the world of banking by 1855. And the producerism enunciated by the first writer would become the dominant theme in the critique of banking in southern Indiana.

Despite the aversion to banking enunciated by "Farmers and Patriots Rights," many Hoosiers were forced to depend upon banks. Although in their day-to-day pursuit of the strategy of "surplus produce," they shielded their immediate existence from the grasping hands of the capitalist, their long-term goal of providing for their progeny forced them to sell for cash. All would have preferred gold and silver, but specie was often scarce in the hill country. Even the relatively stable Bank of the United States notes were hard to come by, as Molly Mace, who had a habit to support, revealed: "send in [a letter] some white powder for mine is almost gone and I cant do without it for it is all my life so dont fail the first United States bank I can git hold of I will send you down pay for it."[40] Most bank notes could not travel so well. Mace's brother, Jonathan Hardy, had no money to repay his debts back East despite some success. While his bank notes circulated at 50 percent below par in southern Indiana, they would not be accepted at all in the East.[41] And when the banks failed, it could mean disaster for many Hoosier settlers through the ripple effect. Edward Brush, who had stood security for friends and neighbors, had to pay up as others failed, and he in turn had to request his sister's help in collecting a debt: "I am in as much need of Money now as I can be."[42]

The problems with the value of bank notes exemplified much of what many Hoosiers (and many Americans) disliked about banks. In this period, banks were generally established when a group applied to the state for a charter, granting them certain privileges, not the least of which was limited liability. The investors were required by the charter to deposit a certain sum in specie into the vaults of the bank, and when that sum was acquired, they could open for business. Their primary function was not as a savings institution but rather as a lender, normally for a very short term, although many notes could be renewed. For this reason, the primary beneficiary of their existence was the mercantile class, something which annoyed many farmers. Once they were open for business, they proceeded to lend money, not from their specie reserves, but by issuing notes, which, allegedly, could be redeemed for specie upon application. However, because normally there was little chance that all these notes would be presented at once for redemption, most banks issued far more notes than they had specie on reserve. These notes, used to pay for goods and services, began to be used within communities and might wander great distances. As long as there was confidence in a bank, its notes satisfied the need for a circulating medium. But should a note travel too far from its home or rumors begin about the soundness of a bank, the bank's notes could suddenly lose much of their value. Those holding such notes might be economically broken. Therefore, when a bank's soundness had been called into question, it could precipitate a run on the bank, with far more notes being presented for redemption than the bank had specie. At this point, the bank would "suspend specie payments." Such an act would certainly depress the notes' value further. In the meantime, the bank would be relentlessly pursuing its debtors, demanding payment on the loans they had issued and foreclosing when payment was not made.

The unfairness of this system of banking was evident to many hill country Hoosiers. While the bank could suspend and resume payment of its debt with little fear of legal repercussions, it could completely take away the property—and thus the competency—of any person who owed it money. With the limited liability provisions granted its investors, they never had to put at risk their business or their family home, as did most farmers. Moreover, the fluidity of the value of the notes themselves was especially distressing. While the strategy of surplus produce may well have protected Hoosier farmers from immediate danger, the desire to re-create for their progeny their living situation compelled the hill country yeomanry to accumulate cash for such purchases. The wise ones bought land in small lots over the span of years, never trusting to carry these bank notes for very long. The unlucky and the foolhardy often found themselves holding worthless paper. Finally, persons on the periphery of the commercial society, like many Hoosier farmers, found themselves the target of persons holding devalued paper. Without information, Hoosiers would sometimes acquire bank notes that turned out to be worth less than they believed.

For Hoosier farmers, these problems seemed more than arbitrary. In their trading, they were somewhat at the mercy of the professional merchant, who had more knowledge of the bank note market. While they could often walk away from any particular trade, circumstances sometimes forced them to trade. Moreover, because of the need to provide for their children, farmers could not walk away from a lifetime of trading. Informed by their agrarian-republican ideals of the importance of farming and animated by their firm belief in receiving the fruits of their labor, many farmers resented the merchants' ability to determine not just the value of the goods but the value of the money that they presented. Instead of seeing merely the predictable actions of the marketplace for notes, they believed that merchants and banks—usually owned, after all, by the mercantile class, which was also the major recipient of the loans—were manipulating the value of money to their own ends. Such corruption, with its end in denying farmers the fruits of their labor and sometimes even their farms, was seemingly condoned by the equally corrupt machinations of the legislatures who approved the limited-liability charters in the first place. Both the cabal of the mercantile/banker class and the cabal of the governmental aristocrats—and they were often seen as the same people—were seeking to deny the mass of the people their independence and prosperity.

The Indiana Constitution had denied Hoosiers a close look at the Bank of the United States, which actually was run conservatively and from the mid-1820s on served as a brake on some of the excesses of the smaller banks. Southern Indiana residents did have an early exposure to one of the monstrosities of banking during the brief and infamous existence of the Lexington bank.[43] Hoosiers were also exposed to the dirty world of politics and banking among constitutionally legal banks, thanks to the state bank system.[44] Built on the back of the Bank of Vincennes, which had been established—along with the Madison Farmers' and Mechanics' Bank, which had opted out of the state system—by the territorial legislature, the State Bank of Indiana suffered greatly in the aftermath of the Panic of 1819. Yet fulfilling many Hoosiers' fears, politics had become sordidly involved in bank affairs.

> The bank was suspected as being unfairly managed at the time, and long before the [state government's] money was placed in it. It was generally

believed through the country it would fail, and none but those concerned in
banks, spoke to the contrary.[45]

The Brookville branch of the State Bank was the center of much intrigue. Local lore suggested the sources of animosity against the bank: "What
was known as the aristocratic party of Brookville evidently controlled the
policy of the bank and this may account in part for the opposition which
the bank had to meet."[46] Poor loans by the Vincennes main branch to a
steam mill operation owned by the directors of the Vincennes branch were
just one manifestation of the tendency of the bank to lend money to favor-
ites, among whom were many politicians. During the Panic of 1819, the
Bank of the United States and the Cincinnati Land Office began to refuse
notes issued on Indiana banks, a circumstance which forced the State Bank
at Vincennes and its branches at Corydon, Brookville, and Vevay as well as
the independent Farmers' and Mechanics' Bank in Madison to suspend
specie payment. Even after suspending specie payment, the directors of the
State Bank were busy raiding the surpluses, including federal government
deposits that had been placed in its vaults by Secretary of the Treasury
Crawford in his quiet attempt to build a political machine for 1824. When
the bank failed in late 1822, about two-thirds of the debt owed it was from
the steam mill operations, with almost another 10 percent independently
owed by the bank's directors. Yet in early 1822, long after it was widely recognized that the bank was in deep financial distress, the directors of the
bank declared a 40 percent dividend for some shareholders.[47] The experience of many Hoosiers had been that banks were dens of thieves and that
political intrigue could only make matters worse.

Beyond the swindling that characterized the State Bank, many Hoosiers
held a far deeper suspicion that banks were devices by which aristocrats
attempted to manipulate farmers' lives. A meeting of Washington County
residents resolved that banking threatened their "rights as Republican
people" and ultimately their independence.[48] Some saw the hand of the
Bank of the United States reaching across state lines to distress local banks,
and they raised the specter of the monster.

> We dread the danger arising from a powerful moneyed institution, conduct-
> ing its gigantic operations under the *specious name* of the *United States' Bank.*
> . . . Should their paper become the only circulating medium, and all other
> withdrawn, the nation would necessarily become dependent upon their ca-
> price—must bend to their inclinations or be deprived of that which is so
> essential to their prosperity.

Added the Brookville *Enquirer,* which would support Clay in 1824, protection from the dangers of the Second Bank of the United States lay in a

multitude of local banks: "We must have a paper circulation, if we have any, and the only question is, what kind is to be preferred."[49] Others found more safety in specie and saw a silver lining in the Panic of 1819: "There has been a "damp" in trade since my arrival in this country, I think, partly owing to the insolvent state of our banks; but, however, that evil is rapidly removing and the credit of bank paper is dying every day, in consequence of which, specie is beginning to circulate more fluently."[50] Like many Hoosiers, John Wynn was convinced that specie held its value. Compared to the wide fluctuations of paper money, gold and silver must have seemed stable. Wynn was joined by many Hoosiers in believing that specie was the only legitimate representation of value.

Since many Hoosiers experienced corruption in local banks, not all Hoosiers would have joined the Brookville *Enquirer* in seeing local banks as a means of curbing the grasp of the Bank of the United States. Richard Hopkins, standing for the state legislature, wrote:

> The bank question appears to agitate the public mind; every one begins to know and already has felt the bad effects of this monstrous evil. It has introduced pride, avarice, and idleness, with their concomitant evils on one hand. . . . The introduction of a moneyed aristocracy, immediately growing into so many little monarchies in every town where one is established . . . is a small part of the bad effects of this gigantic evil that has been stalking through our land to the injury of the good citizens. . . . The very principles of banking is corruption; they are generally supported by fraud. . . . The citizens of this great nation, the boast of empires and whose authors is liberty and independence, is almost tottering on the brink of ruin by the introduction of this host of banks and the scourge of mankind.[51]

Identifying the source of the 1819 hard times—"Banks! Banks!! and the rage for speculation"—Lycergus called for the bankers to return to simpler livelihoods:

> Would it not be better, far better, for people, who have already nearly ruined themselves by dealing in speculations and banks—I say, would it not be better for them again to follow the plough and handle the reaping hook; to throw the shuttle and the sledge, and obtain that by industry which they can neither do by speculation or banking—an honest livelihood?[52]

The remedy to the distress caused by the banks was political. Banks existed thanks to privileges granted to them by the government, and some Hoosiers believed that the government, as the sovereign will of the people, should be able to take those privileges away. Understanding "that the people of the state were actually [divided into] parties viz. those in favor of Banks and those opposed to them," T.J.L. wrote to the Salem *Tocsin* to argue that bankers were aristocrats, and the solution was democracy:

> The question then arises, is there a majority of such men [aristocrats] in Indiana? I am certain there is not. Then where lies the blame of the present state of this? in both the representatives and people.[53]

For T.J.L., the masses had to organize to defeat the shadowy party of the few who supported banks. Politics had created the banks; politics could eliminate it.

As the worst problems brought forth by the Panic of 1819 faded into the past and the State Bank folded its operation, banking ceased to be the most emotional question in the politics of the hill country. Just as many Hoosiers desired and John Wynn observed, specie and Second Bank of the United States notes became the circulating medium, although a scarce one as opponents had warned. Nevertheless, banking had served to reinforce among many Hoosiers the feeling that the political economy was threatened by small bands of men, especially those currently in power in Washington and the Indiana capital. Men with such feelings began to coalesce around Jackson in 1824, and with the evidence of the "Corrupt Bargain," Jackson began to represent the outsiders' savior, and he won the presidency in 1828. Three years into his term, when Nicholas Biddle decided to submit the Second Bank of the United States (BUS) for recharter in 1832, he believed that Jackson would not dare veto it with the election approaching. Biddle, safely ensconced in the rapidly commercializing East, perhaps could not understand the great antipathy for banks among so many Westerners and Southerners. Jackson had risen to power on the vague feelings of powerlessness which circulated around banks and banking, and when he chose to veto the BUS recharter, he tapped into those simmering feelings.

While Biddle's recharter bill worked its way through Congress, there were few voices raised in the hill country against continuing the Bank of the United States.[54] It was only with the veto, as Jackson took Biddle's challenge and made the BUS the key issue of the 1832 campaign, that Hoosier Democrats rediscovered their hatred of it. Clay supporters, on the other hand, stood behind the BUS, arguing that the BUS assisted the West and its farmers, lending to them at 7 percent and thus allowing "them to realize a profit of 10, 15, or 20 per cent."[55]

Immediately after the veto, rumors flew that the veto had caused a drop in prices. Denying that there was any such drop, the Salem *Western Annotator* nevertheless said:

> But suppose that the veto has actually caused a fall in the price of wheat, or any other article of agriculture, what does it prove? Only this, that the United

States Bank possesses the power to regulate the price of every article our farmers raise—to build up and pull down whom and when it pleases; and that, if not checked, it will be able to regulate not only our public matters, but everything, even down to our household affairs.[56]

The specter of the bank's entering into household affairs, thus threatening Hoosier farmers' competencies, was a powerful one, and Jacksonian rhetoricians specifically singled out farmers. As Enoch Parr understood it, "The parties shewed themselves affectually to be the Aristocry of Wilth and the Democracy of numbers—in my view it was whether the Bank of the U. S. and the moneyed power elsewhare should rule the republick or the voice of the people."[57] The question of the Bank of the United States was to be determined by the election of 1832.

But the people of the West have too much the spirit of their forefathers— that spirit which proclaimed and maintained the independence of America, to be drove to the polls like the serfs of Europe, and made [to] vote their master's will[.] They will rise in the majesty of their strength, on the first Monday in November next, and burst the chains forged by the Bank to enslave them.[58]

Through most of the hill country of southern Indiana, Jackson's supporters stood by their man in 1832, but in the southeastern part of the state, a slow shift away from Jackson continued. A close examination of Franklin County, which exhibited such a shift, reveals that much of the shift took place in the Brookville Township, the home of the county seat and commercial center of Brookville.[59] Those with business interests who had supported Jackson in 1828 were scared by his policies. In general, the 1832 election, despite its status as a referendum on the Bank of the United States, did not show major shifts in voting; it did not draw large numbers of new voters to the polls nor did the issues repel voters. In many ways, the election served to confirm that the coalition built by Jackson in 1828 responded well to the Bank War, because it symbolized their greatest fears, fears grounded in personal experience with the arbitrariness and corruption of banks.

"The Republic is safe another four years," pronounced Bazil B. Edmonston.[60] Edmonston had earlier written that "Jackson's strength is increasing in this state to a vast amount in consequence of the veto he put on the bank bill to prevent the moneyed aristocratic party in America and the lords in England from swindling away all the labourers' money and drain our specie out of the United States."[61] For Edmonston, as well as for lesser partisans in the hill country, the election of 1832 was of paramount importance, for it confirmed that the Bank of the United States would no longer have power over their lives. Jackson's victory was, in their eyes, a victory of the people over those like Clay who craved money and power and sought to use the government to gain their desires.[62]

As many Whigs saw it, Jackson's exercise of the veto had been an arbitrary exercise of power, but in the people's affirmation of Jackson, they had asserted that his power was legitimate. For many Hoosiers, indeed for many Americans, the power granted to the Second Bank of the United States threatened their independence and thus the potential to replicate their circumstances for their children. And when such a power was not from within their own community or even their state, the potential for power to be exercised arbitrarily and without regard to any morality seemed great. Instead, only the desire for profits moved those who headed and invested in the Bank of the United States, and such a desire could subsume the interests of both the investors' various communities and the nation itself—hence the great emphasis on the patriotism of Jackson, Benton, and others, who would never sell out the country.

BANKING AND INTERNAL IMPROVEMENTS AT THE STATE LEVEL

Yet for many Hoosiers, the question remained, what was to be the alternative to the Bank of the United States? Many thought that once bank notes had disappeared, specie would fill the vacuum, but others asserted: "We are a commercial people." Granted, they argued, there had been bank failures in the past, making some people's prejudices easy to understand, but no prudent banks failed; it was only "necessary to guard in future against mismanagement."[63] Jackson's attack on the Bank of the United States resonated not only with farmers who pursued a strategy of "surplus produce," but also with some of their more market-oriented neighbors, both farmers and merchants. After all, they, too, might fear that a large organization could manipulate the marketplace, and they, too, may have responded to fears that foreign interests might dictate the BUS's policies. The anti-BUS forces may well be seen as two camps, roughly following what later would be seen as "soft-money" and "hard-money" Democrats. Soft-money Democrats tended to support state control of banking; hard-money Democrats fought for a complete return to gold and silver.

The distinctions between the two camps reflected two versions of the "localist ethic," in many ways reflecting different moral horizons. For some, morality could only be regulated in tight local communities, and thus trade at a distance was morally ambiguous and could best be maintained by reliance upon specie, with its seemingly fixed value. Others followed the logic of the Brookville *Enquirer,* in arguing that banks were a legitimate fixture at the state level, where they could be more locally controlled. A third possibility, still in its infancy in 1832, was that private interests could compete, without government privilege, thus regulating themselves through the invisible hand of the marketplace.

These three positions also found manifestation in the internal improvement schemes of the 1830s. Some held to the notion that internal improvements were best achieved by the action of the local government, and the only involvement of the federal and state governments would be in the distribution of federal land moneys (the Three Per Cent Fund) on a per capita basis. Others believed that the state had the legitimate duty to pursue larger internal improvement projects, while only a few at this point believed that private enterprise could undertake alone any projects of such magnitude.

Andrew Jackson's success in limiting the reach of the federal government into the lives of Hoosiers shifted the scene of conflict to the state government, where Jacksonians with broader visions than their more localist friends could join with the more nationalist Whigs-to-be in promoting banking and internal improvement schemes. Localism would continue to play a major part in the construction of both a second State Bank and the Mammoth Internal Improvements Bill, as well as the concurrent fight over *ad valorem* taxation. Many joined Enoch Parr in understanding implicitly, if not logically, the connection between the three:

> It was in the summer of 1834 that a excitement was raised to change the form of taxation to that of the ad valorum system, and with that change Gov. Noble recommended the borrowing of a large sum of money for the purpose of creating a State Bank and amediately on this was recommended the system of internal improvement.[64]

Important in understanding the state debates over these issues would be the recognition that many Hoosier farmers were not engaged in commercial farming, yet depended upon the marketplace to achieve familial goals, and that such farmers were common throughout the state, with heavy concentrations of them in parts of the hill country. For these farmers, all of these schemes amounted to taxation, not on their profits but on their competency. And any threat to their competency was, in their agrarian republican vision, a threat to the nation. In time they would have to modify their strategies, to create the most risk-free means of maintaining their competency and providing for their children. That many people modified their economic strategies to correspond to the changes in banking, taxation, and transportation did not mean that these people necessarily desired the changes.

The debates are best seen through the lens of the localist tradition. The terms of the fights often circulated around geographical distribution, and the debate broached the question of what is the public good, asking how any measures which benefited the populace unevenly could be seen as serving the public good. At the state level, too, the questions tended to take on an individualist cast, tapping into notions of egalitarianism. Whether a road ended in Lawrenceburg or Aurora, or whether a branch bank was located in Jeffersonville or New Albany, all could have a profound impact on identifiable individuals. And because of this impact, questions of "exclusive privilege" took on additional importance.

The rhetoric over the state banks echoed the earlier national debate. Indeed, the impetus for the second State Bank came from Jackson's veto, as the circulating medium in Indiana had been specie and Bank of the United States notes out of its branches in Louisville and Cincinnati. Not surprisingly, some resisted the State Bank in the same terms as they had the Bank of the United States. Enoch Parr remembered the issues of that day:

> Banking is always accompanied with an excess of speculating, and speculating creates no new welth, and of corse the labouring part of the people are fleeced unproceived, and the few is inriched at the expence of the many.

Like many hill country Hoosiers, Parr was not completely opposed to banks, but he sought to protect the mass of the people from their operations.

> It may do to incorporate companies to do a thing that an individual cannot do. And if banks are incorporated and restricted from issuing small notes they might answer a valueable purpose. . . . But if the banks were restricted from issuing notes of a less denomination than fifty dollars or if it was twenty-five dollars then if the banks should stop payment there would be specia enough in the land to answer the purpose of the labouring class of people and speculators would be the greatest sufferer.[65]

Parr, like many Jacksonians, sought to create a certain space for merchants to operate, a realm of the marketplace separate from the ordinary pursuit of day-to-day survival. Indeed, the strategies pursued by many farmers necessitated these two realms. In support of the banks, Senator Graham, representing Jackson, Jennings, and Scott counties, detailed how banks would benefit farmers.

> But, sir, the idea held out that farmers are to be benefitted by borrowing in bank is entirely illusory. Banks are adapted to commercial points where men in trade can use large sums for short periods, but every man who understands the effects and policy of banking, will bear me out in saying that the

only safe course by which farmers can be benefitted by Banks, is that they afford facilities to merchants and traders, and enables them to purchase the farmer's produce, beef, pork, and stock, but whenever I see a farmer borrow money in bank and mortgage his farm as security, I say to myself, "that farm will soon change owners."[66]

Nevertheless, opposition existed to the banks in general and to the State Bank in particular. The Salem *Indiana Phoenix* reported that "we understand that in one or two distant neighborhoods from Salem, in our county, there is some opposition going ahead to the incorporation of a State Bank."[67] Far from the commercial activity of Salem, such neighborhoods saw less need for supporting the activities of merchants.

Supporters of the bank had the edge. Questioning the logic of the distant neighborhoods' opposition, the *Phoenix* acknowledged:

We know that strong objections can be brought against the policy of such a measure at a time like the present; but we must all know that unless something is speadily done to check a worse evil, the whole country goes to ruin. The evil to which we allude, is that of charging from 25 to 50 per cent on money. Give us a bank and usurious practices within its reach will be knocked in the head. Nothing else could induce us at this time to favor the bank project.[68]

As we saw in the case of Cornelius Pering, the *Phoenix* was correct in asserting that lenders would find ways around usury laws, but many hill country denizens could not understand why a bank would prove to be any more scrupulous. State Senator Graham saw the answer in state control: "If the State assumes the responsibility, she should have sufficient controls, such control as would at all times enable her to guard the rights of her citizens."[69] Moreover, many also raised the specter of the state's being flooded by the worthless notes of distant states, beyond the local control of Hoosiers. The promises of the bank were many; the question, as the pro-Jackson Salem *Western Annotator* understood it, was whether the people truly wanted a State Bank.

If [the people] are thoroughly convinced that a State Bank would afford permanent relief, that a fresh spring would be given to industry, and new life imparted to every kind of business, we say let the measure be adopted. But if, on the contrary, all this is not clearly seen—or it is to prove a paralytic on industry—a tax on the resources of the country, let it be resisted.[70]

The gauntlet had been thrown down, and the Jacksonian forces conceded the necessity to respect the will of the people.

Despite much debate, the 1832–33 session of the Indiana General Assembly could not reach agreement on establishing a state bank, and the legislators' having left that business unfinished, most of the electorate perceived that those elected for the 1833–34 term would take up the issue as their first order of business. In the Hill Country, both supporters and foes of Jackson were elected, with Jackson's enemies concentrated in the Ohio Valley and in major commercial areas. Yet pro- and anti-Jackson forces joined together to support the bank bill. The fear of banks did not find expression in the legislature.

Many Jacksonians supported the second State Bank because it was well regulated, and the subsequent history of the bank justified that support. The State Bank was sufficiently local for some Jacksonians, and the vast array of branches satisfied even some extreme localists, especially those from towns blessed with a branch. Because the State Bank's charter mitigated many of the worst features of nineteenth-century banks, it weathered many storms, although state oversight of the bank was sometimes more lax than men like Senator Graham had hoped. Perhaps the greatest testimony to its solid foundation was that it somehow survived the severe financial problems brought about by the second of the great commercial schemes of the 1830s in Indiana, the Mammoth Internal Improvements Bill.

As part of his program to restore government to the people, Andrew Jackson had also questioned some federal involvement in internal improvement projects. While Jackson's position on internal improvements was not hard and fast, he did reinvigorate the notion that governments had only a limited responsibility to provide for internal improvements and that those improvements had to benefit the public generally.[71] New conflicts emerged over state-funded improvements, as some hill country localists who opposed federal internal improvements saw a certain consistency in supporting the more localized projects of the state, which stood to benefit a large bulk of the people. The specific need to appeal to people's localist beliefs forced the state to pursue a program far beyond its means. A shift to a pro–internal improvements stance took place in southern Indiana and, along with massive support from central and northern Indiana, permitted the Mammoth Internal Improvements Bill to pass. However, many other southern Indiana localists argued that the state should not engage in such a massive effort.

Opponents of the internal improvements projects used a number of interrelated points to drive home the problems with the undertaking. Not the least of the reasons was that their particular locale would be bypassed by this allegedly general operation. It was that very localist spirit which had created a program of its size in the first place, as each county sought a project within its own borders. For the most localist, though, even a short distance from the projects seemed to deny people the benefits. Thus, for many opponents, the problem was that the scheme benefited the general public unevenly. Some even recognized that internal improvements tended to benefit specifically those most involved in the marketplace, and people who would rather not use them still suffered higher taxes. These opponents often turned to the more general system of using federal money from lands to finance a series of cheaper roads, which would benefit more people while placing little tax demand on those who did not use them.

However, among the opposition were voices that echoed complaints like those raised against the banks, with suspicions of debt and fears of loss of independence: "It is therefore important . . . that proud ambition shall not bolt over reasonable bounds, and plunge the State into that awful abyss from whence there is not escape—the whirlpool of *debt*."[72] Specters of European aristocracy again entered the rhetoric: "Are the freemen of Dearborn county, who pride themselves in being citizens of Indiana, a state destined at no distant day to be the third or fourth state in the Union, are they willing she shall be mortgaged to the aristocratic lords of Europe?"[73] For others, those who threatened their existence were closer to home: "That course of policy is a bad one which is calculated to immerse the State in debt, and render her *tributary* for ages to some other state—say New York."[74] The language of debt, with its accompanying loss of independence, was transferred from the farmers' own lives to the situation of their state, and with the reintroduction of an aristocracy which sought to control others, the language further paralleled many Hoosiers' personal fears.

In important ways, though, the threat was not just to the sovereignty of the state but to many individuals' own competency, because the changes produced by the internal improvement schemes seemed, to some, to pull them further into the commercial world. With the accompanying scheme of *ad valorem* taxes, some farmers were drawn into a world in which internal improvements located near their property raised the value of their property and thus raised their taxes. *Ad valorem* property taxes, whereby an assessor fixed the value of the property upon which taxes were then paid, replaced classification, whereby land was classified according to quality, upon which a tax was then paid per acre of a given classification. The quality of the land, of course, was only one of the variables that would normally determine its value—proximity to towns, of course, would make land more valuable. Therefore, the movement to *ad valorem* taxation was a movement to a more market-driven notion of value, as opposed to classification, which generally assessed one's ability to cultivate "surplus produce."

Ad valorem taxation first passed in 1833, but the original law establishing it was widely hated. The *Rising Sun Times* denounced it, asserting that two-thirds of the citizenry were opposed.[75] One local resident explained his opposition:

> According to my construction of the law, a man who owns a farm in the vicinity of a grist mill, tannery, distillery, carding machine, &c. must be taxed for that privilege. There is about as much justice in this as there is in taxing one man higher than another, because his land happens to be in the vicinity of a town. If my neighbor chooses to lay off a town on his farm, I must pay more tax, because, for sooth, my land is in the vicinity of it. I could not prevent my neighbor from doing this—I did not desire him to do it—the town cannot benefit me—yet all this argues nothing in the eyes of the lawmakers—I must pay more tax.[76]

Likewise, to be located near one of the new internal improvement projects would raise a person's taxes, even if the farmer did not choose to reap any benefits from it.

For many farmers who pursued the risk-averse strategy of "surplus produce," internal improvements did not promise many benefits. While the state legislature did not propose to tax the people to pay for the improvements, there were other costs involved. The tolls on the new roads, railroads, and canals were deemed sufficient to cover the costs of retiring the bonds sold to build them, and as one proponent noted, such tolls were less than wagon transportation was at the time.[77] Yet as C. W. Hutchen retorted, many farmers did not pay haulage.

> Every farmer needs a wagon and team, and on a good road he may transport his surplus products to the head of market without visible expense, and at a season when his work is not pressing his attention at home. Every dollar thus saved by our own labor is calculated to enrich the state; improve her internal condition, and aid the farmer in his business—and when he is prosperous, the whole country must flourish.[78]

Yet the benefit that many localist-minded Hoosiers saw in internal improvements was not in reducing costs to the producer but in providing a home market, whereby a farmer did not have to leave his family for extended periods of time and risk the dangers of travel and of distant marketplaces.

For profit-minded Hoosiers, the benefits of the system were even greater. Governor Noah Noble of Brookville looked to the Ohio effort and saw the increased land values:

> The money thus procured . . . immediately benefitted the people by being thrown into circulation in payment for labor, materials and subsistence, and as soon as the works were completed, the people and the States were repaid many fold by the increased demands and higher prices for their produce; by the activity imparted to every branch of industry and by the enhancement of the landed property of the country. The additional value alone of the lands in the district of the country intersected by the Miami Canal in Ohio, far exceeds the cost of construction.[79]

While higher prices for "surplus produce" might benefit the multitudes, those who stood to reap the greatest rewards were those most involved in the commercial world. Implicit in Noble's message, however, was the notion that all could find wealth and the means to pay their taxes by selling their land. For Hoosiers who believed that their land secured their independence and who sought to establish their children in a similar situation, such notions of profit must have seemed ludicrous. In many ways, these notions may have reflected the particular vision of Noble and others, who saw many early settlers, especially the squatters, as impediments to an expanding economy. As in the image of the squatter who sold his improvements and moved on, many believed that a policy which drove out the lazy and the improvident would be a benefit to the entire community.

With the rise of the Mammoth Internal Improvements Bill, the question of *ad valorem* taxation was raised again. For many hill country Hoosiers, such taxation was a mixed blessing. While it seemed to tax citizens unfairly for proximity to towns and internal improvements, even if they did not benefit from them, already by 1835 it was apparent to hill country farmers that under such a form of taxation, other parts of the state, because of more improvements and greater commercial potential, would bear more of the burden. Hill country legislators led the fight in 1836 to modify the law's provisions to make it more equitable. In general, the fight followed the newly formed party lines, with Democrats advocating the modifications and Whigs opposing them, but Whig supporters of the measure—necessary because they controlled the House of Representatives—were disproportionately from the hill country, while southern Indiana Democrats voted almost unanimously for the changes.[80] A return to the classification system of taxation may have forced many hill country farmers to pay higher taxes, so they conceded the change, despite lingering ideological doubts about the *ad valorem* basis.

One of the alleged merits of the Mammoth Internal Improvements Bill was that it did not depend upon taxation at all, thus reducing the burden upon the general public and placing the financing on the backs of those who chose to use the new roads, railroads, and canals. This reliance on tolls came about because the initial cries against improvement concentrated on the fact that tax revenues would be going toward projects which would not benefit all taxpayers alike:

> I would ask the editors, of what benefit a railway from Madison to India-napolis, and another from Lawrenceburgh to the same place, and a canal along the valley of Whitewater—of what benefit these contemplated improve-ments can be to the inhabitants of the interior—*those distant from the routes of those thoroughfares?*

To this writer, the authors of such a design were obvious: "Those who ex-pect to be benefitted by the [Mammoth Bill] are the persons, and the only persons, to be found warmly engaged in its support; while all others are opposed to it as being repugnant to the pure principles of Republicanism, and destructive to the interests and subversive of the rights that the gener-ous nature of republican governement is wont to confer."[81]

Despite forcing the plan's designers to promise not to tax the whole state, some continued to oppose it, arguing that government should never act in such a manner as to benefit the few.[82] They prophesied that in pledging the full faith of the state, the state government might well have to reach into its residents' pockets one day, if the revenues from the projects failed to fund the bond payments.

> Now, fellow citizens, I am opposed to *any* bill that commits the *whole* for the benefit of the *few*. I am opposed to anything which is partial in its opera-tions; and I despise the spirit of selfishness in whatever shape I see it. Our state is not able to do justice to all in a scheme of internal improvements. She is already committed for as much as I am willing she shall be—she has bought the Bank up on tick.[83]

For some in southern Indiana, though, the opposition rested on their competitors gaining the advantage of improvements paid for by state dol-lars; much of the original opposition came from commercial centers by-passed by the improvements. The Vevay editor decried the forces of specu-lation that surrounded the Mammoth Bill, but then revealed his deeper motive: "The bill is as extensive as the wildest speculator ever hoped for; but Switzerland County is neglected."[84] Despite the opposition to the in-ternal improvements bill, few said they opposed internal improvements per se.

Most criticisms of the Mammoth Bill did not oppose the notion that government was to provide such improvements, but merely questioned the means, both financial and physical, by which these improvements were provided. Some believed that macadamized roads would have sufficed at a fraction of the cost of the railroads and canals included in the Mammoth Bill, and such roads would "accomodate a much greater portion of the *people*."[85] In urging the building of roads rather than canals and railroads, C. W. Hutchen noted:

> An economical farmer will first erect a good barn; next a commodious dwelling. The former is essential, the latter comfortable. Good turnpike roads are essential; Rail roads and Canals would be comfortable.[86]

For many, the source of funds for such endeavors should be the Three Per Cent Fund, that portion of the proceeds from federal land sales that was given to the state to finance internal improvements.[87] The most radical proposition regarding internal improvements was that the Three Per Cent Funds should pass from the federal government through the state government to local governments, who would best spend it, but this proposition was embraced by only a small minority.

While Democrats would later remember the era as one in which the Whigs had coerced the people into going against their better judgment, both Whigs and Democrats went wholeheartedly for the Mammoth Internal Improvements Bill. Whether pursuing commercial agriculture or merely selling their surplus produce, farmers welcomed the promise of better markets, better often being defined as local ones, within the oversight of the face-to-face community. Much of the hill country had poor water resources for the transportation of goods to market, although its bottom tier of counties bordered the Ohio River. An early traveler noted:

> This state . . . has not sufficient water communication, and thus the inhabitants have no market for their produce. There is not in this state any river of importance, the Ohio which washes its southern border excepted.[88]

Without satisfactory river transportation, travel in Indiana in 1835 was a difficult proposition, and even the most committed localists saw a certain purpose in connecting their neighborhood with more distant ones. Whether it be as macadamized roads or railroads, most Hoosiers believed that it was the proper place of government to build some forms of connection between their various locales. The sale of surplus products was the basis of the reproduction of the family, in the largest sense, and with the promise of no new taxes, the new internal improvements project fit neatly into the risk-averse strategies of many hill country farmers.

In many ways the Mammoth Internal Improvements Bill was mammoth, precisely because of the localist sentiments of many Hoosiers. Believing that the government should pursue no policy that favored one citizen over another, in one fell swoop, Hoosier legislators created a system that served the needs of a large majority of its citizenry, with nearly every county getting a project. And the votes in the Indiana House followed the map of the improvements (see map 4.3).[89] To serve one's county was to vote for a plan in which one's county was included. A Monroe county "voter" remarked that the county "has heretofore been well represented both in the Senate and House. . . . In fact, she has shared largely in the benefits of the Internal Improvements Bill."[90] Many, of course, saw this system as logrolling.[91] However, the system was larger than it needed to be merely to win approval.

In 1837, these questions came to a head in the gubernatorial race. The Democrats did not even field a candidate, and the race was between two Whigs, incumbent governor David Wallace, the major proponent of the Mammoth system, and John Dumont of Switzerland County, bypassed by the internal improvements bill. Democrats gravitated to Wallace in counties where the internal improvements were planned, and Whigs backed Dumont in counties bypassed by the scheme. This tendency was most apparent in southern Indiana, especially along the Ohio and the Wabash (see map 4.4). Nevertheless, a more subtle trend was also apparent. Whereas in the northern half of the state, many seemed to embrace internal improvements although they lived quite far from the routes, the effect was more limited in southern Indiana. Of course, the internal improvements scheme was primarily a means of providing markets for farmers and merchants in central and northern Indiana. The relative lack of enthusiasm in the hill country reflected in part the terrain, which made hill country commercial centers difficult to reach. In addition to the physical difficulties of participating in the market expansion brought about by the internal improvements projects, there were more psychological and moral difficulties. Residents in northern Indiana perhaps were more willing to engage in long-distance trade, trade outside their moral communities.

In many ways, the ambivalence about trade more common in the hill country helps to explain why some southern Indiana communities voted for Dumont despite being on a line of development. In Owen, Monroe, and Lawrence counties, around 60 percent of the voters embraced Dumont, although a road or railroad was planned to connect them to New Albany. In Owen County, a canal leading from Indianapolis to Evansville on the Ohio River was also a possibility.[92] At the more local level, such distinctions also appear. In Franklin County's Whitewater Township, voters supported the Dumont ticket, as did their neighbors to the south in Logan Township, Dearborn County, despite the Whitewater Canal planned through them. Like the counties elsewhere in the hill country, they would have benefited greatly from the improvements—that is, if their residents intended to use them.

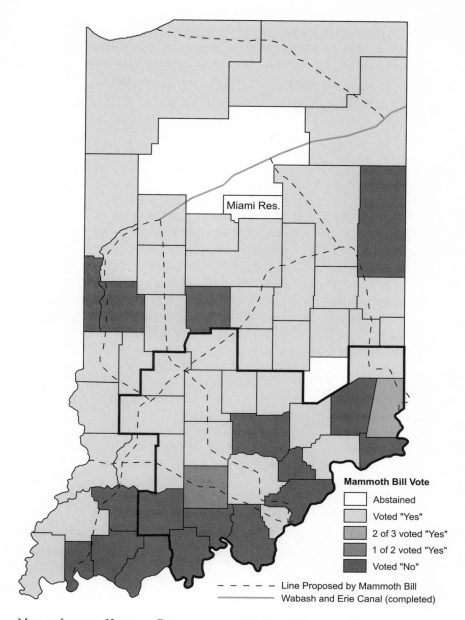

MAP 4.3 INDIANA HOUSE OF REPRESENTATIVES VOTE ON MAMMOTH INTERNAL IMPROVEMENTS BILL, 1836
Derived from Indiana legislature, 1835–36 *House Journal*, 225–32. (Martin/Nation)

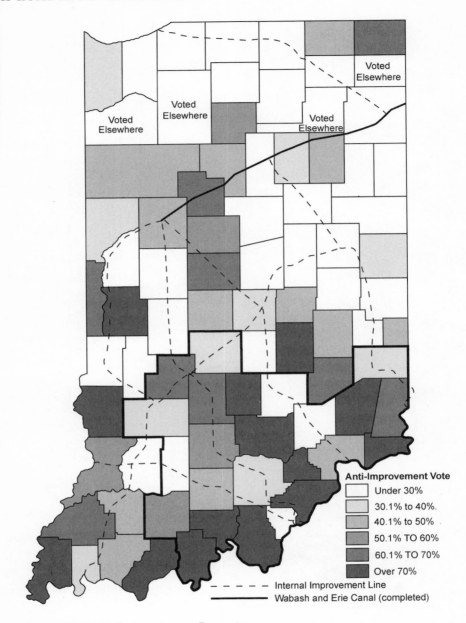

Map 4.4 Indiana Gubernatorial Race, 1837
Derived from *Indiana Election Returns, 1816–1851*, comp. Dorothy Riker and Gayle
Thornbrough (Indianapolis: Indiana Historical Bureau, 1960). (Martin/Nation)

Such a local examination is also instructive in understanding other reasons for support and opposition to the internal improvements projects. In
Franklin County, the major marketplaces tended to support the plan, as
did those areas with relatively flat and fertile plains. In Dearborn County,
Lawrenceburg, beneficiary of all the traffic on the Whitewater Canal, was
solidly for internal improvements, and the commercial center of Rising
Sun, home to one of the most strident editorial voices against the Mam-
moth Bill because it was excluded from its benefits, nevertheless supported
Wallace. The rest of the county, perhaps burnt by the failure to include a
Lawrenceburg and Indianapolis Railroad, got behind Dumont.

There were, then, several ways in which hill country Hoosiers reacted to
the Mammoth Internal Improvements Bill. The bill itself had been defined
in localist terms, attempting to benefit a large number of people by ensuring that most locales received some state aid. Opposition to the bill arose
from both commercial interests angered that their competitors received
special benefits from the state and from farmers who believed that the improvements, coupled with *ad valorem* taxes, threatened their risk-averse
strategy embodied in the phrase "surplus produce." Yet that strategy, with
its long-term goal of creating farms for farmers' progeny, demanded that
farmers take their surplus to market, and thus the internal improvements
scheme also found favor. But because hill country Hoosiers were far more
localist in their orientation, they perceived the benefits of the internal improvement scheme as less general in nature, only affecting the small population near where the improvements were to be laid. The hill country therefore served as the stronghold for both Whig and Jacksonian opponents of
the state internal improvement project.[93]

As we shall see, the failure of the Mammoth Internal Improvements
scheme vindicated the vision of the ultra-Jacksonian opponents of the
project like Enoch Parr.

> From the firs mention of the system of borrowning money upon the credit
> of the state for the purpose Banking or internal improvement I used all the
> influence I was master of to prevent it. And I have made these remark to
> shew the ruinous effect of a state or individual borrowing. But particularly a
> state to borrow money for any proposed object whatever in time of peace is
> to involve the whole or almost the whole in a kind of snatch game to see who
> shall get the most of the money borrowed.

For Enoch Parr, the problems of the state coalesced with his Jeffersonian-
Jacksonian ideas.

> No man that was in the convention that framed the constitution of Indiana intended to give the power to the legislature to borrow ten milion of dollars to squander on a visionary object. Neither did the framers of the constitution of the U.S. grant power to congress to incorperate a banking company altho the aristocrasy has pretend to desern the power and shew it to the people by first shewing the *necessaty* and then the *advantage* and then pretending to act for the *common welfare*. But it is the few, and them the aristocrasy that is advantagd in the end.[94]

With hindsight, Parr's vision was clear. In the more immediate aftermath, Bazil Edmonston likewise praised his son, a state representative, for his opposition to the bill.

> When our internal improvements bill in this state was introduced he went against it. He cursed the bill and swore the State was ruined and his proficy has proved itself to be true. There was only 18 against it and they are rising into a large majority by the wild acts of Wigs, and insolvent debtors before the State is ruined and we are the most divided people on politics you ever witnessed. Friendship, fellowship and neighborship it has don worse, its gotten into the churches and marred the brotherly love. They [the Whigs] steer a course similar to the tories in the Revolutionary War.[95]

Certainly there were voices against the project, and the political world became rancorous. Despite Edmonston's suggestion that neighbors fought with neighbors, the near-unanimity of many sections would suggest that the differences were not so divisive. Many times, the voices in opposition were scattered and ignored.

From a distance many have seen the flaws in the Mammoth Internal Improvements Bill. For both Whigs and Democrats, the eventual failure of the project would engender a certain reluctance to pursue public projects of any scope and a new espousal of private enterprise, although each arrived at these positions by far different routes. After the full ramifications of the program eventually emerged, Hoosiers were reluctant to give the Whigs much power, and Whigs were afraid to exercise it too grandly; moreover, from the internal improvement debacle, Whigs learned the limits of government involvement in the economy. For Democrats the effect was to reinvigorate their fear of activist government—a fear that in the internal improvements debate had been in tension with their belief in government's following the desires of the people. From the humiliating experiences of the state of Indiana with Eastern and foreign financiers, many Democrats relearned the dangers of distant markets and the amorality of the financial world. In response, they, too, would embrace the notion that government should not be involved in the economy, that it was not its place to award benefits and, conversely, to deny privileges.[96]

THE SAVING GRACE FOR THE WHIGS: A FAVORITE SON

For the moment, however, the great debate over internal improvements had little effect on presidential elections. Commenting on the 1836 local election, the *Indiana American* noted that the "result is no test of the strength of parties as the Van Burenites in some townships voted for the Harrison candidates and in other townships, hundreds of Harrison men voted for Van Buren candidates."[97] Neither in 1836 nor in 1840 was Indiana's preference for a president based on the great ideological debates of the day. For the first time, Hoosiers had a native son—well, as native as any of them—running for the highest office in the land: William Henry Harrison. Governor of the Indiana Territory from its inception to 1812, Harrison had personally negotiated, at the point of the gun, for much of the land in the hill country of southern Indiana. After his victory at the Battle of the Tippecanoe, he led United States forces in the invasion of Canada during the War of 1812, culminating in the Battle of the Thames and effectively ending all threats from the original inhabitants of Indiana. If Andrew Jackson had proven his worth by standing up to the British at the Battle of New Orleans, Harrison had proven his worth by leading the only successful American offensive of the war. Hoosiers, many of whom had not even been in Indiana in 1811, could not recall the anger at his endangering the territorial militia by crossing into Indian land and attacking, and they also ignored earlier Hoosiers' constant straining against Harrison's executive authority.[98] Harrison was a known quantity—personal politics—and respected for his achievements. His opponent, Martin Van Buren, had far too many connections to Eastern juntas, the exact associations that excited many Hoosiers' fears.

In the election of 1836, the hill country joined the rest of the state in supporting William Henry Harrison, although with less enthusiasm. Martin Van Buren won only eight of the twenty-three counties in the region, picking up just twelve more of the state's remaining fifty-three, and he polled 5 percent more votes in the hill country than he did in the rest of the state. But only Morgan, Ripley, Franklin, Floyd, and Dearborn counties recorded increased votes from 1832 for the Democratic ticket. Martin Van Buren could not maintain the level of support that Jackson had drawn.

One of the reasons for the small Democratic gains in Franklin, Ripley, and Dearborn counties was the immigration of German Catholics into the region beginning about 1834. A slightly later immigration into Dubois County and then even later into Perry County would begin to prop up Democratic polls in that region, much to the glee of area Democrats like Bazil Edmonston. Democratic editors missed few opportunities to bring the Whig nativist sentiment to the attention of their German readers.

> The federal press has not been sparing of its abuse of the [foreign] class of our citizens. . . . The fact that the Germans generally vote the democratic ticket, and are zealous in their support of democratic principles and our republic institutions . . . has secured to them the hatred of the leaders of the federal clique of this country.[99]

The vituperativeness of some of the Whig leadership against Germans and other immigrants did little to win immigrants' votes.

However, nativism was only part of the story of why German Catholics were Democrats. Like many of their native-born Democratic neighbors in the hill country, German Catholics tended to live on small farms with little surplus produce, yet managed to find the wherewithal to persist and to pass along farms to their offspring. Moreover, while belonging to the Roman Catholic church may seem to be far afield from their neighbors' Primitive Baptist congregation, both these churches stressed a localized morality which demanded humility from its adherents. On the other side of the wide gulf that separated them from the perfectionist sects, which generally found favor among Whigs, neither Primitive Baptists nor German Catholics could accept the postmillennial vision of a human world capable of achieving the kingdom of heaven on earth. Given their shared vision of the limitations of human beings, it was little wonder that neither group was as willing as its more evangelical neighbors to participate widely in the commercial marketplace. Therefore, it was hardly surprising that both could be found supporting a Democratic ticket which warned of the dangers of banks, internal improvements, and other paraphernalia of a commercial society.

Even by 1840, the influx of Germans could hardly budge Harrison's hold on the hill country. In fact, while he drew about the same percentage of votes in the rest of the state, Harrison gained additional support in the hill country, gaining about one and a half percentage points to draw over 53 percent of the vote. Van Buren lost Lawrence, Floyd, and Dearborn counties from his column—doubtless because blame for the Panic of 1837 rested on his shoulders in many commercial centers like New Albany, Aurora, Lawrenceburg, and Rising Sun—although Jackson County rejoined the Democratic column.[100] The election of 1840 was the nadir of the Democratic Party in southern Indiana. Its failing caused Bazil Edmonston to question universal white male suffrage:

> I can ashure you that the result of the late election has almost turned me against . . . the right of free suffrage. But when I reflect that the people have been swindled out of their votes by the most mean bold false calumnays that the midnite spirit of damned spirits could concoct whereby they have been induced to elect a man without principle and without a pledge, hence the political space if left open for him to [suit] his one apetite from the most depotic thro all the monarchel forms down to the liberal principle of Democracy.[101]

That Jackson had run without a pledge was ignored by partisan Edmonston, but the antiparty spirit may have explained the logic of some who voted for both Jackson and Harrison.

Harrison's "Log Cabin" campaign was one that excited voters throughout the country, and in Indiana it prompted a large jump in voter participation. Nearly 85 percent of potential voters showed up at the polls in November, an increase of nearly 15 percent over 1836.[102] Both parties shared in the excitement. Only in Floyd County did the Democrats show an actual loss in supporters; every other hill country county had at least eighty new Democratic voters, and ten counties had three hundred or more new Democrats.[103] Nevertheless, throughout the state most Democratic gains were offset by even larger numbers of new Whig voters.

Harrison's 1840 victory in Indiana had come, surprisingly enough, during an upsurge in Democratic strength in the state.[104] The Democratic Party, which had fused with anti–internal improvement Whigs in 1837, reclaimed the issue for themselves and forged a major victory in 1839, gaining the Indiana House of Representatives, as well as sending five Democrats to the U.S. Congress. But in 1840, the trend reversed itself. In a massive sweep, the Whigs captured seventy-eight seats in the Indiana house, including twenty-six from the hill country, leaving the Democrats with only twenty-two, of which hill country representatives filled eight. There remained bright spots in the hill country like Washington County, in which the Democratic candidate for governor took six of eight townships. Statewide, however, Whig Samuel Bigger thoroughly trounced Tilghman Howard by nearly nine thousand votes.

Harrison's "coattails" worked well in state and local elections held three months before the presidential election; the Whig Party brought to the 1840s a number of new voters. Yet the change was to be a momentary one. Beginning with two special elections early in 1841, voters in Franklin and Sullivan counties replaced Whigs with Democrats in the Indiana House of Representatives. In August 1841, Democrats regained control of the Indiana House, as the hill country sent twenty Democrats and only twelve Whigs, countering the Whig majority from the rest of the state.[105]

GENERAL INCORPORATION AS
ANTIDOTE TO MONOPOLY

Whereas even in 1840, most Hoosiers remembered that Democrats and Whigs had joined together to create the Mammoth system, such memories faded as events unfolded that corresponded to many of the worst fears voiced by more radical Democrats. Faced with financial disaster, hill country Democrats bit their lips and worked to get the state out of the mess that they had helped to create. The final verdict on the Mammoth Internal Improvements Bill would come in the 1851 Constitutional Convention, in which Hoosiers wrote into their new constitution a provision that prevented a repetition of any such undertaking. Understanding the situation as a choice between illegitimate privileges granted by the state and individual initiative, they chose private enterprise, not just within the realm of internal improvements but also in banking and other corporate endeavors. To a certain extent, it was an acquiescence to the modernizing forces of capitalism, but such a capitulation promised to create more localized capitalist entities, responding to local needs and local concerns. More importantly, the hope was that by removing the state from the machinations of the marketplace, the mass of the people could also be removed: no state obligations, no fears of subordinating independent farmers.

Hoosiers had learned all too well during the internal improvement scandal the problems of distant capital. Indiana started its internal improvements scheme just at the wrong time, in the summer of 1836, a scant year before the Panic of 1837 began to dry up the capital markets and the demand for Hoosier surplus produce. Not until late in 1839 would the full impact of the Panic be felt in Indiana, but in that autumn, work on most of the projects ground to a halt. With capital markets dried up, the money no longer flowed even at a rate to pay off the interest on the bonds already issued, let alone to pay contractors and laborers.[106]

To make matters worse, the bonds had been sold under the most corrupt of means. The rules governing the bond sales were completely ignored, as some were sold on credit. In the worst instance of corruption, the Morris Canal and Banking Company, which had acted as the state's agent in many of the bond sales, failed to deliver the receipts to the state. Historian Donald Carmony recently estimated that "at least $3,500,000 was ultimately lost from bonds sold to finance internal improvements for which the state failed to receive the principal therefor."[107] All the worst fears of Hoosier Democrats were to be realized. While the fraud was certainly not the only reason for the failure of the internal improvements scheme—the depression probably was the primary cause and the scheme's large scale clearly contributed—fraud was certainly the most predictable cause. Here were the immoral vultures from afar, from New Jersey, to be exact, who had taken advantage of the bone and sinew of the country, the farmers of the Midwest.

Many of the bonds were sold to legitimate investors on both sides of the Atlantic, and these investors became distraught when the state ceased work on the improvements and, of course, when it ceased to pay the interest on their investments. The state dragged its feet but eventually classified the improvements in order of importance and began to contract completion of some of the projects to private companies. Nevertheless, there still remained the bonded debt. After several years of nonpayment, Charles Butler of the American Land Company was chosen to represent the bondholders in negotiations with the state of Indiana and the state of Michigan, whose internal improvement schemes had suffered a similar fate.[108] Michigan repudiated the fraudulent debt, but also worked to pay off some of its legitimate debts. Indiana continued to procrastinate, but despite some talk abroad about repudiation—"it is not to be denied, that men have sometimes been found in our country, who, if they do not advocate repudiation, at least give countenance to views which must result in repudiation"— Hoosiers in general claimed their desire to repay the entire debt, legitimate and fraudulent.[109] Nevertheless, few Hoosier politicians could be found willing to tax the state to pay the debt, and Charles Butler came away from his first encounter with the Indiana General Assembly in 1846 with a bill that proved unacceptable to bondholders, especially those from across the sea. Swooping down on the legislature in its next session, Butler came away with the modifications demanded by the bondholders, but the legislators incorporated into their 1847 amendment the assertion that they would make no other provision for retiring the bonded debt, thus forcing investors to accept a certain small loss rather than risk a greater loss. Investors were required to turn in the old bonds, and they were issued new bonds for half the principal and interest. Stock in the Wabash and Erie Canal was given for the other half, but bondholders were required to provide additional investment in order to complete the canal to the Ohio River. Guided by a morality which demanded that persons fulfill their obligations to others, Hoosiers nevertheless were not pleased by the demanding air of Butler and the bondholders. As many Hoosiers saw matters, these, too, were immoral people, attempting to manipulate the lives of innocents in their insatiable greed.

> That swindling institution, the Morris Canal and Banking Company, purchased between three and four millions of dollars of our bonds, then broke,

made an assignment, and never paid us one copper.—These bonds naturally found their way into the hands of kindred spirits, London brokers and the New York Wall Street Stock Jobbers, now represented by Mr. Butler.[110]

Jacksonian rhetoric about banks and internal improvements, when coupled with Hoosiers' experiences with such entities, reinforced many southern Indiana residents' doubts of the moral goodness of those in power, especially those beyond the control of their community and the ballot box.

From the moment the Mammoth Bill passed, some Hoosiers had cried out against it. For many of the early protesters, their sentiments may have been connected to their neighborhood's being passed by, but their rhetoric helped to shape the public debates that continued for years to come. Early in the debate, one critic, while conceding that there were projects which the national and state government should pursue, provided that they could be finished quickly and would provide a steady income, nevertheless asserted that "the last and most equitable method of making internal improvements is by the enterprise of individuals and companies possessing surplus capital, who will always seek an investment in stock of this kind whenever there is a fair prospect of gain."[111] Such a prospect was always on the minds of a few hill country Hoosiers. In its first incarnation in 1825, for instance, the Whitewater Canal was proposed as a private endeavor, with the belief that "Eastern capitalists" would invest in such a project.[112] Indeed, even while the legislature was proposing the Mammoth scheme, it also was approving charters for a variety of private roads, canals, and even railroads. With the failure of the state system, many retreated into the belief that individual enterprise was the sole means by which such schemes would be undertaken. The opportunity to institutionalize this approach came with a new state constitution.

In 1850, after several years of effort, the voters called for a constitutional convention. One of the express reasons was to prohibit state indebtedness, a prohibition which found its way into the new state constitution of 1851. Hill country Democrat Daniel Read spoke for many when he asserted, "Experience says, the State has no capacity for any of these departments of business, and it is always cheated and plundered."[113] Quickly Hoosiers began to hail their intelligence regarding governmental aid to internal improvements. Commenting on the plans for a Pacific Railroad, the Brookville *Franklin Democrat* praised the notion, but warned against government involvement.

> If it will pay, individuals will make it, and then only those will put their labor in that shall choose to do it. If it will not pay[,] neither government nor individuals should undertake it. . . . We think the policy of Indiana on inter-

nal improvements to be the correct one[,] leaving them to a willing individual enterprise.[114]

By leaving such enterprises to private initiative, hill country Hoosiers understood that the burdens of such endeavors would only be placed on those who willingly agreed to accept them. In return for accepting the risk, such investors would receive any profits.

Such a scheme contrasted sharply with the universalizing vision of many Whigs, who tended to see these internal improvements in much the same light as their reform efforts, as uplifting the masses. Yet as we have seen, the potential of these internal improvements to benefit everyone in the hill country was uneven. For a farmer pursuing the "safety-first" strategy of marketing surplus produce, the availability of easy transportation was of less importance to his family's overall survival than it was to his profit-minded neighbors. Those who wanted to pursue profit were given, under this new scheme, the opportunity to invest in projects that would benefit them, but without oppressing their less commercially minded neighbors. The Democratic Party, which from its beginning was a coalition party, found in individual enterprise the way to balance the demands of its business supporters as well as its non-market-oriented voters.

Localism remained in the very strategy of "surplus produce," which lowered taxes sought to maintain. Yet it also reappeared in a shift to public support of internal improvements on the county and even township level, a shift which the state condoned. In many ways, this shift was a rewriting of the notion of "general welfare," one which reflected the Democratic electorate's belief that the general improvements sought by the national and state governments primarily benefited the mercantile classes, who sought to trade goods at a distance, but that more localized improvements could improve the "general welfare," by providing outlets for surplus produce. What emerged, therefore, was not a pure form of private enterprise but private enterprise supported by county and municipal governments.

With the demise of the state-directed internal improvements projects, private interests became involved in several projects. The state leased and then sold the Whitewater Canal and the Madison & Indianapolis Railroad. Along the Mammoth Bill's proposed route of a road or railroad from New Albany through Salem, Bedford, Bloomington, and on to Lafayette and Michigan City, both locals and distant investors attempted to build a railroad after the state de-emphasized the Salem line. By 1847, the new private scheme began building a railroad from New Albany to Salem, and over 1,600 Washington County taxpayers—about 60 percent of the actual voters—signed a petition for the county to subscribe $20,000 to the stock of the company.[115]

Such enthusiasm certainly suggested that support for railroads was not limited to the capitalist classes in the hill country. The railroad was built—the county welcomed the first train about three years later—and in 1851, the county congratulated itself on surviving the heavy taxation, reducing its tax rate 80 percent.[116] By 1854, the line had been extended to Michigan City, linking five interior hill country counties to both the Ohio River and the Great Lakes.

The vast number of railroads that were proposed and completed in the hill country in the late 1840s and 1850s helped to convince Hoosiers that they had taken the correct course in relying upon private enterprise to provide the internal improvements desired. One of the most compelling rationales for state involvement in the 1830s had been that the state should undertake projects that were beyond the means of private enterprise or that promised little return for their investment. By 1860, railroad lines, including several equal in scope to the original Mammoth projects, had been completed through the hill country, most notably the Ohio & Mississippi Railroad, linking St. Louis with Cincinnati and points eastward on its sister lines of the Baltimore & Ohio, and thus proving the potential for the private sector. The hill country was rarely a destination for these early lines. Several roads ended in its large towns on the Ohio River, but they reached far north onto the flatlands for much of their traffic. Nevertheless, these lines did serve a majority of hill country counties enroute to more important destinations, and few of the companies were reluctant to accept money from the local citizenry or local governments; more than one road was rerouted thanks to a notable subscription of stock. Only Greene, Brown, and Dubois counties, of the sixteen counties not on the Ohio, did not have rail service by 1860. Certainly the experience with private railroad corporations was not entirely a positive one, but mass disaffection with the railroads remained muted until after the Civil War. Most hill country Hoosiers agreed with Jackson County Representative Samuel T. Wells that "railroads are undoubtedly great blessings to our country when they have the proper restrictions thrown around them, but if they have not those restrictions they are like banks, their power is invincible."[117]

Wells was writing on the occasion of the creation of the new state constitution. If an important impulse of the convention had been to prevent the state from ever again participating in a scheme like the Mammoth Internal Improvements Bill, another purpose was to eliminate the vast flood of local legislation that was encumbering the legislative process. In the minds of many Hoosiers, such local legislation further tended to allow the General Assembly to confer special privileges upon individuals and corporations. Such special privileges were tantamount to monopoly in the minds of many Hoosiers. Samuel Wells saw great relief for the mass of people in the new constitution's end to special and local legislation:

> That provision which provides against special and local legislation we find to be one of our best safeguards. Their rights are protected by it, from encroachments by moneyed aristocracies and monopolies.—Indeed, the delay in the change of our fundamental law was too long—for the foundations of many monopolies have already been laid—railroad charters have been granted all over the land and some of the oldest and most successful of them are now commencing to show what they really are.

Wells noted that "even in our young state, where we have scarcely had time to find out their advantages, [railroads] have a very great influence on the legislature." Wells added: "Under our new constitution the legislature can grant no charters but must enact a general railroad law under which all companies are to organize, and under which they have no exclusive privileges."[118] And for many hill country Hoosiers, just as "exclusive privilege" meant monopoly, so monopoly meant a threat to the successful sustaining of their families. "[Jefferson's] hatred to all monopolies and partial legislation that gave to wealth unjust advantages over labor, enlisted against him all who made their Ledger their bible and their money their god."[119] Opposition to such a threat, now embodied in the monopoly, was a key purpose of the Democratic Party: "It is the party whose endeavor has ever been to maintain the rights of the poor and laboring classes against the exclusive monopoly sought for by the wealthy and arrogant."[120] Monopoly was dangerous because monopolies could dictate prices and wages, thus denying ordinary citizens their birthright independence, and because these corporations had grown so large that they could corrupt the government.

This monopoly threat from corporations had been explicitly part of the demand for the new constitution. Railing against the failure to put a referendum for such a convention on the 1848 ballot, the Brookville *Franklin Democrat* asserted that "this people want the Constitution revised, and their rights protected against the inroads of swindling corporations."[121] Throughout much of the 1840s, southern Indiana legislators led a futile fight in the Indiana General Assembly against corporations and the limited liability of their investors.[122] The fight reached its acme in 1845, in the shadow of Charles Butler's first visit, but the forces were weak, only comprising maybe half of the Democrats from the hill country, with a few stragglers from elsewhere in the state.[123] The lessons from the internal improvements scheme framed the entire debate: Legislator Nathaniel Webber "referred to the conduct of the Morris Canal and Banking Company, as well as to numberous private cases within his own knowledge, to prove the danger and corrupting tendency of all charters, and the necessity of guarding the people against their practices."[124] Corporate "limited liability," by which investors in a corporation were only liable to the extent of their individual investments, was viewed by "ultra-Democrats" as a special privilege and contrasted sharply with the liability of ordinary Hoosier farmers, whose business failings meant the loss of not only their farms but also their homesteads.[125] Some of the animus against corporations was centered in bad experiences. Franklin County's Democratic legislators led the fight against "limited liability" in part because the actions of the White Water Valley Canal Company had created many problems in their locale, as the company issued scrip in payment of its debts, and then placed restrictions on redemption of the scrip.[126] For some in the hill country, though, "individual liability"—where each investor was responsible for a corporation's indebtedness—represented a degree of honesty characteristic of their own dealings. By making individuals liable for all decisions of which they were a part, some Hoosier Democrats believed, they could preclude any individual from undertaking any endeavor of a scale that might necessarily subordinate other individuals.

Yet other hill country legislators, although Democrats, ignored the argument over "individual liability" and forthrightly argued for business interests. Claiming to speak for the people, Democratic Representative Davis of Scott County argued that "individual liability" would effectively ruin business: "His own constituents are interested in a prospective railroad from Columbus to Jeffersonville; and yet, if this principle be adopted by the House, the undertaking might as well be given up at once." Democratic Senator Buell of Dearborn was even more explicit in embracing business interests.

> Mr. Buell reported an act amending the Dearborn Cotton Manufacturing Company, the object of which was to do away with the "individual liability" clause in the charter. Mr. Buell said he regarded the action of the democratic party of this State for the last few years on this subject as calculated to keep manufacturing companies from being established in this State, and as a democrat he was not disposed to stand it any longer.

Although not all were willing to establish "individual liability" as law, there remained a deep underlying suspicion of corporations. In response to Buell's comments, Democratic Senator Berry of Franklin County, a leader in the "individual liability" group, "moved to amend by making the directors individually liable for an excess of indebtedness over the amount of solvent stock," a motion that carried. When a related question arose over whether corporate charters should be written so that they could be revoked, even a Whig representative from Perry County was willing to allow such an action, provided two-thirds of the legislature concurred, and although his amendment was never taken up, the question of charter revocation passed the Indiana House.[127]

For many, distinctions were to be made between banking corporations and those engaged in the pursuit of some public benefit. "It may do to incorporate companies to do a thing that an individual cannot do," Enoch Parr wrote, but he asserted:

> It would be hardly necessary to say democracy teaches no eclusive priviledge no eclusive legislative privilidges for Shavers and Stock jobers to Shave and fleece the poor labouring man and get rich without labour for we know that who ever lives with out labor or gets rich with out labor some body must labour for him and this is not equal rights and equal priviledgs.[128]

Such a distinction between banks and other endeavors, including internal improvements, was often clearly made by hill country residents.

> There is no doubt that chartered Insurance and shaving establishments of all kinds should be well guarded, so as to prevent fraud and imposition upon the people; but why the stockholders of a Road Company—not one in a hundred of which yield three per cent on the capital invested, and which could seldom be started except by a local spirit among those immediately interested—should be subjected to such a penalty as "individual liability" passes our comprehension. The fact is, incorporations to make roads are so seldom profitable, that stock is rarely subscribed in them out of the immediate neighborhood of their locations, where subscribers expect to receive an *indirect* remuneration for their investments, in the enhanced value of their property and agricultural products.

While such an argument was advanced by a Whig newspaper, its emphasis on the localism of such endeavors would suggest the reason why many hill country Democrats found the "ultra-Democrat" line on corporations hard to toe. And this localism provided some of the safety of such endeavors:

> When a Company is chartered, every one in the vicinity of its location must of necessity have some knowledge of its solvency and ability to meet its engagements; and, as no one is *compelled* to deal with it, men should be left to their own volition as to whether they will credit it or not.[129]

While the willingness of some county commissions to turn over public roadbeds to private turnpike companies would mean that some citizens would be compelled to use even so "threatless" a corporation as a road company, it was precisely the perceived lack of compulsion which made general incorporation laws so appealing to many hill country Democrats.

As long as the company was not awarded some exclusive privilege in return for the risk it undertook, there was little threat of monopoly.

In many ways, the increasingly antimonopoly stand of Hoosiers, both Whig and Democrat, with its emphasis on denying exclusive privileges, shifted the emphasis away from fears of manipulation by large corporations and toward the more liberal capitalist fear of competition's being squashed. In sum, this shift led to the passage of the general incorporation laws. With the private sector's providing roads, canals, and railroads, many Hoosiers saw themselves as gaining advantages—not the least of which was more secure markets for surpluses and thus added security—without making any investment, either personally or through the government and its taxation process. Moreover, the new corporations reflected a certain localist base, as the increasing wealth of the region ensured that the major investors were no longer solely outsiders.

Such trends were also evident in the world of banking. The State Bank of Indiana was one of the most secure institutions in the country, and although it suspended specie payment in the aftermath of the Panic of 1837, its broader success helped subdue some Hoosier fears of corporations. Nevertheless, a coalition of Whigs and soft-money Democrats, generally not from the hill country, would work to pass the banking equivalent of the general incorporation law, free banking.

It was only three years after the establishment of the new State Bank of Indiana in 1834 that it underwent its first test in the Panic of 1837. The bank, like the state as a whole, weathered the problems well until 1839, but that did not silence its critics, who were angered by the State Bank's conservative policies.[130] Anti-bank crusaders were enraged by the bank's suspension of specie payment in 1837—the means by which it survived the Panic—and demanded that the state legislature repeal the charter.

> It may by some, probably be esteemed sacrilegious in us to suggest that the Legislature should not *legalize* the *illegal* proceedings of the State Bank of Indiana and Branches. . . . In suspending specie paymens [*sic*], they have set aside law, and assumed a menacing attitude that calls forth a merited rebuke at the hands of the power that gave them life.

But suspension was not the primary reason to end the charter.

> A very decided majority of the people, if we know them, are opposed to the principle of banking, and desire to witness the day that shall put a period to all banks—they would joyously perform the funeral obsequies of the last vestige of the monopolising system.[131]

Until 1839, however, Whigs controlled the legislature, and the 1839 General Assembly spent much of its time confronting the failed internal improvements program.

Moreover, other Democrats saw in "free banking"—the chartering of any bank that met certain requirements—a solution to monopoly power. A narrow majority of Democrats joined with powerful Whigs in bringing the proposal before the state legislature in 1838, but other Whigs, primarily from the central and northern parts of the state, joined over 40 percent of the Democrats in defeating the measure.[132] In many ways, the difference between soft-money and hard-money Democrats reflected a difference over which was the greater evil, private power or state power. For hard-money Democrats, any institution, public or private, that threatened to enslave the individual was to be feared, but for soft-money Democrats, private institutions could only become powerful enough with the assistance of the government, which doled out special privileges.

Even hard-money Democrats could be pragmatic. With their ascent to power in the early 1840s, they did not immediately attempt to dismantle the State Bank. After their legislative sweep of 1839, the Democratic-controlled Committee on the State Bank, chaired by William Bowles of Orange County and including among its six members two other hill country Democrats, found a middle course.[133]

> A metallic currency is not now attainable if desired.—For if we had no issue of paper, our circulation would be supplied from the surrounding States— who would then realize the profit and expose us to the evils.

If the choice was to be locally controlled banks or banks more distant, Democrats would choose the local, precisely the impetus which had first brought the bank into existence: "The operations of our bank must confirm the conviction that is prevailing throughout the country, against conferring on either corporations or government too much power over the property of the community."[134]

In 1843, the Democrats finally gained full control of both the legislative and executive branches, control they would generally maintain into the 1850s, but they did little to change the terms of banking in the state. In his inaugural address, James Whitcomb, the first Democratic governor of the state, identified the banks as the cause of much of the current distress.

> Our State, in common with the rest of the Union, and especially of the western portion of it is experiencing the distress and embarrassment consequent upon a system of overbanking and its natural progeny, over-trading and

deceptive speculation. The wealth of a community, consisting essentially in property, of which the currency is but the representative, it is evident, that an undue increase of the latter by means of a paper circulation, while it enhances the nominal price of former, does not really increase its substantial value.

For Whitcomb, as for many hill country Hoosiers, wealth was property and its value was in its productivity, not in its dollar price. Moreover, the temptation to seek out wealth in such a manner had the potential to violate morality. For Whitcomb, the answer to both the state's difficulties with internal improvements and its residents' difficulties with banks was plain:

> Our consumption having exceeded our income, the balance must be restored by a corresponding excess of our receipts over our expenses. We have been lured to the embrace of debt under the flattering guise of credit, and we can only be extricated by the joint aid of industry and economy. They should again seek the ancient land-marks of frugality and republican simplicity from which too many have unwittingly strayed.[135]

Despite their control of the General Assembly and Governor Whitcomb's animosity toward banks, Democrats did little to change the banking system in the 1840s. They did institute policy and personnel changes that made it palatable for the duration of the 1840s.[136]

Nevertheless, a lingering suspicion of banks remained among Hoosiers, and at the Constitutional Convention of 1851 they forbade the recharter of the State Bank as an enterprise backed by the state and opened the door for free banking. About half the Democrats in the convention, mostly from the southern half of the state, initially opposed all banks, but eventually went along with the final plan.[137] When the General Assembly met in 1851–52 and addressed legislation on free banking, the regional differences re-emerged, as central and northern Indiana Democrats joined a substantial majority of Whigs to pass the first free banking law, which permitted banks to do business on the value of stock in other companies deposited with the state auditor. According to historian William Shade, Hoosier Democrats had temporarily ceased to discuss banking because it threatened to tear their party apart. Governor Joseph Wright signed the free banking bill against his better judgment but immediately began working against the bill.[138] He was joined by hill country Democrats, who questioned the assertions that safeguards in it would protect citizens: "*Our faith in the integrity of poor human nature generally* and bankers in particular, is not sufficiently imbued with the marvelous to receive the doctrine without a great deal of allowance."[139]

Indiana had not been alone in passing free banking laws, and the appearance of notes from distant states caused some consternation.

Their appearance *may* be accounted for on strict commercial principles; but their disappearance too general[ly] smacks of the "*take-in!*" Even, should all things terminate justly, the presence of these strange promises are detrimental to commercial confidence, because of a lack of acquaintance.

Recognizing the trust inherent in commercial relationships, the writer nevertheless doubted the morality of those distant from him.

Free trade, it may be said, demands of us an extension of confidence. All this may be very true; but free trade does not certainly require that elasticity of confidence, necessary to induce the people of Indiana to suffer others to surfeit the market with vagrant promises *to pay* when we have no assurance that those promises are not similar to all other bank promises—merely inducements to quietly wait an auspicious season for general suspension.[140]

Many hill country Hoosiers echoed such fears about trade at a distance.

Yet the free banking law had been passed partially because too many locales in the state were without banking facilities, thus forcing them to depend upon more distant bankers. When a bank was proposed for Brookville, even those who had lambasted free banking as resulting in shinplasters could praise it, because it was to be run by "sound men," a good thing, for "banks need men with means beyond banking investments."[141] And when economic difficulties occurred a year later, the same opponents would praise the Bank of Brookville as "solvent, with well-established men, cautious to protect their reputations."[142] In many ways, free banking responded not merely to antimonopoly sentiments among Hoosiers, but also to a certain localist strain that trusted business more when conducted among men who knew one another's reputation.

The economic difficulties of 1854, however, severely strained the new free banks in the state. When the Cincinnati banks refused to accept Indiana free bank notes in 1854, many Indiana banks failed. Through the problems, hill country Democrats hesitantly stood by the free banks: "We are opposed to all banking systems—they are nothing but legalized swindling machines—but if we must have banks, we prefer the Free Banking system, as it is termed, guarded with proper restrictions, to any other system." Some saw the nefarious hand of capitalists behind the downturn.

The movement against the free banks, is made for the purpose of favoring the re-chartering of the State Bank. Capitalists do not wish to bank upon the free banking principle—they prefer the old system—make up a capital of $100,000 in specie and issue and put into circulation $300,000 in rags; thus enabling them to do a business of $200,000 without any capital, or even security to the bill holders.[143]

Others went further, calling for a return to the "constitutional currency" of gold and silver.

> It is high time that [the people] should demand from their legislators a law which will secure to them a currency free, to some extent, from the power of unprincipled men, one which will preserve a uniform value, in other words, the currency of the constitution, gold and silver.[144]

Through the 1840s and 1850s, the hill country of southern Indiana was the stronghold of the hard-money elements within the state Democratic Party. Despite the occasional allure of development, hill country residents feared some of the entanglements that economic expansion might bring, as their fortunes would become dependent upon the machinations of men and corporations distant from their own lives, beyond the control of local moral communities. In many respects, of course, Hoosiers were merely wise about the prospects of their own lives and their land. Some hill country residents undoubtedly understood that their land could not support intensive commercial farming. Yet to note such self-interest in directing their electoral activity would be both to ignore their willingness to go along with some forms of development—such as the Washington County vote for the New Albany and Salem Railroad—and to ignore their desire to pursue lives that chose security over the accumulation of profits. The persistence of hill country residents in the hill country would suggest that the way of life which they had created there was to their liking. The high price of land in the 1850s would have created ample opportunity for residents to sell out and head west. They did not. Instead, they chose to live in the hills of southern Indiana and protect their way of life through what they considered their God-given right of the ballot, electing Democratic representatives who would ensure that the massive alterations sweeping the economy would not enslave them but would complement the Hoosier strategy of "surplus produce."

THE DEMOCRATIC PARTY ASCENDANT

At the national level, the 1840s and 1850s would see a shift from some of the economic issues of Jackson's day to other issues. Andrew Jackson had won, banishing many of the problems from the national stage, only to have the fights replicated in state and local legislative assemblies. Certainly, some still invoked the cry of "Banks or No Banks" to rally the faithful:

> The Clay worshippers have not thus far defined their position with regard to the kind of Bank they desire the people to vote.—The presumption is, that

like their GREAT MASTER, HENRY CLAY, they advocate a FIFTY MILLION BANK, to be controlled by British capitalists, who thereby would be enabled to fix the price of beef, pork, and the products of American industry, so as to meet the interest and taxes of her Majesty's subjects throughout England and her allies.[145]

Nevertheless, for many Americans and for the Hoosiers of the hill country, the election of 1844 turned primarily on territorial expansion; as public land disappeared in the hill country, parents looked west to find a place for their progeny.

By 1844, much of the public land in southern Indiana had been taken up, and what remained, often swampy low lands, was not worth the $1.25 that the federal government charged. As the supply dwindled and as the children of early settlers reached adulthood, demand increased, and thus prices rose. If a primary purpose of the family's production strategies was to provide for its children, the absence of cheap land placed the entire project in jeopardy. However, to the West lay new lands and new opportunities to replicate the society that they had created in southern Indiana. Oregon, California, Texas—all promised continuation of the way of life Hoosier farmers and their children knew. And the aggressive expansionism of the Democratic Party, never afraid of foreign powers, would hardly stop at the claims of the indigenous peoples of the Plains. New lands like Kansas and Nebraska would be the real destination of many young hill country Hoosiers.

In the 1844 election, Hoosiers continued the swing back to the Democratic Party, which had begun in 1839 and had been interrupted only by the immense personal appeal of Whig candidate William Henry Harrison. After the great outpouring of voters in 1840, even more voters showed up in 1844, especially in the hill country. This swelling of the polls helped lead to a Democratic victory in the state. Seventeen hill country counties (of twenty-five) joined twenty-eight other counties (of sixty-six) in the Democratic column. Significantly, for the first time, the presidential race uniformly attracted more voters than local elections. "Fifty-four forty or fight," and the territorial issues connected with that powerful slogan, spoke to many in the hill country, which by 1844 was confirming its status as the stronghold of the Democratic Party in the state.

Nevertheless, there remained a great diversity within the region, with several areas of strong Whig support. Besides their traditional region of strength in the southeastern part of the state, Whigs continued to draw more votes along the Ohio River in Perry and Crawford counties, as well as in some commercial centers such as Paoli in Orange County and along other rivers and internal improvement projects. Democratic strength was concentrated in more noncommercial areas, often away from major rivers, internal improvement projects, and county seats.[146]

By 1848, the euphoria over territorial expansion had subsided somewhat, and the presidential campaign was not able to stir up the enthusiasm of 1844, although it still outdrew the local elections, and the map of Democratic strength was not significantly redrawn. By 1852, the Democracy grew stronger. Within the hill country, only six counties did not provide Democratic majorities (see map 4.5). In Morgan, Ripley, and Jefferson counties, Franklin Pierce still managed to garner the plurality, and in the three remaining Whig counties along the Ohio River—Harrison, Perry, and Crawford—Pierce fell just 40 votes shy, out of 4,900 cast, of winning all three. In general, Whigs in southern Indiana were growing increasingly dissatisfied with the party. Its tendency to become a sectional party threatened the commercial interests of many southern Indiana Whigs, and without a useful platform to pursue their interests, they dropped out of the electoral process, absenting themselves from the electoral process in some instances.

Throughout the hill country, though, the basic pattern of commercialized areas as Whig and noncommercialized areas as Democratic remained.[147] This trend was most apparent in the western half of the hill country; in the southeastern part of the state, the presence of German immigrants played an important role, as southwestern Franklin County, northern Dearborn County, and northern Ripley County comprised the center of the German settlements. Germans were more localized and less commercial. In general, the measurements of county seats and improved transportation certainly only reflected opportunities, yet, because of the role local citizenry played in establishing seats and various transportation lines, such "improvements" sometimes provided insight into the character of the locale. However, many of the newer rail lines, like the ones that were being built through the heart of the German Catholic settlements in southeastern Indiana, had as their main object the transportation of goods from one urbanizing location to another, and the route they took was dictated as much by the terrain as by the desires of hill country residents. Indeed, commercial areas were as likely to be Democratic as Whig, but noncommercialized areas were three times more likely to be Democratic than Whig. In 1852, Democrats drew significant majorities in the larger towns along the Ohio River: Lawrenceburg, Aurora, Vevay, Madison, New Albany, and Cannelton. A new urban industrial working class was being formed, often constituted by immigrants, and they were being drawn to the egalitarianism and antinativism of the Democrats.[148] While this new dimension to Democratic politics in the hill country would have important ramifications of its own, the farmers of the

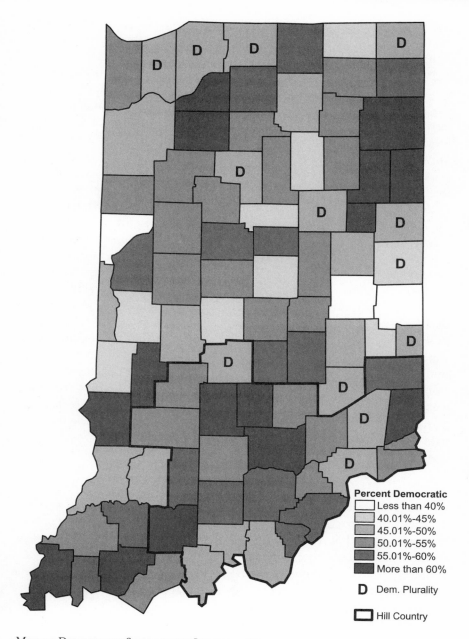

MAP 4.5 DEMOCRATIC STRENGTH IN INDIANA, 1852
Derived from Walter Dean Burnham, *Presidential Ballots, 1836–1892* (Baltimore: Johns Hopkins University Press, 1955). (Boone/Nation)

region, those most removed from the commercial life, continued to find protection in the Democratic Party from those that threatened their way of life.

If John Tyler and James Polk found in territorial expansion an issue that spoke to the needs of many hill country farmers to provide for their progeny, they and the hill country farmers only slowly came to understand that territorial expansion would become a stage upon which questions of the morality and the danger of slavery would be discussed, raising the issue of universalized norms of behavior. In 1850, the answer seemed simple: let the people decide for themselves. That answer had served Hoosier farmers well for many years, and they had constructed structures of moral governance in their communities, both internal and external to the individual. But to many Hoosiers, people were doomed to sin. Only the governance of a tight local community could hold such sinning in check. Persons outside the governance of these communities remained dangerous, and Hoosiers sought to restrict these distant persons' influence upon them, through economic strategies that limited Hoosiers' dependence upon distant marketplaces and distant people and through political action that sought to limit the power over them of people distant from them. Their understanding of their role in the political process was circular. At once threats to their independence were threats to the political order as a whole, but that political order's primary purpose was to protect their independence. In the end, the Constitution and the federal government were to be hailed because they promoted a world in which a white man could expect to rise to a place where he could be free from the enslavement of others, whether of the government or private corporations or of other individuals.

MORAL VISIONS AND TEMPERANCE

The economic issues of banking and internal improvements were resolved by the 1851 Constitution, which specifically forbade any local or special legislation. While seemingly a triumph for the localist outlook—no longer could the legislature interfere in the affairs of counties or townships—the prohibition ironically enough served to eliminate local control over many issues, including the fight over temperance that animated much of the political world in the 1840s and 1850s.

Temperance has often been identified by historians as a significant part of the conflicts that built the Second Party System. In the traditional telling of the story, Whigs proceeded from evangelicalism and political ideology to promote the reform movements of the period. The objects of said reform, often immigrants and almost always nonevangelical, found a home in the Democratic Party. The Democrats, in this telling, were primarily attractive because they opposed the nativists and evangelicals, and ideology, especially regarding economics, played little role in creating the Democratic Party.

The stereotypical images of Upland Southerners and Catholics as overindulgent in alcohol have led many to understand the temperance issue as one that divided wets and drys, but it actually was part of the larger conflict over morality that also informed the localism and the economic positions of many Hoosier farmers. Only with the movement of certain Protestant evangelical sects away from belief in the fallen state of man toward a belief in the perfectibility of man could the huge transformation of Americans' drinking habits have taken place in the nineteenth century. For those who could not embrace the perfectibility of man, the reform measures, especially when they demanded the prohibition of alcohol, seemed to ignore both the impossibility of the task and the possibility of moral rectitude without either tee-totaling or government mandate, and therefore these measures risked trampling the rights of Hoosiers.

> Many true and faithful democrats look upon the cause of temperance as a moral, and not a political question. . . . They treat it as a matter of conscience and as such leave it to the individual and his God. The Democrats do not oppose "search, seizes, confiscation and destruction" of intoxicating drinks because they desire drunkenness, but because their principles are founded on faith in God and confidence in the people; which teaches them to love their fellow men as brethern and not oppress them as enemies—to teach morality by example and precept, not by tortures and penalties—to elevate and enlighten, not to degrade and enslave their race. . . . [T]he right to make, use, buy, and sell the products of the soil and the work shop are his natural rights, and just in proportion as the law deprives him of them, he is thus far shorn of his individual freedom. The only distinction between freeman and slave is that the former acts from his own judgment and the latter from the will of his master.[149]

Certainly for many in southern Indiana the threat to eliminate whiskey as one form for corn to be marketed had the potential to limit their economic pursuits. Others emphasized the actual morality of those opposed to temperance laws: "The democratic party are as temperate as any other party."[150] While Democratic editors derided temperance advocates as "fanatics," they were quick to exclude "those who believe in moral suasion, instead of law-force."[151]

Temperance forces had hounded the Democratic legislature in 1853, and it responded by passing not the Maine-type Prohibition law favored by the reformers but a local option law, following the Democratic tradition of deferring to local authorities. Ironically, the law was struck down by the Indiana Supreme Court because it violated the new constitution's prohibition against local and special laws, which required that all laws be of "general and uniform operation throughout the state," a restriction enacted specifically to prevent the legislature from according special privileges to individuals and corporations.[152]

With the Fusion (Republican/American) ascent to the legislature in 1855, the prohibitory law sought by temperance advocates was finally enacted, over the objections of every Democrat who remained in the House of Representatives. Complaints rang out that the Indiana law was more stringent than the Maine law.

> There is no doubt but the main portion of the law is unconstitutional; and we have no idea it will ever be enforced. But if the law was constitutional it never would or could be enforced in this State. The people of Indiana will never submit to so tyrannical a law as it is.[153]

The law mandated that liquor could be "searched for, seized, confiscated, and destroyed," which to many Hoosiers was a direct violation of their property rights and one which, if upheld, would lead down a slippery slope to losing other property and eventually allow Hoosiers to be enslaved. Almost immediately the law was struck down on those very grounds.[154]

Less than a year later, some hill country reformers decided to take matters into their own hands. In Salem, the county seat of Washington County, a number of women, headed by alleged Know-Nothings, descended on the liquor retailers in the town. They spared two of the groceries, but arriving at the home of German immigrant Werner Zerk, who sold liquor, they secured his person by force and destroyed all his alcohol. In retaliation, another mob formed later that evening, with the intention of destroying the Know-Nothing newspaper offices, but local Democratic leaders Horace Heffren and B. J. Wilson calmed the crowd for the moment. By eleven, however, this mob had returned, and they went to the newspaper office and destroyed it, emptying its contents into the street, as well as vandalizing a shoe shop of one of the original mob's leaders. Retaliation by the Know-Nothing crowd was threatened, and preparations were made to defend the Democratic newspaper's offices, with men arriving from distant parts of the county, "resolving to maintain the Democrat office at all hazards." The physical violence ended with the Democratic editor's thrashing the Know-Nothing editor, who had been vilifying his counterpart for several months.[155]

The fight over temperance had the means to tear southern Indiana communities apart to a degree that banking or internal improvements had not.

The opaque ways in which banking and internal improvements threatened the liberties of Hoosiers were in stark contrast to the tangible threats of the temperance laws. Salem's affray in 1856 would not be the last time that southern Indiana communities would be divided against themselves; it would not be the last time that mobs attempted to enforce their own brand of morality; it would not be the last time that many hill country farmers felt a real menace to their liberty. Despite the greater opacity of the threat, Hoosiers had learned to defend their liberties and the autonomy of their local moral community in the fights over banking and internal improvements, and it was those lessons that they took into the temperance debate and later into the conflict surrounding slavery and secession.

Hoosiers who feared dependency upon the marketplace had already found a home in the Democratic Party, with its attacks on banks, internal improvements, and the moneyed aristocracy in general. These Hoosier farmers, like most members of the Democratic Party, supported free markets; their fear, however, was that markets beyond their local community were not free but controlled by a ruthless plutocracy. For this reason, they opposed the Whigs' commercial expansion, because they believed that it would consolidate the aristocracy's hold on the marketplace, while at the same time raising taxes to pay for internal improvements, thus forcing the farmers to sell more in these suspect markets to acquire the cash necessary to pay their taxes. The Democratic Party promised to loosen the aristocracy's grip on the commercial marketplace, thus making it a more dependable place for Hoosier farmers to trade their surplus produce and thereby acquire the means by which they could provide for their children. Likewise, Hoosier farmers, especially Primitive Baptists and German Catholics, saw reform efforts like temperance as doomed attempts to perfect humanity, a vain and sacrilegious undertaking, but one which finally threatened, in its absolutism and universality, to undermine their localism. For many of these groups, human sin could only be subdued by the oversight of the local moral community. Whether it oversaw drinking or commerce, such a moral community could help mitigate the worst aspects of innate human depravity. The moneyed aristocracy, outside the confines of the local moral community, was as doomed to sin as the drunkard. The center of moral life was the community, and in their politics, many southern Indiana farmers sought unremittingly to ensure that localism was maintained.

Localism, Race, and the Civil War

✿ ✿ ✿ ✿ ✿ ✿

Part and parcel of the conflicts in the northern United States over slavery and the coming of the Civil War were conflicts over universal moral authority. The disparate elements of religious belief, political ideology, and even economic behavior, coalescing as we have seen around localism, found further expression in the debates over the slavery question and in the willingness of hill country Hoosiers to fight to save the Union and later to free the slaves. The localized moral horizons of these Hoosiers limited their sympathy for African American slaves, yet their defense of the Union as the best protector of European Americans' liberty would find many of them enlisting in the Union army. The Civil War would help to expose that contradiction within their minds, yet few would completely abandon their localist worldview.

By 1860, there were many visible changes in southern Indiana, not the least of which were the railroads that crossed the hill country on their way to destinations elsewhere. The 1850s brought a certain stability to the region, for despite the fact that children left the region, the region achieved fairly high persistence in its population. No new waves of migrants arrived, and the German Catholic immigrants of the decade had settled into their lives in the hill country. And during the 1850s, the Democratic Party would continue to shore up its dominance in the region.

The most obvious changes were in the towns of the region. Lawrenceburg, Madison, Jeffersonville, and New Albany, all places where the railroads met the river, continued to grow. But in the hinterlands, where the bulk of hill country peoples still lived, the railroads also accompanied changes. Production rose, with greater surpluses for the marketplace, but productivity grew more slowly than elsewhere in the state. By 1860, in the median county in the hill country, the average farm raised just over 100 bushels more than it needed, while in the median county outside the hill country, the average farm raised nearly 240 bushels more than it consumed. Only six hill counties reported surplus production averaging over 200 bushels per farm, thus earning more than $100 in a year, in a region where a new farm for one's child could cost well over $2,000. The emerging distinctiveness of the region reflected the greater fertility elsewhere in the state, as well as perhaps a greater dedication to the market in the northern two-thirds of the state. Nevertheless, hill country farmers remained fairly even with their northern Indiana neighbors in capital investment, as measured by the value of the farm machinery they had purchased.[1] For most Hoosier farmers north and south, the new farm implements that were just coming on the market were not worth the risk of capital investment; still ensconced in a world of "safety-first" farming, these Hoosier farmers had not yet appreciated the benefits of technology. This quick glance at the agricultural scene would suggest that, despite the influx of railroads, agriculture was only slowly moving toward profit seeking. Practicing safety-first farming, Hoosier farmers were reaping even greater rewards without much greater capital investment: the strategy of "surplus produce" was still paying off.

But with the rising values of farms and the closing of the public domain in the hill country, Hoosier farmers had to look elsewhere to find their children farms of their own. Perhaps the greatest transformation was due to the railroads after all. No longer did the family ties have to be broken as the children moved west. They were only a train ride—well, maybe a transfer or two—away. In the earlier part of the century, the letters back home would end with the lament of seeing each other in heaven. By 1860, these letters would end with plans for visiting the next winter. Geographical space had been diminished, a subversive inroad into these Hoosiers' localism.

For many Hoosiers, their localism still played an important role in their lives. The multitude of churches—sometimes the result of their localist desire to control their own congregations—meant that moral communities no longer corresponded as neatly to geographical neighborhoods, but these Hoosiers still believed in the importance of these moral communities. Because they still believed that immorality could be legitimately curbed only through the vigilance of the local community, the localism of these Hoosiers would continue to find expression in their lives.

SLAVERY AND RACE

Questions over slavery tapped into people's willingness to exercise moral authority at a distance, to impose some universal moral standard.[2] For Hoosiers raised in traditions that tended to see humans as depraved and incapable of living up to any such standard, such a notion as imposing morality seemed ludicrous; only under the careful watch care of the congregation and clergy could the worst impulses of humans be subdued. While all might share certain standards of behavior—imbedded in the Scriptures—their enforcement was best undertaken by friends and neighbors. To do otherwise would be to understate the depravity of humanity, while the absolutism of universal moral authority tended to strip each situation of its uniqueness and each offender of his individuality. By understanding this reluctance, we can better see why hill country Hoosiers, although many loathed slavery, were reluctant to act in any way to ensure its demise.

Hoosiers, many of whom were Upland Southerners, hated both slavery and African Americans. Many had left the South precisely because their dreams could not exist concurrent with the institution of slavery.[3] Southern Indiana was the endpoint for the greatest deviation from the prevailing east-to-west pattern found east of the Rockies.[4] The breaking of this pattern would suggest that these new Hoosiers disagreed with their Southern brethren about slavery. Certainly that was the case for Quakers and Scotch-Irish Presbyterians from the Carolinas. For many other new Hoosiers, however, such ready identification with antislavery denominations cannot be made, but their antipathy for the peculiar institution and its leaders was strong. From Vevay on the Ohio River, Charles Sealsfield reported:

> [The emigrants from Kentucky] would have remained, had it not been for the insolent behaviour of their more wealthy neighbors, who, in consequence of those emigrants having no slaves and being thus obliged to work for themselves, not only treated them as slaves, but even encouraged their own blacks to give them every kind of annoyance and to rob them—for no other reason than they dislike having paupers as neighbors.[5]

Unlike those Southerners who would move more due west into Mississippi and Alabama, the Upland Southerners who came to southern Indiana did not believe that slavery was essential to their political and social rights, as expressed in their local community.[6] Ardent Jacksonian C. W. Hutchen saw that "slavery is an evil, all will admit," for it "destroys energy, and creates idleness and dissipation." In nonslaveholding states, there were enterprising and industrious inhabitants, but in the slaveholding states, "the great mass of the people are 'too proud to beg, too honest to steal, and too lazy to work' and hence they content themselves with what they may happen to have about them."[7]

Southern-born Hoosiers not only forbade slavery in the state but sought within their local moral communities, the churches, to cut ties with congregations of their faiths that admitted slaveholders. Notably this separation occurred within the various Baptist sects, who in the early days still had ties to churches in Kentucky. In 1822, for instance, the Sharon Baptist Church asked its association to admonish the Kentucky Association, "on the principles of slaveholding."[8] Sinking Springs Baptist Church attempted to sever any contact with slaveholding churches when it "agreed to instruct our messengers to the next Lost River association to support the proposition (if such should be made) to request Blue River Association to bear testimony against the practis of slavery in their Kentucky correspondence."[9] For Lost River Association to correspond with Blue River Association, which in turn corresponded with slaveholding associations, was to taint Sinking Spring's worship. The line was drawn: slavery was sinful, and its practitioners could not be part of hill country moral communities. Having moved away from the cries of pain and anguish and severed their ties to those who perpetrated it, Hoosiers were absolved in their own minds from complicity in the peculiar institution.

Whereas Hoosiers were not averse to ridding their communities of the stain of slavery, they were nevertheless loath to deal with slavery outside their own communities. Any attempt to do so risked engaging in universal moral compulsion. People could not be forced to do good, but they could choose to curb their worst impulses. Hill country Hoosiers, who suffered under the admonition of the New England churches, certainly had little reason to do likewise to their Southern brethren.

Hatred of slavery often went hand in hand with hatred of African Americans. In seeking to exclude slavery, Hoosiers hoped to exclude African Americans, and from the beginning of the state, legislation was introduced limiting the emigration of freed African Americans to Indiana. In 1831, Indiana followed Ohio in limiting African Americans' rights further, animated in part by fears that portions of Cincinnati's large black population would migrate across the state line; the Indiana law did not prohibit African Americans from entering the state but just required that they post a $500 bond to guarantee that they would not become public charges.[10]

In the 1850s, many Whigs cum Republicans joined their neighbors in the Democratic Party in seeking ways to exclude African Americans from their communities. The Free Soil spirit sought to keep the frontier lily-white.[11] There were elements within the Republican Party that sought some form of equality for African Americans, and a sizeable number of Republicans sought the end of slavery, though without asserting equality for slaves. But racism pervaded the entire culture, North and South, Democrat and Whig/Republican, Catholic and Protestant, farmer and manufacturer.

This racism was reflected in the new Indiana constitution, written in 1851. Until this point, the state legislature had resisted efforts to erect additional barriers to freed people's coming to Indiana, but the new constitution specifically forbade any further migration of blacks to Indiana. The constitutional convention mandated that Hoosiers vote separately on the black exclusion clause, and so the racial feeling of Indiana was taken. Residents of the southern half of Indiana were nearly unanimous in their demand for racial exclusion. In the hill country, only five counties did not tally at least 90 percent of their population in favor of exclusion. Ripley County was the most open county in the hill country, but with 79 percent of its population voting to bar African Americans, Ripley was hardly progressive, and much the same point must be made about the rest of the state. In all but four counties the exclusion clause achieved a majority; in 70 percent of northern Indiana counties it had at least a two-to-one margin.[12] Throughout the state of Indiana, as throughout the United States, a clear majority sought to bar African Americans from their communities.

Racism, of course, was at the heart of this desire. Believing as they did in the special destiny of Americans of European descent, they excluded African Americans as incompatible with that vision. In a letter to the editor upon "The Negro Question," one *American Eagle* correspondent asserted that if a man who reflects upon this question "has common sense, and five grains of honesty about him, associated with a prurient [prudent?] regard for the character and welfare of the white race, he will, in all human probability, take a bold and fearless stand against the Abolitionist doctrines"; after all, a physiological contrast between the races would reveal how "ape-like" blacks were.[13] As time progressed, the emphasis on the animalistic qualities would grow stronger, the hatred and fear more profound, and the distinctions between men of different colors more pronounced.

For many hill country Democrats, their theology taught them to expect differences in humanity. Whereas for some perfectionist evangelicals, it was necessary to rescue both African and European and elevate them to achieve God's plan on earth, Catholics and Primitive Baptists were far more willing to accept God's world as he seemed to have handed it to them, including the degradation of enslaved African Americans. God worked in mysterious ways. These hill country Democrats saw the situation of slaves as natural and foreordained.

In many respects, this stance of both the Baptists and the Catholics reflected their roots in an earlier frame of mind, in which hierarchy was acceptable because all men were fallen; while this mind-set never understood the world in racial terms, its lesson about acquiescence in an individual's fate reinforced later racial notions to naturalize the slaves' condition. For much the same reason that Hoosier Baptists questioned missions to the indigenous peoples and to other European Americans, they wondered if God intended the African American to be saved; if He did, surely He would save him. And with doctrines like Daniel Parker's "Two-Seedism," which posited that humanity had roots in two seeds—one from God, one from Satan—it became easy for some to see the world as divided into two races, one good, one evil. Such an extreme idea was held only among a small minority, but for both Catholics and Primitive Baptists, fallen man deserved little better than the fate of the slave.

Nevertheless, Hoosiers were also racists. In Dubois County, by 1860 dominated by German Catholics, a nonpartisan meeting resolved:

> We hold to no equality with the Negro, and we will have no social intercourse with them, for we look upon them as an inferior race and believe that the Almighty never intended the races to amalgamate.[14]

But Germans also hated slavery. Joseph Thie reported that his father voted Whig once, because they promised to end slavery. However, Thie's father believed that the freed African Americans were not to amalgamate but were to be settled elsewhere.[15] In Dubois County, Christina Katterhenry saw the Civil War as God's punishment for slavery. For many Germans, slavery must have felt like a danger. They, too, did not belong, as much Nativist literature reminded them. And if the institution of slavery stood, they might find themselves first as second-class citizens and later perhaps as slaves. Having left Europe with its caste system still intact, German Catholics had embraced the white equality espoused by the Democratic Party; they did not wish to return to the kind of world they had left behind.[16]

Hill country Germans were not alone in opposing slavery while seeking to keep their distance from African Americans. For many Hoosiers, like many Democrats in the North, the races were far different—perhaps even of different origin—and the African race was incapable of enjoying liberty, at least not on the American plan, for natural law had defined the race's destiny in Africa and given it a particular set of rights and privileges. This naturalism had helped to define the colonization projects, as European Americans hypothesized about the distinctions between Africans and Europeans.[17] In many respects, naturalism paralleled the predestination of the Calvinist tradition of Primitive Baptists. By understanding the slaves' condition as the result of the immutable workings of either God or nature, the inferior caste of the Africans became self-evident, even while some could dismiss slavery as unnatural or un-Christian. The final blow to African Americans came from the circular nature of the reasoning: their subordinated status showed them as incapable of achieving equality. Indeed, for many Democrats, a corollary of that idea—only those who achieved liberty were capable of holding it—had animated them to resist all the intrusions upon their liberties from banks and the moneyed aristocracy. The United States was to be a white man's land, inhabited by those capable of achieving and retaining their liberty.[18]

Ironically, free African Americans had lived in southern Indiana from its earliest settlement by the European Americans. However, during the 1850s, the trend was reversed, as African Americans left the hill country.[19] What drove African Americans away? The Fugitive Slave Act of 1850 certainly made southern Indiana, with its close proximity to the slaveholding South, a more dangerous place for African Americans, both legally free and runaway. But hate and the violence that followed from it certainly must bear much of the burden.[20] The Civil War would only exacerbate these trends. In Washington County, the 1850s had seen a decline from 272 African Americans to 187, but by 1870 there were only 18 remaining, most of whom would quickly leave. The murder of two African Americans undoubtedly sped many departures. John Williams, who owned his own 160-acre farm, was shot in cold blood in 1864, for no apparent reason. Another man was killed for continuing to attend a white church.[21] In the 1860s and 1870s, hundreds more African Americans left the hill country, and other counties and towns in the region joined Washington County in banning African Americans extralegally from their locales.[22] The hill country, especially in its rural regions, had become lily-white.

This exodus occurred concurrent with a rising crescendo of racist rhetoric in southern Indiana. As the sectional crisis increased, African Americans in southern Indiana became a visible symbol of what was threatening to tear the nation apart and because that nation and its constitution served as the best guarantee of liberty, African Americans became a threat to European Americans' own freedom. Moreover, the debate over slavery had energized certain racial theories, theories which further demonized African Americans living in the hill country.

Racism explained the antipathy of hill country Hoosiers for African Americans, but it failed to explain why many of them seemingly chose to permit slavery in the territories, territories where their children looked for their future. After all, much of the popularity of the Free Soil movement, which became the Republican Party, proceeded from the hope that it would exclude African Americans, both free and slave, from the territories. To prevent a Civil War, Lincoln himself was willing to compromise to permit slavery in perpetuity in those states where it already existed in return for excluding it from all new lands. In this way, Lincoln—who grew up just outside the hill country in Spencer County, the son of Primitive Baptist parents—echoed the southern Indiana reluctance to interfere in the moral communities of the South. But hill country Hoosiers also believed that the new communities forming on the frontier were also beyond their moral scope: they should be allowed to decide for themselves the question of slavery.

LOCALISM AND POPULAR SOVEREIGNTY

Popular Sovereignty expressed Hoosiers' belief in democracy, their experience with self-government, and their understanding that morality was not universal but local. Democracy, they believed, asserted that each white man was equal and capable of governing himself. Such a man did not need the assistance of some elite from elsewhere to guide his decisions. In their territorial period, Hoosiers had survived such elite guidance, and they had quickly taken advantage of every possibility of slipping from such control. They also had chafed under the admonitions of New England missionaries, whose very presence questioned their ability to seek their own religion. And now, in the debates over slavery in the new territories, another unholy alliance between Eastern evangelicals and Eastern aristocrats threatened to impose their own universal standards on the children of hill country Hoosiers who moved onto these new lands.

Among Northerners the question of slavery in the territories was, at the heart of it, a conflict between those who saw slavery as an absolute wrong and those who could not abide a world governed by absolutes. For many, absolutes were a source of tyranny. Stephen Douglas, Popular Sovereignty's most vocal advocate, condemned uniformity as against the vision of the Founding Fathers:

> Our Government was not formed on the idea that there was to be uniformity of local laws or local institutions. . . . [Our fathers] foresaw that the great diversity of climate, of production, of interests, would require a corresponding diversity of local laws and local institutions.[23]

Douglas placed great emphasis on the construction of morality within tightly bound local communities.

For this reason, Hoosiers could be pleased with the notion of Popular Sovereignty and with the leadership of Stephen Douglas, even while their children made plans to move to Kansas or Nebraska. Opposed to slavery and opposed to blacks, emigrating Hoosiers could trust that their own exercise of self-government would create a society in keeping with their needs and desires. In their eyes, they should have the same opportunities afforded their parents, and their parents who remained in the hill country shared this belief: "[T]he Nebraska bill . . . leaves the question of slavery open for the people who settle the territory to settle."[24] In the minds of southern

Indiana Hoosiers, the principle of Popular Sovereignty was intricately linked to their own struggles against aristocracy.

> The extension of the right of suffrage has at every step met with determined opposition and yet it has always proved to be a blessing, and none of the troubles promised by the opponents have been realized. . . . And when the people of the Territories shall have had the opportunity to exercise their in-alienable rights, it will prove so much superior to the old apprentice system, that all will wonder that it had not been changed half a century sooner.[25]

When it appeared that the Buchanan administration was going against the principle during the Kansas constitutional question, Hoosiers reaffirmed Popular Sovereignty: "The Administration will fail to find the great mass of the party satisfied with the admission of Kansas with any constitution that may be framed for her unless the constitution be submitted to a vote of her people."[26] When the choice appeared to be the Democratic Party or the principle of local governance through Popular Sovereignty, Hoosiers chose principle.

They also chose principle over the potential of their children's sharing their new homes with African American slaves. While conceding the evil of slavery, some even saw it as a red herring, obscuring the great debate over the right of the people to govern themselves.[27] And fighting the Lecompton constitution, southern Indiana Democrats reaffirmed their adherence to the notion that the wishes of the people were the highest law: "We have yet to see the first Lecompton Democrat who maintains that the institution of slavery is the real wish, express or implied, of a majority of the *bona fide* settlers of Kansas."[28] Some Hoosiers did argue that not to allow the Lecompton constitution was to interfere with the sovereign affairs of Kansas's citizens.[29] Most hill country Hoosiers, however, believed that the principle of Popular Sovereignty was their best guarantee of creating a society consistent with their morals, and they believed that it provided the best opportunity for their children to re-create on the Great Plains the kind of communities in which they had matured.

Despite the evident tensions brewing beneath the surface of the Democratic Party in southern Indiana, the mid-1850s were numerically its most dominant period. The demise of the Whig Party had left the opposition somewhat directionless. Many former Whigs floated into the American Party at first, scared of the sectional character of the new Republican Party. At the state level, these two parties fused in 1854, forming a Fusion Ticket that attracted votes from parts of the hill country, but what was most evident was that the central portion of the hill country remained as the core of the Democratic Party in the state. In many respects, the 1856 election continued the success of the Democratic Party in southern Indiana begun in 1852, although subtle fissures were appearing. Only five hill counties failed to give Democrats an absolute majority, and all but three counties gave Democrats a plurality. At the township level, the established pattern remained the same. While Democrats and Republicans/Americans split the commercial townships, the Democrats had overwhelming appeal in non-commercial areas.[30]

The biggest difficulty for the Democratic Party in southern Indiana was several prominent Party politicians' support of the Buchanan administration and thus, in the minds of southern Indiana residents, of the Southern slaveholders. Jesse Bright, who represented the state in the U.S. Senate, and William English, who engineered the compromise on the Lecompton constitution, resided in Jefferson and Scott counties, respectively. English had attempted to walk the thin line between remaining friends with the administration and staying loyal to his constituents' wishes. But to most Hoosiers, Senator Bright served Southern slaveholders; indeed, Bright was one himself, for he held slaves on a Kentucky farm. A powerful member of the Senate, he had been instrumental in Buchanan's nomination, and he used this influence. The 1858 elections would see some hill country Democrats become disgusted by the administration's actions, and in several of the congressional races, anti-Lecompton Democrats ran against administration candidates, with one avowedly anti-Lecompton Democrat, John G. Davis, actually winning. Lecompton supporters did not bother to run a candidate in one congressional district, and the Democratic split in another opened the way for a Republican to win. Two other administration candidates won, including William English, and the English Bill seemed to have successfully defined a middle ground between support of the party and adherence to principle.[31]

The split between the Buchananites and the Douglasites would have an effect in the 1860 election. The election in the hill country belonged to the Douglas Democrats. In ten of the hill country's twenty-five counties, Northern Democrats still retained an absolute majority, and they gained a plurality in five more (map 5.1). Interestingly enough, many strong Republican counties in the hill country also provided support for the Southern Democratic ticket. One reason, of course, was that Southern Democrats drew votes away from Douglas, thus allowing for a Republican plurality. But a second reason had to do with the nature of the local Democratic Party. In counties like Scott, Jefferson, and Monroe in which local Democratic leaders had supported the Buchanan wing of the party, many of those leaders also supported John Breckinridge for president in 1860 and were able to deliver some votes for him. But such local pro-slavery leadership,

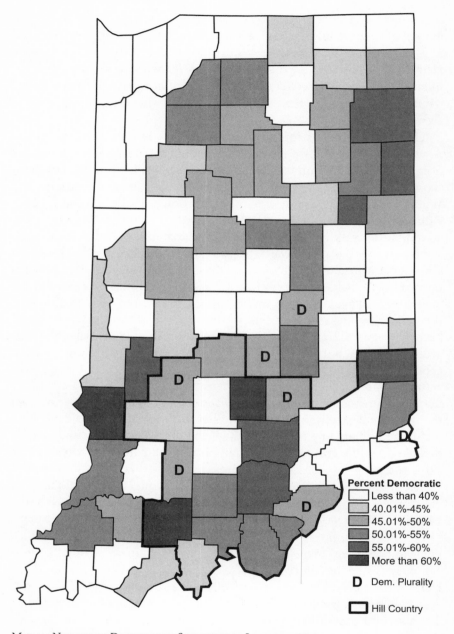

MAP 5.1 NORTHERN DEMOCRATIC STRENGTH IN INDIANA, 1860
Derived from Walter Dean Burnham, *Presidential Ballots, 1836–1892* (Baltimore: Johns
Hopkins University Press, 1955). (Boone/Nation)

most scandalously in the person of Jesse Bright, also seems to have driven some Democrats into the Republican Party, swelling its ranks.[32]

However, the most important element in southern Indiana elections remained the extent of commercialization, although 1860 introduced a new twist. At the township level, noncommercial areas were tallied in the Northern Democratic column; commercial townships generally voted for the other three tickets.[33] In the past, Democrats had split the commercial areas with their opposition, while maintaining a firm grasp on the noncommercial areas, but in 1860, Northern Democrats barely managed to win a third of the commercial townships, despite the increasing number of railroads through traditional Democratic strongholds like German Catholic settlements. For instance, the New Albany & Salem Railroad, which had extended itself from Salem to Gosport, Owen County, and points north, had along its route only seven townships which gave a majority to Douglas, out of twenty-one through which it passed. The New Albany and Salem delivered much of its freight to the Ohio, on which it was shipped south. Persons along this route, as well as others living in more commercialized areas, voted their pocketbooks in the 1860 election, seeing either in the expansive Republican vision new opportunities or in the Southern Democratic and Constitutional Unionist platforms the maintenance of their commercial ties to the South. For Douglas Democrats, however, the issue was far more localized, still tied into their ability and their children's ability to govern themselves: it was a vision of the Union, but one which saw the Union as the best guarantor of individual liberty and local autonomy.

THE SECESSION CRISIS

Douglas and the Northern Democrats lost, of course. To some hill country Hoosiers, secession was a predictable result of the Republican victory—they understood their Southern brethren—but war probably was not. Situated on what they perceived as the border, they disliked secession, but feared war. In their predicament, they urged compromise at almost any cost; some even preferred dissolution to coercion, but they were the minority. The rumors of war brought meetings and declarations from throughout the hill country.[34]

When the sectional crisis reached its crescendo, hill country farmers joined the rest of the nation in searching for the guilty. Most notable to many of these Democrats was the sectional character of the Republican Party.

Our forefathers warned us against sectionalism—and predicted, if acted upon, it would destroy our government. The Republicans would not heed the warning—they elected their man, and the horrors of a civil war is upon us.[35]

Others connected the Republicans' sectionalism to their willingness to ignore the Constitution, as interpreted in the Dred Scott decision.

> Abraham Lincoln, President of the United States was elected by a sectional party, who by their platform denied the right of citizens of certain States to settle and take with them their property, and hold it in the organized Territories of the United States, which was common property, belonging alike to all the states while Territories, or until State Governments are formed and admitted into the Union, either with or without slavery, as the citizens of each territory might determine.[36]

Some interpreted the Supreme Court's rulings more broadly, arguing that the United States was to be governed by whites: "This is a government made by the white man and for the white man; and that none but white men should ever exercise a governing influence therein."[37] Aaron Stryker privately wrote: "Our Country is gone up unless our Republicans will agree to come down on a Constitutional Basis that will satisfy the South."[38] The Constitution, with its direct references to slavery, was more important to Hoosiers than distant and degraded slaves, and protection of the Constitution was of paramount importance.

Agreement on the role of the South in creating the crisis was harder to find, and it was constantly changing, although after Confederates fired upon federal troops at Fort Sumter, many in southern Indiana began to argue that the South was guilty, too. Even before the violence began, some recognized that Southern fire-eaters shared the blame with Republican abolitionists, even while they dealt with the jumble of their own thoughts and emotions about the Civil War that they perceived on the horizon.

> But I do believe that if some of the Extreme Abolitionists in the North and some of the Extreme Southern fire-eaters were to get together and fight and kill one another, it would be a gods [?ser]vice I am aware though that such cannot be the case if there is fighting done they are the very men that will stand back and cooly look.[39]

At its deepest root, this Hoosier feared his own ultimate powerlessness and resented having to fight a war that fanatics had started through overextension of their own power. Some Hoosiers worked to affect the outcome, though. Those at a mass meeting of Orange, Dubois, and Martin counties judged the bulk of the Southern people to be faithful to the Union and thus unfairly being coerced by Northern extremists.

> We believe the people of the Southern states are and have ever been content to remain in the Union, and under the Constitution as handed down to us

by our revolutionary fathers. We deeply sympathize with them in their unwilling resistance to an incoming administration which, by a perverted construction of the Constitution, tending to destroy the rights of the people, of the States and the peace, prosperity, and happiness of the whole people of the Republic.[40]

But the Union sentiments were as real for most hill country Hoosiers as they asserted they were for most Southerners. Few joined the Brookville *Franklin Democrat* in asserting that the "Union was voluntary": "Let us peacably brake up rather than endeavor by blood shed to force a state to remain in the Union."[41] Many joined in declaring that the "maintenance of Federal Union transcends party ends and aims."[42] William Holman, one of the region's Democratic congressmen, wrote to his constituents: "But if this Union cannot be preserved by such sacrifices [as in the Crittenden Compromise], I am still *unwilling* at any time or under any circumstances whatever that this Union be dissolved."[43]

Their devotion to Union came precisely from the long-cherished belief that the Union served as the best protection for individual liberty and local autonomy. Many Hoosiers further recognized that the secession of the Southern states would weaken the Democratic Party within the federal government, thus permitting the Republicans—still Federalists in these Hoosiers' minds—to seize control of the government and execute their nefarious plot to deprive the common man of his rights. After all, in the Republican defiance of the Fugitive Slave Law, had they not proven their complete disregard for the Constitution?

> Will [Indiana] go with the Northern states? Will she be willing to cut loose from all her natural allies and form new ones with States that have, by open violations of the Constitution, brought about this state of things? . . . We think not.[44]

Others saw the situation not just as the work of a flawed party but as part of a longer conspiracy pitting one region against another.[45] Whether the crisis had been caused by region or party, Hoosiers felt the issue was their own rights. For many hill country Hoosiers, given their moral and racial distance from the plight of the slave, the notion that equality and justice were an African American's birthright was completely alien. Solely at issue was that their own personal equality and justice were being threatened by the ascendancy of a government that had proven its disregard for the Constitution.[46]

Despite the multitude of voices among southern Indiana Democrats, one aspect remained constant: these Hoosier farmers judged the events by the impact on their own lives. Whether supporting peaceful secession or restoration of the Union, southern Indiana Democrats looked to protect their constitutional rights and their communities as they understood them. Their differences, from this perspective, seemed less important than their similarities, and indeed, except for a few rabid War Democrats and a couple of decided Southern sympathizers, Democrats in southern Indiana found the means to coexist with one another, providing a solid opposition to Republican outrages while disagreeing over the prosecution of the war. Part of the reason for this unity was that the southern Indiana Democratic Party remained in the middle of the party, with few War Democrats or Southern sympathizers to polarize the issue.

SOUTHERN INDIANA SUPPORT FOR THE WAR

Although several important studies argue otherwise, the mythology that southern Indiana was peculiarly pro-Southern in orientation lives on.[47] For a variety of reasons, Democrats, especially those in southern Indiana, have been smeared by the charge of disloyalty. Certainly the most notable reason for this distortion came from partisan history. As the victors, the Republicans wrote the history, and in their history, Democrat was often equated with pro-Southern. Democrats were placed in the difficult position of being both loyal and yet retaining what they understood as a moral, if not constitutional, responsibility to voice opposition to the government's actions. Republicans found in this opposition a demagogic platform upon which they could advance their party's prospects, and the history of Democratic disloyalty was therefore initially written on the campaign trail.

For both Republicans and later historians who wished to emphasize such sentiments, there were some hill country Democrats who voiced stridently pro-Southern comments. Situated on what they believed would be the border between the two nations, some Hoosiers looked south to their natural allies and proposed that they be included in the new Southern nation. A Union meeting in Perry County resolved:

> That if no concession and compromises can be obtained, and a disunion shall be unfortunately made between the Northern and Southern states, then the commercial, manufacturing, and agricultural interests of this county require us to say that we cannot consent that the Ohio river shall be the boundary line of contending nations, and we earnestly desire that if a line is to be drawn between the North and the South, that line shall be found north of us.[48]

Congressman-elect James Cravens privately proposed that a new state of Jackson be formed from southern Indiana and Illinois, for the interests of that region were with the South.[49] Kentucky's remaining in the Union subdued such rhetoric, of course, but proposals like Craven's remained available to those questioning the loyalty of southern Indiana.

Statements before the war often emphasized these Southern connections. In the Indiana legislature, Washington County's Vermont-born state senator, Horace Heffren, asserted that he would

> leave my native land—my hearthstone—my wife and family—and rather become a private in the Southern army, fighting for equal rights and privileges, rather than be the Commander-in-Chief of an Abolition army that would be compelled to go to the South to shed the blood of those who dare to raise their arms for freedom and liberty—for justice and self-preservation.[50]

When war came, however, Heffren became a major in the Union army. Nevertheless, suspicions continued to follow him, and he was implicated in fifth column activity, even turning state's evidence in the course of the investigation in 1864. Less notable men also revealed their private desires to fight for the South: "If this noble Union of Ours does ever come to Cival War I would if I had to fight at all I would go South and help our Southern Brethren."[51] Like Horace Heffren, many other hill country Hoosiers, despite their earlier declarations, joined the Union army. The prewar rhetoric did not fit with their war behavior, but such evidence rarely convinced others that southern Indiana was loyal.

The editor of the Paoli *American Eagle,* who had seconded the sentiments of the Perry County Union meeting—that if the Union could not be preserved, the line should be drawn north of Perry County—argued that trade with the South made it southern Indiana's natural ally, but that Union remained the best outcome.

> Situated as the great State of Indiana is, there is no telling the value of the Union to her citizens . . . all her navigable streams flowing to the Southern states, by aid of which our people find an easy and cheap conveyance for their surplus products to a certain market.[52]

Despite their strategy of "surplus produce" to limit their dependence upon the commercial marketplace, many southern Indiana farmers sought to sell that surplus, generally on Southern markets, to achieve their long-term goals. Nevertheless, because many hill country farmers were generally less commercially oriented, the threat of losing their markets perhaps was not so great.[53] In the 1860 election, areas which showed more commercial interest had gone either Republican or Southern Democrat; Douglas Democrats attracted the noncommercial vote, suggesting that preservation of the Union remained the primary desire of many hill county residents. The talk of joining the South was often a recognition of commercial ties, but it was usually a contingency plan, to be adopted only if the Union had peacefully divided against these Hoosiers' desires. Preserving the Union, however, may well have been in the best interest of Hoosier commerce. When war came and Kentucky did not secede, Hoosiers' own plans for "secession" were mostly laid aside in haste. In its stead came demands that the Mississippi be quickly reopened. Many Hoosiers saw in reuniting the means to continue their lives as they had lived before the war.

> The state of Indiana on account of geographical position and commercial interest, never will consent to any settlement upon a basis of disunion, or a policy which shall separate her from the States bordering upon the Mississippi river. Her highest interest demands the perpetuation of the Union, and especially, that the great valley of the Mississippi from its source to its mouth shall remain under one government and one flag.[54]

The interests of trade propelled Hoosiers, both Democratic and Republican, into their Unionist stance, not toward a pro-Southern position.

Other reasons have also been put forward to explain the allegedly pro-Southern stance of southern Indiana, but most are as ambiguous as the commercial ties. Some have pointed to the leadership of Jesse Bright and, to a lesser extent, William English, but Bright was repudiated in much of the hill country by Douglas Democrats, and the Republicans were in ascendancy in the areas over which Buchanan Democrats had exercised the greatest control. Following the brother-versus-brother theme of the Civil War, others have pointed to familial ties, but while these undoubtedly troubled some individuals, many had been far removed from the South for many years. "Southern Brethren" was the favorite phrase, but when Vermont-born Horace Heffren could use similar rhetoric, its specificity was lost. After all, as one Dubois County speaker put it, Southerners were his brethren, but they were wrong, and "the only way to convince them of their error is to thrash it out of them."[55] Like commercial ties, familial ties played a role in the hill country's response to the sectional crisis, but in that role it generally supported the maintenance of the Union.

When the war came, Democrats and Republicans in the hill country were of similar mind. In fact, in the period from the election to the war, hill country Republicans typically had joined the Democrats in calling for some sort of peaceful resolution that maintained the Union.[56] In many respects, hill country Republicans shared with their Democratic neighbors familial and commercial ties to the South.[57] Hill country Hoosiers of both parties seemed more willing to compromise and overlook the other issues at hand, all in the interest of saving the Union. In its initial phase, they understood that the war was to restore the Union and to punish those who had resorted to violence to speed its demise, and these twin purposes were supported by Republican and Democrat alike.

Such shared purpose did not last long. Hoosier Republicans never quite trusted the sincerity of their Democratic neighbors, always condemning them for not volunteering for the army, and they were quick to uncover evidence that treasonable fifth column activity was being perpetrated in the state and especially in large parts of the hill country. In actuality, Southern sympathizers were scattered throughout the state and did not represent anything but a small minority of the peoples of the hill country.[58] Many who did join alleged fifth column groups did not do so for the largely delusional "Northwest Conspiracy" that filled the heads of a select few of the leaders, but as mutual protection societies that served to guard their civil liberties, threatened by the federal and state government. In large measure, they believed that the measures undertaken by Abraham Lincoln and Indiana's governor, Oliver P. Morton, were antirepublican and destined to strip hill country Hoosiers of their chosen way of life and of their rights guaranteed by the Constitution; such fears were reinforced when emancipation of the slaves was proclaimed, tapping deep into their racist fears that elevation of the African American would threaten their economic independence and universal white equality.

In many respects, the rise of allegedly pro-Southern organizations was the result of a self-fulfilling prophecy of the Republican administration of Governor Morton. Fearful that internal dissent would destroy the war effort from within, Morton used his power to root out those whom Republicans believed disloyal. Nevertheless, such actions signaled to many Hoosiers that their civil liberties and even their lives were in danger. In response, they often formed local organizations that served as protection from, as they claimed, any Confederates who would cross the Ohio River. But their abstract language about protecting liberty served as a warning to the Republican administration: "to protect the rights and property of our people against the depredations of lawless men or bands."[59] In response, the Morton administration often would not recognize them as the local militia, refusing to issue them arms. The Morton administration's actions played an important role in developing a network of resistance in the hill country.

Republican rhetoric angered some Hoosiers. From Brownstown, Isaac Ireland reported threats.

> Everybody is Traitors an Toryes that Dont Sancton the Ablition ware against Slavery The Chickago Plat Form Denies the South the Right to the Comon Teritory and places the Negro on Equality with the Wite man I am sorry that

> Thare Ever was a Sectional Man elected President We are repay the Reward
> Now . . . The Same Party that oposed the Mexican ware are the same party
> that urgin the extermination of the South and wanting the Negroes freed.
> The Republicans threaten to hang Every Body that dont Believe as they do.[60]

Yet Ireland's comments revealed that Morton was not alone in projecting
fears upon his opposition: few Republicans in Indiana supported African
American equality. In the summer of 1861, the notion that the war was
being fought over slavery was merely the wish of the abolitionist wing of
the Republican Party, but it was the uppermost fear of many Democrats.
Few who had volunteered for the army did so to end slavery. But the fear of
African American equality was a part of the calculation for those who opposed the war and thus refused to enlist.

In the hill country, as elsewhere, failure to enlist became the most obvious sign of disloyalty.[61] That some remained safe at home particularly
rankled soldiers, and their letters from the front were filled with indict-
ments of their neighbors who had not volunteered. The deprivation of army
life animated their anger. Soldier Joseph Hotz focused on his neighbors'
getting rich and living in relative luxury.

> You say that they did not draft in our township; I wish they had done it
> because there are a goodly number of lazy bones there with a big mouth who
> fight at home behind the whiskey glass. . . . I wish the low Germans would have
> to go soon, because they already made a lot of money with their bacon.[62]

For most, however, those who chose not to come were traitors of the
worst ilk, and the draft promised to force them to defend their country.

> I herd there was a draft took place in Ind the 18th of the presant month I
> hope that is so for there is some secesh and traitors back thair that will live
> under the government but wont support it.[63]

Even their mothers joined in the demand: "I hope they will draft some or
all of those that lean so much to the South."[64] When the draft actually did
come, the troops were happy that the Copperheads were conscripted.

> I received your letter a few days ago giving an account of those who were
> drafted at home and the news really did me good. Others got letters from
> home stating who were drafted in their counties and it was about the same
> way, nearly all Butternuts. The news has made rejoicing in the regiment.[65]

Back at home, Republican politicians such as Alexander Dunihue also
rejoiced that they could draft Butternuts, yet described the fears of Copperhead rebellion.

> We have a draft for 500 hundred thousand more but [Lawrence] county has to furnish only 180 Gibson[?] Township (butternut) 57, Bono (do.) 37, Indian Creek 25, Spice Valley none, Marion 37, Marshall 25, Perry none, Pleasant Run 4. The butternuts are all armed with Revolvers, in this county and in fact throughout the Western States.[66]

A close associate of the Republican administration, Dunihue reported that the governor had spies in all the lodges of the Knights of the Golden Circle and the Sons of Liberty, and that the government knew all the leaders and most of the members.[67] Dunihue's concerns revealed that Republicans were sincere in their fears, not merely using them for political hay, but he, like most Republicans, failed to understand that the Sons of Liberty and even the Knights of the Golden Circle appealed to other Hoosiers not because they supported the rebellion, but because these groups were the means to resist the oppression of the Republican administrations of Lincoln and Morton.

While some failed to enlist because they believed the war was just a means of oppression of themselves and their Southern brethren, others chose not to enlist for far more mundane reasons, including one which reached deep into the familial traditions of southern Indiana: their mother would not permit it. While the gendered nature of this prohibition was itself unusual, its basis in parental authority was not. In her reminiscences, Lucille Carr Marshall recalled her father's failure to enlist; Marshall was therefore troubled that her father, the descendant of some of Indiana's earliest settlers, did not fight. Marshall's paternal grandmother,

> Nancy, intense in her own rectitude, believed war to be wrong and those who took part in it, guilty of great sin. During the years of the Civil War, she went serenely to church to watch the baptizings and to sing the hymns. She said for all to hear that the North had no right to fight the South. Oh, slavery was wrong, everybody knew that, of course, but the southern people would take care of freeing the slaves if they were left alone. Were they not good folks? Did not many of the family's cousins live below the Ohio River? Could she think of permitting her own sons to go down to the South against them?[68]

Like many in southern Indiana, Nancy Carr did worry about fighting family members, but even more evident in her refusal to fight was her insistence that slavery was a local matter, sinful yes, but beyond the pale of her local community, and that even to eliminate a sin, it was not permissible to sin in another way by fighting. Nor was Nancy Carr the only mother to stop her sons from volunteering. In the German Catholic community of Huntingburg, not all who wanted to enlist could.

> The sons of my sister also had enough self-denial in regard to their lives to
> offer them, if need be, for the precious freedom and honor of the Fatherland
> and would gladly have gone [to war]. But the mother could not make the
> sacrifice, and since they are Christian youths they did not want to go against
> the wishes of their parents and are therefore still here.[69]

Why this German American mother refused to permit her sons to volunteer was not evident as it was with Nancy Carr, but in both cases familial obligations were deemed more important than duty to country.

German Catholics were the one identifiable group of Democrats in southern Indiana who did not generally enlist at the rate of others. In Franklin County in 1862, the townships with heavy German populations were forced to resort to a draft to meet their obligations.[70] German Catholics, who so often were Democrats, did not volunteer at the rates of their American-born neighbors, but they could hardly be accused of wishing not to fight their Southern brothers, and their dependence upon the market, let alone the Southern market, was relatively less, too.[71] While certainly Germans' desire to avoid war, which reminded them of European tyranny, was important, they, too, desired to remain within their local communities, with less regard for those like the enslaved Africans who lived elsewhere.

Republicans, of course, believed that the failure to enlist was only one indication of Democratic disloyalty, and they were quick to point to other examples, some quite serious, of treason in the hill country and elsewhere. In many respects, fears of Democratic disloyalty prompted Republicans, when faced with these episodes of traitorous activity, to respond with overwhelming force, which in turn confirmed Democrats' worst fears about Republicans' intent to destroy the white man's civil liberties, leading Democrats to organize resistance to this oppression, evidence to Republicans of Democratic disloyalty, thus beginning the cycle over again.[72]

Not surprisingly, however, it was the draft which provoked the greatest amount of armed resistance. To some Hoosiers, conscription was unconstitutional. Any form of the draft seemed likely to replicate the tyranny that had plagued Europe.[73] Indeed, for some hill country residents, it was worse: "The feudal ages had their priviliged orders, but even then the Baron was the first to risk his own life." Through the draft, the rich forced the poor man to leave his family and defend the wealthy. Resistance was promised: "If this conscription act is to be put in force, we advise Gov. Morton . . . to come himself, with his whole force, direct to Franklin county, for there may be trouble here." The problem with the draft was that it enslaved men, white men who had the right to be free:

I should just like to see an American citizen who had got so low that he
would stand like a dumb slave while his master lashed—not to a reasonable
task like the "sweet scented" negro—but to death. But perhaps I had better
say no more at present lest some man who has *three hundred dollars* will
denounce me as a traitor.[74]

For many poorer Hoosiers, the ability of the wealthy to purchase substi-
tutes confirmed that the purpose of the draft was to enslave poor whites,
part of the grander plan that elevated blacks while degrading whites. Threats
of resistance to the draft were heard throughout the region. John
McPheeters's wife reported the growing resistance in Stamper's Creek Township, Orange County: "A great many in Stamper's Creek twp say they will
shoot the man who comes to enroll their names."[75] Enrollment officers
throughout the state, including the hill country, were threatened, and sometimes those threats were carried out.[76] Armed resistance, of course, exacerbated the conflicts within Hoosier communities, because it confirmed the
Republicans' worst fears.

Yet resistance was scattered over a large area and over the four years of
the Civil War. Certain counties were the scene of recurring problems—
Brown, Greene, and Martin—but in general, the notion of highly organized groups planning systematic resistance and rebellion did not fit the
highly individualized nature of much of the resistance that did occur. Republicans often gave a partisan or treasonous twist to affairs that were personal and local in nature. Any illegal activity at all was connected to disloyalty. Southern Indiana had always had some difficulties with gangs, who
had hideouts in the more remote parts of the region, and during the Civil
War, these gangs were assumed by the Republican authorities to be part of
the "Copperhead" conspiracy.[77] In their search for disloyalty, the Morton
administration spied "secesh" everywhere.

Of course, the alleged "secesh" in southern Indiana sometimes proudly
wore butternut pins, the symbol of their opposition to the policies of the
Republican administrations in Washington and Indianapolis, and this proud
display antagonized administration supporters to the point of violence.
"Butternut" was the name that Hoosier Democrats adopted from the several used to deride them, in reference to the dye derived from the butternut
which they used to dye their home-spun clothes.[78] The Paoli *American Eagle*
drove home the point with its discussion of "Butternut Clothing":

In some neighborhoods in this county, there is some homes so intensely *loyal*
that they denounce their neighbors as Southern sympathizers and traitors,
because they wear brown Jeans—an article of clothing that has probably been

worn, in the West, to a greater extent than any other color. They denounce them thus, because they are Democrats, and that such colored goods are used by the rebels.[79]

Clothing worn for decades in the West and dyed with butternut stain separated those who pursued honest labor from those who sought to enslave them. By wearing a butternut pin itself, much as others elsewhere wore copperhead pins, Hoosier Democrats engaged in symbolic resistance to the tyranny of the Republican administrations. No act of resistance in southern Indiana inspired such overwhelming response. In both resistance and response, there were no gender boundaries.

> What is the meaning of that suit of Martha Alford in court? We heard she was fined [three] dollars for taking a butternut breast pin off one of the Canon Girls I suppose the Gove will remit the fine If he does not we [at the headquarters of the 12th Indiana Volunteers] propose sending her a testimonial if she was unjustly prosecuted.[80]

In Harrison County, a similar incident took place when Republican women attacked a girl wearing a butternut pin, but the incident turned ugly, and after the shooting ended, a man was dead. It was not the only death in the state over a small pin.[81] Nothing, however, symbolized the depth of the differences in the hill country better than the willingness to kill over a small nut.

Acts of individual and mob terrorism angered and hurt hill country Hoosiers, and many of these Democrats suspected that the Republican administrations were behind them or at least turned a deaf ear. However, hill country Hoosiers especially feared the actions of the government in limiting civil liberties. The cycle of government oppression's fueling civil resistance, which in turn initiated greater government oppression was primarily, as the model would suggest, within the realm of the government's actions, not those of various individuals or even mobs. Hill country resistance sometimes brought massive response from government troops—a regiment to Monroe County, a battalion to Brown—and these occupations of the hill country often only served to raise the stakes. Many Hoosiers believed that these occupation forces had ulterior motives. When a regiment was sent to Monroe County to recover the enrollment lists, residents of neighboring Greene County, one of the hotbeds of active resistance in the hill country, believed that such a large force probably intended to "invade" their county to suppress political dissent, and so a large number of armed Greene Countians allegedly gathered at the county line to repel the invaders. They did not choose to confront the regiment, perhaps having little problem with the army's ostensible task of recovering the enrollment list; yet their choice to defend their county line conforms neatly to the hill country belief in the sanctity of locale: they would not engage in aggression, but would repel any invasion.[82]

Martial law, of course, was what Hoosiers had feared from the beginning. Despite the "invasions" of the hill country, martial law was never declared anywhere in the state. But Hoosier vision saw further than their borders, and they feared that military rule could come to Indiana. Speaking about the 1864 elections, the Brookville *Franklin Democrat* asserted that Governor Morton "is using every effort to induce Lincoln to proclaim martial law in the State and make our election a farce and a juggle—as was done in Kentucky, Missouri, and Delaware."[83] Despite martial law's not being declared, during the prosecution of the alleged "Northwest Conspirators," military tribunals served as courts, rather than the civil courts, which were still open.[84] For some Hoosiers, these trials served as the confirmation of their worst fears that military tyranny could rule their lives; for others details of an actual "conspiracy" overcame their earlier trepidation about the antidissent campaign.

The most troubling aspect of the Republican administrations' campaign against disloyalty came early and in many respects served as the basis for most of the organized attempts to suppress dissent in southern Indiana: the suspension of the writ of habeas corpus. When the suspension was extended in 1862 to cover Indiana, the condemnations doubled.

> The Constitution guarantees us protection against unlawful arrests, and a trial by jury; the Writ of Habeus Corpus *secures* us these blessings. To comprehend how much depends upon this security it may be sufficient to know that without it, any of us could be seized, incarcerated in prison, and executed without trial, without law. We would be subject to these enormities by a vicious neighbor or any unscrupulous power who might conceive it in their interest, or the satisfaction of their hatred, thus to dispose us, and we could have no remedy—no relief.

Liberty was no longer a right but depended upon the capriciousness of those in power, and thus, "we have been hurled from the high pedestal of Freemen to the low condition of slaves."[85] With the suspension of the writ of *habeas corpus* came a multitude of arbitrary arrests, which the hill country soon discovered were used to quell what they considered legitimate political activity. In Seymour, Indiana, during a debate among the candidates for the Indiana legislature, an army officer in the audience took offense at the statements of the Democratic candidate, Jason Brown, and arrested him, dragging him to Indianapolis. The federal marshal there thought the charges insubstantial and had Brown released, whereupon he returned to Jackson County and defeated his Republican opponent in the election of 1862.[86]

The election of 1862 was the first opportunity for hill country residents to vote their minds on the Civil War, and they joined others from other parts of the state in a resounding shift to the Democratic Party, despite the Republicans' attempt to join with "War Democrats" in a Union party.[87] Most of the southern half of the state, including the hill country, elected Democrats to the Indiana House of Representatives (see map 5.2); the hill country selected twenty-two Democrats and only five Republicans to join the evenly split seventy-two remaining seats in the rest of the state. Only in areas of traditional Whig/Republican strength did the administration maintain its hold, mainly because its support there had been so strong originally. In October 1862, long before much of the active extralegal resistance began, hill country Hoosiers had acted to put a curb on what they perceived to be the threat to their civil liberties and way of life posed by the Republican administrations in both Indianapolis and Washington, thanks to the opportunity for the legislature to elect a U.S. Senator. Yet when the Democratic-dominated legislature got to Indianapolis, they found their ability to legislate limited by Republican maneuvering.[88]

For hill country Hoosiers, the loss of any legitimate means by which to participate in government was just one of a number of sacred rights that the Republican administrations had denied them: suspension of the writ of habeas corpus; conscription; disruption of the freedom of the press, freedom of speech, and the right to assemble peacefully; military tribunals; and martial law. In my brief excursion through these perceived offenses, I have not tried to establish cause and effect, but rather to re-create the context in which hill country Hoosiers, whose belief systems I have already explored in such detail, were immersed. Understanding their worldview before the Civil War, we can hardly be surprised that they reacted the way they did during the Civil War. Perhaps southern Indiana Democrats were a little naive, but these offenses against rights that they held sacred reinforced their earlier fears about the Republican Party and its desire to impose its absolute, universal moral values, so necessary for the expanding commercial economy it wished to usher in. For some, actually only a minority of hill country Democrats, active resistance to these threats seemed the required response.

RESISTING A CONFEDERATE INVASION

Perhaps the most ironic result of these intimations of southern Indiana disloyalty was that it might have lured Confederate troops across the Ohio

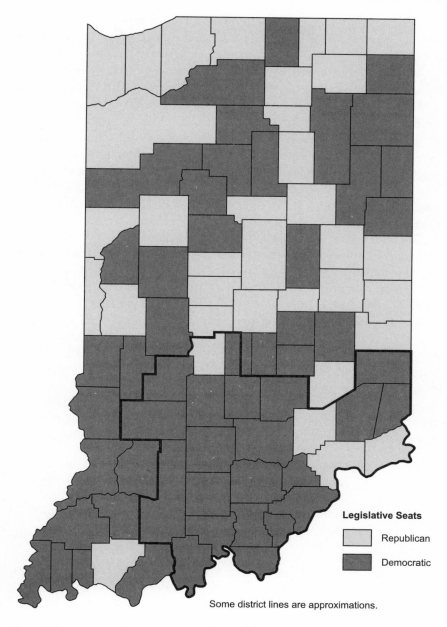

Legislative Seats

Republican

Democratic

Some district lines are approximations.

MAP 5.2 ELECTION FOR INDIANA HOUSE OF REPRESENTATIVES, 1862
Derived from *A Biographical Directory of the Indiana General Assembly,* comp. and ed.
Rebecca A. Shepherd et al., vol. 1 (Indianapolis: Select Committee on the Centennial
History of the Indiana General Assembly and the Indiana Historical Bureau, 1980).
(Martin/Nation)

River, in the belief that they would not meet much resistance. There were three raids into the state, one by Confederate irregulars in 1862 at Newburgh, in Warrick County outside the hill country, and two in 1863 into the heart of the hill country, one a small cavalry excursion led by Thomas Hines, and on the heels of it, a larger cavalry raid by Hines's superior, John Hunt Morgan.

Morgan appeared at Brandenburg, Kentucky, with two thousand cavalrymen, and they ferried across to Harrison County, Indiana. Like Hines, Morgan was acting without orders, but he proceeded through the hastily assembled militia of three hundred men at Corydon and north into Washington County, where again the citizenry gallantly formed some resistance, only to be shoved aside by overwhelming force. The rest of the state breathed easier when Morgan turned eastward, but the hill country felt the brunt of his raid, as he swept through Jennings, Ripley, and Dearborn counties, whose citizens all made futile efforts to repel the invaders.[89]

Despite efforts by Republicans to identify collaborators in the hill country, there was ample evidence that most Hoosiers were deeply angered by the Confederate invasion and fought against overwhelming odds in their effort to protect their homes. For hill country Democrats, their actions during the raids revealed their loyalty to the Union, but the Republicans were not so sure. Hines's raid especially looked peculiar, its military objective obscure, but that did not disturb most hill country Hoosiers, who jousted among themselves for the credit of capturing Hines's men. The Paoli *American Eagle* claimed the honor for ordinary citizens, including Orange County's own, as opposed to the organized Home Guard, which of course had the taint of the Morton administration. Democrats the state over asked their Republican neighbors to rethink the question of loyalty.

> When Hinds's [*sic*] band passed here every man in the vicinity, that had a gun, turned out—and when the second alarm was given, the people from every part of the county rushed to Paoli, to aid in driving out the invaders. There was but one feeling manifested throughout the large concourse of people—and that was to defend our soil to the last. Men and neighborhoods that had been denounced as southern sympathizers turned out promptly.[90]

The question of defending one's own home spoke directly to the southern Indiana localist tradition. At the beginning of the war, the Paoli *American Eagle* had claimed that "not a man in the Northern States would suffer such an invasion [by the South]—no matter how strong their sympathies might be with the South."[91] One soldier wrote home to hope that "now is the time for the men that are at home that always said the[y] would enlist when the time come—and now is the time—to catch [Morgan] before he has time to get out of the state."[92] Lucille Carr Marshall's father, who had remained home at the bidding of his mother, Nancy, responded likewise:

> Then word came of Morgan's Raid. Aunt Becky ran to the garden with a spade and the family silverware. . . . Four or five men hurried up our hill on horseback, seeking volunteers to turn Morgan back. Father quickly unhitched a horse from a wagon, leaving its teammate standing in harness while he ran upstairs for a rifle. Nancy did not interfere. This was defense of home; it was not warfare.[93]

The indiscriminate destruction and violence meted out by Morgan's raiders certainly consolidated support for the war effort in the region. William Orr, a soldier in the army, suspected as much:

> I want you to let me no what the people in Washington County think of John Morgan and his Band of thieves and robers. I guess the Copperheads wont think so much of the southern confederacy since John Morgan made a raid up there.
>
> The raids, by threatening Hoosiers' homes and way of life, solidified the aversion that many in southern Indiana already had for the secessionist cause.[94]

THE FIGHT FOR UNION

As we have already seen, most hill country Hoosiers supported the Union, but their understanding of the purpose and scope of the Union often differed from that of their Republican neighbors, even as they found general agreement with those same neighbors on the condition of the African American and on slavery within the South.[95] Many had entered the army to preserve the Union, much as their Republican neighbors would, but they did not believe that preserving the Union necessitated changing it. More importantly, they believed that the Union existed as the best protector of their individual freedoms and local autonomy.

The complexity of southern Indiana Democratic thought about the war often led to nearly contradictory emotions. Hoosier Democrats sought the middle ground, condoning neither secession nor abolition.

> Encouraging news from the army for the Last few days and if we don't meet with any reverses we may soon expect to see our union once more in a flourishing condition if we can ondly kill Abolitionist for no doubt they are responsible for the war All such men as Sumner, Lovejoy, Giddings, Hale, Julian and several others who are urging the Presadent and Conggress for an

> unconditional Emancipation of the States are just as bad men as Jeff Davis +
> Co. for their doctrine destroys the Constitution at once so I cannot see that
> they are any better than secesh.[96]

Whereas little love was lost for the Southern secessionists, there was no love at all for the abolitionists, precisely because, with their universal moral absolutism, they were in effect disunionists. Many Hoosiers supported the Union precisely as a guarantor of personal independence and local autonomy. This ironic twist was perhaps Andrew Jackson's greatest legacy. In defending the Union against the Nullificationists, Jackson had given voice to the feeling that the Union was somehow sacred. But it was in Jackson's exercise of the veto power that he most clearly displayed this negative vision of federal power: in the Jacksonian vision, the power of the federal government was only to be unleashed in the defense of liberty, to curb all other powers. By not exercising power in a positive manner—the Whig vision of expanding the economy, for instance—the federal government, as Democrats understood it, thus became incapable of acting capriciously, of favoring one group over another, and thereby denying the second its liberty. In only exercising its power in response to great threats to liberty, the federal government was thus limited, incapacitated from threatening liberty itself. The Union was, to Hoosier Jacksonian Tilghman Howard, the "greatest guarantee" of "the liberty of the people."[97] And so the Union remained for the three decades before the Civil War.

With the approach of war, Hoosiers reexamined their devotion to Union, but in the promise of the Union they still found the greatest protection for their freedom.

> Our liberty and independence is at stake. If a dissolution of the Union takes
> place, and civil war follows, where will the people of Indiana look to for
> protection. What power will or can, in such a state of things, secure to them
> the blessings and privileges they now enjoy under the Constitution and in
> the Union.[98]

So hill country Hoosiers marched off to save the Union. But the Union they wished to save did not need to be transformed to be saved. All their Southern brethren required was a good thrashing, but saving the Union also necessitated silencing the abolitionists.

> We as citizens of a common Union, are always ready to obey the require-
> ments of the Constitution, and will uphold and maintain the Union and the
> Constitution against all their enemies, come they in what guise they will,
> either as Secessionists or Abolitionists.[99]

For most hill country Hoosiers, their statements about the Union were not merely the hollow patriotic declamations of people accused of disloyalty, but reflected their understanding of the importance of the Union in protecting their liberties.

The Union and the Constitution were so important that hill country Hoosiers tended to call for speedy reunification without fundamental change. While their honor would not permit them to concede every point to the South—they especially urged that the South pledge itself to oppose future secession before reentry—Indiana Democrats saw few impediments to the successful negotiation of peace and reconciliation.[100] Few southern Indiana Democrats could be labeled Peace Democrats, but many held the abolitionists responsible for some of the problems. To their mind, both secession and abolition threatened the Union and the Constitution.

The beliefs of hill country Hoosiers were extremely localist in nature, and whether they volunteered or whether they refused to participate in the war or even chose to resist actively some aspects of the war effort, they followed their conscience and their Constitution, a document which they understood to protect the rights of free men. Sometimes there was little difference in thought between those who fought the war and those who were recognized at home as active dissenters:

> You spoke of D. M. Hill in your last as being a butternut i got a leter from him giving his views on the war i think if the people was all near write as he is we would have a beter prospect for the future than we have now.[101]

Other soldiers found themselves in the middle, neither abolitionist nor rabidly copperhead.

> I am between two fires the democrats censures me and say I am abolitionist becaus I am for the prosecution of this war let it cast what it may and becaus I am in favor of using the negro to the best advantage he can be used if they will fight let them do it I will not grumble a bit if a negro gets killed instead of me, so push them in.
>
> Again Republicans are down on me and say I am a secesh . . . because I am still a democrat.[102]

Of course, other soldiers did condemn those who remained at home. Some soldiers were already Republicans; others had been converted in the ranks. But there was a range of opinions within the army and no sharp dividing line between those who stayed and those who went to war.

The issue for most hill country Hoosiers, both those who fought and those who remained at home, was to maintain, as historian Kenneth Stampp would put it, the "Union as it was."[103] With "all the Predecessors of Mr. Lincoln ... it was universally acknowledged that the General Government had no power over domestic or local affairs of the respective States, and all held that the Union being "found in spirit of mutual concession and compromise" could only be maintained, by a "constant exercise of the same concilliatory and friendly impulse."[104] Concerned primarily about their own communities, Hoosiers saw the division that was ripping them apart, and they looked for the culprits. Needless to say, the culprits were outsiders—particularly the "General Government"—who had intruded into local affairs, a direct conflict with many Hoosiers' understanding of the Constitution, which served to protect localities from outside interference. Moreover, to Hoosiers, these outsiders, who wore the time-honored guise of "Republican" but held much more to the Whig-Federalist vision, introduced foreign ideas and encouraged a desire for power and wealth among their neighbors. The war was part of a Republican program that was destroying their communities.

Hill country Democrats argued that while the Republican administrations had, on the one hand, trampled the rights of ordinary Hoosiers, on the other hand, they had introduced all sorts of far-reaching legislation which, while Southern Democrats had been in Congress, could have never become law: tariffs, national banks, large-scale federal aid to railroads. These were issues which had historically troubled hill country Hoosiers, and with their passage, some Hoosiers began to believe that the Republicans had precipitated the war precisely to establish their program. Democrats noted the calls for a new United States Bank early in the war effort —"times demand such an institution"—and were quick to retort: "If the people want low prices for their labor and products, they will favor the establishing of such a bank." They added: "Recollect that Gen. Jackson rid you of this pest—and warned you against permitting the establishment of another."[105] In the midst of their denunciations of the tyranny and abuses current, Washington County Democrats included "greenbacks" among the crimes which the Republicans had foisted on the people in order to enslave them.[106] Such fears of capitalist ascendancy continued in the immediate postwar years. One Democratic candidate hoped the party would continue its fight against wealth, no matter who the local convention chose:

Whatever be the decision of the party in convention, I shall ever be found supporting the principles inscribed on our old banner let it be borne by whom it may. There is no time for family quarrels, for the fiery hoofs of the war horse of negro-equality can already be heard in the distance as a tornado which shall obliterate the last vestige of state rights, and overwhelm the poor whites with the burthens of taxation to support capitalists and the bondocracy in cash.[107]

Before the war, the rhetoric demanding resistance to capitalist expansion often implied enslavement of poor whites, but the emancipation of the slaves had given the rhetoric an additional racist overtone, one which began to pervade everything hill country Democrats would write.

The Republicans, Hoosier Democrats never tired of noting, disregarded the Constitution and thus destroyed the Union. Equating abolitionists with Republicans, Democrats pointed to the abolitionists' disregard for the Constitution's Fugitive Slave Clause as evidence of their willingness to ignore the Constitution in their endeavor to establish their absolute moral values. Never recognizing that enslaved African Americans might have rights, indeed, were suffering from the same sort of nondemocratic institution—intent on stripping humans of their liberties—that would have normally inspired many Jacksonians to use the power of the federal government to curb it, Hoosier Democrats could only see in the disregard of the Constitution a threat that other rights, both state and individual, guaranteed under that contract might also be in danger.

At the announcement of the Emancipation Proclamation, hill country Hoosiers rose in protest. Their worst fears, that the war for the Union would turn into a war to abolish slavery, were realized.[108] To many Hoosiers, slavery was a domestic institution outside the oversight of the federal government, and to abolish it in any state was a deliberate interference by the federal government in local affairs. Again, the fears revolved around what Democrats perceived as the potential for continued interference in local arrangements.

Yet, as we have already seen, hatred for the African American had crept into even postwar condemnations of the capitalist aristocracy of bondholders. Beyond any inability of southern Indiana residents to see that African Americans had rights that deserved protecting, Hoosiers began to attribute to these freed slaves a more direct danger to themselves. The earliest steps toward emancipation drew a comparison to the loss of liberties of whites: "We have always been of the belief that the freeing of negroes involved, of necessity, the enslaving of the white race, and hence it does not surprise us that this attempted change in the status of the negro is accomplished by a corresponding change in the status of white men."[109] Much as some Southern whites saw the enslaved African American as their protection from the grasp of the capitalist, who, as long as he had a steady nonwhite labor source, would continue to accept peaceful coexistence with an independent white yeomanry, many Hoosiers believed that the freeing of the slaves and their entry into society would serve to degrade white labor and thus destroy the common equality that had marked all European American men. "We shall oppose negroes coming into Indiana and settling, for such a policy will destroy the wages of the laboring white man—compelling him to become worse than a slave."[110] Hill country Hoosiers believed that the only place where equality could reign was where African Americans were not. Believing that their equality rested on the absence of slave owners and capitalists who exploited labor, they feared a world in which a "servile" class like African Americans would create the proper conditions for capitalist endeavors. James W. Owens made clear the connections between universal white equality and African debasement: "If to think a poor man is good as a rich one, if to value a white man more than a negro, makes one a copperhead, then, *oh, but I'm a Copper.*"[111]

While some Hoosiers linked their economic concerns with African American freedom and formed their opposition on their own loss of freedom, others resorted to the basest forms of racism. Opposition to the Emancipation Proclamation brought forth some outrageous contentions. One meeting concluded,

> That the Proclamation of Abraham Lincoln, freeing all the slaves in certain States and parts of States, is an unwarranted usurpation of power, a violation of the Constitution, and an act which should be treated with scorn and contempt by every lover of this country; by every man, who is opposed to rapine, butchery, and every species of crime at which humanity revolts.[112]

Stamper's Creek Democrats agreed, resolving that Lincoln "consigns the women and children of the South to servile insurrection, assassination and butchery, rapine and murder, by a barbarous, inferior and servile race, is inhuman, disgraceful, and contrary to all the usages of civilized warfare, justly earning for its author the execration of mankind."[113] In their racialized sympathy for the Southerners in rebellion against them, hill country Hoosiers marked out new lines of community, of "us."

Even some Hoosiers in the army recoiled at the Proclamation. Days after Lincoln issued the statement, Isaac Rowland wrote his father that "i am out fighting to free the negroes whitch dont set very well on my stomache just now."[114] John Hardin also reported dissent in the ranks, but he argued that "if it will put the rebellion down I will fully concent to it. anything in the world that will restore peace to our country."[115] While Indiana did not secede as some prophesied, the proclamation led to a drop in enrollment and the expansion of the draft in southern Indiana, which further angered many Hoosiers. In Springfield Township, Franklin County, some citizens met in 1864 to voice opposition to the draft.

Whereas, it appears to be the fixed determination of the present administration to accept of no terms of settlement of our national troubles, short of an unqualified abolition of slavery throughout the States; and for the purpose of accomplishing this object solely the President has ordered that five hundred thousand men be raised by conscription.[116]

The Emancipation Proclamation angered many, yet other events would mitigate its effect on the 1864 election in southern Indiana.

Perhaps the most notable of these events was the actual arrest of several Hoosiers for involvement in the "Northwest Conspiracy." Among these were prominent hill country Democrats: Horace Heffren of Washington County, William Bowles of Orange County, and Andrew Humphries of Greene County. Humphries was probably unfairly accused, but he was found guilty along with the others when Heffren turned state's evidence and reported what he knew. Heffren apparently was aware of the grandiose plans of some of the conspirators, although his own role remained quite obscure. Bowles was one of the grandiose, and he was guilty of treason. Actual guilt or innocence, however, was not as important as what the public perceived, and with respected Democrats like Heffren turning state's evidence, many could easily believe that the Republicans, after all, were correct in their assertions of fifth column activity.

Therefore, despite the Emancipation Proclamation, Democrats did not build much upon their 1862 gains in southern Indiana, regaining only Scott and Greene counties. In 1864, seventeen hill counties gave their tally to the Democrats. Various townships and counties may have shifted, but the more general patterns of voting remained the same in southern Indiana, which continued to be a Democratic stronghold. The rest of the state, however, swung strongly back into the Republican column, thus muting hill country political voices.

PRIMITIVE BAPTISTS AND THE CIVIL WAR

The war had a profound effect on the communities of southern Indiana. Partisan politics took on a new cast. No longer was it possible really to defer to the decision of the electorate. It was people's loyalty and their love of liberty that were in question. The partisan politics, the question of loyalty or disloyalty, the conflicting visions of freedom—all spilled over into other aspects of southern Indiana life. Families were divided by these conflicts. And many a church was, too.

The Civil War inspired several separations among "Primitive" Baptists. Unity Baptist Church, near Hardinsburg, in Washington County, was led by Charles Sands, a preacher who participated in at least one Union meeting before the Civil War.[117] In 1862, Unity placed on its books a set of "Political Resolutions," which immediately earned them the enmity of neighboring churches and precipitated a split within the Unity congregation.[118] After the war's close, the minority and majority parties were able to patch up their differences:

> We do now jointly agree that as we in former days lived pleasantly and in fellowship one with another and desiring not to so act that we may not longer reproach the cause but in all difference to bear much and suffer long ever seeking each others good and Religious welfare cultivating the noble principles of peace love and harmony that the lost influence of society may be regained that the discipline of Gods house may be regarded and the house of Christ healed.[119]

The congregation of Unity tried to heal the wounds of the war.

In a Franklin County "Primitive" Baptist church, there was never any actual division during the war, but the wounds festered. Early in 1865, Big Cedar Grove Baptist Church received Elder W. H. T. Perdue after his relation of a conversion experience; he could not get a letter of dismission because of the war in the South whence he came.[120] Perdue stirred up some trouble during a short tenure, praying for the North and those in authority. After leaving for a church in Tipton County, Perdue returned, but was not readmitted to the church, because "he had sold this church to the Missionary Baptists."[121] Missionary Baptists were antithetical to "Primitive" Baptists, who were often called antimissionary Baptists, because they believed that missionary work was unscriptural. Missionary Baptists, by contrast, had a far more liberal view of evangelical work, believing that God sent them out to proselytize and, for those with a postmillennial bent, to prepare His kingdom on earth. Perdue apparently polarized the congregation. John P. Brady wrote to Joab Stout:

> I do feel that our church is in a deplorable situation at present, with scarcely one ray of hope for the immediate future.
> In some respects it seems quite apparent that our house, or Church is divided against itself, and if so, the future is plainly fore-told.[122]

When Big Cedar Grove Church chose its pastors in 1869, a miscount which swung one pastorship from the Perdue supporters—Joab Stout, actually—to the antimissionary group—Brother A. L. Thurston—angered many in an already angry congregation divided over missionary work.[123] At the original election, slanders flew, and Brother Ira Stout called another member a "Rebel." Stout, the Democratic paper retorted, "*fit bled* and *died* for the country in the way of a secret police for Springfield Township."[124] Two months later the local Republican paper chimed in, arguing that the problem began when the "'copperhead' element" in the church was angered by Perdue's political creed.[125] The war had not been left behind in the hill country. The deeper cultural issue which underlay the "Primitive" Baptist aversion to missionary movements had also animated the "Copperhead" aversion to the war and abolitionism. It was a question of moral horizons: What sort of responsibility did an individual and a community have to those outside the neighborhood, outside the watch care of the congregation?

The Civil War would play its own role in the destruction of localism. By dividing communities like Big Cedar Grove, the conflicts created by the war destroyed some of what made localism viable. The war had other effects, as it accelerated the process of nationalism, making the Union more than just a protector of civil liberties. Much was changing in other facets of Hoosier life, and the limited horizons of localism were slowly pushed and pulled. The Democratic Party, a national organization, demanded greater allegiance to itself than to one's locale; in return, it promised to protect the citizen's independence, much as the rural neighborhood cum community once had. And the white race expanded many Hoosiers' notion of "we," an expansion which allowed American-born Hoosiers to welcome German Catholics to the hill country, while nevertheless permitting them to engage in the most scurrilous of race-baiting and even racial violence, as they drove African Americans from longtime homes in the region.

Changes were also happening in the society and economy. Railroads and other forms of modern transportation had created new links across the nation, allowing Hoosiers to become more integrated into the marketplace, buying more and more consumer goods. And these new forms of transportation allowed the children of hill country residents to remove to distant territories without leaving their families behind forever; if family had been the building block of hill country communities, that families could continue contact even though they no longer lived in the neighborhood meant that "community" would be redefined outside of geographical space, but within familial space.

Yet these changes would be incremental, as there remained remarkable stability in the society. The Democrats still predominated, nonevangelical Christians still had voice, and "surplus produce" still defined the way most hill country Hoosiers farmed.

Epilogue

The division in the Big Cedar Grove Church was not the only one that tore southern Indiana communities apart in the postwar years. The Civil War drove an important wedge, as hill country Hoosiers, insufficient in their devotion to the Union, began to be labeled traitors. Throughout the region, contention and strife began to surface, and differences that before the war were often handled through the legislative and judicial processes found extralegal forms of expression, through gangs, mob violence, and the formation of vigilante committees. By the late nineteenth century, distinctions between southern Indiana and the rest of the state had crystallized, in part because the rest of the state had changed, while southern Indiana continued to embrace a more traditional worldview. Nevertheless, change was occurring in southern Indiana, creating conflicts within their communities.

Perhaps nothing came to distinguish the hill country of southern Indiana more from the rest of the state than in its agricultural production. By 1880, central Indiana had developed into one of the world's great mixed farming regions, but the hill country lagged behind.[1] Many hill country farms were still barely managing to bring any kind of surplus at all; eleven counties produced deficits. But hill country Hoosiers were more likely to own their own land. Not wishing to risk a purely commercial enterprise, many southern Indiana farmers were convinced that their traditional hog-and-corn strategy, while not lucrative, worked best to ensure their independence. Among them, others were attempting to catch up with their neighbors to the north, buying machinery, draining fields, and increasing surpluses.

Yet the momentous yields of the flatlands of Indiana and the profits from tobacco elsewhere in the Ohio Valley reinvigorated the common refrain about the lack of ambition of southern Indiana residents. Even among the residents of the region, this complaint resounded:

> The population of Washington County is on the decrease. What is the matter? The cause for this can be summed up in three words: Lack of Enterprise.[2]

This correspondent detected "some" enterprise in the county seat of Salem—not surprising among the merchant classes—but found it lacking in the townships, among the farmers. As the consumer culture gained ascendancy, it illuminated the reluctance of the southern Indiana farmer to fully participate in the market and thus to purchase the myriad consumer goods being produced. Hill country Hoosiers were tagged with the label of poverty. Were they poor? Only if poverty is defined by the lack of consumer luxuries.[3] In 1880, the production levels in southern Indiana were sufficient to keep most farm families fed, the land provided lumber for fuel and shelter, water was plentiful, and the work of women in butter and eggs probably provided much of the funds for clothing.

Southern Indiana's image as poor and uncivilized was made worse by the extralegal violence that periodically erupted in the region. Lynching and Regulator activity would help to define the hill country of southern Indiana.[4] Before the Civil War, lynching had been rare in southern Indiana, but Regulator activity—the mass visitation of the community on an unsavory neighbor, which might include some form of violence, but often was merely the threat of violence, a warning to leave the community—had always been available as the last resort of the community. The Civil War had broken down some of the trust that held together communities, and in the immediate aftermath of the war, deadly violence became increasingly common in southern Indiana. The initial source of this reign of terror began in Jackson County, and from there, lynching and other forms of violent extralegal justice spread throughout the hill country.

Jackson County's immediate justification for the lynching was that fourteen murders had occurred within two years.[5] Vigilante committees were organized, with the "best citizens of the county," and two alleged rapist-murderers were lynched. When the Reno Gang robbed an express train near Seymour, ten gang members were killed in three incidents. Before they had finished in 1869, the Jackson County vigilante committee had murdered seventeen men. Their actions found copycats throughout southern Indiana. When Delos Heffren, brother of confederate sympathizer Horace Heffren, committed murder in Salem in 1873, Washington County lynched him. From 1865 through 1898, at least sixty persons were lynched in the hill country of southern Indiana. The tide against lynching, at least of whites, was finally turned in 1897, after five men accused of minor felonies were taken from the Ripley County jail and hanged. The public revulsion in the rest of the state propelled the enactment of two antilynching laws.[6]

Hill country Hoosiers who engaged in lynching cared little about public opinion outside the region; they saw their attempts as necessary for maintaining their communities. There had been a breakdown in the traditional forms of regulating the community, such as church discipline, and the criminal justice system had proven inadequate.[7] Likewise, many hill country Hoosiers justified the growth of Regulator activity as necessary for maintaining morality and decency within their communities. The Regulators "are not a gang of lawless ruffians as one would suppose from reading of their proceedings, but farmers who propose to make the lazier, shiftless population behave themselves."[8]

Regulator activity focused not so much on serious crimes as upon violations of what its participants considered the moral code of the community: drunkenness, adultery, wife beating, and laziness. The punishment was a whipping, but some of these were so severe that they were nearly fatal. Regulator activity had its first burst of activity in the postbellum period in 1873, but then quieted down to a mild level of activity—an incident every other year or so. The late 1880s and early 1890s were the heyday of vigilantism, with well over fifty incidents that have come to my notice, and the activity would continue through 1912, moving slowly north and settling in Monroe and Bartholomew counties.[9]

Those who initiated the Regulator activity hoped, sincerely I believe, that by reestablishing their moral authority in the communities of the hill country, they would help to modernize the region. Yet their willingness to resort to violence revealed how tradition bound even these alleged upstanding citizens were. In Harrison and Crawford counties, at least, the local Regulators were intimately connected to the Republican Party and may have had their organizational roots in the pro-Union secret organizations which had sought to ferret out their pro-Confederate neighbors—they tended to perceive that those who were Democrats were also those content to lead dissipated lives.[10]

For many hill country Hoosiers, the Democratic Party continued to respond to their needs, fighting the radical money questions when they needed to be fought.[11] Although in several counties the tide had shifted to the Republicans, the region as a whole remained strongly Democratic. More important, thanks in large measure to the careful balance that hill country Democrats maintained during the Civil War between loyalty to country and opposition to the administration, the two-party system had remained alive in Indiana, allowing the Democrats to represent the interests of hill country farmers: there was little waving of the "bloody-shirt" in the hill country. In the process, southern Indiana Democrats balanced the Republicans in the northern two-thirds of the state, making Indiana a swing state in national elections.

By the early twentieth century, these Democrats represented hill country farmers who were increasingly impoverished. Falling commodity prices meant that hill country farmers would get insufficient income to achieve their familial goals, even if they could eke out some form of subsistence. Moreover, the limitations of the land were being reached. A century of cultivation took a toll on its fertility; by 1935, soil erosion in most of the hill country exceeded 50 percent, with Crawford County registering over 99 percent.[12] Timber sustained some farms in the latter part of the nineteenth century and into the twentieth, and other extractive industries—notably limestone in Monroe and Lawrence counties and coal in Greene County—would help to support some of the region's communities. Slowly land would be taken out of cultivation. This process was accelerated by the Depression and the subsequent New Deal programs, which dealt a terrible blow to the surplus produce strategy, and it was aided by federal and state purchases of large tracts during the New Deal and into World War II, including three very large military facilities and the Hoosier National Forest, now encompassing 196,000 acres.[13]

Yet worldviews die out much more slowly than their material basis. To visit southern Indiana today is still to encounter strong elements of ways of thinking that were transplanted and molded in the nineteenth century. And since these worldviews were not unique to southern Indiana, they can be found throughout this nation and beyond.

Notes

Abbreviations

Edmonston Papers	Bazil B. Edmonston Papers, Indiana Division, Indiana State Library, Indianapolis
Genealogy Division	Genealogy Division, Indiana State Library, Indianapolis
IHS	Indiana Historical Society
Indiana Division	Indiana Division, Indiana State Library, Indianapolis
Lilly Library	Lilly Library, Indiana University, Bloomington
Mace Collection	Benjamin Mace Collection, Indiana Division, Indiana State Library, Indianapolis
Pering Papers	Pering Family Papers, Indiana Division, Indiana State Library, Indianapolis
Smith Library	William Henry Smith Library, Indiana Historical Society, Indianapolis
State Archives	Indiana State Archives, Indianapolis
WCHS	Washington County Historical Society, Salem, Ind.

Introduction

1. This has been made most apparent for regions in the rural Midwest by William Cronon, *Nature's Metropolis: Chicago and the Great West* (New York: W. W. Norton, 1991), which traces the development of Chicago in relation to the development of its hinterlands.

2. Lawrence Kohl, *The Politics of Individualism: Parties and the American Character in the Jacksonian Era* (New York: Oxford University Press, 1989). Many supporters of integration and progress had their particular concerns about the changes being wrought, but they tended to focus on the danger of liberty turning into license, with a secondary concern about the weak being crushed. See Daniel Walker Howe, *The Political Culture of the American Whigs* (Chicago: University of Chicago Press, 1979); Christopher Clark, *The Roots of Rural Capitalism: Massachusetts, 1780–1860* (Ithaca, N.Y.: Cornell University Press, 1990); Paul Johnson, *A Shopkeeper's Millennium: Society and Revivals in Rochester, New York, 1815–1837* (New York: Hill and Wang, 1978), and Ronald Walters, *American Reformers, 1815–1860* (New York: Hill and Wang, 1978).

3. This ambivalence showed up in muted hindsight among the residents of western New York, as detailed in Carol Sheriff's *Artificial River: The Erie Canal and the Paradox of Progress, 1817–1862* (New York: Hill and Wang, 1996).

4. Martin Bruegel, *Farm, Shop, Landing: The Rise of a Market Society in the Hudson Valley, 1780–1860* (Durham, N.C.: Duke University Press, 2002); Clark, *Roots of Rural Capitalism;* Susan E. Gray, *The Yankee West: Community Life on the Michigan Frontier* (Chapel Hill: University of North Carolina Press, 1996); and Stephanie McCurry, *Masters of Small Worlds: Yeoman Households, Gender Relations, and the Political Culture of the Antebellum South Carolina Low Country* (New York: Oxford University Press, 1995).

5. James Bergquist, "Tracing the Origins of a Midwestern Culture: The Case of Central Indiana," *Indiana Magazine of History* 77 (1981): 1–32; and John Lauritz Larson, "Pigs in Space; or, What Shapes America's Regional Cultures?" in *The American Midwest: Essays on Regional History,* ed. Andrew R. L. Cayton and Susan E. Gray (Bloomington: Indiana University Press, 2001).

6. Andrew R. L. Cayton and Peter S. Onuf, *The Midwest and the Nation: Rethinking the History of an American Region* (Bloomington: Indiana University Press, 1990). Cayton

and Susan Gray concede that the largest groups of dissenters from this tradition were in southern Ohio, Indiana, and Illinois. See Cayton and Gray, "The Story of the Midwest: An Introduction," in their edited volume *The American Midwest*, 13–14. The other essays in this volume make a series of strong ruminations about the regional identity of the Midwest.

7. In contrast to the focus on self-identity in Cayton and Gray, eds., *The American Midwest*, Appalachian studies has generally focused more on outsiders' construction of region, perhaps because the localism of Appalachian residents limited their sense of regional identity. See Henry Shapiro, *Appalachia on Our Mind: The Southern Mountains and Mountaineers in the American Consciousness, 1870–1920* (Chapel Hill: University of North Carolina Press, 1978); David Whisnant, *All That Is Native and Fine: The Politics of Culture in an American Region* (Chapel Hill: University of North Carolina Press, 1983); Allan Batteau, *The Invention of Appalachia* (Phoenix: University of Arizona Press, 1993); and Altina Waller, "Feuding in Appalachia: Evolution of a Cultural Stereotype," in *Appalachia in the Making: The Mountain South in the Nineteenth Century*, ed. Mary Beth Pudup, Dwight B. Billings, and Altina Waller (Chapel Hill: University of North Carolina Press, 1995), 347–76.

8. Cayton and Gray, "The Story of the Midwest: An Introduction," 13–15.

9. Gray, *The Yankee West*; Don Harrison Doyle, *The Social Order of a Frontier Community* (Urbana: University of Illinois Press, 1978); Susan Sessions Rugh, *Our Common Country: Family Farming, Culture, and Community in the Nineteenth-Century Midwest* (Bloomington: Indiana University Press, 2001); and Kim Gruenwald, *River of Enterprise: The Commercial Origins of Regional Identity in the Ohio Valley, 1790–1850* (Bloomington: Indiana University Press, 2002).

10. The tendency for politics to follow ethnic, religious, and cultural lines was well detailed by a group labeled the "ethno-cultural" historians. As a good entry point, see Ronald Formisano, "The Invention of the Ethnocultural Interpretation," *American Historical Review* 99 (April 1994): 453–77. Summing up the pertinent findings for my work is Robert P. Swierenga, "Ethnoreligious Political Behavior in the Mid-Nineteenth Century: Voting, Values, Cultures," in *Religion and American Politics*, ed. Mark Noll (New York: Oxford University Press, 1990).

11. The evangelical-Whig-capitalist mode has been explicated by Paul Johnson, *A Shopkeeper's Millennium*, and Howe, *The Political Culture of the American Whigs*. A shorter overview is Howe, "The Evangelical Movement and Political Culture in the North during the Second Party System," *Journal of American History* 77 (March 1991): 1216–39. Also suggestive are Thomas L. Haskell, "Capitalism and the Origins of the Humanitarian Sensibility," *American Historical Review* 90 (April 1985): 339–61 and (June 1985): 547–66; Nathan Hatch, *The Democratization of American Religion* (New Haven, Conn.: Yale University Press, 1989); and Kohl, *The Politics of Individualism*.

12. Charles Sellers makes a splendid effort in *The Market Revolution: Jacksonian America, 1815–1846* (New York: Oxford University Press, 1991), but he saddles himself with the unfortunate categories of Arminian and Antinomian, which prove to obscure as much as they illuminate. Like Sellers, many others have tried to explain away the presence of Catholics in the Second Party system. Kathleen Neils Conzen has addressed some of these issues in "German Catholic Communalism and the American Civil War: Exploring the Dilemmas of Transatlantic Political Integration," in *Bridging the Atlantic: The Question of American Exceptionalism in Perspective*, ed. Elisabeth Glaser and Hermann Wellenreuther (Washington, D.C.: German Historical Institute, by Cambridge University Press, 2002).

1. The Land and Its Peoples

1. Enoch Parr, "Memoir of Enoch Parr," *Indiana Magazine of History* 22 (December 1926): 373–77.

2. Allan Bogue, *From Prairie to Corn Belt* (1963; Chicago: Quadrangle Books, 1968), 51–52; James Henretta, "Families and Farms: Mentalité in Pre-Industrial America," *William and Mary Quarterly*, 3rd ser., 35 (January 1978): 3–22.

3. Henry Nash Smith, *Virgin Land* (1950; Cambridge: Harvard University Press, 1970), 123–44; Richard Slotkin, *The Fatal Environment* (1985; Middletown, Conn.: Wesleyan University Press, 1987), 60–76.

4. On the contemporary poverty of southern Indiana, see James Madison, *The Indiana Way* (Bloomington: Indiana University Press, and Indianapolis: Indiana Historical Society, 1986), table 4, 287.

5. For a sampling of travelers' comments on land quality, see Morris Birkbeck, *Notes on a Journey in America* (Philadelphia: Caleb Richardson, 1817), 107–108: David Thomas, *Travels through the Western Country in the Summer of 1816* (Auburn, N.Y.: Printed by David Rumsey, 1819), 121; George Hunter, *The Western Journals of Dr. George Hunter, 1795–1805*, ed. John Francis McDermott, vol. 53, part 4, new series, of the *Transactions* of the America Philosophical Society (Philadelphia: American Philosophical Society, 1963), 26; Edmund Dana, *Geographical Sketches on the Western Country Designed for Emigrants and Settlers* (Cincinnati: Looker, Reynolds, 1819), 122; Elias Pym Fordham, *Personal Narrative of Travels . . . 1817–1818*, ed. Frederic Austin Ogg (1818; Cleveland: Arthur H. Clark, 1906), 156; and Henry Vest Bingham, "The Road West in 1818: The Diary of Henry Vest Bingham," ed. Marie George Windell, *Missouri Historical Review* 40 (October 1945): 47.

6. For pre-encounter settlements, see James H. Kellar, *An Introduction to the Pre-History of Indiana* (Indianapolis: Indiana Historical Society, 1973).

7. John R. Swanton, *The Indian Tribes of North America,* Smithsonian Institution, Bureau of American Ethnology, Bulletin 145 (Washington, D.C.: Government Printing Office, 1952), 232, 240.

8. Erminie Wheeler-Voegelin, *Ethnohistory of Indian Use and Occupancy in Ohio and Indiana prior to 1795,* 2 vols. (New York: Garland, 1974), 2:309–10.

9. Bill Gilbert, *God Gave Us This Country* (New York: Atheneum, 1989), 192.

10. Erminie Wheeler-Voegelin, Emily J. Blasingham, and Dorothy R. Libby, *An Anthropological Report on the Miami, Wea, and Eel River Indians* (New York: Garland, 1974), 193–97. See also the *Atlas of Great Lakes Indian History* (Norman: Published for the Newberry Library by the University of Oklahoma Press, 1987).

11. John Swanton, in *Indian Tribes,* claims that the Osage were originally in the Ohio Valley (272), as well as the Mosopelea.

12. William J. Eccles, "Iroquois, French, British: Imperial Rivalry in the Ohio Valley," in *Pathways to the Old Northwest* (Indianapolis: Indiana Historical Society, 1988), 20–24. On Iroquois claims, see Francis Jennings, *The Ambiguous Iroquois Empire* (New York: W. W. Norton, 1984).

13. For these movements and "alliances," see Richard White, *The Middle Ground: Indians, Empires, and Republics in the Great Lakes Region, 1650–1815* (Cambridge: Cambridge University Press, 1991).

14. James Clifton, *The Prairie People: Continuity and Change in Potawatomi Indian Culture, 1665–1965* (Lawrence: University of Kansas Press, 1977), 158–61.

15. White, *The Middle Ground,* 469.

16. Quoted in Gilbert, *God Gave Us This Country,* 177.

17. On Harrison's treaties, see Robert M. Owens, "Jeffersonian Benevolence on the Ground: The Indian Land Cession Treaties of William Henry Harrison," *Journal of the Early Republic* 22 (Fall 2002): 405–35; John Barnhart and Dorothy Riker, *Indiana to 1816: The Colonial Period* (Indianapolis: Indiana Historical Society, 1971), 337–40, 375–76; Bert Anson, *The Miami Indians* (Norman: University of Oklahoma Press, 1970), 146–53; Harvey Lewis Carter, *The Life and Times of Little Turtle: First Sagamore of the Wabash* (Urbana: University of Illinois Press, 1987), 170–78; Clinton Alfred Weslager, *The Delaware Indians: A History* (New Brunswick, N.J.: Rutgers University Press, 1972), 338–40; Madison, *The Indiana Way,* 37–40.

18. Alfred A. Cave, "The Shawnee Prophet, Tecumseh, and Tippecanoe: A Case Study of Historical Myth-Making," *Journal of the Early Republic* 22 (Winter 2002): 636–73, makes the case that Tippecanoe was not much of a setback for the Pan-Indian alliance and the Prophet's reputation. Adding to Cave's notion of myth-making, Barnhart and Riker have noted that immediate reaction among Hoosiers to Harrison's foray into "Indian Country" was mixed. Many thought that Harrison had led his men into danger without good reason. See Barnhart and Riker, *Indiana to 1816,* 392–97.

19. James Madison, *The Indiana Way,* 29.

20. See John C. Hudson, "North American Origins of Middlewestern Frontier Populations," *Annals of the Association of American Geographers* 78 (September 1988): 403 (fig. 5).

21. Gregory S. Rose, "Upland Southerners: The County Origins of Southern Migrants to Indiana by 1850," *Indiana Magazine of History* 82 (September 1986): 242–63. The impact of Upland Southerners is traced in Richard Lyle Power, *Planting Corn Belt Culture: The Impress of the Upland Southerner and Yankee in the Old Northwest,* IHS Publications, vol. 17, no. 4 (Indianapolis: Indiana Historical Society, 1953); and Nicole Etcheson, *The Emerging Midwest: Upland Southerners and the Political Culture of the Old Northwest, 1787–1861* (Bloomington: Indiana University Press, 1997).

22. U.S. Census of Population, manuscript schedule, Franklin and Washington counties, Indiana, 1820–50, microfilm, National Archives, Washington, D.C. This map is peculiar, in that it excludes Kentucky and Ohio in uncovering the pattern. I was led to the idea of constructing the map in this way because James Bergquist argued that in southwestern Ohio, future emigrants for central Indiana paused and participated in the amalgamation of Upland Southern and Mid-Atlantic cultures, in many ways the essence of Midwestern culture. See Bergquist, "Tracing the Origins of a Midwestern Culture: The Case of Central Indiana," *Indiana Magazine of History* 77 (1981): 1–32.

23. Sister Mary Gilbert Kelly, O.P., *Catholic Immigrant Colonization Projects in the United States, 1815–1860* (New York: U.S. Catholic Historical Society, 1939), 63–84.

24. James Albert Woodburn, *The Scotch-Irish Presbyterians in Monroe County, Indiana,* IHS Publications, vol. 4, no. 8 (Indianapolis: Edward J. Hecker, 1910).

25. Walter Hachthauser, "The History of Lutheranism in Southern Indiana," *Concordia Historical Institute Quarterly* 15 (1942): 46–59, 89–90; John Bodnar, review of *The Belgians of Indiana,* by Henry Verslype, *Indiana Magazine of History* 85 (December 1989): 353; Alice L. Green, "French Settlements in Floyd County," *Indiana Magazine of History* 11 (1915): 67–69; and Pierret Dufour, "Early Vevay," *Indiana Magazine of History* 20 (1924): 1–36, 306–45, 364–94. For a broad overview of ethnic diversity in the Middle West and its implications, see Jon Gjerde, *The Minds of the West: Ethnocultural Evolution in the Rural Middle West, 1830–1917* (Chapel Hill: University of North Carolina Press, 1997).

26. Emma Lou Thornbrough, *The Negro in Indiana,* Indiana Historical Collections, vol. 37 (Indianapolis: Indiana Historical Bureau, 1957); Gregory Rose, "The Distribution of

Indiana's Ethnic and Racial Minorities in 1850," *Indiana Magazine of History* 87 (September 1991): 224–60; Xenia Cord, "Black Rural Settlements in Indiana before 1860," IHS *Black History News and Notes,* no. 27 (February 1987): 4–8.

27. U.S. Census of Population, manuscript schedule, Franklin and Washington counties, 1820, microfilm, National Archives.

28. U.S. Census of Population, manuscript schedule, Franklin and Washington counties, Indiana, 1820, 1840, and 1850, microfilm, National Archives. No information on occupation was taken in the 1830 census. The figures for Washington County in 1850 dropped laborers from two railroad camps who fell into the random sample (there were three in the county in that year). With them, Washington County would have had about 68 percent of the workforce as farmers.

29. For those persisting from 1830, over 90 percent of employed persisters were farmers in 1850 in both counties. And for 1840 persisters, 86 percent of Washington County and 81 percent of Franklin County residents were farmers in 1850.

30. *Brookville Enquirer,* 5 September 1820.

31. Brookville *Franklin Democrat,* 29 March 1850.

32. Drew McCoy, *The Elusive Republic* (Chapel Hill: Published for the Institute of Early American History and Culture by the University of North Carolina Press, 1980), esp. 68. Cf. James Kloppenberg "The Virtues of Liberalism: Christianity, Republicanism, and Ethics in Early American Political Discourse," *Journal of American History* 74 (June 1987): 9–33; and Joyce Appleby, *Capitalism and the New Social Order* (New York: New York University Press, 1984).

33. Technique suggested by Michael J. O'Brien's *Grassland, Forest, and Historical Settlement: An Analysis of Dynamics in Northeast Missouri* (Lincoln: University of Nebraska Press, 1984). Land purchases drawn from *Indiana Land Entries,* vol. 1: *Cincinnati District,* comp. Margaret Waters (1948; Knightstown, Ind.: Bookmark, 1977); U.S. Land Office, Jeffersonville records, microfilm, State Archives, Indianapolis; and Washington County, Tract Entry Book, Recorder's Office, Washington County Courthouse, Salem, Ind.

34. Linking *Indiana Land Entries,* vol. 1: *Cincinnati District,* and U.S. Census of Population, manuscript schedule, Franklin County, 1820.

35. Stephen F. Strausberg, *Federal Stewardship on the Frontier: The Public Domain in Indiana* (New York: Arno Press, 1979). See also Malcolm J. Rohrbough, "The Land Office Business in Indiana, 1800–1840," in *This Land of Ours: The Acquisition and Disposition of the Public Domain* (Indianapolis: Indiana Historical Society, 1978), 39–59; and Rohrbough, *The Land Office Business: The Settlement and Administration of American Public Lands, 1789–1831* (New York: Oxford University Press, 1968).

36. Washington County, Tract Entry Book; Jeffersonville records, Tract Book #3, U.S. Land Office, microfilm, State Archives.

37. Salem *Western Annotator,* 12 January 1833. See Strausberg, *Federal Stewardship,* 352–57; Thomas Le Duc, "History and Appraisal of U.S. Land Policy to 1862," in *Land Use Policy and Problems in the United States,* ed. Howard Ottoson (Lincoln: University of Nebraska Press, 1963), 3–27; and Rohrbough, "The Land Office Business in Indiana."

38. *Indiana Land Entries,* vol. 1: *Cincinnati District,* 20–21.

39. William Faux, *Memorable Days in America: Being a Journal of a Tour to the United States,* vols. 11 and 12 of *Early Western Travels, 1748–1846,* ed. Reuben Gold Thwaites (New York: AMS Press, 1966), 11:241–42.

40. Cf. Robert E. Ankli, "Farm-Making Costs in the 1850s," *Agricultural History* 48 (January 1974): 51–70; and Jeremy Atack, "Farm and Farm-Making Costs Revisited," *Agricultural History* 56 (October 1982): 663–76.

41. Watson Family Letters, in *Twenty-four Letters from Labourers in America to Their Friends in England*, Sutro Branch, California State Library Occasional Papers Reprint Series no. 1, prepared by H. Bruner, P. Radin, and A. Yedida, 5–14.

42. Strausberg, *Federal Stewardship*, 65.

43. *Indiana Land Entries*, vol. 1: *Cincinnati District;* Washington County, Tract Entry Book; and Jeffersonville Land Office, Tract Book #3.

44. Paul Wallace Gates, "Land Policy and Tenancy in the Prairie Counties of Indiana," in *Landlords and Tenants on the Prairie Frontier* (Ithaca, N.Y.: Cornell University Press, 1973), 112.

45. Bogue, *From Prairie to Corn Belt,* 49.

46. Washington County census records were not split into townships until 1840, so definitive statements about residence in a given township cannot be made until that year. Therefore, it is difficult to distinguish farmers from county seat capitalists. Washington County Historical Society *Newsletter,* vols. 10–12 (December 1989–March 1991).

47. U.S. Census of Population, manuscript schedule, 1820–40, Franklin and Washington counties, Indiana, microfilm, National Archives.

48. And the census marshal may well have missed one of the two "absent" purchasers, Charles Carter; he appeared in Gibson Township in 1860 at the head of a large family.

49. See the various articles of Paul Wallace Gates collected in *Landlords and Tenants on the Prairie Frontier,* particularly "Land Policy and Tenancy in the Prairie Counties of Indiana" and "Hoosier Cattle Kings."

50. Gates, "Land Policy and Tenancy," in his *Landlords and Tenants,* 112. See also August B. Reifel, *History of Franklin County, Indiana* (1915; Evansville, Ind.: Unigraphics, 1971), 135; and Noah J. Major, *Pioneers of Morgan County,* ed. Logan Esarey, IHS Publications, vol. 5, no. 5 (Indianapolis: Edward J. Hecker, 1915), 233.

51. Franklin County 1833 Tax Roll, microfilm, Genealogy Division.

52. John Henry, Vincennes, to Mary Henry, Washington, Ky., [n.d.], Short-Henry Papers, Smith Library.

53. Contrast the development of Michigan and Illinois described in John Haegar, *The Investment Frontier* (Albany: State University of New York Press, 1981).

54. *Brookville Enquirer,* 1 August 1820.

55. Benjamin and Mary Mace, Lexington, Ind., to Parents [Benjamin and Rebecca Mace], Tewksbury, Mass., n.d., Mace Collection.

56. John Hicks, "Pioneer Life in Owen County," 1985 *Yearbook* of the Society of Indiana Pioneers, 12.

57. Elisha Hughes, Franklin County, to Father and Friends, 23 January 1824, Elisha Hughes Collection, Smith Library.

58. George Kennedy, Fairfield P.O., Franklin County, to Leonard Pickle, 21 February 1836, George Kennedy Collection, Smith Library.

59. Bingham, "The Road West in 1818," 49.

60. Thomas Hulme, "Mr. Hulme's Journal . . . ," in *A Year's Residence in the United States of America,* by William Cobbett (1828; New York: Augustus M. Kelley, 1969), 468.

61. Jacob and Charlotte Weaver, Vevay, Ind., to Johannes Weaver, New York, 28 March 1815, Jacob Weaver Collection, Smith Library.

62. Land contracts may also explain how in the tax records, persons were taxed for improvements without owning any land to improve. See Franklin County Tax Duplicates, 1844 and 1845, Auditor's Office, Franklin County Courthouse, Brookville, Ind.

63. Figures derived from samples drawn from the 1820 manuscript census, compared with land entries and deeds. U.S. Census of Population, manuscript schedule, 1820, Franklin

County, microfilm; Franklin County, General Index to Deeds, Recorder's Office, Franklin County Courthouse, Brookville, Ind.; *Indiana Land Entries*, vol. 1: *Cincinnati District*, 16–21, 58–60, 78, 124, 141–43, and 153–54. An additional problem arises in that deed records do not denote transferal of land through inheritance; therefore, all of these estimations for landlessness are undoubtedly understated.

64. Figures are adjusted to take into account persons who bought property from the federal government but who had not yet been added to the tax rolls.

65. Again, this is based on a not so dubious assumption that everyone who shares a last name is related. In the Highland Township 1835 Tax Assessment Roll in Smith Library, in which everyone, landowners and landless alike, was listed by section, I found only one instance where two persons with the same last name did not live in the same section.

66. Gates, "Land Policy and Tenancy," in his *Landlords and Tenants*, 111.

67. A provocative overview on squatting is Robert W. McCluggage, "The Pioneer Squatter," *Illinois Historical Journal* 82 (Spring 1989): 47–54. Squatting well may have been pursued by a more transient population—indeed, the very stereotype of squatter is that of a transient. Such transients would never have purchased land; therefore, my research design would not uncover them. My question, however, remains: to what extent was squatting one of the strategies pursued by the more permanent residents of southern Indiana?

68. In both census years, those identified as squatters made up about 4 percent of the sample. This analysis is based on some dubious assumptions, but is nevertheless instructive. I assume that anyone who had purchased private land before he purchased public land was probably leasing that private land or buying it on contract from the moment he settled in the county. I further assume that anyone who had family in the county was probably working the family's lands in common.

69. As to land contracts, no one who was landless in 1821 would enter a deed in the next nine years.

70. *Indiana Land Entries*, vol. 1: *Cincinnati District*, 142.

71. Highland Township, Franklin County, 1835 Tax Assessment Roll, Smith Library.

72. Jerold L. Shively, *Soil Survey of Franklin County, Indiana* (Washington, D.C.: U.S. Department of Agriculture, Soil Conservation Service, 1989), map 51, 117.

73. U.S. Census of Agriculture, manuscript schedule, 1850, Franklin County, microfilm, State Archives.

74. Joseph Hewitt [Springfield Township, Franklin County] to father, 7 May 1853, Joseph Hewitt Collection, Smith Library.

75. William Jones, Wooster, to Messrs. George and Levi Jennings, 9 June 1833, Jennings Family Papers, Smith Library.

76. Susannah Hines Pering, Bloomington, Ind., to L. Edwards, Chard, England, 27 August 1833, transcript, 30–31, Pering Papers.

77. James D. Davidson and Greenlee Davidson, "Documents: Diaries of James D. Davidson and Greenlee Davidson during Visits to Indiana," *Indiana Magazine of History* 34 (June 1928): 133 (25 October 1836).

78. William Newnham Blane, *An Excursion through the United States and Canada during the Years 1822–1823, by an English Gentleman* (London: Printed for Baldwin, Cradock, and Joy, 1824), 146.

79. Bazil B. Edmonston, Jasper, Ind., to Benjamin R. Edmonston, Waynesville, Hayward County, N.C., 24 December 1833, transcript, Edmonston Papers.

80. Blane, *An Excursion*, 140–41.

81. Parr, "Memoir," 421–24.

82. Franklin County, 1844 Tax Duplicate.

83. Washington County, 1844 Tax Duplicate, Auditor's Office, Washington County Courthouse, Salem, Ind. For a full statistical overview, see my dissertation, Richard Nation, "Home in the Hoosier Hills: Agriculture, Politics, and Religion, 1810–1870" (Ph.D. diss., University of Michigan, 1995), tables 2.5 and 2.6, 637.

84. U.S. Census of Population, manuscript schedule, 1850, Franklin and Washington counties, Indiana, microfilm, National Archives.

85. Certainly nothing precludes both an agricultural ladder and the family system detailed in this chapter. See Jeremy Atack, "The Agricultural Ladder Revisited: A New Look at an Old Question with Some Data for 1860," *Agricultural History* 63 (Winter 1989): 1–25.

86. See my dissertation, Nation, "Home in the Hoosier Hills," table 2.11, 638.

87. Cf. Sean Hartnett, "The Land Market on the Wisconsin Frontier: An Examination of Land Ownership Processes in Turtle and LaPrairie Townships, 1839–1890," *Agricultural History* 65, no. 4 (Fall 1991): 38–77, esp. 70–72.

88. To establish persistence rates, I am using the older method of linking names to censuses, despite Donald Parkerson's questioning of its validity. My main interest is in establishing that persistence took place at a greater rate than in many other places in the Midwest at the same time or at the same stage in development, and since these other figures were derived in a similar manner, I will assume that the flaws in the methodology will have approximately the same effect on my figures as it did theirs. See Parkerson, "How Mobile Were Nineteenth-Century Americans?" *Historical Methods* 15 (1982): 99–109.

89. Figures were derived from U.S. Census of Population, manuscript schedule, 1820–50, microfilm, National Archives; and U.S. Census of Population, manuscript schedule, 1860, computer file, IHS. Figures were derived by assuming a 10 percent error rate in linking from one census to the next, a figure suggested by work in later, more detailed censuses. Alternatively, a similar number appears by ignoring all people who have one of the twenty-five most common surnames in early Indiana.

90. See, e.g., Merle Curti et al., *The Making of an American Community: A Case Study of Democracy in a Frontier County* (Stanford, Calif.: Stanford University Press, 1959), 69; John Mack Faragher, *Sugar Creek: Life on the Illinois Prairie* (New Haven, Conn.: Yale University Press, 1986), 249n; and Bogue, *From Prairie to Corn Belt*, 25–26. See also Kenneth Winkle, *The Politics of Community: Migration and Politics in Antebellum Ohio* (New York: Cambridge University Press, 1988).

91. See my dissertation, Nation, "Home in the Hoosier Hills," table 2.18, 641.

92. Linking Highland Township, Franklin County, Tax Rolls for 1833 and 1835.

93. The chi-square statistic calculates a significance of family on persistence greater than P.90.

94. In much of this, I would concur with Don Harrison Doyle's assessment of Jacksonville, Ill., in *The Social Order of a Frontier Community* (Urbana: University of Illinois Press, 1978), in which he details how a small number of less transient elites formed the core of the community. Southern Indiana differed, I would suggest, because this core elite was larger—thanks to less migration—more centered around family, encompassed most landowners and their extended families, and therefore was more egalitarian.

95. Carole Shammas, "Anglo-American Household Government in Comparative Perspective," *William and Mary Quarterly*, 3rd ser., 52 (January 1995): 104–44. For evidence of patriarchy in Eastern households, see Christopher Clark, *The Roots of Rural Capitalism: Massachusetts, 1780–1860* (Ithaca, N.Y.: Cornell University Press, 1990) and Nancy Grey Osterud, *Bonds of Community: The Lives of Farm Women in Nineteenth-Century New York* (Ithaca, N.Y.: Cornell University Press, 1991); for Southern households, see Stephanie McCurry, *Masters of Small Worlds: Yeoman Households, Gender Relations, and*

the Political Culture of the Antebellum South Carolina Low Country (New York: Oxford University Press, 1995).

96. A quick survey of the 1850 census suggests that, in Washington County, well over half of the adult males who were not heads of households were living in relatives' households; in Franklin County, the percentage was over 80 percent. Another quick survey of twenty-year-olds suggests an explanation for the difference. In Washington County, far more young males, both landed and unlanded, had married and thus lived in their own households. Finally, at most 10 percent of all unlanded twenty-year-olds lived in nonrelatives' households.

97. John Modell, "Family and Fertility on the Indiana Frontier," *American Quarterly* 23, no. 5 (1971): 615–34.

98. Joseph Wynn, *Biography of Joseph Alexander Wynn* (Greensburg, Ind.: Baptist Observer, n.d.), 12.

99. This obligation could cross the miles; see Lewis Peleg, New Providence, Ind., to James Gere, Groton, Conn., 8 September 1830, Indiana History Manuscripts, Lilly Library.

100. Bazil B. Edmonston, Dubois County, to Col. Ninian Edmonston, Haywood County, N.C., 9 January 1831, transcript, Edmonston Papers.

101. Asa and Rachel Rosenbarger [Harrison County] to Rudolph and Barbary Rosenberger [*sic*], Virginia, 22 August 1835, in Asa Rosenbarger, *Word from the West: A Letter to Rudolph Rosenberger in Virginia, from His Son in Indiana, 1835* (privately printed, 1951).

102. See Mace Collection.

103. Brookville *Indiana American,* 21 May 1841.

104. Major, *Pioneers of Morgan County,* 301–303.

105. Letter from John and Mary Watson, Aurora, Dearborn County, to Father and Mother, Stephen Watson Sr., Sedlescomb, near Battle, Sussex, Old England, 28 April 1823, in *Twenty-four Letters,* 10.

106. Portia Everett, "The Weaker Sex," in *Legends of Franklin County* (Brookville, Ind.: Whitewater, 1958), n.p. I relate this story, not because I believe it to be true, but because it was passed along; it must have resonated in some way for Franklin County residents.

107. J. S. Wynn, Palestine, Ind., to Mattie J. Stout, 19 October 1856, Martha Stout Papers, Smith Library.

108. Hicks, "Pioneer Life," 13.

109. Parr, "Memoir," 380–82, quotation 381. That wives were necessary did not mean that there was no affection; see, e.g., J. P. Woodward, Springville, to L. A. Wolf, Mauckport, Harrison County, 10 November 1844, Woodward Manuscripts, Lilly Library.

110. Modell, "Family and Fertility," 632.

111. Ibid., 625.

112. Rental agreement, John Wheeler and Fanny Booth, Elijah Zenor Papers, Smith Library.

113. Father Joseph A. Thie, *Enochsburg and St. John's Church,* 19.

114. John Mack Faragher, "Sugar Creek Community," in *The Countryside in the Age of Capitalist Transformation,* ed. Steven Hahn and Jonathan Prude (Chapel Hill: University of North Carolina Press, 1984).

2. Religion and the Localist Ethic

1. Ethnocultural political historians have already recognized the link between Catholics and Calvinistic Baptists, whom I will call Primitive Baptists. See Richard Jensen, "The Religious and Occupational Roots of Party Identification: Illinois and Indiana in the 1870s,"

Civil War History 16 (December 1970): 325–43, esp. 331. See also Jensen, *The Winning of the Midwest: Social and Political Conflict, 1888–1896* (Chicago: University of Chicago Press, 1971); Paul Kleppner, *The Cross of Culture: A Social Analysis of Midwestern Politics, 1850–1900* (New York: Free Press, 1970); and Robert P. Swierenga, "Ethnoreligious Political Behavior in the Mid-Nineteenth Century: Voting, Values, Cultures," in *Religion and American Politics,* ed. Mark Noll (New York: Oxford University Press, 1990).

2. Nathan Hatch, *The Democratization of American Christianity* (New Haven, Conn.: Yale University Press, 1989).

3. George Leavitt, Crawford County, to parents, J. N. C. Leavitt, Esq., Chichester, N.H., 15 September 1848, Leavitt manuscripts, Lilly Library.

4. Lucinda Kittredge, Salem, Ind., to Wakefield Gale, Eastport, Maine, 21 March 1833, Wakefield Gale Collection, Smith Library.

5. B. C. Cressy, Salem, Ind., to Absalom Peters, New York, 7 June 1830, photostat, American Home Missionary Society Papers, Indiana Division, Indiana State Library (originals, Hammond Library, Chicago Theological Seminary).

6. Salem Presbyterian Church Records, 1817–53, 21 May 1842, transcript, Presbyterian Church Records, WCHS.

7. Joseph Hewitt, Mount Carmel, Franklin County, to father, 14 October 1853, transcript, Joseph Hewitt Collection, Smith Library.

8. John W. Parsons, China, Jefferson County, to Absalom Peters, New York, 20 February 1833, photostat, American Home Missionary Society Papers, Indiana Division, Indiana State Library.

9. Hughes, Franklin County, to Father and Friends, 23 January 1824, Elisha Hughes Collection, Smith Library.

10. U.S. Census, Social Statistics, manuscript schedule, 1850, State Archives.

11. U.S. Census Office, *The Seventh Census of the United States, 1850* (1853; reprint, New York: Arno Press, 1976), 799–807, corrected by consulting original manuscripts: U.S. Census, Social Statistics, manuscript schedule, 1850, State Archives. See Linda K. Pritchard, "The Spirit in the Flesh: Religion and Regional Economic Development," in *Belief and Behavior: Essays in the New Religious History,* ed. Philip R. Vandemeer and Robert Swierenga (New Brunswick, N.J.: Rutgers University Press, 1991), 93.

12. P. I. Beswick, near Beanblossom, Monroe County [later Brown County], to Asbury Wilkinson, 12 August 1839, Asbury Wilkinson Collection, Smith Library.

13. U.S. Census Office, *The Seventh Census of the United States, 1850,* 799–807.

14. Based on church records for Washington and Franklin counties preserved at the Smith Library, Genealogy Section, Indiana Division, and WCHS.

15. On "feminization" of religion, see, though fraught with problems, Ann Douglas, *The Feminization of American Culture* (New York: Knopf, 1978); also Nancy Cott, *The Bonds of Womanhood* (New Haven, Conn.: Yale University Press, 1977); and Harry S. Stout and Catherine A. Brekus, "Declension, Gender, and the 'New Religious History,'" in *Belief and Behavior: Essays in the New Religious History,* ed. Philip R. Vandemeer and Robert Swierenga (New Brunswick, N.J.: Rutgers University Press, 1991).

16. Records of Big Cedar Grove Baptist Church, 1858, transcript, Genealogy Division.

17. In much the same way, in the Catholic Church, the priests noted the size of their congregations in terms of family. See, e.g., the letter of 23 December 1844 from Father Kundeck, reporting his missionary successes, in Frances G. Holweck, "Two Pioneer Indiana Priests," *Mid-America,* n.s., 1 (July 1929): 73.

18. Edward Eggleston, *The Hoosier Schoolmaster* (1871; Bloomington: Indiana University Press, 1984), 103.

19. George Knight Hester, "Narratives of the Reverend George Knight Hester and His Wife, Benee (Briggs) Hester," *Indiana Magazine of History* 22 (June 1926): 169–75. Cf. Eli Farmer's similar struggles in "Eli Farmer Autobiography," Eli Farmer Manuscripts, Lilly Library, 85–90.

20. Enoch Parr, "Memoir of Enoch Parr," *Indiana Magazine of History* 22 (December 1926): 398–401.

21. Ibid., 404–19.

22. Robert Wilken, O.F.M., *A Historical Sketch of the Holy Family Church and Parish* (1937; Oldenburg: n.p., 1987), 55–56.

23. The best overview of the religious environment out of which many hill country Hoosiers had come is John Boles, *The Great Revival* (Lexington: University Press of Kentucky, 1972). See also Paul Conkin, *Cane Ridge* (Madison: University of Wisconsin Press, 1990); and Christine Heyrman, *Southern Cross: The Beginnings of the Bible Belt* (New York: Alfred A. Knopf, 1997).

24. U.S. Census, Social Statistics, manuscript schedule, 1860, Washington County, State Archives.

25. *Memoir of Priscilla Cadwallader* (1862; reprint, Salem, Ind.: Overman, 1901); and William Forster, *Memoirs of William Forster,* ed. Benjamin Seebohm, 2 vols. (London: Alfred W. Bennett, 1865), 1:344–45. See Thomas Hamm, *The Transformation of American Quakerism: Orthodox Friends, 1800–1907* (Bloomington: Indiana University Press, 1988).

26. Sidney Ahlstrom, *A Religious History of the American People* (New Haven, Conn.: Yale University Press, 1972), 277–78; for a more specific study in Indiana, although outdated and, I believe, severely biased, see James Albert Woodburn, *The Scotch-Irish Presbyterians of Monroe County, Indiana,* IHS Publications, vol. 4, no. 8 (Indianapolis: Edward J. Hecker, 1910). See also *History of Washington County, Indiana* (1884; reprint, Paoli: Stout's Print Shop, 1965), 829.

27. Richard Simons, "A Utopian Failure," *Indiana History Bulletin* 18 (January 1941): 98–114.

28. Sister Mary Gilbert Kelly, O.P., *Catholic Immigrant Colonization Projects in the United States, 1815–1860,* U.S. Catholic Historical Society, Monograph Series 17 (New York: U.S. Catholic Historical Society, 1939), 79.

29. Gary Ward Stanton, "Brought, Borrowed, or Bought: Sources and Utilization Patterns of the Material Culture of German Immigrants in Southeastern Indiana, 1837–1860" (Ph.D. diss., Indiana University, 1985), 96n65.

30. B[azil] B. Edmonston, Jasper, Ind., to Col. Ninian Edmonston, Waynesville, Haywood County, N.C., 21 October 1839, transcript, Edmonston Papers.

31. Bazil B. Edmonston, Jasper, Ind., to Ninian Edmonston and Family, Waynesville, Haywood County, N.C., 18 May 1839, transcript, Edmonston Papers. For Protestant attitudes about Catholics in another part of southern Indiana, see C. Walker Gollar, "Early Protestant-Catholic Relations in Southern Indiana and the 1842 Case of Roman Weinzaepfel," *Indiana Magazine of History* 95 (1999): 233–54.

32. Kelly, *Catholic Immigrant Colonization Projects,* 72–73, citing *Berichte der Leopoldinen-Stiftung im Kaisethume Österreich,* XIV, 67–68, letter of 5 August 1840.

33. Father Kundeck, letter of 27 July 1842, reprinted in Frances S. Holweck, "Two Pioneer Indiana Priests," 76–78.

34. While traditional Catholic history, with its institutional emphasis, has tended to emphasize too greatly the role of priests and the rest of the hierarchy, it would be a mistake, in a revolt against such history, to ignore the major role played by priests in the particular instance of the two major centers of German Catholic settlement in southern Indiana. Stanton, "Brought, Borrowed, or Bought," 86–87, makes a similar point.

35. German Protestant pastors may have played similar roles. See the mention of Pastor Tölke in a letter from a midcentury German immigrant to Greene County, Hermann Bullerman, reproduced in James R. Kuppers and Karl M. Gabriel, eds., "Beginning Anew: Immigrant Letters from Indiana," *Indiana Magazine of History* 95 (1999): 340–45.

36. Robert Frederick Trisco, *The Holy See and the Nascent Church in the Middle Western United States, 1826–1850*, Analecto Gregoroiana, vol. 125 (Rome: Gregorian University Press, 1962), 262–74.

37. Kelly, *Catholic Immigrant Colonization Projects*, 64–76; Juliet Anne Niehaus, "Ethnic Formation and Transformation: The German Catholics of Dubois County, Indiana, 1838–1979" (Ph.D. diss., New School for Social Research, 1981), 95–100; and Holweck, "Two Pioneer Indiana Priests," 63–78. Holweck reproduces a number of Kundeck's letters to the Leopoldine Foundation. See also Sister Mary Carol Schroeder, O.S.F., *The Catholic Church in the Diocese of Vincennes, 1847–1877*, Catholic University of America Studies in American Church History, vol. 35 (Washington, D.C.: Catholic University of America Press, 1946).

38. Cf. Stanton, "Brought, Borrowed, or Bought," 87, with Schroeder, *The Catholic Church in the Diocese of Vincennes*, 25.

39. Kelly, *Catholic Immigrant Colonization Projects*, 82–83.

40. Stanton, "Brought, Borrowed, or Bought," 87.

41. Kelly, *Catholic Immigrant Colonization Projects*, 83.

42. Ibid.

43. Ibid., 72.

44. Schroeder, *The Catholic Church in the Diocese of Vincennes*, 96. On lay control, see David Gerber, "Modernity in the Service of Tradition: Catholic Lay Trustees at Buffalo's St. Louis Church," *Journal of Social History* 15, no. 4 (Summer 1982): 655–84; and Patrick Carey, "The Laity's Understanding of the Trustee System," *Catholic Historical Review* 64 (July 1978): 356–77.

45. Niehaus, "Ethnic Formation and Transformation," 109.

46. On German Catholic communalism, see Kathleen Neils Conzen, "German Catholic Communalism and the American Civil War: Exploring the Dilemmas of Transatlantic Political Integration," in *Bridging the Atlantic: The Question of American Exceptionalism in Perspective*, ed. Elisabeth Glaser and Hermann Wellenreuther (Washington, D.C.: German Historical Institute, by Cambridge University Press, 2002). See also Conzen, "Mainstreams and Side Channels: The Localization of Immigrant Cultures," *Journal of American Ethnic History* 11 (1991): 5–20.

47. A point which Jay Dolan, writing in *American Catholic Experience: A History from Colonial Times to the Present* (Garden City, N.Y.: Doubleday, 1985), 168, draws from Joseph White's study of German immigrants in Cincinnati: "Religion and Community: Cincinnati Germans, 1814–1870" (Ph.D. diss., University of Notre Dame, 1980).

48. Father Joseph Kundek to Hamilton Smith [president (?) of Cannelton Co.], 28 May 1851, Hamilton Smith Manuscripts, Lilly Library.

49. Minutes of Lost River Regular Baptist "Old Union" Church, Washington [and Orange] County, 18, transcript, Baptist Church Records, WCHS.

50. Minutes of the Sinking Spring Baptist Church, Washington County, 3rd Saturday, February 1844, transcript, Baptist Church Records, WCHS.

51. For a somewhat different understanding of church discipline, see Gregory Wills, *Democratic Religion: Freedom, Authority, and Church Discipline in the Baptist South, 1785–1900* (New York: Oxford University Press, 1997).

52. Minutes of Elim (New Providence) Baptist Church, 1816–56, Washington County, 8 November 1823–17 September 1824, transcript, 18–20, Baptist Church Records, WCHS.

53. Minutes of Delaney's Creek Regular Baptist Church, Washington County, transcript, 8, Baptist Church Records, WCHS.

54. Minutes of Lost River Regular Baptist "Old Union" Church, Washington County, transcript, 18, Baptist Church Records, WCHS. Emphases mine.

55. Minutes of Elim (New Providence) Baptist Church, 1816–56, Washington County, 12 July 1823, transcript, Baptist Church Records, WCHS.

56. Minutes of Lost River Baptist Church, Washington (and Orange) County, 3rd Saturday, July 1837, transcript, Baptist Church Records, WCHS.

57. Record of Blue River Baptist Church, Washington County, 28 June 1851, transcript, Baptist Church Records, WCHS.

58. First Christian Church, Salem, Ind., First Record Book, 7 February 1843–27 March 1843, transcript, Christian Church Records, WCHS.

59. Record of Blue River Baptist Church, Washington County, 1847–70, 4 September 1865, transcript, Baptist Church Records, WCHS.

60. Ibid., March 1863.

61. Woodburn, *Scotch-Irish Presbyterians,* 500.

62. *The Doctrines and Discipline of the Methodist Episcopal Church* (New York, 1808), 48, cited in William Warren Sweet, *The Methodists,* vol. 4 of *Religion on the American Frontier* (1946; New York: Cooper Square, 1964), 643. Note how bringing suit and being a glib salesman are lumped with fighting.

63. Arminius, "Short Sketches," *Methodist Quarterly Review* 5 (September 1822): 351, cited in Charles A. Johnson, *The Frontier Camp Meeting: Religion's Harvest Time* (Dallas: Southern Methodist University Press, 1955), 177.

64. Minutes of Elim (New Providence) Baptist Church, 1816–56, Washington County, transcript, April 1833, Baptist Church Records, WCHS.

65. Livonia Presbyterian Church, Sessional and Other Records, 1828–71, December 1830, transcript, Presbyterian Church Records, WCHS.

66. Records of Big Cedar Grove Church, Franklin County, 13 October 1856, microfilm, Indiana Division. It may be Ansel Reese.

67. Minutes of Elim (New Providence) Baptist Church, 1816–56, Washington County, January 1848–September 1849, transcript, 58–59, Baptist Church Records, WCHS. My suspicion is that Alvis was not properly contrite, perhaps believing that his innocence before the secular court had some bearing on his innocence before God.

68. First Christian Church, Salem, Ind., First Record Book, 7 February 1843–27 March 1843, transcript, Christian Church Records, WCHS.

69. Ibid., 11 January 1844, transcript, 2, Christian Church Records, WCHS.

70. Allen Wiley, "Methodism in Southeastern Indiana," *Indiana Magazine of History* 23 (March 1927): 14–15.

71. See Nation, "Home in the Hoosier Hills," map 2.5, 576.

72. One might envision such a purely geographical church as having a majority of members from its immediate environs, with gradually fewer members as the geographical distance from the church increases.

73. Timothy L. Smith, "The Ohio Valley: Testing Ground for America's Experiment in Religious Pluralism," *Church History* 60 (1991): 461–79.

74. Hatch, *The Democratization of American Religion.*

75. Peter Onuf, *Statehood and Union: A History of the Northwest Ordinance* (Bloomington: Indiana University Press, 1987).

76. Parr, "Memoir," 411.

77. Nevertheless, Baptists, and especially Primitive Baptists, were very much engaged in theological debates, even while they were the greatest advocates of the laity's ability to preach.

78. Donald Mathews, "Evangelical America—The Methodist Ideology," in *Rethinking Methodist History,* ed. Russell Richey and Kenneth Rowe (Nashville: Kingswood Books, 1985).

79. Ibid., 97–98.

80. Ibid., 92.

81. Paul Johnson, *A Shopkeeper's Millennium: Society and Revivals in Rochester, New York, 1815–1837* (New York: Hill and Wang, 1978).

82. See Thomas L. Haskell, "Capitalism and the Origins of the Humanitarian Sensibility," Parts 1 and 2, *American Historical Review* 90 (April 1985): 339–61 and (June 1985): 547–66.

83. Eggleston, *Hoosier Schoolmaster,* 153, 158.

84. Allen Wiley, another southern Indiana Methodist minister, bears out Eggleston's portrayal of a shift in Methodism. See Wiley, "Methodism in Southeastern Indiana," *Indiana Magazine of History* 23 (1927): 3–62, 130–216, 239–332, 393–466. See also the forthcoming work by John Wigger, which builds on the final chapter of his *Taking Heaven by Storm: Methodism and the Rise of Popular Christianity in America* (Urbana: University of Illinois Press, 1998), presented in draft form at the 2003 Society for Historians of the Early American Republic conference, Columbus, Ohio: "Methodism and the Development of Ohio Valley Religion."

85. Hatch, *Democratization of American Christianity,* chap. 7.

86. For a recent attempt to compare reform in the North and South, see John W. Quist, *Restless Visionaries: The Social Roots of Antebellum Reform in Alabama and Michigan* (Baton Rouge: Louisiana State University Press, 1998).

87. The Methodist hierarchy did arouse some animus among its laity. In the Methodist Protestant schism of the 1820s, some in southern Indiana joined Methodists throughout the nation in revolting against the authority of the Methodist hierarchy in running local churches. Hatch, *Democratization of American Christianity,* 205–206. Since Hatch details a Methodist shift toward "respectability," I would suggest that the Methodist Protestants were simply continuing down the earlier path and refusing to shift; for the Primitive Baptists, I intend to make just that point below. One Methodist clergyman who was troubled by the hierarchy was Eli Farmer. See the "Autobiography of Eli Farmer," Eli Farmer manuscripts, Lilly Library, 227–28, 231, 238, 250.

88. Elizabeth K. Nottingham, *Methodism and the Frontier: Indiana Proving Ground* (New York: Columbia University Press, 1941), 170.

89. Charles Sellers, *The Market Revolution: Jacksonian America, 1815–1846* (New York: Oxford University Press, 1991), 216.

90. See Lawrence Kohl, *The Politics of Individualism: Parties and the American Character in the Jacksonian Era* (New York: Oxford University Press, 1989).

91. Record of Blue River Baptist Church, 1847–70, Franklin Township, Washington County, 28 June 1851, transcript, Baptist Church Records, WCHS.

92. I will use "Primitive" to indicate the whole of conservative Baptists, despite some indication that it appears to have been a particular sect of conservative Baptists. See Lemuel

Potter, *Labor and Travels of Elder Lemuel Potter* (Evansville, Ind.: Keller Printing Company, 1894), 138. Potter, a member of Old School Baptists, lambastes the Primitive Baptists for not believing in Baptist doctrine.

93. Byron Lambert, *The Rise of the Antimission Baptists: Sources and Leaders, 1800–1840* (New York: Arno Press, 1980); Donald Mathews, *Religion in the Old South* (Chicago: University of Chicago Press, 1977); and Bertram Wyatt-Brown, "The Antimission Movement in the Jacksonian South," *Journal of Southern History* 36 (November 1970), which Wyatt-Brown has substantially rewritten in "Paradox, Shame, and Grace in the Backcountry," in his *The Shaping of Southern Culture: Honor, Grace, and War, 1760s–1880s* (Chapel Hill: University of North Carolina Press, 2001).

94. Eggleston, *Hoosier Schoolmaster*, 102.

95. Parsons, China, Jefferson County, to Rev. Absalom Peters, New York, 20 February 1833, photostat, American Home Missionary Society Papers, Indiana Division.

96. Lambert, *Rise of the Antimission Baptists*, chap. 1.

97. T. Scott Miyakawa, *Protestants and Pioneers: Individualism and Conformity on the American Frontier* (Chicago: University of Chicago Press, 1964), 154, 158; Wyatt-Brown, "The Antimission Movement," 524. See also James Rhett Mathis, "'Can Two Walk Together Unless They Be Agreed?' The Origins of the Primitive Baptists, 1800–1840" (Ph.D. diss., University of Florida, 1997).

98. John Cady, *The Origin and Development of the Missionary Baptist Church in Indiana* (Franklin, Ind.: Franklin College, 1942) and "The Religious Environment of Lincoln's Youth," *Indiana Magazine of History* 37 (March 1941): 16–30.

99. *Minutes of the Eighth Annual Meeting of the Lost River Association, September 1833* (Salem: E. Patrick's Print., 1833).

100. Minutes of Elim (New Providence) Baptist Church, 1816–56, Polk Township, Washington County, 1819, transcript, Baptist Church Records, WCHS.

101. Ibid., December 1841, transcript.

102. For the distinction, see Lemuel Potter, *Labor and Travels*, 187, where he quotes a letter from R. C. Keele. See also Randy K. Mills, "The Struggle for the Soul of Frontier Baptists: The Anti-Mission Controversy in the Lower Wabash Valley," *Indiana Magazine of History* 94 (1998): 303–22.

103. Wilson Thompson, *Autobiography of Elder Wilson Thompson* (Elizabethtown, Ill.: R. L. Nelson, 1979), 446–48.

104. *Minutes of the Blue River Association, 1825* (Salem, Ind.: Eleazer Wheelock, 1825).

105. Records of Unity Baptist Church, 1st Saturday in August 1858, transcript, Baptist Church Records, WCHS.

106. "Minutes of White Water Regular Baptist Association" [1852], Brookville *Franklin Democrat*, 3 September 1852. Emphasis on "entangling alliances" added.

107. *Minutes of White Water Regular Baptist Association* [1855] (Brookville, Ind.: C. B. Bentley, 1855).

108. *Minutes of the Blue River Association, 1825*.

109. Parr, "Memoir," 402–403.

110. Minutes of Sinking Spring Baptist Church, September 1817–February 1844 [*sic*], second Saturday in July 1858, transcript, Baptist Church Records, WCHS.

111. Records of Unity Baptist Church, 1818–58, first Saturday in June 1858, transcript, Baptist Church Records, WCHS.

112. Records of Lost River Baptist Church, 1814–51, 17 January 1834 [actually 1835], transcript, Baptist Church Records, WCHS.

113. *Minutes of the Blue River Association, 1825.*

114. Ibid.

115. *Minutes of the Lost River Association, 1826* (Salem, Ind.: Ebenezer Patrick, 1826).

116. Minutes of Sinking Spring Baptist Church, September 1817–February 1844, second Saturday in July 1858, transcript, Baptist Church Records, WCHS.

117. "Minutes of the White Water Regular Baptist Association" [1852], Brookville *Franklin Democrat*, 3 September 1852.

118. *Minutes of the Lost River Association, 1826.*

119. Joel Hume and Benomi Stinson, *A Debate on the Doctrine of Atonement,* reported by Wm. Loach (Cincinnati: E. Morgan, 1863), 88–89.

120. "Minutes of White Water Regular Baptist Association" [1852], Brookville *Franklin Democrat*, 3 September 1852.

121. *Minutes of the Eighth Annual Meeting of the Lost River Association, September, 1833.*

122. *Minutes of the . . . White-Water Regular Baptist Association, 1840.*

123. Hume and Stinson, *A Debate on the Doctrine of Atonement,* 120–21.

124. Perhaps the best way to make this point is to note that there are Christian faiths which believe that in the Bible all is revealed.

125. Records of the Unity Baptist Church, 1st Saturday in June 1858, transcript, Baptist Church Records, WCHS. Emphasis mine. Note that they do not condemn "opinions" not based on the Gospels, but merely forbid imposing these opinions on others.

126. Obviously, the two religions had very different roads to salvation, and the impact of those differences on their worldviews has been explored from Weber to the present. Nevertheless, I would submit that the impact of the Calvinist/Catholic split on salvation had become fairly insignificant in America circa 1850. In addition, the contrition demanded of the Catholics had its parallels in the Primitive Baptist demand that its congregants confess their sins to the membership and ask for forgiveness. And the final goal of both faiths was to keep God's children in the church.

127. Records of Lost River Baptist Church, 9 December 1820, transcript, Baptist Church Records, WCHS.

3. "Surplus Produce" and Market Exchange

1. Livonia Presbyterian Church, Sessional and Other Records, 1828–71, 3 December 1830, transcript, Presbyterian Church Records, WCHS. Emphasis mine.

2. For another view of agriculture in the Hoosier hills, see Howard Nicholson, "Swine, Timber, and Tourism: The Evolution of an Applachian Community in the Middle West, 1830–1930" (Ph.D. diss., Miami University, 1992).

3. Christopher Clark, *The Roots of Rural Capitalism: Massachusetts, 1780–1860* (Ithaca, N.Y.: Cornell University Press, 1990), and Allan Kulikoff, *The Agrarian Origins of American Capitalism* (Charlottesville: University Press of Virginia, 1992). Important corrections to Kulikoff's and Clark's generally solid interpretations are in Richard Lyman Bushman, "Markets and Composite Farms in Early America," *William and Mary Quarterly,* 3rd ser., 55 (July 1998): 351–74; Joyce Appleby, "The Vexed Story of Capitalism Told by American Historians," *Journal of the Early Republic* 20 (2000): 487–521; and Naomi Lamoreaux, "Rethinking the Transformation to Capitalism in the Early American Northeast," *Journal of American History* 90 (2003): 437–61. Strong recent work includes the evocative Martin Bruegel, *Farm, Shop, Landing: The Rise of a Market Society in the Hudson Valley, 1780–1860*

(Durham, N.C.: Duke University Press, 2002), and Susan Sessions Rugh, *Our Common Country: Family Farming, Culture, and Community in the Nineteenth-Century Midwest* (Bloomington: Indiana University Press, 2001).

4. For the early period, Kenneth Lockridge, *A New England Town,* expanded ed. (New York: W. W. Norton, 1985) and, in the later period, Robert Wiebe, *The Search for Order* (New York: Hill and Wang, 1967); Steven Hahn, *The Roots of Southern Populism* (New York: Oxford University Press, 1983); and Bruce Palmer, *"Man over Money"* (Chapel Hill: University of North Carolina Press, 1980).

5. Christopher Waldrep, "'So Much Sin': The Decline of Religious Discipline and the 'Tidal Wave of Crime,'" *Journal of Social History* 23, no. 3 (Spring 1990): 535–52, incorporated into his *Night Riders: Defending Community in the Black Patch, 1890–1915* (Durham, N.C.: Duke University Press, 1993).

6. Thomas Bender, *Communities and Social Change in America* (New Brunswick, N.J.: Rutgers University Press, 1978); and Don Harrison Doyle, *The Social Order of a Frontier Community* (Urbana: University of Illinois Press, 1978), 12–13.

7. Kim Gruenwald tells the story of early commercialization well in *River of Enterprise: The Commercial Origins of Regional Identity in the Ohio Valley, 1790–1850* (Bloomington: Indiana University Press, 2002).

8. Noah J. Major, *Pioneers of Morgan County,* ed. Logan Esarey, IHS Publications, vol. 5, no. 5 (Indianapolis: Edward J. Hecker, 1915), 395; John Scott, of Centreville, Ind., *The Indiana Gazetteer or Topographical Dictionary,* IHS Publications, vol. 18, no. 1 (1826; Indianapolis: Indiana Historical Society, 1954), 101.

9. William Newnham Blane, *An Excursion through the United States and Canada during the Years 1822–1823, by an English Gentleman* (London: Printed for Baldwin, Cradock, and Joy, 1824), 144–45.

10. Enoch Honeywell Diary, Enoch Honeywell Collection, Indiana Division.

11. Margaret Walsh, *The Rise of the Midwestern Meat Packing Industry* (Lexington: University Press of Kentucky, 1982).

12. Brookville *Indiana American,* 28 November 1834.

13. Harrison Burns, *Personal Recollections of Harrison Burns, as Written in 1907,* IHS Publications, vol. 25, no. 2 (Indianapolis: Indiana Historical Society, 1975), 13–14.

14. Scott, *Indiana Gazetteer,* 34.

15. Ibid., 101. Women's work—butter and eggs—was not quantified.

16. U.S. Census Office, *Compendium of the Eleventh Census, 1890* (Washington, D.C.: Government Printing Office, 1892–97), 17–18.

17. Morris Birkbeck, *Notes on a Journey in America* (Philadelphia: Caleb Richardson, 1817), 103.

18. William Faux, *Memorable Days in America; Being a Tour of the United States,* vols. 11 and 12 of *Early Western Travels, 1748–1846,* ed. Reuben Gold Thwaites (New York: AMS Press, 1966), 11:204.

19. Patrick Henry Jameson, "These Years Serve to Remind Me," 1970 *Yearbook* of the Society of Indiana Pioneers, 13.

20. Faux, *Memorable Days,* 11:234.

21. G[eorge] C. Leavitt, Crawford County, to parents, J. N. C. Leavitt, Esq., Chichester, N.H., 23 February 1847, Leavitt manuscripts, Lilly Library. Leavitt goes on to undercut himself, reporting that over half the population marketed goods in New Orleans every year.

22. In a subsequent letter, Leavitt added that "the great ambition of most people on setting out in life is to have 40 acres of land which can be bought at the land office for $50 and erect theron a log cabin and if they have corn & pork to do them[,] as the expressin is[,] they are satisfied." George Leavitt, Crawford County, to parents, J. N. C. Leavitt, Esq., Chichester, N.H., 15 September 1848, Leavitt manuscripts, Lilly Library.

23. Richard Lee Mason, *Narrative of Richard Lee Mason* (1819; New York: Charles Frederick Hearman, [1915]), 34.

24. [Baynard Rush Hall], *The New Purchase,* by Robert Carleton, pseud., ed. James Albert Woodburn (1843; Princeton, N.J.: Princeton University Press, 1916), 219.

25. Charles Sealsfield, *The Americans as They Are,* (London: Hurst, Chance, 1828), 58–59. Actually, by this time there were plenty of apple trees in the vicinity of Troy.

26. Lori Merish, "'The Hand of Refined Taste' in the Frontier Landscape: Caroline Kirkland's *A New Home, Who'll Follow?* and the Feminization of American Consumerism," *American Quarterly* 45 (December 1993): 485–523. See also David Blanke, *Sowing the American Dream: How Consumer Culture Took Root in the Rural Midwest* (Athens: Ohio University Press, 2000).

27. H. H. Pleasant, "Crawford County," *Indiana Magazine of History* 18 (September 1922): 249.

28. Brookville *Indiana American,* 10 July 1857.

29. William W. Borden, "Personal Reminiscences," in *Catalogue of the Borden Museum* (New Albany: Tribune, 1901), 11.

30. Sealsfield, *The Americans as They Are,* 59.

31. Faux, *Memorable Days,* 11:203–204, also 237.

32. Jan de Vries has proposed renaming the changes often called the industrial revolution to be the "industrious revolution," noting how industriousness changed household-level production. See his "The Industrial Revolution and the Industrious Revolution," *Journal of Economic History* 54 (June 1994): 249–73.

33. Birkbeck, *Notes on a Journey,* 106.

34. Faux, *Memorable Days,* 11:234.

35. Susannah Hines Pering, Bloomington, Ind., to L. Edwards, Chard, England, 27 August 1833, transcript, 30, Pering Papers.

36. [Hall], *The New Purchase,* 263.

37. Lewis Peleg, New Providence, Ind., to James Gere, Groton, Conn., 8 September 1830, Indiana History Manuscripts, Lilly Library. Peleg added that girls did not think it a "disgrace to roll logs, pile Brush, hoe corn, &tc. And be brough up like savages without knowing B from a Broomstick."

38. On servant problems, see Faye Dudden, *Serving Women* (Middletown, Conn.: Wesleyan University Press, 1983), 44–71.

39. Lorenzo Chapin, Leavenworth, Ind., to Jonathan Wales, Whalestown, N.Y., 30 January 1820, Lorenzo Chapin Papers, Smith Library.

40. George Kennedy, Fairfield P.O., Franklin County, to Leonard Pickle, 21 February 1836, George Kennedy Collection, Smith Library.

41. Asa and Rachel Rosenbarger [Harrison County] to Rudolph and Barbary Rosenberger [*sic*], Virginia, 22 August 1835, in Asa Rosenbarger, *Word from the West: A Letter to Rudolph Rosenberger in Virginia, from His Son in Indiana, 1835* (privately printed, 1951).

42. Jehiel Goltry, Spencer, Six-Mile P.O., Jennings County, to George Humphrey, Fairport, Chemung County, N.Y., 10 December 1840, Jehiel Goltry Papers, Indiana Division.

43. Charles R. Arms [near Fredonia, Ind.] to Richard Arms, Brand, Vt., 6 August 1844, in "A Vermont Emigrant Living in Crawford County Writes Home" (1844), *Indiana Source Book*, vol. 3, ed. Willard Heiss (Indianapolis: Indiana Historical Society, 1982), 150.

44. Mason, *Narrative*, 35–36.

45. Forster, *Memoirs*, 1:345.

46. This paragraph follows Gordon Wood's study on the transition from a monarchical and feudal understanding of the purpose of work to the democratic and consumerist understanding. See Wood, *The Radicalism of the American Revolution* (New York: Knopf, 1992), 33–36. John Crowley has provided a broad sketch of widespread notions of comfort in "The Sensibility of Comfort," *American Historical Review* 104 (June 1999): 749–82. More work needs to be done on the changing notions of what comfort entails.

47. Faux, *Memorable Days*, 11:234.

48. My discussion of "surplus produce," with its distinction between trade governed by the local community and surpluses marketed on distant, amoral markets, parallels the distinction drawn by Christopher Clark in *The Roots of Rural Capitalism* between trade at a distance and the "local ethic of exchange" (28–38). I have chosen to follow the lead of Daniel Vickers, to interpret the words Hoosiers used to describe their economic behavior, looking at the notion of "surplus produce" in much the way Vickers considers "competency," and see within it both the ideals of capitalism as well as an attempt to mitigate the risks of the market and of farming. Vickers, "Competency and Competition: Economic Culture in Early America," *William and Mary Quarterly*, 3rd ser., 47 (January 1990): 3–29.

49. Vickers, "Competency and Competition," 3.

50. For "safety-first" farming, see Gavin Wright, *The Political Economy of the Cotton South* (New York: W. W. Norton, 1978), 62–74. See also Clarence H. Danhof, *Change in Agriculture: The Northern United States, 1820-1870* (Cambridge: Harvard University Press, 1969), and Anne Mayhew, "A Reappraisal of the Causes of Farm Protest, 1870–1900," *Journal of Economic History* 32 (June 1972): 464–75. None of Wright's argument is inconsistent with Jeremy Atack and Fred Bateman's findings for the northern United States in 1860. See Atack and Bateman, "Self-Sufficiency and the Origins of the Marketable Surplus in the Rural North, 1860," *Agricultural History* 58 (July 1984): 296–313; Atack and Bateman, *To Their Own Soil: Agriculture in the Antebellum North* (Ames: Iowa State University Press, 1987); and Atack and Bateman, "Yeoman Farming: Antebellum America's Other 'Peculiar Institution,'" in *Agriculture and National Development: Views on the Nineteenth Century*, ed. Lou Ferleger (Ames: Iowa State University Press, 1990).

51. Burns, *Recollections*, 18. The Vawters were perhaps the most prominent family in Jennings County at the time and also prominent in Baptist church circles.

52. Richard S. Fisher, *Indiana: In Relation to Its Geography, Statistics, Institutions, County Topography* (New York: J. H. Colton, 1852), 74.

53. "Governor's Message," Brookville *Indiana American*, 8 December 1843.

54. Salem *Indiana Phoenix*, 4 April 1833.

55. Bazil B. Edmonston, Jasper, Ind., to Ninian Edmonston, Waynesville, Haywood County, N.C., 18 May 1839, transcript, Edmonston Papers.

56. Faux, *Memorable Days*, 11:267.

57. Salem *Indiana Farmer*, 26 July 1822.

58. Paoli *American Farmer*, 28 January 1858.

59. George Kennedy, Fairfield P.O., Franklin County, to Leonard Pickle, 21 February 1836, George Kennedy Collection, Smith Library.

60. Bloomington *Post*, 26 July 1839.

61. John B. Durham [Medora, Ind.?] to Samuel W. Durham, Marion, Iowa, 28 March 1852, Mary Durham Collection, Indiana Division.

62. S. A. Ferrall, *A Ramble of Six Thousand Miles through the United States of America* (London: Effingham Wilson, 1832), 87.

63. Birkbeck, *Notes on a Journey,* 102.

64. Susannah Hines Pering, Bloomington, Ind., to L. Edwards, Chard, England, 27 August 1833, transcript, 31, Pering Papers.

65. Dorothea Kline McCullough, "'By Cash and Eggs': Gender in Washington County during Indiana's Pioneer Period" (Ph.D. diss., Indiana University, 2001). See also Elizabeth Perkins, "The Consumer Frontier: Household Consumption in Early Kentucky," *Journal of American History* 78 (September 1991): 486–510; for the later period, see Blanke, *Sowing the American Dream.*

66. Burns, *Recollections,* 19.

67. Brookville *Indiana American,* 10 July 1857.

68. Jacob Weaver [Switzerland County] to Johannes Weaver [New York], 5 August 1822, Jacob Weaver Collection, Smith Library.

69. Clark and Parmelia Sanderson, Dunham's Station P.O., Jackson County, to nephew and niece [David and Mary Ann Ireland?], September 1855, James Ireland Collection, Smith Library.

70. Jameson, "These Years Serve to Remind Me," 25–26.

71. Bazil B. Edmonston, Jasper, Dubois County, to Ninian Edmonston, Esq., Raughley, Wake County, N.C., 8 December 1832, transcript, Edmonston Papers.

72. Isaac Reed, "The Autobiography of Isaac Reed," *Indiana Magazine of History* 78 (June 1982): 206.

73. Jameson, "These Years Serve to Remind Me," 27.

74. James N. Reader, Mauckport, Ind., to Jacob Brandenberg, 26 November 1858, Jeha Brandenburg Papers, Indiana Division. Reader also warned: "Be careful that you are not robbed or killed."

75. George and Elizabeth Faucett, Orange County, to Abel and Alunia (?) Faucett and Family [Greene County?], 22 December 1853, Abel J. Faucett Papers, Smith Library.

76. John Parker, Jackson County, to Uncle, Aunt, & cousins [David Ireland], 5 February 1860, James Ireland Collection, Smith Library. Emphasis mine.

77. Benjamin and Mary Mace, Ontario (?), to Brother Ely Mace, Tewksbury, Mass., 10 November 1816, Mace Collection.

78. Benjamin and Mary Mace, Lexington, Ind., to parents, Benjamin and Rebecca Mace, Tewksbury, Mass., n.d., Mace Collection.

79. Mary J. Mace, Peavine, Washington County, to Isaac Mace, Hartland, N.Y., 9 September 1818, Mace Collection.

80. Jonathan Hardy, Jefferson County, to Benjamin Mace and wife & children, Tewksbury, Mass., 29 November 1821, Mace Collection.

81. Molly Mace to Parents, Brothers, and Sisters, Peter Hardy, Sandowne, N.H., 22 January 1820, Mace Collection.

82. Benjamin and Mary Mace, Washington County (New Lexington P.O., Scots County), to Parents, Benjamin Mace, Tewksbury, Mass., 10 September 1820, Mace Collection.

83. Jonathan Hardy, Jefferson County, to Benjamin Mace and wife & children, Tewksbury, Mass., 29 November 1821, Mace Collection.

84. Benjamin and Mary Mace, Washington County (New Lexington P.O., Scott County), to Parents, Benjamin Mace, Tewksbury, Mass., 10 September 1820, Mace Collection.

85. Thomas H. Greer, "Economic and Social Effects of the Panic of 1819 in the Old Northwest," *Indiana Magazine of History* 44 (September 1948): 227–43.

86. Faux, *Memorable Days,* 236.

87. Jacob Weaver [Switzerland County] to Johannes Weaver [Blooming Dale, Hurley, N.Y.], 30 July 1820, Jacob Weaver Collection, Smith Library.

88. Brookville *Indiana American,* 10 October 1834.

89. Jesse Hamilton, Ripley County, to James and Agnes Crandall, Danville, Ill., 10 April 1860, John Watts Hamilton Collection, Smith Library.

90. Bazil B. Edmonston, Jasper, Dubois County, to Ninian Edmonston, Esq., Raughley, Wake County, N.C., 8 December 1832, transcript, Edmonston Papers.

91. Fisher, *Indiana,* 74

92. Brookville *Franklin Democrat,* 29 October 1852.

93. See Robert E. Ankli, "Farm-Making Costs in the 1850s," *Agricultural History* 48 (January 1974): 51–70. See also Judith Klein, "Farm-Making Costs in the 1850s: A Comment," *Agricultural History* 48 (January 1974): 71–74; and Jeremy Atack, "Farm and Farm-Making Costs Revisited," *Agricultural History* 56 (October 1982): 663–76.

94. Samuel Brown, *The Western Gazetteer; or, Emigrant's Dictionary* (Auburn, N.Y.: Printed by H. C. Southwick, 1817), 55. See also Edmund Dana, *Geographical Sketches on the Western Country Designed for Emigrants and Settlers* (Cincinnati: Looker, Reynolds, 1819), 110.

95. Elisha Hughes to Father and Friends, 23 January 1824, Elisha Hughes Collection, Smith Library. See also Asa and Rachel Rosenbarger [Harrison County] to Rudolph and Barbary Rosenberger [*sic*], Virginia, 22 August 1835, in Asa Rosenbarger, *Word from the West.*

96. Washington County Estate Book, 1829–31, WCHS; and Franklin County Probate Order Book 1 (A), County Clerk's Office, Franklin County Courthouse, Brookville, Ind.

97. U.S. Census of Agriculture, manuscript schedule, 1850, Franklin and Washington counties, Indiana, microfilm, State Archives. The discrepancies between the two counties reflected different marshals' definitions of what constituted a farm. As a percentage of those growing corn, in Franklin County, 85 percent grew wheat and 65 percent grew oats, while in Washington County, the numbers are each less than a percentage point lower.

98. Samuel Whedon [Jackson County] to Brother & Sister, Mr. Whedon, Seneca Township, Ontario County, N.Y., 29 June 1829, Samuel Whedon Collection, Smith Library. Frequency of sweet potatoes based on U.S. Census returns, published and manuscript.

99. Burns, *Recollections,* 20–21.

100. George Fitzhugh, Madison, Ind., to Miss E. K. Fitzhugh, Windsor, near Baltimore, Maryland, 21 August 1838, George Fitzhugh Papers, Indiana Division.

101. John Bradbury, *Travels in the Interior of America in the Years 1809, 1810, and 1811,* 2nd ed., vol. 5 of *Early Western Travels, 1748–1846,* ed. Reuben Gold Thwaites (New York: AMS Press, 1966), 284.

102. Jameson, "These Years Serve to Remind Me," 7–8.

103. Note how something that becomes part of the "surplus production" strategy gets placed in the fields, part of the man's domain, and not in the garden, the woman's domain.

104. Jameson, "These Years Serve to Remind Me," 14–15. See also Mrs. Karl Tafel, "Latin Farmers in Indiana," *Indiana Magazine of History* 45 (December 1949): 414–15.

105. Burns, *Recollections,* 22.

106. Enoch Honeywell, "Diary," in *Travel Accounts of Indiana, 1679–1961,* comp. Shirley S. McCord (Indiana Historical Collections, vol. 47. [Indianapolis]: Indiana Historical

Bureau, 1970), 78. Original manuscript in Indiana Division. See also Ferrall, *A Ramble of Six Thousand Miles,* 89–90; and letter from Elisha Hughes to Father and Friends, 23 January 1824, Elisha Hughes Collection, Smith Library.

107. Charles R. Arms [near Fredonia, Ind.] to Richard Arms, Brand, Vt., 6 August 1844, in "A Vermont Emigrant Living in Crawford County Writes Home" (1844), *Indiana Source Book,* vol. 3, ed. Willard Heiss (Indianapolis: Indiana Historical Society, 1982), 150.

108. U.S. Census of Agriculture, manuscript schedule, 1850, Franklin County, microfilm, State Archives; and U.S. Census Office, *Seventh Census of the United States, 1850* (1853; New York: Arno Press, 1976).

109. Bradbury, *Travels in the Interior,* 303. See also Asa and Rachel Rosenbarger [Harrison County] to Rudolph and Barbary Rosenberger [*sic*], Virginia, 22 August 1835, in Asa Rosenbarger, *Word from the West.*

110. Based on U.S. Census of Agriculture, manuscript schedule, 1850, Franklin and Washington counties, Indiana, microfilm, State Archives.

111. The amount of beef cattle is hard to determine from the census, because only "other cattle" over one year old were enumerated. That a number of farms had milk cows, but no "other cattle," would suggest that the males inevitable in the dairying process had been disposed of in some way before enumeration or their first birthday.

112. Jameson, "These Years Serve to Remind Me," 13.

113. Washington County Estate Book, 1829–31, WCHS; Franklin County Probate Order Book 1 (A), November 1830–February 1835, and Franklin County Probate, Complete Record 8, 1851–52, County Clerk's Office, Franklin County Courthouse, Brookville, Ind.

114. Burns, *Recollections,* 21.

115. See Robert E. Gallman, "Self-Sufficiency in the Cotton Economy of the Antebellum South," *Agricultural History* 44 (January 1970): 5–23; and Raymond C. Battalio and John Kagel, "The Structure of Antebellum Southern Agriculture: South Carolina, a Case Study," *Agricultural History* 44 (January 1970): 25–37. The heavy migration from the Upland South may explain the dairy deficiency that Atack and Bateman as well as I have detected in Indiana. Atack and Bateman, *To Their Own Soil,* 146–61 and 201–24.

116. Indiana legislature, 1851–52 *Senate Journal,* 1767–68.

117. Based on examination of extant Commissioners' Records and Order Books. Auditor's Office, Franklin County Courthouse, Brookville, Ind.; Auditor's Office, Washington County Courthouse; and Genealogy Division. See also the Brookville *Franklin Democrat,* 12 May 1854.

118. Noah Major, *The Pioneers of Morgan County,* 254.

119. H. H. Pleasant, *A History of Crawford County, Indiana* (Glendale, Calif.: Arthur H. Clarke, 1926), 349. Pleasant is referring, in this instance, to an incident in the 1880s.

120. The only real danger to a hog was the bear, as recounted in "The Autobiography of David Osborn, Senior (1807–93)," http://www.boap.org/LDS/Early-Saints/DOsborn.html, accessed 21 May 2003.

121. Cornelius Pering, Bloomington, Ind., to S. Edwards, Chard, Somerset, England, 27 August 1832, transcript, Pering Papers.

122. Burns, *Recollections,* 21.

123. Charles R. Arms [near Fredonia, Ind.] to Richard Arms, Brand, Vt., 6 August 1844, in "A Vermont Emigrant," 150.

124. U.S. Census of Agriculture, manuscript schedule, 1850, Franklin and Washington counties, Indiana, microfilm, State Archives.

125. Aaron Stryker, Brownstown, Ind., to David Ireland & wife, 15 January 1854, James Ireland Collection, Smith Library.

126. Susannah Hines Pering, Bloomington, Ind., to L. Edwards, Chard, England, 27 August 1833, transcript, 31, Pering Papers.

127. Jameson, "These Years Serve to Remind Me," 14.

128. For a description of the making of hominy, see Burns, *Recollections*, 23–24.

129. The corn bushel equivalencies are arrived at by the methods in Atack and Bateman, *To Their Own Soil*, 201–24 and notes, using a random sample drawn for four southern Indiana townships from the manuscript of the U.S. Census of Agriculture, manuscript schedule, 1850, Franklin and Washington counties, Indiana, microfilm, State Archives. For more detail on production, see my dissertation, Nation, "Home in the Hoosier Hills," 273–75.

130. Values based on letter from James N. Goodnow, Vernon, Jennings County, to John Goodnow, Hobart, N.Y., 23 December 1849, James N. Goodnow Papers, Smith Library.

131. U.S. Census, Social Statistics, manuscript schedule, 1850, State Archives. Washington County allegedly only had one-third of its crop, while Franklin County had its "usual" crop.

132. James N. Goodnow, Vernon, Jennings County, to John Goodnow, Hobart, N.Y., 23 December 1849, James N. Goodnow Papers, Smith Library.

133. See letters from Samuel Whedon [Jackson County] to Brother & Sister, Mr. Whedon, Seneca Township, Ontario County, N.Y., 29 June 1829, Samuel Whedon Collection; Jacob Weaver, Switzerland County, to Johannes Weaver, New York, 5 May 1816, Jacob Weaver Collection; and Joseph Hewitt, Drewersburg, Franklin County, to Father, Ireland, 12 June 1856, Joseph Hewitt Collection, all in Smith Library.

134. Washington County Estate Book, 1829–31, WCHS; Franklin County Probate Order Book 1 (A), November 1830–February 1835, County Clerk's Office, Franklin County Courthouse, Brookville, Ind. Timony Flint, *A Condensed Geography and History of the Western States, or the Mississippi Valley*, 2 vols. (1828; Gainesville: Scholars' Facsimiles and Reprints, 1970), 2:156.

135. Paoli *American Eagle*, 24 November 1859.

136. On the complex relationship between commercially minded farming and the ethic of soil improvement, see Steven Stoll, *Larding the Lean Earth: Soil and Society in Nineteenth-Century America* (New York: Hill and Wang, 2002).

137. Faux, *Memorable Days*, 236.

138. The complex story of household production of textiles is told in Adrienne Hood, "The Material World of Cloth: Production and Use in Eighteenth-Century Rural Pennsylvania," *William and Mary Quarterly*, 3rd ser., 53 (January 1996): 43–66; and Laurel Thatcher Ulrich, *The Age of Homespun: Objects and Stories in the Creation of an American Myth* (New York: Alfred A. Knopf, 2001). See also Michael Zakim, "Sartorial Ideologies: From Homespun to Ready-Made," *American Historical Review* 106 (December 2001): 1553–86.

139. Fortescue Cuming, *Sketches of a Tour to the Western Country*, vol. 4 of *Early Western Travels, 1748–1846*, ed. Reuben Gold Thwaites (1810; New York: AMS Press, 1966), 262.

140. Thomas Jefferson Brooks, "Hindostan, Greenwich, and Mount Pleasant: The Pioneer Towns of Martin County—Memoirs of Thomas Jefferson Brooks," ed. George Wilson, *Indiana Magazine of History* 16 (December 1920): 290.

141. John Hicks, "Pioneer Life in Owen County, Indiana," 1985 *Yearbook* of the Society of Indiana Pioneers, 11.

142. Flint, *A Condensed Geography and History,* 141. See also *History of Washington County* (1884; Paoli, Ind.: Stout's Print Shop, 1965), 696.

143. Jacob Weaver [Switzerland County] to Johannes Weaver, Blooming Dale, Hurley, N.Y., 6 July 1817, Jacob Weaver Collection, Smith Library.

144. Washington County Estate Book, 1829–31, and Franklin County Probate Order Book 1 (A). On sharing, see Warder W. Stevens, *Centennial History of Washington County* (1916; reprint, Evansville, Ind.: Unigraphics, 1967), 146. The paucity of weaving machinery appraised in the probate records has often been noted. In several instances in the records I examined, the widow's portion had already been removed, with just a dollar figure given. I would surmise that since many widows often turned to textile manufacturing to support themselves, perhaps this is the case elsewhere. One might even suggest that, albeit contrary to law, many appraisers recognized looms and wheels as the wife's property. No one, I believe, can immerse himself in probate records for long without recognizing how much the values and methods reflect not the letter of the law but local customs. Such is the point of Andrew Hoag, "Probate Relationships and the Establishment of Wood County, Ohio, 1820–1840" (Ph.D. diss., University of Michigan, 1991).

145. Stevens, *Centennial History,* 146.

146. Burns, *Recollections,* 23.

147. John and Mary Watson, Aurora, Dearborn County, to Father and Mother, Stephen Watson Sr., Sedlescomb, near Battle, Sussex, Old England, 9 March 1825, in *Twenty-four Letters from Labourers in America to Their Friends in England,* prepared by H. Bruner, P. Radin, and A. Yedida, Sutro Branch, California State Library Occasional Papers reprint series no. 1 (n.d.), 10.

148. Salem *Indiana Farmer,* 1 June 1822.

149. Salem *Western Annotator,* 4 May 1833.

150. U.S. Census Office, *Compendium of the Enumeration of the Inhabitants and Statistics of the United States* (Washington, D.C.: Thomas Allen, 1841); U.S. Census Office, *The Seventh Census of the United States, 1850.* Information on the number of farms in each county in 1850 drawn from U.S. Census Office, *Statistical View of the United States.*

151. Washington County Estate Book, 1829–31; Franklin County Probate Order Book 1 (A); and U.S. Census of Agriculture, manuscript schedule, 1850, Franklin and Washington counties, Indiana, microfilm, State Archives.

152. Governor Joseph Wright, *An Address Delivered by Gov. Joseph A Wright . . . to the District Agricultural Society, Composed of the Counties of Washington and Orange* (Indianapolis: Austin H. Brown & Co., Printers, 1854), 5–9.

153. U.S. Census Office, *Compendium of the Enumeration of the Inhabitants and Statistics of the United States* (Washington, D.C.: Thomas Allen, 1841); U.S. Census Office, *The Seventh Census of the United States, 1850.* Information on the number of farms in each county in 1850 drawn from U.S. Census Office, 7th Census, 1850, *Statistical View of the United States.*

154. Washington County Estate Book, 1829–31, WCHS; Franklin County Probate Order Book 1 (A), November 1830–February 1835, County Clerk's Office, Franklin County Courthouse, Brookville, Ind.; and U.S. Census of Agriculture, manuscript schedule, 1850, Franklin and Washington counties, Indiana, microfilm, State Archives.

155. Tafel, "Latin Farmers in Indiana," 414.

156. J[oseph] and L[ydia] Miller [Jackson County] to D[avid] and M[ary] Ireland, n.d., James Ireland Collection, Smith Library.

157. Account books surveyed can be found at Smith Library, Indiana Division, and WCHS.

158. Tafel, "Latin Farmers in Indiana," 414.

159. Burns, *Recollections*, 24.

160. Thomas Jefferson Brooks, "Hindostan, Greenwich, and Mount Pleasant: The Pioneer Towns of Martin County—Memoirs of Thomas Jefferson Brooks," ed. George Wilson, *Indiana Magazine of History* 16 (1920): 290.

161. Kulikoff, *Agrarian Origins*, 30–32. Nancy Grey Osterud, in her synthetic essay introducing a special issue of *Agricultural History* devoted to women in American agriculture, seconds Kulikoff on the conflicting interests. See Osterud, "Gender and the Transition to Capitalism in Rural America," *Agricultural History* 67 (Spring 1993): 14–29. Gloria Main has pointed out that capitalist relations offered "wives and children a possible escape from patriarchal control." Main, review of *The Agrarian Origins of American Capitalism*, by Allen Kulikoff, *American Historical Review* 99 (February 1994): 294.

162. Mary Ryan, *Cradle of the Middle Class* (Cambridge: Cambridge University Press, 1981).

163. See Major, *Pioneers of Morgan County*, 301–303.

164. In "The Homespun Paradox: Market-Oriented Production of Cloth in Eastern Canada in the Nineteenth Century," *Agricultural History* 76 (2002): 28–57, Béatrice Craig, Judith Rygiel, and Elizabeth Turcotte note that in eastern Canada, homespun continued to find a market because it was heavier and warmer than goods produced elsewhere.

165. Dorothea Kline McCullough puts a different spin on women's work and the market economy in her dissertation, "'By Cash and Eggs,'" esp. chap. 4, dealing with women and commercialization, but our accounts are not in conflict. Clearly one of the appeals of women's textile manufacturing was its usefulness both for the family and for the market, just as the surplus produce model suggests.

166. *Rising Sun Times*, 11 April 1835.

167. Vevay *Village Times and Switzerland County News*, 13 October 1836; Brookville *Franklin Democrat*, 29 October 1852.

168. George Knight Hester, "Narratives of the Rev. George Knight Hester and His Wife, Benee (Briggs) Hester," *Indiana Magazine of History* 22 (June 1926): 141.

169. John and Mary Watson, Aurora, Dearborn County, to Father and Mother, Stephen Watson Sr., Sedlescomb, near Battle, Sussex, Old England, 15 June 1822, in *Twenty-four Letters*, 10.

170. For instance, see John Voorhees's estate list, where a share in a cross-cut saw is listed. Franklin County Probate Order Book 1 (A), November 1830–February 1835, 108.

171. Major, *Pioneers of Morgan County*, 258.

172. Cornelius Pering, Bloomington, Ind., to S. Edwards, Chard, Somerset, England, 27 August 1832, transcript, Pering Papers.

173. Benjamin and Mary Mace, Lexington, Ind., to Parents [Benjamin and Rebecca Mace], Tewksbury, Mass., n.d., Mace Collection.

174. Burns, *Recollections*, 25.

175. Ibid., 26.

176. Blane, *An Excursion*, 141.

177. *Brookville Enquirer*, 7 November 1820.

178. Salem *Western Annotator*, 12 January 1833.

179. Burr Banks ledger, Ledgers, WCHS.

180. Links made between U.S. Census of Population, manuscript schedule, 1850, Franklin and Washington counties, Indiana, microfilm, National Archives, and U.S. Census of Population, manuscript schedule, 1860, Franklin and Washington counties, computer file, IHS. See Jeremy Atack, "The Agricultural Ladder Revisited: A New Look at an Old Question with Some Data for 1860," *Agricultural History* 63 (Winter 1989): 1–25.

181. Benjamin and Mary Mace, Washington County (New Lexington P.O., Scott County), to Parents, Benjamin Mace, Tewksbury, Mass., 10 September 1820, Mace Collection.

182. See ledger of Andrew Shirk, 1841–49, 272, Andrew Shirk Collection, Smith Library.

183. Account books in WCHS, Indiana Division, and Smith Library.

184. U.S. Census of Agriculture, manuscript schedule, 1850, Franklin and Washington counties, Indiana, microfilm, State Archives.

185. Vevay *Weekly Messenger,* 11 July 1834.

186. Court cases about the time of 1820, 1840, and 1860 censuses were linked to individuals in the census. In Washington County, court cases drawn from [Circuit] Court Record, October 1818–December 1822; Washington County [Circuit] Court [Record], 1840–41; Washington County Common Pleas Minutes, 1859–60; and [Circuit Court] Minutes Book, 1852–61; all in the Clerk's Office, Washington County Courthouse, Salem, Ind. In Franklin County, court cases drawn from [Circuit Court] Civil Order Book 2, 1818–20; Circuit Court Order Book 6, August 1839–February 1841; Circuit Court Order Book 13, 1857–62; Court of Common Pleas, Order Book 3, 1858–61; all in Clerk's Office, Franklin County Courthouse, Brookville, Ind.

187. Justice of the peace dockets for several townships in Washington County are available at the WCHS.

188. The same could be said for the associate judges on the local circuit court, but it appears that they were concerned about legal form. See the notes of Enoch Parr, one such lay associate judge, "Memoir of Enoch Parr," *Indiana Magazine of History* 22 (December 1926): 431–53.

189. [Hall], *The New Purchase,* 214–15.

190. For one from an even later period, see Account Book of Joseph Jackson, 1875–85, Metamora, Ind., 33, Joseph Jackson Collection, Smith Library.

191. Ledger, 1821–31, Washington County, WCHS.

192. John Ketcham to Absalom Morgan, 14 November 1844, Monroe County Indiana History Manuscripts, Lilly Library.

193. Hicks, "Pioneer Life in Owen County," 12–13.

194. [Hall], *New Purchase,* 215.

195. Hester, "Narratives," 140.

196. Michael Merrill, "Cash Is Good to Eat: Self-Sufficiency and Exchange in the Rural Economy of the United States," *Radical History Review* 15 (Winter 1977): 42–71.

197. See ledger of Andrew Shirk, 1856–60, 43, Andrew Shirk Collection, Smith Library.

198. Cornelius Pering, Bloomington, Ind., to S. Edwards, Chard, Somerset, England, 27 August 1832, transcript, Pering Papers.

199. Brookville *Franklin Democrat,* 29 March 1850.

200. George and Elizabeth Faucett, Orange County, to Abel and Alunia (?) Faucett and Family [Greene County?], 22 December 1853, Abel Faucett Papers, Smith Library. For another part of this story, see Anna Bruner Eales, ed., "Paoli and Placerville: Correspondence of a Hoosier in the Gold Rush," *Indiana Magazine of History* 95 (1999): 30.

201. Based on examination of deed records in Washington County Courthouse, Salem, Ind.; and Franklin County Courthouse, Brookville, Ind.

202. J. N. O. [Jno., meaning John?] Hughes, Elizabethtown [Bartholomew County], Ind., to Ezekiel Tyner [Franklin County], 27 July 1841, Ezekiel Tyner Papers, Smith Library.

203. Aaron S. Bullard, Vernon, Ind., to Joseph Bullard, Grand Rapids, 11 April 1847, Aaron Bullard Collection, Smith Library.

204. Records of Unity Baptist Church, 1818–58, 21 (1st Saturday in March 1857), transcript, Baptist Church Records, WCHS.

205. Livonia Presbyterian Church, Sessional and Other Records, 1828–71, 3 September 1859, transcript, Presbyterian Church Records, WCHS.

206. Paoli *True American,* 11 March 1843, 18 March 1843, 29 December 1843.

207. Vevay *Weekly Messenger,* 11 July 1835.

208. Salem *Indiana Farmer,* 1 June 1822.

209. *Brookville Enquirer,* 7 November 1820.

210. Note attached from John Sloan to letter from C. H. Sloan [New Albany?] to mother and father, Jacob Hunt, Portland, Maine, 18 November 1842, Hunt manuscripts, Lilly Library.

211. Jacob Weaver [Switzerland County] to Johannes Weaver [Blooming Dale, Hurley, N.Y.], 30 July 1820, Jacob Weaver Collection, Smith Library.

212. *Rising Sun Times,* 11 July 1835.

213. George Leavitt, Crawford County, to parents, J. N. C. Leavitt, Esq., Chichester, N.H., 23 February 1847, Leavitt manuscripts, Lilly Library.

214. Paoli *True American,* 29 December 1843.

215. Diary of Horace Stow, 11, manuscript, Horace Stow Collection, Smith Library.

216. Tafel, "Latin Farmers in Indiana," 415.

217. George Faucett, Orange County, to Abel Faucett, Greene County, 3 January 1841, Abel J. Faucett Collection, Smith Library.

218. Joseph W. Ancoin, Parish of Assumption, La., to George Kapps, Dubois County, 27 January 1860, George Kapp Collection, Smith Library.

219. Thomas Jefferson Brooks, "Hindostan, Greenwich, and Mount Pleasant," 290.

220. Robert Wilken, O.F.M., *A Historical Sketch of the Holy Family Church and Parish* (1937; Oldenburg: n.p., 1987), 79.

221. Hicks, "Pioneer Life in Owen County," 12.

222. Samuel Gibson Brown, "Flatboat Letters from Samuel Gibson Brown," 1965 *Yearbook* of the Society of Indiana Pioneers, 20.

223. Indianapolis *Indiana Daily State Journal,* 10 December 1845, quoting the Louisville *Journal,* reprinted in *Progress after Statehood: A Book of Readings,* comp. Pamela J. Bennett and Shirley S. McCord, Indiana Historical Collections, vol. 49 (Indianapolis: Indiana Historical Bureau, 1974), 495–97.

224. Worthington *Valley Times,* 27 January 1859, reprinted in *Progress after Statehood: A Book of Readings,* 482–83.

225. Salem *Washington Democrat,* 19 June 1857.

226. Definition of competency from Daniel Vickers, "Competency and Competition: Economic Culture in Early America," 3.

227. The other papers cited above were Whig/American/Republican.

4. The Politics of Localism

1. John Ashworth, *"Agrarians" and "Aristocrats": Party Political Ideology in America, 1837–1846* (Cambridge: Cambridge University Press, 1987). For the broader cultural context, see David Roediger, *Wages of Whiteness: Race and the Making of the American Working Class* (London: Verso, 1991).

2. Daniel Feller, *The Public Lands in Jacksonian America* (Madison: University of Wisconsin Press, 1984); and Harry Scheiber, *Ohio Canal Era: A Case Study of Government and the Economy, 1820–1861* (Athens: Ohio University Press, 1969).

3. Lawrence Kohl, *The Politics of Individualism: Parties and the American Character in the Jacksonian Era* (New York: Oxford University Press, 1989).

4. See Robert P. Swierenga, "Ethnoreligious Political Behavior in the Mid-Nineteenth Century: Voting, Values, Cultures," in *Religion and American Politics,* ed. Mark Noll (New York: Oxford University Press, 1990), and Richard Jensen, "The Religious and Occupational Roots of Party Identification: Illinois and Indiana in the 1870s," *Civil War History* 16 (December 1970): 325–43.

5. This position is most ably synthesized by Harry Watson, *Liberty and Power: The Politics of Jacksonian America* (New York: Hill and Wang, 1990).

6. For an overview of the voluminous literature on this subject, see Ronald Formisano, "The Invention of the Ethnocultural Interpretation," *American Historical Review* 99 (April 1994): 453–77.

7. Paul Johnson, *A Shopkeeper's Millennium: Society and Revivals in Rochester, New York, 1815–1837* (New York: Hill and Wang, 1978), helped lead the way on a synthesis of Whig economic and religious appeals. Charles Seller's *The Market Revolution: Jacksonian America, 1815–1846* (New York: Oxford University Press, 1991) has made an initial attempt to bridge Democratic economic concerns with the party's ethnic and religious makeup.

8. In the earlier period, see Thomas P. Slaughter, *The Whiskey Rebellion* (New York: Oxford University Press, 1986) and Ronald Formisano, *The Transformation of Political Culture: Massachusetts Parties, 1790s–1840s* (New York: Oxford University Press, 1983). For the late nineteenth century, see James Turner, "Understanding the Populists," *Journal of American History* 67 (September 1980): 354–73; and, most importantly for this study, Melvyn Hammarberg, *The Indiana Voter: The Historical Dynamics of Party Allegiance during the 1870s* (Chicago: University of Chicago Press, 1977). In Southern politics during the antebellum period, both Mills Thornton and Harry Watson have detected a similar schism. J. Mills Thornton III, *Politics and Power in a Slave Society: Alabama, 1800–1860* (Baton Rouge: Louisiana State University Press, 1978), and Harry Watson, *Jacksonian Politics and Community Conflict* (Baton Rouge: Louisiana State University Press, 1981). In this context, also see John Stilgoe's discussion of the "metropolitan corridor" formed by the railroads, in his *Metropolitan Corridor* (New Haven, Conn.: Yale University Press, 1983).

9. James Kloppenberg, "The Virtues of Liberalism: Christianity, Republicanism, and Ethics in Early American Political Discourse," *Journal of American History* 74 (June 1987): 9–33. See also Daniel Rodgers, "Republicanism: The Career of a Concept," *Journal of American History* 89 (June 1992): 11–38.

10. Brookville *Franklin Democrat,* 29 October 1852. Compare this remark with Drew McCoy's description of republicanism in *The Elusive Republic* (Chapel Hill: Published for the Institute of Early American History and Culture by the University of North Carolina Press, 1980), 68.

11. William H. English, *Address of Honorable William H. English, Delivered at Livonia, Indiana, before the Washington and Orange County Agriculture Society, October 15, 1857* (Washington, D.C.: Congressional Globe Office, 1858).

12. Enoch Parr, "Memoir of Enoch Parr," *Indiana Magazine of History* 22 (December 1926): 384.

13. David Krueger, "Party Development in Indiana, 1800–1832" (Ph.D. diss., University of Kentucky, 1974), chap. 2.

14. This discussion based primarily on Krueger, "Party Development," 59–69. See also Peter Onuf, *Statehood and Union: A History of the Northwest Ordinance* (Bloomington: Indiana University Press, 1987); and John D. Barnhart, *Valley of Democracy* (Lincoln: University of Nebraska Press, 1953).

15. Parr, "Memoir," 379. This quotation confirms Nicole Etcheson's argument about the importance of manliness in the political culture of Upland Southerners: Etcheson, *The Emerging Midwest: Upland Southerners and the Political Culture of the Old Northwest, 1787–1861* (Bloomington: Indiana University Press, 1997), 27–39.

16. Patrick Henry Jameson, "These Years Serve to Remind Me," 1970 *Yearbook* of the Society of Indiana Pioneers, 16.

17. Corydon *Indiana Gazette*, June 22, 1820, quoted in *Indiana Magazine of History* 13 (1917): 112–13, reprinted in *Readings in Indiana History*, comp. Gayle Thornbrough and Dorothy Riker, Indiana Historical Collections, vol. 36 (Indianapolis: Indiana Historical Bureau, 1956), 506–507.

18. Corydon *Indiana Gazette*, 1 March 1821, quoted in *Indiana Magazine of History* 13 (1917): 113, reprinted in *Readings in Indiana History*, 507–508.

19. Cited by "To the Electors of Franklin and Fayette Counties," *Brookville Enquirer*, 21 October 1820. Emphasis added.

20. "To the Electors of Franklin and Fayette Counties," *Brookville Enquirer*, 21 October 1820.

21. Brookville *Franklin Democrat*, 17 July 1857.

22. On antiparty sentiment in the neighboring state of Illinois, see Gerald Leonard, *The Invention of Party Politics: Federalism, Popular Sovereignty, and Constitutional Development in Jacksonian Illinois* (Chapel Hill: University of North Carolina Press, 2002).

23. Parr, "Memoir," 386.

24. James Huston, *Securing the Fruits of Labor: The American Concept of Wealth Distribution, 1765–1900* (Baton Rouge: Louisiana State University Press, 1998), 19–20.

25. Corydon *Indiana Gazette*, 9 July 1823, citing the Indianapolis *Gazette*, quoted in Logan Esarey, "Pioneer Politics in Indiana," *Indiana Magazine of History* 13 (June 1917): 113–14.

26. David Krueger, "Party Development in Indiana," follows Logan Esarey, "Pioneer Politics in Indiana," *Indiana Magazine of History* 13 (June 1917): 99–128, on this point. My discussion rests on both.

27. Newspaper support is discussed in Thomas W. Howard, "Indiana Newspapers and the Presidential Election of 1824," *Indiana Magazine of History* 63 (1967): 177–206.

28. Derived from Huston, *Securing the Fruits of Labor*, chaps. 2 and 3.

29. In this study, election returns will not be cited. Most county-level results were obtained from *Indiana Election Returns, 1816–1851*, comp. Dorothy Riker and Gayle Thornbrough, Indiana Historical Collections, vol. 40 (Indianapolis: Indiana Historical Bureau, 1960); and from Walter Dean Burnham, *Presidential Ballots, 1836–1892* (Baltimore: Johns Hopkins University Press, 1955). The township level results come from thirty-one different sources. The full bibliography can be found in my dissertation, Richard Nation, "Home in the Hoosier Hills: Agriculture, Politics, and Religion, 1810–1870" (Ph.D. diss., University of Michigan, 1995), 647–49.

30. I take the measure of popular sentiment despite the recent warning of Glenn Altschuler and Stuart Blumin that there was not true enthusiasm for politics in the period: *Rude Republic: Americans and Their Politics in the Nineteenth Century* (Princeton, N.J.: Princeton University Press, 2000). See the replies to their initial article, "Limits of Political

Engagement in Antebellum America: A New Look at the Golden Age of Participatory Democracy," *Journal of the American History* 84 (1997): 855–85, especially Harry L. Watson, "Humbug? Bah! Atlschuler and Blumin and the Riddle of the Antebellum Electorate," *Journal of the American History* 84 (1997): 886–93.

31. *Rising Sun Times,* 28 March 1835.

32. In *The Emerging Midwest,* Nicole Etcheson asserts, and I agree, that among Upland Southerners in the Midwest, "region of origin did not determine party loyalty in the Jacksonian period" (40). The portrait she draws of the Upland Southerners' political culture, however, seems more reminiscent of the Jacksonians than the Whigs cum Republicans. I do note below ways in which I believe even southern Indiana Whigs shared views more similar to their neighboring Democrats than to northern Indiana Whigs, which may be the similarity to which Etcheson points us.

33. Parr, "Memoir," 383.

34. Speech of Miles C. Eggleston, Brookville *Franklin Repository,* 4 December 1827; on Ray and his exchange with Jackson, see Krueger, "Party Development," 183–84, 195–99.

35. Parr, "Memoir," 383.

36. Nevertheless, *McCulloch* v. *Maryland* would have voided any such provision in 1819.

37. Vincennes *Western Sun,* 3 February 1816.

38. Brookville *Franklin Democrat,* 3 November 1854.

39. Brookville *Franklin Democrat,* 9 February 1855.

40. Molly Mace [Washington County] to Parents, Brothers, and Sisters, Peter Hardy, Sandowne, New Hampshire, 22 January 1820, Mace Collection.

41. Jonathan Hardy, Jefferson County, to Benjamin Mace and wife & children, Tewksbury, Mass., 29 November 1821, Mace Collection.

42. Edward Brush to sister, 1 November 1822, Edward Brush Collection, Smith Library.

43. David Thomas, *Travels through the Western Country in the Summer of 1816* (Auburn, N.Y.: Printed by David Rumsey, 1819), 119. See also Samuel Brown, *The Western Gazetteer; or, Emigrant's Dictionary* (Auburn, N.Y.: Printed by H. C. Southwick, 1817), 61; and Timothy Flint, *A Condensed Geography and History of the Western States, or the Mississippi Valley,* 2 vols. (1828; Gainesville: Scholars' Facsimiles and Reprints, 1970), 2:171.

44. Logan Esarey, *State Banking in Indiana, 1819–1875,* Indiana University Studies, no. 15 (Bloomington, 1912). Recent coverage of the constitutional and legislative history of early Indiana can be found in Donald F. Carmony, *Indiana, 1816–1850: The Pioneer Era,* vol. 2 of *The History of Indiana* (Indianapolis: Indiana Historical Society, 1998).

45. Salem *Indiana Farmer,* 26 July 1822.

46. August B. Reifel, *History of Franklin County, Indiana.* (1915; reprint, Evansville, Ind.: Unigraphics, 1971), 323.

47. R. C. Buley, *The Old Northwest,* 2 vols. (Bloomington: Indiana University Press, 1950), 1:571–73, 584, 594–97.

48. Carmony, *Indiana, 1816–1850,* 329, citing Vincennes *Western Sun,* 5 June 1819.

49. Brookville *Enquirer and Indiana Telegraph,* 14 January 1820.

50. John Wynn, Brookville, Franklin County, to Thomas Legg, Broughton, Near Stikesley, Yorkshire, Old England, 26 October 1821, in John Wynn, "From Whitewater to Yorkshire," 1961 *Yearbook* of the Society of Indiana Pioneers, 9.

51. Madison *Indiana Republican,* 27 July 1820. Hopkins lost his bid for office, not surprisingly in the leading commercial center in the state, one whose bank had not "failed," although it did suspend specie payments.

52. Corydon *Indiana Gazette,* 21 August 1819. See also George McCaslin's letter, Madison *Indiana Republican,* 20 July 1820.

53. Salem *Tocsin,* 8 April 1820.

54. See, for example, the Salem *Western Annotator,* which tracked the bill through Congress with little comment. With the president's veto, however, it urged that the message "needs but to be read to be appreciated, and although it may be condemned by those *interested* in the re-charter, the reckless opponents of the President, and the monied aristocracy, its doctrines and its author will be sustained by the American people" (1 August 1832).

55. Madison *Indiana Republican,* 11 October 1832.

56. Salem *Western Annotator,* 18 August 1832.

57. Parr, "Memoir," 383.

58. Salem *Western Annotator,* 8 September 1832.

59. Brookville *Indiana American,* 8 November 1844.

60. Bazil B. Edmonston, Jasper, Dubois County, to Ninian Edmonston, Esq., Raughley, Wake County, N.C., 8 December 1832, transcript, Edmonston Papers.

61. Bazil B. Edmonston, Jasper, Dubois County, to Ninian Edmonston, Waynesville, N.C., 11 September 1832, transcript, Edmonston Papers.

62. Bazil B. Edmonston, Jasper, Dubois County, to Ninian Edmonston, Esq., Raughley, Wake County, N.C., 8 December 1832, transcript, Edmonston Papers.

63. *Brookville Inquirer,* 26 April 1833.

64. Parr, "Memoir," 385.

65. Parr, "Memoir," 384. See also the paper Parr would have read, the Salem *Western Annotator,* 4 May 1833.

66. "Mr. Graham's Speech on the Bank Bill, delivered in the Senate of the Indiana Legislature, on the 24th of January, 1833," Salem *Indiana Phoenix,* 27 February 1833.

67. Salem *Indiana Phoenix,* 3 January 1833.

68. Ibid.

69. "Mr. Graham's Speech on the Bank Bill, delivered in the Senate of the Indiana Legislature, on the 24th of January, 1833," Salem *Indiana Phoenix,* 27 February 1833.

70. Salem *Western Annotator,* 4 May 1833.

71. Madison *Indiana Republican,* 11 October 1832.

72. Col. Hutchen's Circular, Brookville *Indiana American,* 25 July 1834. Hutchen lost the election but went on to become the most radical Democratic editor in southern Indiana.

73. *Rising Sun Times,* 25 July 1835.

74. Letter from C. W. Hutchen, "White-Water Canal," Brookville *Indiana American,* 19 September 1834.

75. *Rising Sun Times,* 21 February 1835.

76. *Rising Sun Times,* 28 March 1835.

77. "Mr. Conwell's Opinion," Brookville *Indiana American,* 25 July 1834. Conwell defeated C. W. Hutchen in the state representative election.

78. Letter from C. W. Hutchen, "White-Water Canal," Brookville *Indiana American,* 19 September 1834.

79. Indiana Legislature, 1834–35 *House Journal,* 14.

80. Indiana Legislature, 1835–36 *House Journal,* 357–61.

81. *Rising Sun Times,* 3 March 1835.

82. "Col. Hutchen's Circular," Brookville *Indiana American,* 25 July 1834.

83. *Rising Sun Times,* 25 July 1835.

84. Vevay *Weekly Messenger,* 16 January 1836.

85. *Rising Sun Times,* 27 January 1836.

86. "Col. Hutchen's Circular," Brookville *Indiana American,* 25 July 1834.

87. *Rising Sun* Times, 3 March 1835.

88. Charles Sealsfield, *The Americans as They Are* (London: Hurst, Chance, 1828), 34–35.

89. Harry Scheiber tells a similar tale for Ohio in *Ohio Canal Era.*

90. Bloomington *Indiana Gazette,* 10 June 1836.

91. For a prominent example, see "Mr. Dumont's Address to a Meeting of Switzerland County Farmers and Other Citizens," Vevay *Village Times and Switzerland County News,* 6 April 1837.

92. Routes had not been completely laid out, but a railroad or road through Lawrence and Monroe was mandated, and there really was no other way for the Central Canal to go but through Owen County.

93. Whig Eli Farmer claimed he opposed the scheme. "Eli Farmer Autobiography," Eli Farmer mss, Lilly Library, 192, 197.

94. Parr, "Memoir," 385–86.

95. B. B. Edmonston, Jasper, Dubois County, to Col. Ninian Edmonston, Waynesville, Haywood County, N.C., 18 September 1839, transcript, Edmonston Papers.

96. John Lauritz Larson, *Internal Improvement: National Public Works and the Promise of Popular Government in the Early United States* (Chapel Hill: University of North Carolina Press, 2001).

97. Brookville *Indiana American,* 5 August 1836.

98. See John Barnhart and Dorothy Riker, *Indiana to 1816: The Colonial Period* (Indianapolis: Indiana Historical Society, 1971), 392–97.

99. Brookville *Franklin Democrat,* 9 September 1842.

100. In Dearborn County, the German townships remained the Van Buren stronghold, although Manchester Township recorded the same number of votes for each candidate. It was less German than the others. There was a small drop in Logan Township, but Kelso recorded a huge increase in support for Van Buren.

101. Bazil B. Edmonston, Jasper, Dubois County, to Enoch Edmonston, Rushville, Ill., 2 December 1840, transcript, Edmonston Papers.

102. James Madison, *The Indiana Way* (Bloomington: Indiana University Press, and Indianapolis: Indiana Historical Society, 1986), appendix B, 330.

103. Despite Harrison County's 404 new Democratic voters, it had 538 new Whig supporters as well.

104. The surge in Whig voters here is in keeping with Michael Holt's assessments of the electoral realignment in 1840, but it seems more temporary in Indiana than elsewhere, thanks to the Mammoth Bill. Holt, "The Election of 1840, Voter Mobilization, and the Emergence of Jacksonian Voting Behavior," in William J. Cooper et al., eds., *A Master's Due: Essays in Honor of David Herbert Donald* (Baton Rouge: Louisiana State University Press, 1985). See also Ronald Formisano, "The New Political History and the Election of 1840," *Journal of Interdisciplinary History* 23 (Spring 1993): 661–82; and Holt, *The Rise and Fall of the Whig Party: Jacksonian Politics and the Onset of the Civil War* (New York: Oxford University Press, 1999).

105. In 1841, Whigs maintained their hold on the Hoosier delegation to the U.S. Congress, as Congressmen were elected in a special May election that year rather than in August with the rest of the Indiana local elections. While the special Congressional election attracted fewer voters for both parties than the previous year's presidential election, in the

exclusively local elections—state senator was the highest office—later in August of 1841, Democratic turnout recorded a huge increase over the Congressional race, compared with just a few extra Whigs who made it to the polls.

106. Logan Esarey, *Internal Improvements in Early Indiana,* IHS Publications, vol. 5, no. 2 (Indianapolis: Edward J. Hecker, 1912). See also Lee Newcomer, "A History of the Indiana Internal Improvement Bond," *Indiana Magazine of History* 32 (June 1936); Donald F. Carmony, "Historical Background of the Restrictions against State Debt in the Indiana Constitution of 1851," *Indiana Magazine of History* 47 (June 1951): 129–42; and John Lauritz Larson, "To Try to Make a State of It: Indiana's Mammoth Internal Improvements Bill," *Proceedings of the Indiana Academy of Social Sciences,* 3rd ser., 22 (1987): 77–84.

107. Carmony, *Indiana, 1816–1850,* 42. Esarey, *Internal Improvements,* suggests that around $2 million were stolen and another $4 million were purchased with securities that proved to be worthless, 123–24. The problem with figures is explained by John Lauritz Larson, *Internal Improvement,* 290n35.

108. On Butler's activity, see John David Haeger, *The Investment Frontier: New York Businessmen and the Economic Development of the Old Northwest* (Albany: State University of New York Press, 1981).

109. Governor Bigger's message, Brookville *Indiana American,* 9 December 1842.

110. Vevay *Indiana Palladium,* 27 February 1847; see also Brookville *Indiana American,* 24 December 1841.

111. *Rising Sun Times,* 10 January 1835.

112. Larson, "To Try to Make a State of It," 79. Governor Ray supported the endeavor because it had "no design upon the public purse."

113. Indiana Constitutional Convention, *Debates and Proceedings of the Convention for the Revision of the Constitution of the State of Indiana,* 2 vols. (Indianapolis: A.H. Brown, 1850–[1851]), vol. I, 678.

114. Brookville *Franklin Democrat,* 16 September 1853.

115. Washington County Commissioner's Records, 21 December 1847, transcript, Genealogy Division. To put the signatures into a different perspective, they represented over 46 percent of the men over the age of 21 resident in the county in 1850.

116. Washington County Commissioner's Record, 5 June 1851, transcript, Genealogy Division.

117. Samuel T. Wells, Indianapolis, to Samuel W. Durham, Marion, Lynn County, Iowa, 7 February 1852, Mary Durham Papers, Indiana Division.

118. Ibid.

119. Brookville *Franklin Democrat,* 2 June 1854.

120. Brookville *Franklin Democrat,* 2 July 1852.

121. Brookville *Franklin Democrat,* 14 July 1848.

122. Similar fights occurred in other states at the same time. See Herbert Ershkowitz and William G. Shade, "Consensus or Conflict? Political Behavior in the State Legislatures during the Jacksonian Era," *Journal of American History* 58 (December 1971): 591–621.

123. Perusal of the House journals reveals many amendments regarding "limited liability," but few votes were recorded. For one vote, see Brookville *Indiana American,* 12 January 1846.

124. Brookville *Indiana American,* 26 December 1845. Webber did not represent the hill country.

125. For some of the debates, see the Brookville *Indiana American,* 26 December 1845 and 2 January 1846.

126. See Brookville *Indiana American,* 26 December 1845. On the scrip and the problems it caused, see Brookville *Indiana American,* 11 November 1842 and 19 September 1845.

127. Brookville *Indiana American,* 26 December 1845.

128. Parr, "Memoir," 385, 387.

129. Brookville *Indiana American,* 26 December 1845.

130. For the following discussion of banking in Indiana, I rely upon William G. Shade, *Banks or No Banks: The Money Issue in Western Politics, 1837–1865* (Detroit: Wayne State University Press, 1972). For additional context, see James Rogers Sharp, *The Jacksonians versus the Banks: Politics in the States after the Panic of 1837* (New York: Columbia University Press, 1970).

131. Charlestown *Indianan,* reprinted in Brookville *Indiana American,* 1 September 1837. Editorial note is replicated from the *American.*

132. See Shade, *Banks or No Banks,* 70–75.

133. Paoli *True American,* 28 February 1840.

134. Paoli *True American,* 28 February 1840.

135. James Whitcomb, "Inaugural Address," Brookville *Indiana American,* 15 December 1843. Contrast Whitcomb's vision with that of his predecessor, Samuel Bigger: "In [convertible paper currency] is laid the foundation of the true credit system, which is our surest protection against actual monopolies of capitalists. Credit constitutes the capital of the poor man, bestowed upon him as the reward of his enterprise and integrity. With it he can compete successfully with wealth in all its forms. Without it, labor and property would be brought entirely within the heartless grasp of individual wealth, whose operation can never be under the control of legislation" (Shade, *Banks or No Banks,* 98).

136. Madison, *The Indiana Way,* 89, citing his own work on Indianapolis business and the State Bank.

137. Shade, *Banks or No Banks,* 139–41.

138. Ibid., 170–71.

139. Brookville *Franklin Democrat,* 28 January 1853. Emphasis mine.

140. Brookville *Franklin Democrat,* 21 January 1853.

141. Brookville *Franklin Democrat,* 11 March 1853. On "shinplasters," see 21 January 1853.

142. Brookville *Franklin Democrat,* 17 February 1854.

143. Paoli *American Eagle,* 10 November 1854.

144. Brookville *Franklin Democrat,* 20 April 1855.

145. Paoli *True American,* 28 June 1844.

146. Using county seats, the Ohio River, the White River, and the internal improvement lines completed by 1844 as the basis of commercial activity, I have evaluated, by chi-square test, townships as Whig and Democratic on the basis of commercial or noncommercial location and have determined that the relationship is significant to $P_{.90}$.

147. For the region, the relationship between Whig and Democratic, commercial and noncommercial, defined as above, had a chi-square significance of $P_{.995}$ for the 1852 election.

148. Lawrence M. Lipin, *Producers, Proletarians, and Politicians: Workers and Party Politics in Evansville and New Albany, Indiana, 1850–1867* (Champaign: University of Illinois Press, 1993).

149. Brookville *Franklin Democrat,* 30 June 1854.

150. Paoli *American Eagle,* 18 June 1852.

151. Paoli *American Eagle,* 11 June 1852.

152. Emma Lou Thornbrough, *Indiana in the Civil War Era, 1850–1880,* vol. 3 of *The History of Indiana* (Indianapolis: Indiana Historical Bureau and Indiana Historical Soci-

ety, 1965), 58. See also Suzanne Thurman, "Cultural Politics on the Indiana Frontier: The American Home Missionary Society and Temperance Reform," *Indiana Magazine of History* 94 (1998), 285–302.

153. Paoli *American Eagle*, 16 February 1855. As evidence of the Democrats' willingness to regulate the liquor trade, the same article warned that if the law was struck down, the liquor trade would be "wide open."

154. Thornbrough, 68–69.

155. New Albany *Ledger,* reprinted in Paoli *American Eagle,* 1 May 1856.

5. Localism, Race, and the Civil War

1. U.S. Census Office, *Agriculture of the United States in 1860; Compiled from the Original Returns of the Eighth Census* (Washington, D.C.: Government Printing Office, 1864).

2. Thomas Haskell, "Capitalism and the Origins of the Humanitarian Sensibility," *American Historical Review* 90 (April 1985): 339–61 and (June 1985): 547–66.

3. Philip J. Schwarz, *Migrants against Slavery: Virginians and the Nation* (Charlottesville: University Press of Virginia, 2001).

4. John C. Hudson, "North American Origins of Middlewestern Frontier Populations," *Annals of the Association of American Geographers* 78 (September 1988): 395–413.

5. Charles Sealsfield, *The Americans as They Are* (London: Hurst, Chance, 1828), 32–33.

6. On this see J. Mills Thornton III, *Politics and Power in a Slave Society: Alabama, 1800–1860* (Baton Rouge: Louisiana State University Press, 1978).

7. *Brookville Inquirer,* 3 May 1833.

8. Sharon Baptist Church, Washington Township, Washington County, 3 August 1822, Baptist Church Records, WCHS. Xeroxes of clippings from Salem *Democrat*, May–July 1907.

9. Minutes of Sinking Spring Baptist Church, Posey Township, Washington County, 3rd Saturday, April 1827, transcript, Baptist Church Records, WCHS. Cf. minutes of the Elim (New Providence) Baptist Church, 1816–56, Polk Township, Washington County, 8 June 1822, 13 July 1822, transcript, Baptist Church Records, WCHS.

10. Emma Lou Thornbrough, *The Negro in Indiana,* Indiana Historical Collections, vol. 37 (Indianapolis: Indiana Historical Bureau, 1957), 60.

11. See Eric Foner, *Free Soil, Free Labor, Free Men* (Oxford: Oxford University Press, 1970); and Eugene Berwanger, *The Frontier against Slavery: Western Anti-Negro Prejudice and the Slavery Extension Controversy* (Urbana: University of Illinois Press, 1967).

12. *Indiana Election Returns, 1816–1851,* comp. Dorothy Riker and Gayle Thornbrough, Indiana Historical Collections, vol. 40 (Indianapolis: Indiana Historical Bureau, 1960).

13. Paoli *American Eagle,* 5 November 1857.

14. Jasper *Courier,* 27 February 1861, cited in G. R. Tredway, *Democratic Opposition to the Lincoln Administration in Indiana,* Indiana Historical Collections, vol. 48 (Indianapolis: Indiana Historical Bureau, 1973), 2.

15. Father Joseph A. Thie, *Enochsburg and St. John's Church: Notes of Father Joseph A. Thie* (privately printed, 1976), 12. See also Christina Katterhenry, Huntingburg, Ind., to Uncle, Aunt, Cousins and Nieces [Germany], 25 November 1861, in Christina Katterhenry, "Letter from Huntingburg," trans. Paul F. Roller, *Indiana History Bulletin* 49, no. 2 (February 1972): 23.

16. David Roediger's point about the racial appeal of the Democrats to immigrants holds well here. See Roediger, *Wages of Whiteness: Race and the Making of the American Working Class* (London: Verso, 1991).

17. Such distinction could have meant no more than different but equal, but by the time of the Civil War, it generally implied inferiority.

18. See Jean Baker, *Affairs of Party* (Ithaca, N.Y.: Cornell University Press, 1983), esp. 177–211.

19. See Bruce Bigelow, "The Cultural Geography of African Americans in Antebellum Indiana," IHS *Black History News and Notes* 88 (May 2002): 4–7.

20. For one example of pre–Civil War violence, see Richard F. Nation, "Violence and the Rights of African Americans in Civil War–Era Indiana: The Case of James Hays," *Indiana Magazine of History* 100 (September 2004): 215–30.

21. Thornbrough, *Negro in Indiana,* 225.

22. Ibid., 224–27.

23. Quoted in Baker, *Affairs of Party,* 187, citing Paul Angle, *Created Equal: The Complete Lincoln–Douglas Debates* (Chicago: University of Chicago Press, 1958), 18–19. My debt to Baker on this question of Popular Sovereignty, uniformity, and localism is immense. James Huston, in "Democracy by Scripture versus Democracy by Process: A Reflection on Stephen A. Douglas and Popular Sovereignty," *Civil War History* 43 (September 1997), notes the importance of majoritarianism in the debate.

24. Paoli *American Eagle,* 28 April 1854.

25. Brookville *Franklin Democrat,* 31 March 1854.

26. Brookville *Franklin Democrat,* 25 December 1857.

27. Brookville *Franklin Democrat,* 31 March 1854.

28. Salem *Washington Democrat,* 25 February 1858.

29. See ibid., and Brookville *Franklin Democrat,* 9 February 1858.

30. Chi-square significant to P.$_{99}$. Cf. Richard H. Steckel, "Migration and Political Conflict: Precincts in the Midwest on the Eve of the Civil War," *Journal of Interdisciplinary History* 28 (1998): 583–603.

31. Elmer Duane Elbert, "Southern Indiana Politics on the Eve of the Civil War, 1850–1861" (Ph.D. diss., Indiana University, 1967), chap. 2.

32. Ibid., 225–26.

33. Chi-square statistic is significant to P.$_{995}$.

34. Elbert, "Southern Indiana Politics," chap. 5.

35. Paoli *American Eagle,* 18 April 1861.

36. "Proceedings of the Orange County Democratic Meeting," n.d., Sesquicentennial MSS, Indiana Division. This manuscript is probably a handwritten transcription from the Salem *Washington Democrat* of the proceedings of a 7 May 1863 meeting of the Democrats of Stamper's Creek, Orange County.

37. "Mass Meeting of Orange, Martin, and Dubois Counties," Paoli *American Eagle,* 14 February 1861.

38. Aaron Stryker, Brownstown, to David Ireland, 29 January 1861, James Ireland Family Papers, Smith Library. See also Brookville *Franklin Democrat,* 30 November 1860.

39. D. F. Wilson, Brownstown, Ind., to David Ireland, 11 February 1861, James Ireland Family Papers, Smith Library.

40. "Mass Meeting of Orange, Martin, and Dubois Counties," Paoli *American Eagle,* 14 February 1861.

41. Brookville *Franklin Democrat,* 4 January 1860, 25 January 1860.

42. "Union Meeting of the Citizens of Washington and Orange Counties," Paoli *American Eagle,* 6 February 1861.

43. Brookville *Franklin Democrat,* 25 January 1860.

44. Paoli *American Eagle,* 17 January 1861. The *American Eagle* actually remained pro-Union throughout the war.

45. See, e.g., the New Albany *Daily Ledger*, 21 November 1860, excerpted in *Progress after Statehood: A Book of Readings*, comp. Pamela J. Bennett and Shirley S. McCord, Indiana Historical Collections, vol. 49 (Indianapolis: Indiana Historical Bureau, 1974), 177–78; see also Brookville *Franklin Democrat*, 10 May 1861.

46. Cf. Thomas E. Rodgers, "Liberty, Will, and Violence: The Political Ideology of the Democrats of West-Central Indiana during the Civil War," *Indiana Magazine of History* 92 (1996): 133–59.

47. Kenneth Stampp, *Indiana Politics during the Civil War* (1949; Bloomington: Indiana University Press, 1978); Tredway, *Democratic Opposition;* and Frank L. Klement, *Copperheads in the Middle West* (Chicago: University of Chicago Press, 1960). Robert Churchill, "The Sons of Liberty Conspiracy, 1863–1864," *Prologue* 30 (1998): 294–303, questions this historiography, but his portrait of dissent in southern Indiana does not differ much from my own. See also Stephen E. Towne and Bruce Bigelow, "Democratic Opposition to the Lincoln Administration in Indiana: The Polls and the Press," *Journal of the Indiana Academy of the Social Sciences* 5 (2001): 71–82.

48. Paoli *American Eagle*, 10 January 1861.

49. Stampp, *Indiana Politics*, 56.

50. Indianapolis *Daily State Sentinel*, 9 February 1861, quoted in Elbert, "Southern Indiana Politics," 184.

51. D. F. Wilson, Brownstown, Ind., to David Ireland, 11 February 1861, James Ireland Family Papers, Smith Library.

52. Paoli *American Eagle*, 17 January 1861.

53. Cf. Terry W. Clinton, "'Let Commerce Follow the Flag': Trade and Loyalty to the Union in the Ohio Valley," *Ohio Valley History* 1 (Spring 2001): 2–14.

54. Salem *Washington Democrat*, 19 February 1863, transcript, Washington County Democratic Papers, Sesquicentennial MSS, Indiana Division.

55. Jasper *Courier*, 2 October 1861, quoted in Tredway, *Democratic Opposition*, 56.

56. This assertion is drawn from a reading of Elbert, "Southern Indiana Politics," chap. 5, who sees the similarities but emphasizes the differences.

57. In his study, which covers all of the southern half of Indiana, Duane Elbert has discovered that Republicans were slightly more likely to be from the South than Democrats. Elbert, "Southern Indiana Politics," 209, table 2.

58. Klement, *Copperheads in the Middle West;* Stampp, *Indiana Politics;* and Tredway, *Democratic Opposition.*

59. Paoli *American Eagle*, 25 April 1861. See also the series of announcements of groups like the Fairfield Independent Guards in the Brookville *Franklin Democrat* in the spring and summer of 1861.

60. Isaac Ireland, Brownstown, to brother [David Ireland?], 21 July 1861, James Ireland Family Papers, Smith Library.

61. Thomas E. Rodgers, "Republicans and Drifters: Political Affiliation and Union Army Volunteers in West-Central Indiana," *Indiana Magazine of History* 92 (1996): 321–45.

62. Joseph Hotz, Little Rock, Ark., to Maria Hotz [near Vallonia, Jackson County], 5 September [or October] 1864, trans. Angela Weidlich, Joseph Hotz Papers, Smith Library.

63. Gilbert Denny, Helena, Ark., to father [Washington County], 21 August 1862, Gilbert Denny Papers, Smith Library.

64. Sarah Vanmeter, Blooming Grove, Franklin County, to Chris, 18 August 1862, Joel Vanmeter Papers, Smith Library.

65. William Hobbs, Atlanta, to wife Mary Hobbs, 17 October 1864, William Hobbs Papers, Smith Library.

66. Alexander H. Dunihue, Bedford, Ind., to Charles [Dunihue], 9 August 1864, Alexander H. Dunihue Papers, Indiana Division. Punctuation added to clarify statistics. There was no Gibson Township in Lawrence County.

67. Alexander H. Dunihue, Bedford, Ind., to Charles [Dunihue], 11 August 1863, Alexander H. Dunihue Papers, Indiana Division.

68. Lucille Carr Marshall, *I, Alone, Remember,* IHS Publications, vol. 18, no. 3 (Indianapolis: Indiana Historical Society, 1956), 272–73.

69. Christina Katterhenry, Huntingburg, Ind., to Uncle, Aunt, Cousins, and Nieces [Germany], 25 November 1861, in Christina Katterhenry, "Letter from Huntingburg," trans. Paul F. Roller, 23. Editorial notes are Roller's.

70. Brookville *Franklin Democrat,* 12 September 1862, 10 October 1862.

71. For a nuanced understanding of German Catholics and the Civil War, see Kathleen Neils Conzen, "German Catholic Communalism and the American Civil War: Exploring the Dilemmas of Transatlantic Political Integration," in *Bridging the Atlantic: The Question of American Exceptionalism in Perspective,* ed. Elisabeth Glaser and Hermann Wellenreuther (Washington, D.C.: German Historical Institute, by Cambridge University Press, 2002). For Dubois County, see Elfrieda Lang, "The Germans of Dubois County, Their Newspapers, Their Politics, and Their Part in the Civil War," *Indiana Magazine of History* 42 (September 1946): 229–48. See Frank L. Klement, "Catholics as Copperheads during the Civil War," *Catholic Historical Review* 80 (1994): 36–57.

72. For further discussion see Tredway, *Democratic Opposition,* with its nearly encyclopedic recounting of the various threats to liberty and the willingness of Hoosiers throughout the state, but especially in the southern half, to resist.

73. See Tredway's discussion in *Democratic Opposition,* 13–16.

74. Brookville *Franklin Democrat,* 6 March 1863.

75. Mollie H. McPheeters [Livonia] to John S. McPheeters, 18 June 1863, John S. McPheeters Papers, Smith Library.

76. For one such incident in Monroe County, see Tredway, *Democratic Opposition,* 91.

77. Ibid., 72–73.

78. Ibid., 52–53. Its connection to the Confederacy came about because Confederate enlisted men provided their own uniforms, homespun and dyed by their wives.

79. Paoli *American Eagle,* 14 May 1863.

80. William Houghton, Headquarters, 12th Indiana Volunteers, to Father, 22 November 1863, William Houghton Papers, Smith Library.

81. Tredway, *Democratic Opposition,* 53.

82. Ibid., 91–93. Tredway cites the Bloomfield *Southern Indianan.*

83. Brookville *Franklin Democrat,* 23 September 1864.

84. This use of the military tribunal while the civil courts remained open eventually made it to the Supreme Court, which in *Ex Parte Milligan* ruled the trial illegal.

85. Brookville *Franklin Democrat,* 25 September 1863. Note the source of problems would be a "vicious neighbor." See also "Proceedings of the Orange County Democratic Meeting," n.d., and Salem *Washington Democrat,* 19 February 1863, transcript, Washington County Democratic Papers, both in Sesquicentennial MSS, Indiana Division.

86. Tredway, *Democratic Opposition,* 20.

87. For a nuanced alternative explanation of the Democratic shift in 1862, see Jamie L. Carson et al., "The Impact of National Tides and District-Level Effects on Electoral Outcomes: The U.S. Congressional Elections of 1862–63," *American Journal of Political Science* 45 (2001): 887–98.

88. For a discussion of the conflicts the Democratic legislature had with the Republican governor, see Stampp, *Indiana Politics*, 176–85.

89. For a detailed recent discussion, see Scott Roller, "Business as Usual: Indiana's Response to the Confederate Invasions of the Summer of 1863," *Indiana Magazine of History* 88 (1992): 26–48.

90. Paoli *American Eagle*, 2 July 1863.

91. Paoli *American Eagle*, 25 April 1861.

92. Steven E. Woodworth, ed., *The Musick of the Mocking Birds, the Roar of the Cannon: The Civil War Diary and Letters of William Winters* (Lincoln: University of Nebraska Press, 1998), 66.

93. Marshall, *I, Alone, Remember*, 273.

94. William Orr, Stevenson, Ala., to father and mother [Washington County], 18 August [1863], Civil War Letters, Sesquicentennial Manuscript Project, Smith Library. See also two letters in the John S. McPheeters Papers, Smith Library: Mollie H. McPheeters to Dr. John S. McPheeters, 21 June 1863; and G. M. McPheeters to Friend, 7 July 1863.

95. For southern Indiana Republicans' feelings about African Americans and slavery before the Civil War, see Elbert, "Southern Indiana Politics," 200–202.

96. Aaron Stryker, Brownstown, Ind., to David Ireland, 23 February 1862, James Ireland Family Papers, Smith Library.

97. Tilghman Howard, "An Indiana Democrat of Southern Origin Speaks for the Union, 1832," ed. Chase Mooney, *Indiana Magazine of History* 58 (June 1962): 143–44.

98. Paoli *American Eagle*, 17 January 1861.

99. Salem *Washington Democrat*, 19 February 1863, transcript, Washington County Democratic Papers, Sesquicentennial MSS, Indiana Division.

100. "Proceedings of the Orange County Democratic Meeting," n.d., Sesquicentennial MSS, Indiana Division.

101. Isaac Rowland, Toon Station, Tenn., to Companion, 5 January 1863, Rowland-Shilliday Papers, Smith Library.

102. John Hardin, Vicksburg, Miss., to John and Luly A. Hardin, 11 October 1863, John Hardin Letters, Sesquicentennial Manuscripts Project, Smith Library.

103. Stampp, *Indiana Politics*, xvii.

104. Brookville *Franklin Democrat*, 4 November 1864.

105. Paoli *American Eagle*, 15 August 1861.

106. Salem *Washington Democrat*, 19 February 1863, transcript, Washington County Democratic Papers, Sesquicentennial MSS, Indiana Division.

107. Leander Davis, Chestnut Hill, Ind., to John Hardin, 23 May 18[6]6, Civil War Letters, Sesquicentennial Manuscripts Project, Smith Library. See also Brookville *Franklin Democrat*, 6 October 1866.

108. "Proceedings of the Orange County Democratic Meeting," n.d., Sesquicentennial MSS, Indiana Division.

109. Brookville *Franklin Democrat*, 31 October 1862. An epitaph was appended: "Here lies a nation, which, in endeavoring to give liberty to four millions of negroes that didn't want it, *lost its own*." Note the incredible notion that slaves did not want to be free, a notion which speaks to hill country Hoosiers' belief that any who wanted freedom and were capable of it could get it.

110. Paoli *American Eagle*, 3 August 1865. See Roediger, *Wages of Whiteness*, and Thornton, *Politics and Power*.

111. Brookville *Franklin Democrat*, 17 April 1863.

112. Salem *Washington Democrat,* 19 February 1863, transcript, Washington County Democratic Papers, Sesquicentennial MSS, Indiana Division.

113. "Proceedings of the Orange County Democratic Meeting," n.d., Sesquicentennial MSS, Indiana Division.

114. Isaac Rowland, Jackson, Tenn., to Father, 5 January 1863, Rowland-Shilliday Papers, Smith Library. See also David P. Craig, Suffolk, Va., to Mary Ella Craig, 25 January 1863, David P. Craig Papers, Indiana Division; and Vivian Zollinger, "'I Take My Pen in Hand': Civil War Letters from Owen County, Indiana, Soldiers," *Indiana Magazine of History* 93 (1997): esp. 173–82.

115. John J. Hardin, Memphis, Tenn., to father, John Hardin, Esq., 26 January 1863, Hardin Letters, Sesquicentennial Manuscripts Project, Smith Library.

116. Brookville *Franklin Democrat,* 12 August 1864.

117. Paoli *American Eagle,* 13 June 1861.

118. Minutes of Sinking Spring Baptist Church, 3rd Saturday, May 1863, transcript, Baptist Church Records, WCHS.

119. Record Book of Unity Regular Baptist Church, 17 December 1866, transcript, 11, Baptist Church Records, WCHS.

120. Minutes of Big Cedar Grove Church, Book 2, 1865–71, microfilm, Big Cedar Grove Baptist Church Records, Indiana Division.

121. "History of the Big Cedar Grove Church and Cemetery, 1817–1969," [11], manuscript, Indiana Division.

122. J. P. Brady, Cedar Grove to Joab Stout, 28 December 1868, Joab Stout Papers, Smith Library.

123. For division having to do with missionary work, see "History of the Big Cedar Grove Church and Cemetery, 1817–1969," [8], manuscript, Indiana Division.

124. Brookville *Franklin Democrat,* 23 April 1869.

125. Brookville *Indiana American,* 25 June 1869.

Epilogue

1. U.S. Census Office, *U.S. Census of Agriculture, 1880* (Washington, D.C.: Government Printing Office, 1883). Of the twenty-five hill country counties, production actually decreased in ten counties between 1850 and 1880, although two had significant urban centers; seven more counties had only modest gains of less than one hundred bushels, with six more coming in with gains of between one hundred and two hundred bushels. Only one hill country county, Morgan, was in the top half of the state in production gains in this period.

2. "New Philadelphia," from "O," Salem *Democrat,* 4 April 1891.

3. For a cogent discussion on how poverty is constructed, see Walter Precourt, "The Image of Appalachian Poverty," in *Appalachia and America,* ed. Allan Batteau (Lexington: University Press of Kentucky, 1983).

4. For a sharp analysis of how outsiders defined and disseminated the image of feuding as characteristic of Appalachia, see Altina Waller, "Feuding in Appalachia: Evolution of a Cultural Stereotype," in *Appalachia in the Making: The Mountain South in the Nineteenth Century,* ed. Mary Beth Pudup, Dwight B. Billings, and Altina Waller (Chapel Hill: University of North Carolina Press, 1995), 347–76.

5. Brookville *Franklin Democrat,* 19 April 1867, citing the New Albany *Ledger.*

6. Clifton Phillips, *Indiana in Transition: The Emergence of an Industrial Commonwealth, 1880–1920,* vol. 4 of *The History of Indiana* (Indianapolis: Indiana Historical Bureau and Indiana Historical Society, 1968), 376.

7. See Christopher Waldrep, "'So Much Sin': The Decline of Religious Discipline and the 'Tidal Wave of Crime,'" *Journal of Social History* 23, no. 3 (Spring 1990): 535–52, now incorporated into his book *Night Riders: Defending Community in the Black Patch, 1890–1915* (Durham, N.C.: Duke University Press, 1993).

8. *New York Times,* 12 October 1887, 2.

9. Madeleine Noble, "The White Caps of Harrison and Crawford County, Ind.: A Study in the Violent Enforcement of Morality" (Ph.D. diss., University of Michigan, 1973).

10. See ibid., 11, 29; and H. H. Pleasant, *A History of Crawford County, Indiana* (Glendale, Calif.: Arthur H. Clark, 1926).

11. On this, see William G. Carleton, "The Money Question in Indiana Politics, 1865–1890," *Indiana Magazine of History* 42 (June 1946): 207–28; and Carleton, "Why Was the Democratic Party in Indiana a Radical Party, 1865–1890?" *Indiana Magazine of History* 42 (September 1946): 207–28.

12. Ellen Sieber and Cheryl Ann Munson, *Looking at History: Indiana's Hoosier National Forest Region, 1600 to 1950* (1992; Bloomington: Indiana University Press, 1994), 86.

13. Hoosier National Forest, "What's in the 1991 Plan?" http://www.fs.fed.us/r9/hoosier/planningdocs/plan-whats_in_plan.htm, accessed 06/21/04.

INDEX

Page numbers in italics indicate illustrations.

abolitionists, disdain for, 198–199, 214–215, 217
account books, 115–118
ad valorem property taxes, 149, 153–155; defined,
  153
Adams, John Quincy, 137–139
African Americans: in hill country, 16, 192; attempts to exclude from Indiana, 184–190;
  violence against, 192; exodus from hill country, 192. *See also* racism
agricultural ladder, 29–30
agricultural societies, 94
agriculture: primary occupation, 16; and natural disasters, 90–91; food production, 96–105,
  103, 186–187, 222; cash crops, 104; machinery,
  105, 187; wool and flax production, 107–109
Alford, Martha, 208
Allen, Thomas, 39
Alvis, James, 55
American (Know-Nothing) Party, 184, 194–195
American Home Missionary Society, 39, 65–66;
  tied to Federalist Party, 66
American Land Company, 167–168
Anderson, Uriah, 55–56
aristocracy, moneyed, 128, 137, 146, 171
Arms, Charles, 85, 98, 101
artisans, 84–85, 115
Aurora, Ind., 164, 180
Austro-Hungarian Leopoldine Foundation, 48

Bank of Brookville, 177
Bank of the United States, Second, 93, 128, 139–
  141, 143–148; recharter vetoed, 146–147
Bank of Vincennes, 141
banking, aversion to, 139–152
banking, free, 176–177; defined, 175; and local-
  ism, 177
Banks, Burr, 115–116
Baptist Church, 40, 43–44, 51, 52–53, 54, 56, 59,
  61, 63–74; against slavery, 188–189. *See also*
  Primitive Baptists
barter, 116
Bartholomew Co., Ind., 102, 119, 224
Bedford, Ind., 169
Belgian immigrants, 16
Berry, George, 172
Bethlehem Baptist Church, 69
Big Cedar Grove Baptist Church, 41, 55, 56, *57*,
  220–221, 222
Bigger, Samuel, 87, 165
Birkbeck, Morris, 83, 84, 86, 87, 88, 89
Black Hawk's War, 90
Blane, William Newnham, 27–28
Bloomington, Ind., 84, 88, 169
Blue River Baptist Association, 69, 70, 71, 189
Blue Spring, Ind., 47

Bollin, John, 116–117
Booth, Fanny, 35
Borden, William, 83
Bowers, Jemima Parr, 6–8
Bowers, Joseph, 6–7
Bowers, Solomon, 6–8
Bowles, William: on State Bank, 175; arrested as
  Northwest conspirator, 219
Bradbury, John, 109
Brady, John P., 220
Bright, Jesse, 195, 197, 202
Brookville, Ind., 18, 20, 80, 144, 147, 177
Brown County, Ind., 40, 88, 170, 207, 208
Brown, Jason, 209–210
Brown, Samuel Gibson, 124–125
Brown Township, Washington County, Ind., 116
Brownstown, Ind., 101
Brush, Edward, 141–142
Bullard, Aaron S., 120
Bullard, Joseph, 120
Burns, Harrison, 80, 87, 89–90, 97, 98–99, 100,
  101, 108, 110
Butler Township., Franklin County, Ind., 116
Butler, Charles, 167–168, 171
Butternuts, 207–209

California, 179
Campbell, Alexander, 40, 44, 45, 59
Cannelton, Ind., 180
capitalism, 86, 113; and community, 78–79; and
  local merchants, 126
Carr, Nancy, 205, 213. *See also* Nancy Carr Parr
cash crops, 104
Caswell and Drew, 22
Chapin, Lorenzo, 84
Chastain, George, 18
Chasteen, Nancy, 55
cholera, 90
church discipline, 51–56, 141
Church of the Brethren, 16, 40
Cincinnati, Ohio, 18, 101
Civil War: Fort Sumter, effect on attitudes, 198;
  draft, 204–209; local conflict over, 208–209,
  219–221; martial law, fear of, 209–210; and
  nationalism, 221
Clark, William, 19
Clark's Military Grant, 12–13, 14
Clarksville, Ind., 14
Clay, Henry, 134, 137, 146, 178, 179
Cliff, Thomas, 117
Cobbett, William, 88
Combs, Hannah, 52
commercial development: early, 80–81; cash
  crops, 104; and women, 110–111

269

Index

Index

Index

RICHARD F. NATION is Assistant Professor of
History at Eastern Michigan University.